Escort & Lynx Owners Workshop Manual

by Larry Warren
and John H Haynes Member of the Guild of Motoring Writers

Models covered
2-door Hatchback, 4-door Liftback and 4-door Station
Wagon with 1.3 or 1.6 liter engine (including EFI and
Turbocharged engines). 1981 through 1985.

ISBN 1 85010 122 1

ABCDE
FGHIJ
KLMNO

Printed in England *(1L1–789)*

THE
BOOK

AUTOMOTIVE
PARTS &
ACCESSORIES
ASSOCIATION   MEMBER

Haynes Publishing Group
Sparkford Nr Yeovil
Somerset BA22 7JJ England

Haynes Publications, Inc
861 Lawrence Drive
Newbury Park
California 91320 USA

D1456466

Acknowledgements

Special thanks are due to Ford Motor Company for the supply of technical information and certain illustrations. Champion Spark Plug Company supplied the illustrations showing the various spark plug conditions. The bodywork repair photos were provided by Holt Lloyd Limited.

About this manual

Its purpose

The purpose of this manual is to help you get the best value from your vehicle. It can do so in several ways. It can help you decide what work must be done even if you choose to get it done by a dealer service department or a repair shop; it provides information and procedures for routine maintenance and servicing; and it offers diagnostic and repair procedures to follow when trouble occurs.

It is hoped that you will use the manual to tackle the work yourself. For many simpler jobs, doing it yourself may be quicker than arranging an appointment to get the vehicle into a shop and making the trips to leave it and pick it up. More importantly, a lot of money can be saved by avoiding the expense the shop must pass on to you to cover its labor and overhead costs. An added benefit is the sense of satisfaction and accomplishment that you feel after having done the job yourself.

Using the manual

The manual is divided into Chapters. Each Chapter is divided into numbered Sections, which are headed in bold type between horizontal lines. Each Section consists of consecutively numbered paragraphs.

The two types of illustrations used (figures and photographs) are referenced by a number preceding their captions. Figure reference numbers denote Chapter and numerical sequence in the Chapter; i.e. Fig. 12.4 means Chapter 12, figure number 4. Figure captions are followed by a Section number which ties the figure to a specific portion of the text. All photographs apply to the Chapter in which they appear, and the reference number pinpoints the pertinent Section and paragraph.

Procedures, once described in the text, are not normally repeated. When it is necessary to refer to another Chapter, the reference will be given as Chapter and Section number; i.e. Chapter 1/16. Cross reference given without use of the word 'Chapter' apply to Sections and/or paragraphs in the same Chapter. For example, 'see Section 8' means in the same Chapter.

Reference to the left or right of the vehicle is based on the assumption that one is sitting in the driver's seat facing forward.

Even though extreme care has been taken during the preparation of this manual, neither the publisher nor the author can accept responsibility for any errors in, or omissions from, the information given.

Introduction to the Ford Escort and Mercury Lynx

This front-drive design features unitized construction and 4-wheel independent suspension. Models are available in 2-door, 4-door and station wagon body styles.

The cross-mounted four-cylinder engine drives the front wheels through either a 4-speed manual or 3-speed automatic transaxle by way of unequal length driveshafts. The rack-and-pinion steering gear is mounted behind the engine and is available with power assist. Brakes are discs in front and drum-type at the rear with vacuum assist optional.

Contents

1981 Ford Escort SS 2-door hatchback (front) and 4-door station wagon

1981 Mercury Lynx 4-door station wagon

1981 Mercury Lynx LS 2-door hatchback

1981 Ford Escort GLX 2-door hatchback

1982 Ford Escort GLX 4-door hatchback

General dimensions, capacities and weights

Refer to Chapter 13 for specifications related to 1983 thru 1985 models

---

Dimensions
Overall length
2-door hatchback .... 163.9 in
4-door liftback and station wagon .... 165.0 in

Overall height .... 53.3 in

Width .... 65.9 in

Wheelbase .... 94.2 in

Capacities
Engine oil
All models .... 4.0 US qts

Cooling system
Standard .... 6.3 US qts
With air conditioning .... 6.4 US qts

Manual transaxle lubricant .... 5.0 US pts

Automatic transaxle fluid .... 10.0 US qts

Fuel tank capacity
Standard .... 10.0 US gal
Optional .... 11.3 US gal

Curb weight   **lbs**
2-door hatchback 2008
4-door liftback and station wagon 2128

Spare parts and vehicle identification numbers

Buying spare parts

Spare parts are available from many sources, which generally fall into one of two categories — authorized dealer parts departments and independent retail auto parts stores. Our advice concerning spare parts is as follows:

Authorized dealer parts department: This is the best source for parts which are peculiar to your vehicle and not generally available elsewhere (i.e. major engine parts, transmission parts, trim pieces, etc). It is also the only place you should buy parts if your vehicle is still under warranty, as non-factory parts may invalidate the warranty. To be sure of obtaining the correct parts, have your vehicle's engine and chassis numbers available and, if possible, take the old parts along for positive identification.

Retail auto parts stores: Good auto parts stores will stock frequently needed components which wear out relatively fast (i.e. clutch components, exhaust systems, brake parts, tune-up parts, etc). These stores often supply new or reconditioned parts on an exchange basis, which can save a considerable amount of money. Discount auto stores are often very good places to buy materials and parts needed for general vehicle maintenance (i.e. oil, grease, filters, spark plugs, belts,

touch-up, paint, bulbs. etc). They also usually sell tools and general accessories, have convenient hours, charge lower prices, and can often be found not far from your home.

Vehicle identification numbers

Regardless from which source parts are obtained, it is essential to provide correct information concerning the vehicle model and year of manufacture plus the engine serial number and the vehicle identification number (VIN). The accompanying illustrations show where these important numbers can be found.

1FABP42D9BH100001

VEHICLE IDENTIFICATION NUMBER

The vehicle identification number is affixed to the dash panel and is visible through the windshield

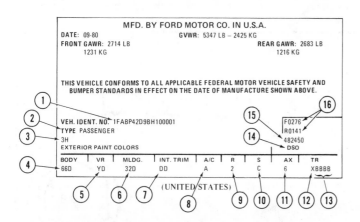

The Certification label is located on the left front door post

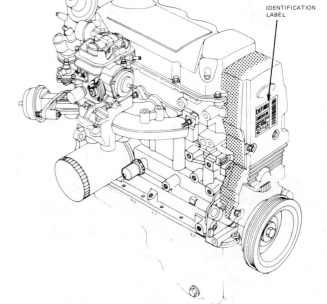

Engine identification label location

1 Vehicle identification number
2 Vehicle type
3 Paint
4 Body type code
5 Vinyl roof
6 Body side moulding
7 Trim code
8 Air conditioning
9 Radio
10 Sun/Moon roof
11 Axle ratio
12 Transmission
13 Springs — Front L and R, Rear L and R (4 codes)
14 District sales office
15 Order number
16 Accessories

Maintenance techniques, tools and working facilities

Basic maintenance techniques

There are a number of techniques involved in maintenance and repair that will be referred to throughout this manual. Application of these techniques will enable the home mechanic to be more efficient, better organized and capable of performing the various tasks properly, which will ensure that the repair job is thorough and complete.

Fasteners

Fasteners, basically, are nuts, bolts, studs and screws used to hold two or more parts together. There are a few things to keep in mind when working with fasteners. Almost all of them use a locking device of some type; either a lock washer, locknut, locking tab or thread adhesive. All threaded fasteners should be clean and straight, with undamaged threads and undamaged corners on the hex head where the wrench fits. Develop the habit of replacing damaged nuts and bolts with new ones. Special locknuts with nylon or fiber inserts can only be used once. If they are removed, they lose their locking ability and must be replaced with new ones.

Rusted nuts and bolts should be treated with a penetrating fluid to ease removal and prevent breakage. Some mechanics use turpentine in a spout-type oil can, which works quite well. After applying the rust penetrant, let it "work" for a few minutes before trying to loosen the nut or bolt. Badly rusted fasteners may have to be chiseled or sawed off or removed with a special nut breaker, available at tool stores.

If a bolt or stud breaks off in an assembly, it can be drilled and removed with a special tool commonly available for this purpose. Most automotive machine shops can perform this task, as well as other repair procedures (such as repair of threaded holes that have been stripped out).

Flat washers and lock washers, when removed from an assembly should always be replaced exactly as removed. Replace damaged washers with new ones. Always use a flat washer between a lock washer and any soft metal surface (such as aluminum), thin sheet metal or plastic.

Fastener sizes

For a number of reasons, automobile manufacturers are making wider and wider use of metric fasteners. Therefore, it is important to be able to tell the difference between standard (sometimes called U.S., English or SAE) and metric hardware, since thay cannot be interchanged.

All bolts, whether standard or metric, are sized according to diameter, thread pitch and length. For example, a standard $\frac{1}{2}$ – 13 x 1 bolt is $\frac{1}{2}$ inch in diameter, has 13 threads per inch and is 1 inch long. An M12 – 1.75 x 25 metric bolt is 12 mm in diameter, has a thread pitch of 1.75 mm (the distance between threads) and is 25 mm long. The 2 bolts are nearly identical, and easily confused, but they are not interchangeable.

In addition to the differences in diameter, thread pitch and length, metric and standard bolts can also be distinguished by examining the bolt heads. To begin with, the distance across the flats on a standard bolt head is measured in inches, while the same dimension on a metric bolt is measured in millimeters (the same is true for nuts). As a result, a standard wrench should not be used on a metric bolt and a metric wrench should not be used on a standard bolt. Also, standard bolts have slashes radiating out from the center of the head to denote the grade or strength of the bolt (which is an indication of the amount of torque that can be supplied to it). The greater the number of slashes, the greater the strength of the bolt (grades 0 through 5 are commonly used on automobiles). Metric bolts have a property class (grade) number, rather than a slash, molded into their heads to indicate bolt strength. In this case, the higher the number the stronger the bolt (property class numbers 8.8, 9.8 and 10.9 are commonly used on automobiles).

Strength markings can also be used to distinguish standard hex nuts from metric hex nuts. Standard nuts have dots stamped into one side, while metric nuts are marked with a number. The greater the number of dots, or the higher the number, the greater the strength of the nut.

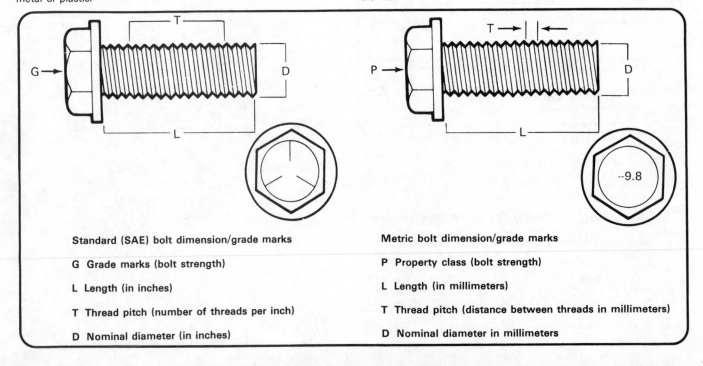

Standard (SAE) bolt dimension/grade marks

G Grade marks (bolt strength)

L Length (in inches)

T Thread pitch (number of threads per inch)

D Nominal diameter (in inches)

Metric bolt dimension/grade marks

P Property class (bolt strength)

L Length (in millimeters)

T Thread pitch (distance between threads in millimeters)

D Nominal diameter in millimeters

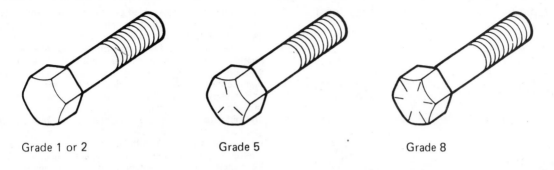

Grade 1 or 2   Grade 5   Grade 8

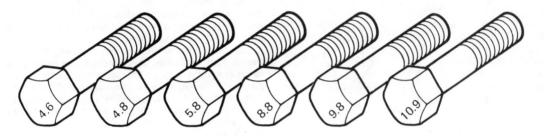

Bolt strength markings (top – standard/SAE, bottom – metric)

Metric studs are also marked on their ends according to property class (grade). Larger studs are numbered (the same as metric bolts), while smaller studs carry a geometric code to denote grade.

It should be noted that many fasteners, especially Grades 0 through 2, have no distinguishing marks on them. When such is the case, the only way to determine whether it is standard or metric is to measure the thread pitch or compare it to a known fastener of the same size.

Since fasteners of the same size (both standard and metric) may have different strength ratings, be sure to reinstall any bolts, studs or nuts removed from your vehicle in their original locations. Also, when replacing a fastener with a new one, make sure that the new one has a strength rating equal to or greater than the original.

Tightening sequences and procedures

Most threaded fasteners should be tightened to a specific torque value (torque is basically a twisting force). Over-tightening the fastener can weaken it and lead to eventual breakage, while under-tightening can cause it to eventually come loose. Bolts, screws and studs, depending on the materials they are made of and their thread diameters, have specific torque values (many of which are noted in the Specifications Section at the beginning of each Chapter). Be sure to follow the torque recommendations closely. For fasteners not assigned a specific torque, a general torque value chart is presented here as a guide. As was previously mentioned, the sizes and grade of a fastener determine the amount of torque that can safely be applied to it. The figures listed here are approximate for Grade 2 and Grade 3 fasteners (higher grades can tolerate higher torque values).

	Ft-lb	Nm
Metric thread sizes		
M-6	6 to 9	9 to 12
M-8	14 to 21	19 to 28
M-10	28 to 40	38 to 54
M-12	50 to 71	68 to 96
M-14	80 to 140	109 to 154
Pipe thread sizes		
1/8	5 to 8	7 to 10
1/4	12 to 18	17 to 24
3/8	22 to 33	30 to 44
1/2	25 to 35	34 to 47
U.S. thread sizes		
1/4 - 20	6 to 9	9 to 12
5/16 - 18	12 to 18	17 to 24
5/16 - 24	14 to 20	19 to 27
3/8 - 16	22 to 32	30 to 43
3/8 - 24	27 to 38	37 to 51
7/16 - 14	40 to 55	55 to 74
7/16 - 20	40 to 60	55 to 81
1/2 - 13	55 to 80	75 to 108

Grade	Identification
Hex Nut Grade 5	3 Dots
Hex Nut Grade 8	6 Dots

Standard hex nut strength markings

Class	Identification
Hex Nut Property Class 9	Arabic 9
Hex Nut Property Class 10	Arabic 10

Metric hex nut strength markings

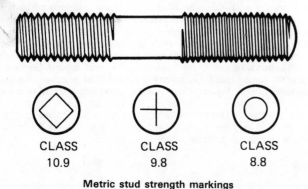

| CLASS 10.9 | CLASS 9.8 | CLASS 8.8 |

Metric stud strength markings

Fasteners laid out in a pattern (i.e. cylinder head bolts, oil pan bolts, differential cover bolts, etc.) must be loosened and tightened in a definite sequence to avoid warping the component. Initially, the bolts or nuts should be assembled finger-tight only. Next, they should be tightened one full turn each, in a criss-cross or diagonal pattern. After each one has been tightened one full turn, return to the first one and tighten them all one half turn, following the same pattern. Finally, tighten each of them one-quarter turn at a time until they all have been tightened to the proper torque value. To loosen and remove them the procedure would be reversed.

Component disassembly

Component disassembly should be done with care and purpose to help ensure that the parts go back together properly. Always keep track of the sequence in which parts are removed. Make note of special characteristics or markings on parts that can be installed more than one way (such as a grooved thrust washer on a shaft). It is a good

idea to lay the disassembled parts out on a clean surface in the order that they were removed. It may also be helpful to make simple sketches or take instant photos of components before removal.

When removing fasteners from an assembly, keep track of their locations. Sometimes threading a bolt back in a part, or putting the washers and nut back on a stud, can prevent mixups later. If nuts and bolts cannot be returned to their original locations, they should be kept in a compartmented box or a series of small boxes. A cupcake or muffin tin is ideal for this purpose, since each cavity can hold the bolts and nuts from a particular area (i.e. oil pan bolts, valve cover bolts, engine mount bolts, etc.). A pan of this type is especially helpful when working on assemblies with very small parts (such as the carburetor, alternator, valve train or interior dash and trim pieces). The cavities can be marked with paint or tape to identify the contents.

Whenever wiring looms, harnesses or connectors are separated, it's a good idea to identify them with numbered pieces of masking tape so that they can be easily reconnected.

Gasket sealing surfaces

Throughout any vehicle, gaskets are used to seal the mating surfaces between two parts and keep lubricants, fluids, vacuum or pressure contained in an assembly.

Many times these gaskets are coated with a liquid or paste-type gasket sealing compound before assembly. Age, heat and pressure can sometimes cause the two parts to stick together so tightly that they are very difficult to separate. Often the assembly can be loosened by striking it with a soft-faced hammer near the mating surfaces. A regular hammer can be used if a block of wood is placed between the hammer and the part. Do not hammer on cast parts or parts that could be easily damaged. With any particularly stubborn part, always recheck to see that every fastener has been removed.

Avoid using a screwdriver or bar to pry apart an assembly, as they can easily mar the gasket sealing surfaces of the parts (which must remain smooth). If prying is absolutely necessary, use an old broom handle, but keep in mind that extra clean-up will be necessary if the wood splinters.

After the parts are separated, the old gasket must be carefully scraped off and the gasket surfaces cleaned. Stubborn gasket material can be soaked with rust penetrant or treated with a special chemical to soften it so that it can be easily scraped off. A scraper can be fashioned from a piece of copper tubing by flattening and sharpening one end. Copper is recommended because it is usually softer than the surfaces to be scraped, which reduces the chance of gouging the part. Some gaskets can be removed with a wire brush, but regardless of the method used, the mating surfaces must be left clean and smooth. If for some reason the gasket surface is gouged, then a gasket sealer thick enough to fill scratches will have to be used upon reassembly of the components. For most applications, a non-drying (or semi-drying) gasket sealer should be used.

Hose removal tips

Caution: *If equipped with air conditioning, do not ever disconnect any of the a/c hoses without first de-pressurizing the system.*

Hose removal precautions closely parallel gasket removal precautions. Avoid scratching or gouging the surface that the hose mates against or the connection may leak. This is especially true for radiator hoses. Because of various chemical reactions, the rubber in hoses can bond itself to the metal spigot that the hose fits over. To remove a hose, first loosen the hose clamps that secure it to the spigot. Then, with slip joint pliers, grab the hose at the clamp and rotate it around the spigot. Work it back and forth until it is completely free, then pull it off (silicone or other lubricants will ease removal if they can be applied between the hose and the spigot). Apply the same lubricant to the inside of the hose and the outside of the spigot to simplify installation.

If a hose clamp is broken or damaged, do not re-use it. Do not reuse hoses that are cracked, split or torn.

Tools

A selection of good tools is a basic requirement for anyone who plans to maintain and repair his or her own vehicle. For the owner who has few tools, if any, the initial investment might seem high, but when compared to the spiraling costs of professional auto maintenance and repair, it is a wise one.

To help the owner decide which tools are needed to perform the tasks detailed in this manual, the following tool lists are offered:

Maintenance and minor repair, Repair and overhaul and *Special.* The newcomer to practical mechanics should start off with the *Maintenance and minor repair* tool kit, which is adequate for the simpler jobs performed on a vehicle. Then, as his confidence and experience grow, he can tackle more difficult tasks, buying additional tools as they are needed. Eventually the basic kit will be expanded into the *Repair and overhaul* tool set. Over a period of time, the experienced do-it-yourselfer will assemble a tool set complete enough for most repair and overhaul procedures and will add tools from the *Special* category when he feels the expense is justified by the frequency of use.

Maintenance and minor repair tool kit

The tools in this list should be considered the minimum for performance of routine maintenance, servicing and minor repair work. We recommend the purchase of combination wrenches (box end and open end combined in one wrench); while more expensive than open-ended ones, they offer the advantages of both types of wrench.

Combination wrench set ($\frac{1}{4}$ in to 1 in or 6 mm to 19 mm)
Adjustable wrench – 8 in
Spark plug wrench (with rubber insert)
Spark plug gap adjusting tool
Feeler gauge set
Brake bleeder wrench
Standard screwdriver ($\frac{5}{16}$ in x 6 in)
Phillips screwdriver (No.2 x 6 in)
Combination pliers – 6 in
Hacksaw and assortment of blades
Tire pressure gauge
Grease gun
Oil can
Fine emery cloth
Wire brush
Battery post and cable cleaning tool
Oil filter wrench
Funnel (medium size)
Safety goggles
Jack stands (2)
Drain pan

Note: *If basic tune-ups are going to be a part of routine maintenance, it will be necessary to purchase a good quality stroboscopic timing light and a combination tachometer/dwell meter. Although they are included in the list of Special tools, they are mentioned here because they are absolutely necessary for tuning most vehicles properly.*

Repair and overhaul tool set

These tools are essential for anyone who plans to perform major repairs and are in addition to those in the *Maintenance and minor*

repair tool kit. Included is a comprehensive set of sockets which, though expensive, will be found invaluable because of their versatility (especially when various extensions and drives are available). We recommend the $\frac{1}{2}$ in drive over the $\frac{3}{8}$ in drive. Although the larger drive is bulky and more expensive, it has the capability of accepting a very wide range of large sockets (ideally, the mechanic would have a $\frac{3}{8}$ in drive set and a $\frac{1}{2}$ in drive set).

Socket set(s)
Reversible ratchet
Extension – 10 in
Universal joint
Torque wrench (same size drive as sockets)
Ball pein hammer – 8 oz
Soft-faced hammer (plastic/rubber)
Standard screwdriver ($\frac{1}{4}$ in x 6 in)
Standard screwdriver (stubby – $\frac{5}{16}$ in)
Phillips screwdriver (No.3 x 8 in)
Phillips screwdriver (stubby – No.2)
Pliers – vise grip
Pliers – lineman's
Pliers – needle nose
Pliers – spring clip (internal and external)
Cold chisel – $\frac{1}{2}$ in
Scriber
Scraper (made from flattened copper tubing)
Center punch
Pin punches ($\frac{1}{16}$, $\frac{1}{8}$, $\frac{3}{16}$ in)
Steel rule/straight edge – 12 in
Allen wrench set ($\frac{1}{8}$ to $\frac{3}{8}$ in or 4 mm to 10 mm)
A selection of files
Wire brush (large)
Jack stands (second set)
Jack (scissor or hydraulic type)

Note: *Another tool which is often useful is an electric drill motor with a chuck capacity of $\frac{3}{8}$ in (and a set of good quality drill bits).*

Special tools

The tools in this list include those which are not used regularly, are expensive to buy, or which need to be used in accordance with their manufacturer's instructions. Unless these tools will be used frequently, it is not very economical to purchase many of them. A consideration would be to split the cost and use between yourself and a friend or friends. In addition, most of these tools can be obtained from a tool rental shop on a temporary basis.

This list contains only those tools and instruments widely available to the public, and not those special tools produced by vehicle manufacturers for distribution to dealer service departments. Occasionally, references to the manufacturer's special tools are included in the text of this manual. Generally, an alternative method of doing

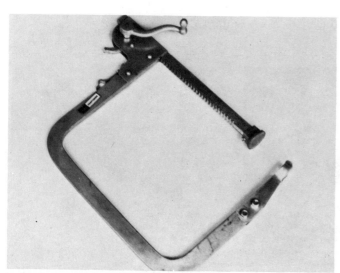

Valve spring compressor

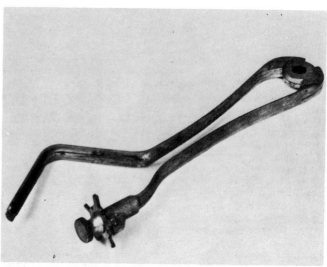

Piston ring groove cleaning tool

Piston ring compressor

Piston ring removal/installation tool

Cylinder ridge reamer

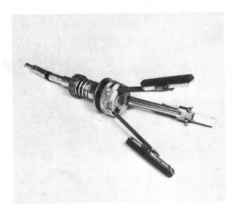
Cylinder bore hone

Cylinder bore gauge

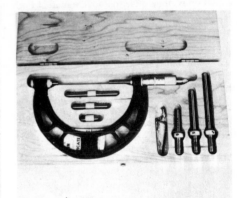
Micrometer set

Dial caliper

Hydraulic lifter removal tool

Universal-type hub puller

Dial indicator set

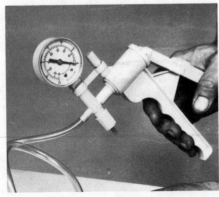
Hand-operated vacuum pump

Brake shoe spring tool

the job without the special tool is offered. However, sometimes there is no alternative to their use. Where this is the case, and the tool cannot be purchased or borrowed, the work should be turned over to the dealer, a repair shop or an automotive machine shop.

Valve spring compressor
Piston ring groove cleaning tool
Piston ring compressor
Piston ring installation tool
Cylinder compression gauge
Cylinder ridge reamer
Cylinder surfacing hone
Cylinder bore gauge
Micrometer(s) and/or dial calipers
Hydraulic lifter removal tool
Balljoint separator
Universal-type puller
Impact screwdriver
Dial indicator set
Stroboscopic timing light (inductive pickup)
Hand-operated vacuum/pressure pump
Tachometer/dwell meter
Universal electrical multi-meter
Cable hoist
Brake spring removal and installation tools
Floor jack

Buying tools

For the do-it-yourselfer who is just starting to get involved in vehicle maintenance and repair, there are a couple of options available when purchasing tools. If maintenance and minor repair is the extent of the work to be done, the purchase of individual tools is satisfactory. If, on the other hand, extensive work is planned, it would be a good idea to purchase a modest tool set from one of the large retail chain stores. A set can usually be bought at a substantial savings over the individual tool prices (and they often come with a tool box). As additional tools are needed, add-on sets, individual tools and a larger tool box can be purchased to expand the tool selection. Building a tool set gradually allows the cost of the tools to be spread over a longer period of time and gives the mechanic the freedom to choose only those tools that will actually be used.

Tool stores will often be the only source of some of the special tools that are needed, but regardless of where tools are bought, try to avoid cheap ones (especially when buying screwdrivers and sockets) because they won't last very long. The expense involved in replacing cheap tools will eventually be greater than the initial cost of quality tools.

Care and maintenance of tools

Good tools are expensive, so it makes sense to treat them with respect. Keep them in a clean and usable condition and store them properly when not in use. Always wipe off any dirt, grease or metal chips before putting them away. Never leave tools lying around in the work area. Upon completion of a job, always check closely under the hood for tools that may have been left there (so they don't get lost during a test drive).

Some tools, such as screwdrivers, pliers, wrenches and sockets, can be hung on a panel mounted on the garage or workshop wall, while others should be kept in a tool box or tray. Measuring instruments, gauges, meters, etc. must be carefully stored where they cannot be damaged by weather or impact from other tools.

When tools are used with care and stored properly, they will last a very long time. Even with the best of care, tools will wear out if used frequently. When a tool is damaged or worn out, replace it; subsequent jobs will be safer and more enjoyable if you do.

For those who desire to learn more about tools and their uses, a book entitled *How to Choose and Use Car Tools* is available from the publishers of this manual.

Working facilities

Not to be overlooked when discussing tools is the workshop. If anything more than routine maintenance is to be carried out, some sort of suitable work area is essential.

It is understood, and appreciated, that many home mechanics do not have a good workshop or garage available, and end up removing an engine or doing major repairs outside (it is recommended that the overhaul or repair be completed under the cover of a roof).

A clean, flat workbench or table of suitable working height is an absolute necessity. The workshop should be equipped with a vise that has a jaw opening of at least 4 inches.

As mentioned previously, some clean, dry storage space is also required for tools, as well as the lubricants, fluids, cleaning solvents, etc. which soon become necessary.

Sometimes waste oil and fluids, drained from the engine or transmission during normal maintenance or repairs, present a disposal problem. To avoid pouring oil on the ground or into the sewage system, simply pour the used fluids into large containers, seal them with caps and deliver them to a local recycling center or disposal facility. Plastic jugs (such as old anti-freeze containers) are ideal for this purpose.

Always keep a supply of old newspapers and clean rags available. Old towels are excellent for mopping up spills. Many mechanics use rolls of paper towels for most work because they are readily available and disposable. To keep the area under the vehicle clean, a large cardboard box can be cut open and flattened to protect the garage or shop floor.

Whenever working over a painted surface (such as when leaning over a fender to service something under the hood), always cover it with an old blanket or bedspread to protect the finish. Vinyl covered pads, made especially for this purpose, are available at auto parts stores.

Jacking and towing

Jacking

The jack supplied with the vehicle should only be used for raising the car for changing a tire or placing jackstands under the frame. **Under no circumstances should work be performed beneath the vehicle or the engine started while this jack is being used as the only means of support.**

All vehicles are supplied with a scissors type jack which fits into a notch in the vertical rocker panel flange nearest to the wheel being changed.

The car should be on level ground with the wheels blocked and the transaxle in Park (automatic) or Reverse (manual). Pry off the hub cap (if equipped) using the tapered end of the lug wrench. Loosen the wheel nuts one half turn and leave them in place until the wheel is raised off the ground.

Place the jack under the side of the car in the jacking notch. Use the supplied wrench to turn the jackscrew clockwise until the wheel is raised off the ground. Remove the wheel nuts, pull off the wheel and replace it with the spare.

With the beveled side in, replace the wheel nuts and tighten them until snug. Lower the vehicle by turning the jackscrew counter-clockwise. Remove the jack and tighten the nuts in a diagonal fashion. Replace the hubcap by placing it into position and using the heel of your hand or a rubber mallet to seat it.

Towing

The vehicle can be towed with all four wheels on the ground provided speeds do not exceed 35 mph and the distance is not over 50 miles, otherwise transmission damage can result.

Towing equipment specifically designed for this purpose should be used and should be attached to the main structural members of the car and not the bumper or brackets.

Safety is a major consideration when towing and all applicable state and local laws must be obeyed. A safety chain system must be used for all towing.

While towing, the parking brake should be fully released and the transmission should be in Neutral. The steering must be unlocked (ignition switch in the Off position). Remember that power steering and power brakes will not work with the engine off.

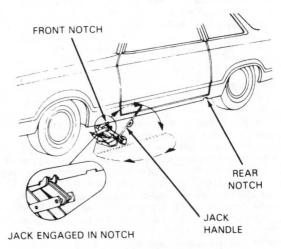

USE APPROPRIATE NOTCH (FRONT OR REAR)

FRONT NOTCH

REAR NOTCH

JACK HANDLE

JACK ENGAGED IN NOTCH

Chassis jacking points

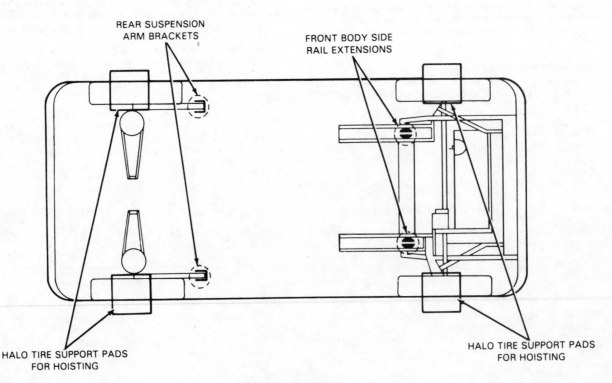

REAR SUSPENSION ARM BRACKETS

FRONT BODY SIDE RAIL EXTENSIONS

HALO TIRE SUPPORT PADS FOR HOISTING

HALO TIRE SUPPORT PADS FOR HOISTING

Frame lifting points

Automotive chemicals and lubricants

A number of automotive chemicals and lubricants are available for use in vehicle maintenance and repair. They represent a wide variety of products ranging from cleaning solvents and degreasers to lubricants and protective sprays for rubber, plastic and vinyl.

Contact point/spark plug cleaner is a solvent used to clean oily film and dirt from points, grime from electrical connectors and oil deposits from spark plugs. It is oil free and leaves no residue. It can also be used to remove gum and varnish from carburetor jets and other orifices.

Carburetor cleaner is similar to contact point/spark plug cleaner but it is a stronger solvent and may leave a slight oily residue. It is not recommended for cleaning electrical components or connections.

Brake system cleaner is used to remove grease or brake fluid from brake system components (where clean surfaces are absolutely necessary and petroleum-based solvents cannot be used); it also leaves no residue.

Silicone based lubricants are used to protect rubber parts such as hoses, weatherstripping and grommets, and are used as lubricants for hinges and locks.

Multi-purpose grease is an all purpose lubricant used whenever grease is more practical than a liquid lubricant such as oil. Some multi-purpose grease is colored white and specially formulated to be more resistant to water than ordinary grease.

Bearing grease/wheel bearing grease is a heavy grease used where increased loads and friction are encountered (i.e. wheel bearings, universal joints, etc.).

High temperature wheel bearing grease is designed to withstand the extreme temperatures encountered by wheel bearings in disc brake equipped vehicles. It usually contains molybdenum disulfide, which is a 'dry' type lubricant.

Gear oil (sometimes called gear lube) is a specially designed oil used in differentials, manual transmissions and manual gearboxes, as well as other areas where high friction, high temperature lubrication is required. It is available in a number of viscosities (weights) for various applications.

Motor oil, of course, is the lubricant specially formulated for use in the engine. It normally contains a wide variety of additives to prevent corrosion and reduce foaming and wear. Motor oil comes in various weights (viscosity ratings) of from 5 to 80. The recommended weight of the oil depends on the seasonal temperature and the demands on the engine. Light oil is used in cold climates and under light load conditions; heavy oil is used in hot climates and where high loads are encountered. Multi-viscosity oils are designed to have characteristics of both light and heavy oils and are available in a number of weights from 5W-20 to 20W-50.

Oil additives range from viscosity index improvers to slick chemical treatments that purportedly reduce friction. It should be noted that most oil manufacturers caution against using additives with their oils.

Gas additives perform several functions, depending on their chemical makeup. They usually contain solvents that help dissolve gum and varnish that build up on carburetor and intake parts. They also serve to break down carbon deposits that form on the inside surfaces of the combustion chambers. Some additives contain upper cylinder lubricants for valves and piston rings.

Brake fluid is a specially formulated hydraulic fluid that can withstand the heat and pressure encountered in brake systems. Care must be taken that this fluid does not come in contact with painted surfaces or plastics. An opened container should always be resealed to prevent contamination by water or dirt.

Undercoating is a petroleum-based tar-like substance that is designed to protect metal surfaces on the under-side of a vehicle from corrosion. It also acts as a sound deadening agent by insulating the bottom of the vehicle.

Weatherstrip cement is used to bond weatherstripping around doors, windows and trunk lids. It is sometimes used to attach trim pieces as well.

Degreasers are heavy duty solvents used to remove grease and grime that accumulate on engine and chassis components. They can be sprayed or brushed on and, depending on the type, are rinsed with either water or solvent.

Solvents are used alone or in combination with degreasers to clean parts and assemblies during repair and overhaul. The home mechanic should use only solvents that are non-flammable and that do not produce irritating fumes.

Gasket sealing compounds may be used in conjunction with gaskets, to improve their sealing capabilities, or alone, to seal metal-to-metal joints. Many gaskets can withstand extreme heat, some are impervious to gasoline and lubricants, while others are capable of filling and sealing large cavities. Depending on the intended use, gasket sealers either dry hard or stay relatively soft and pliable. They are usually applied by hand, with a brush, or are sprayed on the gasket sealing surfaces.

Thread cement is an adhesive locking compound that prevents threaded fasteners from loosening because of vibration. It is available in a variety of types for different applications.

Moisture dispersants are usually sprays that can be used to dry out electrical components such as the distributor, fuse block and wiring connectors. Some types can also be used as treatment for rubber and as a lubricant for hinges, cables and locks.

Waxes and polishes are used to help protect painted and plated surfaces from the weather. Different types of paint may require the use of different types of wax or polish. Some polishes utilize a chemical or abrasive cleaner to help remove the top layer of oxidized (dull) paint in older vehicles.

Troubleshooting

Contents

---

1 Engine will not rotate when attempting to start

1 Battery terminal connection loose or corroded. Check the cable terminals at the battery; tighten or clean corrosion as necessary.
2 Battery discharged or faulty. If the cable connectors are clean and tight on the battery posts, turn the key to the On position and switch on the headlights and/or windshield wipers. If these fail to function, the battery is discharged.
3 Automatic transaxle not fully engaged in Park or manual transaxle clutch not fully depressed.
4 Broken, loose or disconnected wiring in the starting circuit. Inspect all wiring and connectors at the battery, starter solenoid (at lower right side of engine) and ignition switch (on steering column).
5 Starter motor pinion jammed on flywheel ring gear. If manual transaxle, place gearshift in gear and rock the vehicle to manually turn the engine. Remove starter (Chapter 5) and inspect pinion and flywheel (Chapter 5) at earliest convenience.
6 Starter solenoid faulty (Chapter 5).
7 Starter motor faulty (Chapter 5).
8 Ignition switch (Chapter 5).

---

2 Engine rotates but will not start

1 Fuel tank empty.
2 Battery discharged (engine rotates slowly). Check the operation of electrical components as described in previous Section (see Chapter 1).
3 Battery terminal connections loose or corroded. See previous Section.
4 Carburetor flooded and/or fuel level in carburetor incorrect. This

will usually be accompanied by a strong fuel odor from under the hood. Wait a few minutes, depress the accelerator pedal all the way to the floor and attempt to start the engine.

5   Choke control inoperative (Chapter 4).

6   Fuel not reaching carburetor. With ignition switch in Off position, open hood, remove the top plate of air cleaner assembly and observe the top of the carburetor (manually move choke plate back if necessary). Have an assistant depress accelerator pedal fully and check that fuel spurts into carburetor. If not, check fuel filter (Chapters 1 and 4), fuel lines and fuel pump (Chapter 4).

7   Excessive moisture on, or damage to, ignition components (Chapter 5).

8   Worn, faulty or incorrectly adjusted spark plugs (Chapter 1).

9   Broken, loose or disconnected wiring in the starting circuit (see previous Section).

10 Distributor loose, thus changing ignition timing. Turn the distributor as necessary to start the engine, then set ignition timing as soon as possible (Chapter 5).

11 Ignition condenser faulty (Chapter 5).

12 Broken, loose or disconnected wires at the ignition coil, or faulty coil (Chapter 5).

3   Starter motor operates without rotating engine

1   Starter pinion sticking. Remove the starter (Chapter 5) and inspect.

2   Starter pinion or engine flywheel teeth worn or broken. Remove the inspection cover at the rear of the engine and inspect.

4   Engine hard to start when cold

1   Battery discharged or low. Check as described in Section 1.

2   Choke control inoperative or out of adjustment (Chapter 4).

3   Carburetor flooded (see Section 2).

4   Fuel supply not reaching the carburetor (see Section 2).

5   Carburetor worn and in need of overhauling (Chapter 4).

5   Engine hard to start when hot

1   Choke sticking in the closed position (Chapter 1).

2   Carburetor flooded (see Section 2).

3   Air filter in need of replacement (Chapter 4).

4   Fuel not reaching the carburetor (Section 2).

6   Starter motor noisy or excessively rough in engagement

1   Pinion or flywheel gear teeth worn or broken. Remove the inspection cover at the rear of the engine and inspect.

2   Starter motor retaining bolts loose or missing.

7   Engine starts but stops immediately

1   Loose or faulty electrical connections at distributor, coil or alternator.

2   Insufficient fuel reaching the carburetor. Disconnect the fuel line at the carburetor and remove the filter (Chapter 1). Place a container under the disconnected fuel line. Observe the flow of fuel from the line. If little or none at all, check for blockage in the lines and/or replace the fuel pump (Chapter 4).

3   Vacuum leak at the gasket surfaces or the intake manifold and/or carburetor. Check that all mounting bolts (nuts) are tightened to specifications and all vacuum hoses connected to the carburetor and manifold are positioned properly and are in good condition.

8   Engine 'lopes' while idling or idles erratically

1   Vacuum leakage. Check mounting bolts (nuts) at the carburetor and intake manifold for tightness. Check that all vacuum hoses are connected and are in good condition. Use a doctor's stethoscope or a length of fuel line hose held against your ear to listen for vacuum leaks while the engine is running. A hissing sound will be heard. A soapy water solution will also detect leaks. Check the carburetor and intake manifold gasket surfaces.

2   Leaking EGR valve or plugged PCV valve (see Chapter 6).

3   Air cleaner clogged and in need of replacement (Chapter 1).

4   Fuel pump not delivering sufficient fuel to the carburetor (see Section 7).

5   Carburetor out of adjustment (Chapter 4).

6   Leaking head gasket. If this is suspected, take the vehicle to a repair shop or dealer where this can be pressure checked without the need to remove the heads.

7   Timing chain or gears worn and in need of replacement (Chapter 1).

8   Camshaft lobes worn, necessitating the removal of the camshaft for inspection (Chapter 2).

9   Engine misses at idle speed

1   Spark plugs faulty or not gapped properly (Chapter 1).

2   Faulty spark plug wires (Chapter 1).

3   Carburetor choke not operating properly (Chapter 4).

4   Sticking or faulty emissions systems (see Troubleshooting in Chapter 3).

5   Clogged fuel filter and/or foreign matter in fuel. Remove the fuel filter (Chapter 3) and inspect.

6   Vacuum leaks at carburetor, intake manifold or at hose connections. Check as described in Section 8.

7   Incorrect speed or idle mixture (Chapter 4).

8   Incorrect ignition timing (Chapter 1).

9   Uneven or low cylinder compression. Remove plugs and use compression tester as per manufacturer's instructions.

10 Engine misses throughout driving speed range

1   Carburetor fuel filter clogged and/or impurities in the fuel system (Chapter 4). Also check fuel output at the carburetor (see Section 7).

2   Faulty or incorrectly gapped spark plugs (Chapter 1).

3   Incorrectly set ignition timing (Chapter 1).

4   Check for a cracked distributor cap, disconnected distributor wires or damage to the distributor components (Chapter 1).

5   Leaking spark plug wires (Chapter 1).

6   Emission system components faulty (Chapter 6).

7   Low or uneven cylinder compression pressures. Remove spark plugs and test compression with gauge.

8   Weak or faulty EEC ignition system (see Chapter 5).

9   Vacuum leaks at carburetor, intake manifold or vacuum hoses (see Section 8).

11 Engine stalls

1   Carburetor idle speed incorrectly set (Chapter 1).

2   Carburetor fuel filter clogged and/or water and impurities in the fuel system (Chapter 4).

3   Choke improperly adjusted or sticking (Chapter 1).

4   Distributor components damp, points out of adjustment or damage to distributor cap, rotor etc. (Chapter 5).

5   Emission system components faulty (Troubleshooting section, Chapter 6).

6   Faulty or incorrectly gapped spark plugs Chapter 5). Also check spark plug wires (Chapter 1).

7   Vacuum leak at the carburetor, intake manifold or vacuum hoses. Check as described in Section 8.

8   Valve lash incorrectly set (Chapter 2).

12 Engine lacks power

1   Incorrect ignition timing (Chapter 1).

2   Excessive play in distributor shaft. At the same time check for worn or maladjusted contact rotor, faulty distributor cap, wires, etc. (Chapter 5).

3   Faulty or incorrectly gapped spark plugs (Chapter 1).

4   Carburetor not adjusted properly or excessively worn (Chapter 4).
5   Weak coil or condensor (Chapter 5).
6   Faulty EEC system coil (Chapter 5).
7   Brakes binding (Chapter 9).
8   Automatic transaxle fluid level incorrect, causing slippage (Chapter 7).
9   Manual transaxle clutch slipping (Chapter 7).
10   Fuel filter clogged and/or impurities in the fuel system (Chapter 4).
11   Emission control system not functioning properly (Chapter 6).
12   Use of sub-standard fuel. Fill tank with proper octane fuel.
13   Low or uneven cylinder compression pressures. Test with compression tester, which will detect leaking valves and/or blown head gasket.

13 Engine backfire

1   Emission system not functioning properly (Chapter 6).
2   Ignition timing incorrect (Section 1).
3   Carburetor in need of adjustment or worn excessively (Chapter 4).
4   Vacuum leak at carburetor, intake manifold or vacuum hoses. Check as described in Section 8.
5   Valve lash incorrectly set, and/or valves sticking (Chapter 2).

14 Pinging or knocking engine sounds on hard acceleration or uphill

1   Incorrect grade of fuel. Fill tank with fuel of the proper octane rating.
2   Ignition timing incorrect (Chapter 5).
3   Carburetor in need of adjustment (Chapter 4).
4   Improper spark plugs. Check plug type with that specified on tune-up decal located inside engine compartment. Also check plugs and wires for damage (Chapter 6).
5   Worn or damaged distributor components (Chapter 5).
6   Faulty emission system (Chapter 6).
7   Vacuum leak. (Check as described in Section 8).

15 Engine 'diesels' (continues to run) after switching off

1   Idle speed too fast (Chapter 5).
2   Electrical solenoid at side of carburetor not functioning properly (not all models, see Chapter 4).
3   Ignition timing incorrectly adjusted (Chapter 1).
4   Air cleaner valve not operating properly (Chapter 4).
5   Excessive engine operating temperatures. Probable causes of this are: malfunctioning thermostat, clogged radiator, faulty water pump (see Chapter 3).

Engine electrical

16 Battery will not hold a charge

1   Alternator drivebelt defective or not adjusted properly (Chapter 1).
2   Electrolyte level too low or too weak (Chapter 5).
3   Battery terminals loose or corroded (Chapter 5).
4   Alternator not charging properly (Chapter 5).
5   Loose, broken or faulty wiring in the charging circuit (Chapter 5).
6   Short in vehicle circuitry causing a continual drain on battery.
7   Battery defect internally.

17 Ignition light fails to go out

1   Faulty in alternator or charging circuit (Chapter 5).
2   Alternator drivebelt defective or not properly adjusted (Chapter 5).

18 Ignition light fails to come on when key is turned

1   Ignition light bulb faulty (Chapter 10).

2   Alternator faulty (Chapter 5).
3   Fault in the printed circuit, dash wiring or bulb holder (Chapter 10).

Engine fuel system

19 Excessive fuel consumption

1   Dirty or choked air filter element (Chapter 1).
2   Incorrectly set ignition timing (Chapter 1).
3   Choke sticking or improperly adjusted (Chapter 1).
4   Emission system not functioning properly (not all vehicles, see Chapter 6).
5   Carburetor idle speed and/or mixture not adjusted properly (Chapter 4).
6   Carburetor internal parts excessively worn or damaged (Chapter 4).
7   Low tire pressure or incorrect tire size (Chapter 10).

20 Fuel leakage and/or fuel odor

1   Leak in a fuel feed or vent line (Chapter 4).
2   Tank overfilled. Fill only to automatic shut-off.
3   Emission system filter in need of replacement (Chapter 6).
4   Vapor leaks from system lines (Chapter 4).
5   Carburetor internal parts excessively worn or out of adjustment (Chapter 4).

Engine cooling system

21 Overheating

1   Insufficient coolant in system (Chapter 3).
2   Fault in electric fan motor or wiring.
3   Radiator core blocked or radiator grille dirty and restricted (Chapter 3).
4   Thermostat faulty (Chapter 3).
5   Fan blades broken or cracked (Chapter 3).
6   Radiator cap not maintaining proper pressure. Have cap pressure tested by gas station or repair shop.
7   Ignition timing incorrect (Chapter 1).

22 Overcooling

1   Thermostat faulty (Chapter 3).
2   Inaccurate temperature gauge (Chapter 10).

23 External water leakage

1   Deteriorated or damaged hoses. Loosen clamps at hose connections (Chapter 1).
2   Water pump seals defective. If this is the case, water will drip from the water pump body (Chapter 3).
3   Leakage from radiator core or header tank. This will require the radiator to be professionally repaired (see Chapter 3 for removal procedures).
4   Engine drain plugs or water jacket freeze plugs leaking (see Chapters 2 and 3).

24 Internal water leakage

Note: *Internal coolant leaks can usually be detected by examining the oil. Check the dipstick and inside of valve cover for water deposits and an oil consistency like that of a milkshake.*
1   Faulty cylinder head gasket. Have the system pressure-tested professionally or remove the cylinder heads (Chapter 2) and inspect.
2   Cracked cylinder bore or cylinder head. Dismantle engine and inspect (Chapter 2).

25 Water loss

1   Overfilling system (Chapter 3).
2   Coolant boiling away due to overheating (see causes in Section 15).
3   Internal or external leakage (see Sections 22 and 33).
4   Faulty radiator cap. Have the cap pressure tested.

26 Poor coolant circulation

1   Inoperative water pump. A quick test is to pinch the top radiator hose closed with your hand while the engine is idling, then let it loose. You should feel the surge of water if the pump is working properly (Chapter 3).
2   Restriction in cooling system. Drain, flush and refill the system (Chapter 3). If it appears necessary, remove the radiator (Chapter 3) and have it reverse-flushed or professionally cleaned.
3   Fan drivebelt defective or not adjusted properly (Chapter 3).
4   Thermostat sticking (Chapter 3).

Clutch

27 Fails to release (pedal pressed to the floor – shift lever does not move freely in and out of reverse

1   Improper linkage adjustment (Chapter 8).
2   Clutch linkage malfunction (Chapter 8).
3   Clutch disc warped, bent or excessively damaged (Chapter 8).

28 Clutch slips (engine speed increases with no increases in road speed)

1   Linkage in need of adjustment (Chapter 8).
2   Clutch disc oil soaked or facing worn. Remove disc (Chapter 8) and inspect.
3   Clutch disc not seated in. It may take 30 or 40 normal starts for a new disc to seat.

29 Grabbing (juddering) on take-up

1   Oil on clutch disc facings. Remove disc (Chapter 8) and inspect. Correct any leakage source.
2   Worn or loose engine or transmission mounts. These units move slightly when clutch is released. Inspect mounts and bolts.
3   Worn splines on clutch gear. Remove clutch components (Chapter 8) and inspect.
4   Warped pressure plate or flywheel. Remove clutch components and inspect.

30 Squeal or rumble with clutch fully engaged (pedal released)

1   Improper adjustment; no lash (Chapter 8).
2   Release bearing binding on transmission bearing retainer. Remove clutch components (Chapter 8) and check bearing. Remove any burrs or nicks, clean and relubricate before reinstallation.
3   Weak linkage return spring. Replace the spring.

31 Squeal or rumble with clutch fully disengaged (pedal depressed)

1   Worn, faulty or broken release bearing (Chapter 8).
2   Worn or broken pressure plate springs (or diaphragm fingers) (Chapter 8).

32 Clutch pedal stays on floor when disengaged

1   Bind in leakage or release bearing. Inspect linkage or remove clutch components as necessary.
2   Linkage springs being over-traveled. Adjust linkage for proper lash. Make sure proper pedal stop (bumper) is installed.

Manual transaxle
Note: *All the following Sections contained within Chapter 7 unless noted.*

33 Noisy in Neutral with engine running

1   Input shaft bearing worn.
2   Damaged main drive drive gear bearing.
3   Worn countergear bearings.
4   Worn or damaged countergear anti-lash plate.

34 Noisy in all gears

1   Any of the above causes, and/or:
2   Insufficient lubricant (see checking procedures in Chapter 7).

35 Noisy in one particular gear

1   Worn, damaged or chipped gear teeth for that particular gear.
2   Worn or damaged synchronizer for that particular gear.

36 Slips out of high gear

1   Damaged shift linkage.
2   Interference between the floor shift handle and console.
3   Broken or loose engine mounts.
4   Shift mechanism stabilizer bar loose.
5   Damage or worn transaxle internal components.
6   Improperly installed shifter boot.

37 Difficulty in engaging gears

1   Clutch not releasing fully (see clutch adjustment, Chapter 8).
2   Loose, damaged or maladjusted shift linkage. Make a thorough inspection, replacing parts as necessary. Adjust as described in Chapter 7.

38 Fluid leakage

1   Excessive amount of lubricant in transaxle (see Chapter 7) for correct checking procedures. Drain lubricant as required).
2   Side cover loose or gasket damaged.
3   Rear oil seal or speedometer oil seal in need of replacement (Section 6).

Automatic transaxle
Note: *Due to the complexity of the automatic transaxle, it is difficult for the home mechanic to properly diagnose and service this component. For problems other than the following, the vehicle should be taken to a reputable mechanic.*

39 Fluid leakage

1   Automatic transaxle fluid is a deep red color, and fluid leaks should not be confused with engine oil which can easily be blown by air flow to the transmission.
2   To pinpoint a leak, first remove all built-up dirt and grime from around the transaxle. Degreasing agents and/or steam cleaning will achieve this. With the underside clean, drive the vehicle at low speeds so that air flow will not blow the leak far from its source. Raise the vehicle and determine where the leak is coming from. Common areas of leakage are:

a) *Fluid pan:* tighten mounting bolts and/or replace pan gasket as necessary (see Chapter 7)

b) *Rear extension:* tighten bolts and/or replace oil seal as necessary (Chapter 7)

c) *Filler pipe:* replace the rubber seal where pipe enters transaxle case

d) *Transaxle oil lines:* tighten connectors where lines enter transaxle case and/or replace lines

e) *Vent pipe:* transaxle over-filled and/or water in fluid (see checking procedures, Chapter 7)

f) *Speedometer connector:* replace the O-ring where speedometer cable enters transaxle case

40 General shift mechanism problems

1   Chapter 7 deals with checking and adjusting the shift linkage on automatic transaxles. Common problems which may be attributed to maladjustment linkage are:

a) Engine starting in gears other than Park or Neutral
b) Indicator on quandrant pointing to a gear other than the one actually being used
c) Vehicle will not hold firm when in Park position
Refer to Chapter 7 to adjust the manual linkage.

41 Transaxle will not downshift with accelerator pedal pressed to the floor

1   Chapter 7 deals with adjusting the downshift cable or downshift switch to enable the transaxle to downshift properly.

42 Engine will not start in gears other than Park or Neutral

1   Chapter 7 deals with adjusting the Neutral start switches used with automatic transaxle.

43 Transaxle slips, shifts rough, is noisy or has no drive in forward or reverse gears

1   There are many probable causes for the above problems, but the home mechanic should concern himself only with one possibility: fluid level.
2   Before taking the vehicle to a specialist, check the level of the fluid and condition of the fluid as described in Chapter 7. Correct fluid level as necessary or change the fluid and filter if needed. If problem persists, have a professional diagnose the probable cause.

Drive axles

44 Clicking noise in turns

1   Worn or damaged outboard joint. Check for cut or damaged seals. Repair as necessary (Chapter 8).

45 Knock or clunk when accelerating from a coast

1   Worn or damaged inboard joint. Check for cut or damaged seals. Repair as necessary (Chapter 8).

46 Shudder or vibration during acceleration

1   Excessive joint angle. Have checked and correct as necessary (Chapter 8).
2   Worn or damaged inboard or outboard joints. Repair or replace as necessary (Chapter 8).
3   Sticking inboard joint assembly. Correct or replace as necessary (Chapter 8).

Brakes

Note: *Before assuming a brake problem exists, check that the tires are in good condition and are inflated properly (see Chapter 1): the front end alignment is correct (see Chapter 11): and that the vehicle is not loaded with weight in an unequal manner.*

47 Vehicle pulls to one side under braking

1   Defective, damaged or oil-contaminated disc pad on one side. Inspect as described in Chapter 1. Refer to Chapter 9 if replacement is required.
2   Excessive wear or brake pad material or disc on one side. Inspect and correct as necessary.
3   Loose or disconnected front suspension components. Inspect and tighten all bolts to specifications (Chapter 1).
4   Defective caliper assembly. Remove caliper and inspect for stuck piston or damage (Chapter 9).

48 Noise (high-pitched squeak without brake applied)

1   Front brake pads worn out. This noise comes from the wear sensor rubbing against the disc. Replace pads with new ones immediately (Chapter 9).

49 Excessive brake pedal travel

1   Partial brake system failure. Inspect entire system (Chapter 1) and correct as required.
2   Insufficient fluid in master cylinder. Check (Chapter 1) and add fluid and bleed system if necessary (Chapter 9).
3   Rear brakes not adjusting properly. Make a series of starts and stops while the vehicle is in Reverse. If this does not correct the situation remove drums and inspect self-adjusters (Chapter 1).

50 Brake pedal appears spongy when depressed

1   Air in hydraulic lines. Bleed the brake system (Chapter 9).
2   Faulty flexible hoses. Inspect all system hoses and lines. Replace parts as necessary.
3   Master cylinder mountings insecure. Inspect master cylinder bolts (nuts) and torque tighten to specifications.
4   Master cylinder faulty (Chapter 9).

51 Excessive effort required to stop vehicle

1   Power brake booster not operating properly (Chapter 9).
2   Excessively worn linings or pads. Inspect and replace if necessary (Chapter 1).
3   One or more caliper pistons (front wheels) or wheel cylinders (rear wheels) seized. Inspect and rebuild as required (Chapter 9).
4   Brake linings or pads contaminated with oil or grease. Inspect and replace as required (Chapter 1).
5   New pads or linings fitted and not yet 'bedded-in'. It will take a while for the new material to seat against the drum (or rotor).

52 Pedal travels to floor with little resistance

1   Little or no fluid in the master cylinder reservoir caused by: leaking wheel cylinder(s); leaking caliper piston(s); loose, damaged or disconnected brake lines. Inspect entire system and correct as necessary.

53 Brake pedal pulsates during brake application

1   Wheel bearings not adjusted properly or in need of replacement (Chapter 1).
2   Caliper not sliding properly due to improper installation or obstructions. Remove and inspect (Chapter 9).
3   Rotor not within specifications. Remove the rotor (Chapter 9) and

check for excessive lateral run-out and parellelism. Have the rotor professionally machined or replace it with a new one.
4   Out-of-round rear brake drums. Remove the drums (Chapter 9) and have them professionally machined, or replace them.

Suspension and steering

54 Car pulls to one side

1   Tire pressures uneven (Chapter 1).
2   Defective tire (Chapter 1).
3   Excessive wear in suspension or steering components (Chapter 1).
4   Front end in need of alignment (Chapter 11).
5   Front brakes dragging. Inspect braking system as described in Chapter 1.

55 Shimmy, shake or vibration

1   Tire or wheel out of balance or out of round. Have professionally balanced.
2   Loose or worn wheel; bearings (Chapter 1). Replace as necessary (Chapter 11).
3   Shock absorbers and/or suspension components worn or damaged (Chapter 11).

56 Excessive pitching and/or rolling around corners or during braking

1   Defective shock absorbers. Replace as a set (Chapter 11).
2   Broken or weak coil springs and/or suspension components. Inspect as described in Chapter 11.

57 Excessively stiff steering

1   Lack of lubricant in power steering fluid reservoir (Chapter 1).
2   Incorrect tire pressures (Chapter 1).
3   Lack of lubrication at balljoints (Chapter 1).
4   Front end out of alignment.
5   Rack and pinions out of adjustment or lacking lubrication.
6   See also Section 59 'Lack of power assistance'.

58 Excessive play in steering

1   Loose wheel bearings (Chapter 1).
2   Excessive wear in suspension or steering components (Chapter 1).
3   Rack and pinion out of adjustment (Chapter 11).

59 Lack of power assistance

1   Steering pump drivebelt faulty or not adjusted properly (Chapter 1).

2   Fluid level low (Chapter 1).
3   Hoses or pipes restricting the flow. Inspect and replace parts as necessary.
4   Air in power steering system. Bleed system (Chapter 11).

60 Excessive tire wear (not specific to one area)

1   Incorrect tire pressures (Chapter 1).
2   Tires out of balance. Have professionally balanced.
3   Wheel damaged. Inspect and replace as necessary.
4   Suspension of steering components excessively worn (Chapter 1).

61 Excessive tire wear on outside edge

1   Inflation pressures not correct (Chapter 1).
2   Excessive speed on turns.
3   Front end alignment incorrect (excessive toe-in). Have professionally aligned (Chapter 11).
4   Suspension arm bent or twisted.

62 Excessive tire wear on inside edge

1   Inflation pressures incorrect (Chapter 1).
2   Front end alignment incorrect (toe-out). Have professionally aligned (Chapter 11).
3   Loose or damaged steering components (Chapter 1).

63 Tire tread worn in one place

1   Tires out of balance. Balance tires professionally.
2   Damaged or buckled wheel. Inspect and replace if necessary.
3   Defective tire.

64 General vibration at highway speeds

1   Out-of-balance front wheels or tires. Have them profesionally balanced.
2   Front or rear wheel bearings. Check (Chapter 1) and replace as necessary (Chapter 11).
3   Defective tire or wheel. Have them checked and replaced if necessary.

65 Noise – whether coasting or in drive

1   Road noise. No corrective procedures available.
2   Tire noise. Inspect tires and tire pressures (Chapter 1).
3   Front wheel bearings loose, worn or damaged. Check (Chapter 1) and replace if necessary (Chapter 11).
4   Lack of lubrication in the balljoints or tie rod ends (Chapter 1).
5   Damaged shock absorbers or mountings (Chapter 1).
6   Loose wheel nuts. Check and tighten as necessary (Chapter 11).

Safety first!

However enthusiastic you may be about getting on with the job at hand, take the time to ensure that your safety is not jeopardized. A moment's lack of attention can result in an accident, as can failure to observe certain simple safety precautions. The possibility of an accident will always exist, and the following points do not pretend to be a comprehensive list of all dangers; rather, they are intended to make you aware of the risks and to encourage a safety-conscious approach to all work you carry out on your vehicle.

Essential DOs and DON'Ts

DON'T rely on a jack when working under the vehicle. Always use approved jack stands to support the weight of the vehicle and place them under the recommended lift or support points.

DON'T attempt to loosen highly torqued fasteners (i.e. wheel nuts) while the vehicle is on a jack; it may fall.

DON'T start the engine without first checking that the transmission is in Neutral (or Park where applicable) and the parking brake is set.

DON'T remove the radiator cap from a hot cooling system — let it cool or cover it with a cloth and release the pressure gradually.

DON'T attempt to drain the engine oil until you are sure it has cooled to the point that it will not burn you.

DON'T touch any part of the engine or exhaust system until they have cooled down sufficiently to avoid burns.

DON'T siphon toxic liquids (such as gasoline, brake fluid and anti-freeze by mouth, or allow them to remain on your skin.

DON'T inhale brake lining dust — it is potentially hazardous.

DON'T allow spilled oil or grease to remain on the floor — wipe it up before someone slips on it.

DON'T use loose-fitting wrenches or other tools which may slip and cause injury.

DON'T push on wrenches when loosening or tightening nuts or bolts. Always try to pull the wrench towards you. If the situation calls for pushing the wrench away, push with an open hand to avoid scraped knuckles if the wrench should slip.

DON'T attempt to lift a heavy component which may be beyond your capability — get someone to help you.

DON'T rush, or take unsafe shortcuts, to finish a job.

DON'T allow children or animals in or around the vehicle while you are working on it.

DO wear eye protection when using power tools such as a drill, sander, bench grinder, etc., and when working under a vehicle.

DO keep loose clothing and long hair well out of the way of moving parts.

DO make sure that any hoist used has a safe working load rating adequate for the job.

DO get someone to check on you periodically when working alone on a vehicle.

DO carry out tasks in a logical sequence and check that everything is correctly assembled and tightened.

DO remember that your vehicle's safety affects that of yourself and others. If in doubt on any point, get professional advice.

Fire

Remember at all times that gasoline is highly flammable. Never smoke, or have any kind of open flame around, when working on a vehicle. But, the risk does not end there; — a spark caused by an electrical short-circuit, by two metal surfaces contacting each other, or even by static electricity built up in your body under certain conditions can ignite gasoline vapors, which in a confined space are highly explosive.

Always disconnect the battery ground (-) cable before working on any part of the fuel system or electrical systems, and never risk spilling fuel on to a hot engine or exhaust.

It is highly recommended that a fire extinguisher of a type suitable for fuel and electrical fires is kept handy in the garage or workshop at all times. Never try to extinguish a fuel or electrical fire with water.

Fumes

Certain fumes are highly toxic and can quickly cause unconsciousness and even death if inhaled to any extent. Gasoline vapor comes into this category, as do the vapors from some cleaning solvents. Any draining or pouring of such volatile fluids should be done in a well ventilated area.

When using cleaning fluids and solvents, read the instructions carefully. Never use materials from unmarked containers.

Never run the engine of a motor vehicle in an enclosed space such as a garage; exhaust fumes contain carbon monoxide, which is extremely poisonous. If you need to run the engine, always do so in the open air (or at least have the rear of the vehicle outside the work area).

If you are fortunate enough to have the use of an inspection pit, never drain or pour gasoline and never run the engine, while the vehicle is over the pit; the fumes, being heavier than air, will concentrate in the pit with possible lethal results.

The battery

Never create a spark or allow a bare light bulb near the vehicle's battery. It will normally be giving off a certain amount of hydrogen gas, which is highly explosive.

Always disconnect the battery ground cable before working on the fuel or electrical systems.

If possible, loosen the filler caps or cover when charging the battery from an external source. Do not charge at an excessive rate or the battery may burst.

Take care when adding water and when carrying a battery. The electrolyte, even when diluted, is very corrosive and should not be allowed to contact clothing or skin.

Household current

When using an electric power tool, inspection light etc, which operates on household current, always ensure that the tool is correctly connected to its plug and that, where necessary, it is properly grounded. Do not use such items in damp conditions and, again, do not create a spark or apply excessive heat in the vicinity of fuel or fuel vapor.

Secondary ignition system voltage

A severe electric shock can result from touching certain parts of the ignition system (such as the spark plug wires) when the engine is running or being cranked, paticularly if components are damp or the insulation is defective. Where an electronic ignition system is in use, the secondary system voltage is much higher and could prove fatal.

Chapter 1 Tune-up and routine maintenance

Refer to Chapter 13 for information and specifications related to 1981 thru 1985 models

Contents

Specifications

Note: *Additional specifications can be found in the appropriate Chapters.*

Engine oil type .... API classification SE or SF. Consult owners manual for viscosity recommendations

Engine oil capacity .... 3.5 US qts

Engine coolant type .... 50/50 mix of ethylene glycol-based coolant

Radiator capacity
1.3L engine .... 7.4 US pts
1.6L engine .... 8.0 US pts

Automatic transaxle fluid type .... DEXRON II

Automatic transaxle capacity .... 9.8 US qts

Manual transaxle fluid type .... Type F automatic transmission fluid

Manual transaxle capacity .... 5.0 US pts

Power steering pump fluid type .... Type F automatic transmission fluid

Power steering pump capacity .... 1.6 US pts

Wheel bearing grease .... NLGI No. 2

Ignition system .... Consult emissions decal for further information

Spark plug firing order 1-3-4-2

Distributor direction of rotation .... Clockwise

Brakes
Disc pad minimum lining thickness .... $\frac{1}{8}$ in
Drum brake minimum lining thickness .... $\frac{1}{8}$ in

Torque specifications

	Ft-lb	Nm
Carburetor-to-intake manifold	12 to 15	16 to 20
Fuel supply line-to-filter	15 to 18	20 to 24
Fuel filter-to-carburetor	7 to 8	10 to 11

Other recommended lubricants

Hood hinge and latch	Polyethylene grease
Door hinge	Disc brake caliper grease
Clutch pedal pivot bushing	SAE 10W-30 engine oil
Parking brake cable	Polyethylene grease
Weatherstripping	Silicone spray lubricant
Lock cylinders	Graphite lock lubricant

1 General information

Caution: *The electric fan can start at any time, even when the ignition is off. Consequently, the negative battery cable should be disconnected whenever you are working in the vicinity of the fan.*

This vehicle was designed with reduced maintenance in mind and consequently the maintenance schedule varies somewhat from usual automotive practice. For example, the suspension, steering and constant velocity joints are 'lubricated for life' and have no provision for lubrication. These components should not be forgotten however, and should be inspected periodically for leaking, looseness or wear.

Other unusual features of these models are the use of Type F automatic transmission fluid in the manual transmission and the aluminium cylinder head and radiator which make the use of the proper coolant critical.

Consult the General information Section of each Chapter to determine what components may require special maintenance techniques.

2 Introduction

This chapter was designed to help the home mechanic maintain his (or her) car for peak performance, economy, safety and longevity.

On the following pages you will find a maintenance schedule along with Sections which deal specifically with each item on the schedule. Included are visual checks, adjustments and item replacements.

Servicing your car using the time/mileage maintenance schedule and the sequenced Sections will give you a planned program of maintenance. Keep in mind that it is a full plan, and maintaining only a few items at the specified intervals will not give you the same results.

You will find as you service your car that many of the procedures can, and should, be grouped together, due to the nature of the job at hand. Examples of this are as follows:

If the car is fully raised for a chassis inspection for example, this is the ideal time for the following checks: manual transaxle fluid, exhaust system, suspension, steering and the fuel system.

If the tires and wheels are removed, as during a routine tire rotation, go ahead and check the brakes and wheel bearings at the same time.

If you must borrow or rent a torque wrench, you will do best to service the spark plugs and/or repack (or replace) the wheel bearings all in the same day to save time and money.

The first step of this or any maintenance plan is to prepare yourself before the actual work begins. Read through the appropriate Sections for all work that is to be performed before you begin. Gather together all necessary parts and tools. If it appears you could have a problem during a particular job, don't hesitate to ask advice from your local parts man or dealer service department.

Note: *The following maintenance intervals are recommended by the manufacturer. In the interest of vehicle longevity, we recommend shorter intervals on certain operations such as fluid and filter replacements.*

Weekly or every 250 miles (400 km)

Check the engine oil level, adding as necessary
Check windshield wiper blade condition
Check the engine coolant level, adding as necessary
Check the tires and tire pressures
Check the automatic transaxle fluid level
Check the power steering reservoir level
Check the brake fluid level
Check the battery condition
Check the windshield washer level
Check the operation of all lights
Check horn operation

7500 miles (12,000 km)

Check engine oil and filter (Chapter 1)
Check drivebelt tension (Chapter 1)
Check idle speed (Chapter 4)
Check throttle valve (TV) linkage (Chapter 7)
Check air conditioning and heater hoses (Chapter 3)

15,000 miles (24,000 km)

Change engine oil and filter (Chapter 1)
Check drivebelt tension (Chapter 3)

22,500 miles (36,000 km)

Change engine oil and filter (Chapter 1)
Check air conditioning and heater hoses (Chapter 3)
Inspect brake lines and linings (Chapter 9)

30,000 miles (48,000 m)

Change engine oil and filter (Chapter 1)
Drain and replace engine coolant (Chapter 1)
Replace spark plugs (Chapter 1)
Check drivebelt tension (Chapter 3)
Check engine idle (Chapter 4)
Replace carburetor air cleaner (Chapter 1)
Replace crankcase emission filter (Chapter 1)
Clean choke linkage (Chapter 4)
Inspect exhaust system (Chapter 1)
Check throttle valve (TV) linkage (Chapter 7)

37,500 miles (60,000 km)

Change engine oil and filter (Chapter 1)
Check air conditioning and heater hoses (Chapter 3)

45,000 miles (72,000 km)

Change engine oil and filter (Chapter 1)
Check drivebelt tension (Chapter 3)
Check air conditioning and heater hoses (Chapter 3)
Inspect brake lines and linings (Chapter 9)

52,500 miles (84,000 km)

Change engine oil and filter

60,000 miles (96,000 km)

Replace spark plugs (Chapter 1)
Check drivebelt tension (Chapter 1)
Check throttle valve linkage (Chapter 7)
Replace engine timing belt (Chapter 2)
Replace air cleaner element (Chapter 1)
Change engine oil and filter (Chapter 1)
Drain and replace engine coolant (Chapter 1)
Check engine idle speeds (Chapter 4)
Inspect exhaust system and shields (Chapter 1)
Clean choke linkage (Chapter 4)

Severe operating conditions

Severe operating conditions are defined as:
   Frequent short trips or long periods of idling
   Driving at sustained high speeds during hot weather (over 90°F, +32°C)
   Towing a trailer for long distances
   Driving in temperatures below 10°F (-12°C) for 60 or more days
   Driving 2000 miles (3200 km) or more per month
If the vehicle has been operated under severe conditions, follow these maintenance intervals:
Change engine oil and filter every 2000 (3200 km) or two months

Clean and regap the spark plugs every 6000 miles (9600 km)
Drain and refill the automatic transaxle every 22,500 miles (36,000 km) if the vehicle is driven 2000 or more miles per month
Change the air and fuel filters more frequently

3 Fluid levels check

1   There are a number of components on a vehicle which rely on the use of fluids to perform their job. Through the normal operation of the car, these fluids are used up and must be replenished before damage occurs. See the *Recommended Lubricants* specifications for the specific fluid to be used when adding is required. When checking fluid levels it is important that the car is on a level surface.

Engine oil

2   The engine oil level is checked with a dipstick which is located at the side of the engine block. This dipstick travels through a tube and into the oil pan at the bottom of the engine.
3   The oil level should be checked preferably before the car has been driven, or about 15 minutes after the engine has been shut off. If the oil is checked immediately after driving the car, some of the oil will remain in the upper engine components, thus giving an inaccurate reading on the dipstick.
4   Pull the dipstick from its tube and wipe all the oil from the end with a clean rag. Insert the clean dipstick all the way back into the oil pan and pull it out again. Observe the oil at the end of the dipstick. At its highest point, the level should be between the 'Add' and 'Full' marks.
5   It takes approximately 1 quart of oil to raise the level from the 'Add' mark to the 'Full' mark on the dipstick. Do not allow the level to drop below the 'Add' mark as this may cause engine damage due to oil starvation. On the other hand, do not overfill the engine by adding oil above the 'Full' mark as this may result in oil-fouled spark plugs, oil leaks or oil seal failures.
6   Oil is added to the engine after removing a twist-off cap located either on the rocker arm cover or through a raised tube near the front of the engine. The cap should be duly marked 'Engine oil' or similar

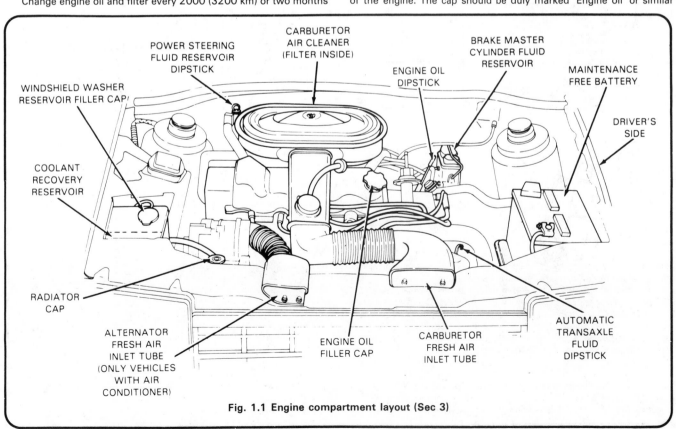

Fig. 1.1 Engine compartment layout (Sec 3)

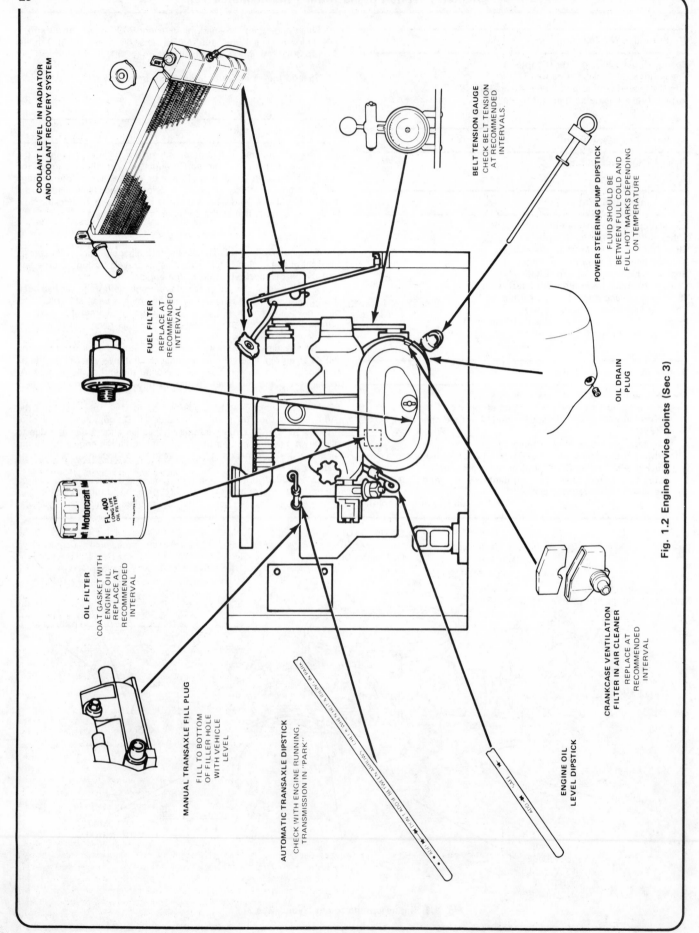

COOLANT LEVEL IN RADIATOR AND COOLANT RECOVERY SYSTEM

BELT TENSION GAUGE
CHECK BELT TENSION AT RECOMMENDED INTERVALS.

POWER STEERING PUMP DIPSTICK
FLUID SHOULD BE BETWEEN FULL COLD AND FULL HOT MARKS DEPENDING ON TEMPERATURE

FUEL FILTER
REPLACE AT RECOMMENDED INTERVAL

OIL DRAIN PLUG

OIL FILTER
COAT GASKET WITH ENGINE OIL. REPLACE AT RECOMMENDED INTERVAL

Motorcraft
FL-400
LONG LIFE
OIL FILTER

MANUAL TRANSAXLE FILL PLUG
FILL TO BOTTOM OF FILLER HOLE WITH VEHICLE LEVEL

AUTOMATIC TRANSAXLE DIPSTICK
CHECK WITH ENGINE RUNNING. TRANSMISSION IN "PARK"

CRANKCASE VENTILATION FILTER IN AIR CLEANER
REPLACE AT RECOMMENDED INTERVAL

ENGINE OIL LEVEL DIPSTICK

Fig. 1.2 Engine service points (Sec 3)

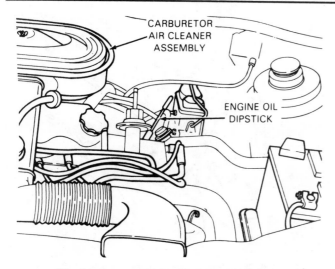

Fig. 1.3 Engine oil dipstick location (Sec 3)

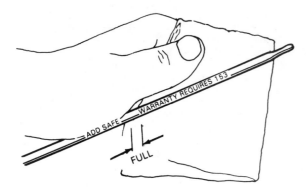

Fig. 1.4 Checking dipstick oil level (Sec 3)

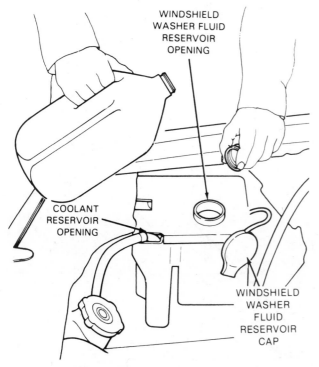

Fig. 1.5 Filling windshield washer reservoir (Sec 3)

wording. An oil can spout or funnel will reduce spills as the oil is poured in.

7   Checking the oil level can also be a step towards preventative maintenance. If you find the oil level dropping abnormally, this is an indication of oil leakage or internal engine wear which should be corrected. If there are water droplets in the oil, or it is milky looking, this also indicates component failure and the engine should be checked immediately. The condition of the oil can also be checked along with the level. With the dipstick removed from the engine, take your thumb and index finger and wipe the oil up the dipstick, looking for small dirt particles or engine filings which will cling to the dipstick. This is an indication that the oil should be drained and fresh oil added (Section 5).

Engine coolant

8   All vehicles are equipped with a pressurized coolant recovery system which makes coolant level checks very easy. A coolant reservoir attached to the inner fender panel is connected by a hose to the radiator cap. As the engine heats up during operation, coolant is forced from the radiator, through the connecting tube and into the reservoir. As the engine cools, this coolant is automatically drawn back into the radiator to keep the correct level.

9   The coolant level should be checked when the engine is cold. Merely observe the level of fluid in the reservoir, which should be at or near the 'Full cold' mark on the side of the reservoir. If the system is completely cooled, also check the level in the radiator by removing the cap. Some systems also have a 'Full hot' mark to check the level when the engine is hot.

10 The coolant level can also be checked by removing the radiator cap. However, the cap should not under any circumstances be removed while the system is hot, as escaping steam could cause serious injury. Wait until the engine has cooled, then wrap a thick cloth around the cap and turn it to its first stop. If any steam escapes from the cap, allow the engine to cool further. Then remove the cap and check the level in the radiator. It should be about 2 to 3 inches below the bottom of the filler neck.

11 If only a small amount of coolant is required to bring the system up to the proper level, regular water can be used. However, to maintain the proper antifreeze/water mixture in the system, both should be mixed together to replenish a low level. High-quality antifreeze offering protection to -20° should be mixed with water in the proportion specified on the container. These vehicles have aluminum cylinder heads and some have aluminum radiators so the use of the proper coolant is critical to avoid corrosion. Do not allow antifreeze to come in contact with your skin or painted surfaces of the car. Flush contacted areas immediately with plenty of water.

12 On systems with a recovery tank, coolant should be added to the reservoir after removing the cap at the top of the reservoir.

13 As the coolant level is checked, observe the condition of the coolant. It should be relatively clear. If the fluid is brown or rust color, this is an indication that the system should be drained, flushed and refilled (Section 28).

14 If the cooling system requires repeated additions to keep the proper level, have the pressure radiator cap checked for proper sealing ability. Also check for leaks in the system (cracked hoses, loose hose connections, leaking gaskets, etc).

Windshield washer

15 The fluid for the windshield washer system is located in a plastic reservoir. The level inside the reservoir should be maintained at the 'Full' mark. The washer and coolant reservoirs are combined in one container with a partition between. Be careful to put fluids in their proper container.

16 An approved washer solvent should be added through the plastic cap whenever replenishing is required. Do not use plain water alone in this system, especially in cold climates where the water could freeze.

Battery

Note: *There are certain precautions to be taken when working on or near the battery; a) Never expose a battery to open flame or sparks which could ignite the hydrogen gas given off by the battery; b) Wear protective clothing and eye protection to reduce the possibility of the corrosive sulfuric acid solution inside the battery harming you (if the fluid is splashed or spilled, flush the contacted area immediately with pelnty of water); c) Remove all metal jewelry which could contact the positive terminal and another grounded metal source, thus causing a short circuit; d) Always keep battery acid out of the reach of children.*

17 Vehicles equipped with maintenance-free batteries require no maintenance as the battery case is sealed and has no removal caps for adding water.

18 If a maintenance-type battery is installed, the caps on the top of the battery should be removed periodically to check for a low water level. This check will be more critical during the warm summer months.

19 Remove each of the caps and add distilled water to bring the level of each cell to the split ring in the filler opening.

20 At the same time the battery water level is checked, the overall condition of the battery and its related components should be inspected. If corrosion is found on the cable ends or battery terminals, remove the cables and clean away all corrosion using a baking soda/water solution or a wire brush cleaning tool designed for this purpose. See Section 30 for complete battery care and servicing.

Brake master cylinder

21 The brake master cylinder is located on the left side of the engine compartment firewall and has a cap which must be removed to check the fluid level.

22 Before removing the cap, use a tray to clean all dirt, grease, etc. from around the cap area. If any foreign matter enters the master cylinder with the cap removed, blockage in the brake system lines can occur. Also make sure all painted surfaces around the master cylinder are covered, as brake fluid will ruin paintwork.

23 Release the clip(s) securing the cap to the top of the master cylinder. In most cases, a screwdriver can be used to pry the wire clip(s) free.

24 Carefully lift the cap off the cylinder and observe the fluid level. It should be approximately $\frac{1}{4}$-inch below the top edge of each reservoir.

25 If additional fluid is necessary to bring the level up to the proper height, carefully pour the specified brake fluid into the master cylinder. Be careful not to spill the fluid on painted surfaces. Be sure the specified fluid is used, as mixing different types of brake fluid can cause damage to the system. See *Recommended Lubricants Specifications* or your owner's manual.

26 At this time the fluid and master cylinder can be inspected for contamination. Normally, the braking system will not need periodic draining and refilling, but if rust deposits, dirt particles or water droplets are seen in the fluid, the system should be dismantled, drained and refilled with fresh fluid.

27 Reinstall the master cylinder cap and secure it with the clip(s). Make sure the lid is properly seated to prevent fluid leakage and/or system pressure loss.

28 The brake fluid in the master cylinder will drop slightly as the brake shoes or pads at each wheel wear down during normal operation. If the master cylinder requires repeated replenishing to keep it at the proper level, this is an indication of leakage in the brake system which should be corrected immediately. Check all brake lines and their connections, along with the wheel cylinders and booster (see Chapter 9 for more information).

29 If upon checking the master cylinder fluid level you discover one or both reservoirs empty or nearly empty, the braking system should be bled (Chapter 9). When the fluid level gets low, air can enter the system and should be removed by bleeding the brakes.

Manual transaxle

30 Manual shift transaxles do not have a dipstick. The fluid level is checked by removing a plug in the side of the transaxle case. Locate this plug and use a rag to clean the plug and the area around it.

31 With the vehicle components cold, remove the plug. If fluid immediately starts leaking out, thread the plug back into the transaxle because the fluid level is airtight. If there is no fluid leakage, completely remove the plug and place your little finger inside the hole. The fluid level should be just at the bottom on the plug hole. Use only specified type F transmission fluid, do not use gear oil.

32 If the transaxle needs more fluid, use a syringe to squeeze the appropriate lubricant into the plug hole to bring the fluid up to the proper level.

33 Thread the plug back into the transaxle and tighten it securely. Drive the car and check for leaks round the plug.

Automatic transaxle

34 The fluid inside the transaxle must be at normal operating temperature to get an accurate reading on the dipstick. This is done by driving the car for several miles, making frequent starts and stops to

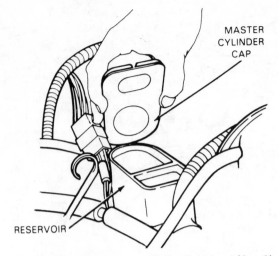

Fig. 1.6 Checking master cylinder fluid level (Sec 3)

MASTER CYLINDER CAP

RESERVOIR

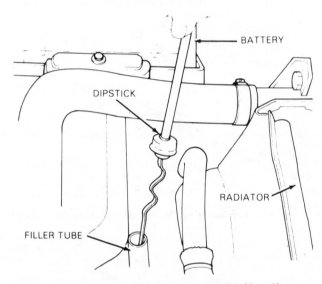

Fig. 1.7 Automatic transaxle dipstick (Sec 3)

BATTERY

DIPSTICK

RADIATOR

FILLER TUBE

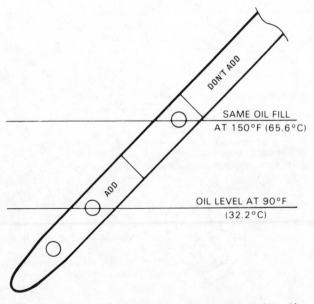

Fig. 1.8 Checking automatic transaxle fluid level (Sec 3)

DON'T ADD

SAME OIL FILL AT 150°F (65.6°C)

ADD

OIL LEVEL AT 90°F (32.2°C)

allow the transaxle to shift through all gears.

35 Park the car on a level surface, place the selector lever in 'Park' and leave the engine running at an idle.

36 Remove the transaxle dipstick (located on the right side, near the rear of the engine) and wipe all the fluid from the end of the dipstick with a clean rag.

37 Push the dipstick back into the transaxle until the cap seats firmly on the dipstick tube. Now remove the dipstick again and observe the fluid on the end. The highest point of fluid should be between the 'Full' mark and $\frac{1}{4}$ inch below the 'Full' mark.

38 If the fluid level is at or below the 'Add mark on the dipstick, add sufficient fluid to raise the level to the 'Full' mark. One pint of fluid will raise the level from 'Add' to 'Full'. Fluid should be added directly into the dipstick guide tube, using a funnel to prevent spills.

39 It is important that the transaxle not be overfilled. Under no circumstances should the fluid level be above the 'Full' mark on the dipstick, as this could cause internal damage to the transaxle. The best way to prevent overfilling is to add fluid a little at a time, driving the car and checking the level between additions.

40 Use only transaxle fluid specified by Ford. This information can be found in the *Recommended Lubricants* Section.

41 The condition of the fluid should also be checked along with the level. If the fluid at the end of the dipstick is a dark reddish-brown color, or if the fluid had a 'burnt' smell, the transaxle fluid should be changed. If you are in doubt about the condition of the fluid, purchase some new fluid and compare the two for color and smell.

Drive axles

42 The drive axle constant velocity joints are lubricated for life at the time of manufacture and it is important to inspect the protective boots for cracks, tears or splits.

43 With the vehicle raised securely, inspect the area around the boots for signs of grease splattering, indicating damage to the boots or retaining clamps.

44 Inspect around the inboard joint for signs of fluid leakage from the transaxle differential seal.

Power steering

45 Unlike manual steering, the power steering system relies on fluid which may, over a period of time, require replenishing.

46 The reservoir for the power steering pump will be located near the front of the engine, can be mounted on either the left or right side.

47 The power steering fluid level should be checked only after the car has been driven, with the fluid at operating temperature. The front wheels should be pointed straight ahead.

48 With the engine shut off, use a rag to clean the reservoir cap and the areas around the cap. This will help to prevent foreign material from falling into the reservoir when the cap is removed.

49 Twist off the reservoir cap which has a built-in dipstick attached to it. Pull off the cap and clean the fluid at the bottom of the dipstick with a clean rag. Now reinstall the dipstick assembly to get a fluid level reading. Remove the dipstick/cap and observe the fluid level. It should be at the 'Full hot' mark on the dipstick.

50 If additional fluid is required, pour the specified lubricant directly into the reservoir using a funnel to prevent spills.

51 If the reservoir requires frequent fluid additions, all power steering hoses, hose connections, the power steering pump and the steering box should be carefully checked for leaks.

---

4 Tire and tire pressure checks

1 Periodically inspecting the tires can not only prevent you from being stranded with a flat tire, but can also give you clues as to possible problems with the steering and suspension systems before major damage occurs.

2 Proper tire inflation adds miles to the lifespan of the tires, allows the car to achieve maximum miles per gallon figures, and helps the overall riding comfort of the car.

3 When inspecting the tire, first check the wear on the tread. Irregularities in the tread pattern (cupping, flat spots, more wear on one side than the other) are indications of front end alignment and/or balance problems. If any of these conditions are found you would do best to take the car to a competent repair shop which can correct the problem.

4 Also check the tread area for cuts or punctures. Many times a nail

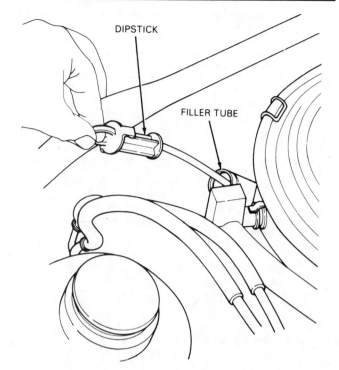

Fig. 1.9 Power steering dipstick location (Sec 3)

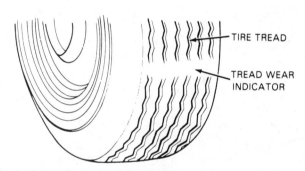

Fig. 1.10 Tread wear indicators which run across the tread when the tire is in need of replacement (Sec 4)

or tack will embed itself into the tire tread and yet the tire will hold its air pressure for a short time. In most cases, a repair shop or gas station can repair the punctured tire.

5 It is also important to check the sidewalls of the tire, both inside and outside. Check for the rubber being deteriorated, cut or punctured. Also inspect the inboard side of the tire for signs of brake fluid leakage, indicating a thorough brake inspection is needed immediately.

6 Incorrect tire pressure cannot be determined merely by looking at the tire. This is especially true for radial tires. A tire pressure gauge must be used. If you do not already have a reliable gauge, it is a good idea to purchase one and keep it in the glove box. Built-in pressure gauges at gas stations are often unreliable. If you are in doubt as to the accuracy of your gauge, many repair shops have 'master' pressure gauges which you can use for comparison purposes.

7 Always check tire inflation when the tires are cold. Cold, in this case, means the car has not been driven more than one mile after sitting for three hours or more. It is normal for the pressure to increase 4 to 8 pounds or more when the tires are hot.

8 Unscrew the valve cap protruding from the wheel or hubcap and firmly press the gauge onto the valve stem. Observe the reading on the gauge and check this figure against the recommended tire pressure listed on the tire placard.

9 Check all tires and add air as necessary to bring all tires up to the recommended pressure levels. Do not forget the spare tire. Be sure to

reinstall the valve caps which will keep dirt and moisture out of the valve stem mechanism.

5   Engine oil and filter change

1   Frequent oil changes may be the best form of preventative maintenance available for the home mechanic. When engine oil ages it gets diluted and contaminated which ultimately leads to premature parts wear.

2   Although some sources recommend oil filter changes every other oil change, we feel that the minimal cost of an oil filter and the relative ease with which it is installed dictates that a new filter be used whenever the oil is changed.

3   The tools necessary for a normal oil and filter change are: a wrench to fit the drain plug at the bottom of the oil pan; an oil filter wrench to remove the old filter; a container with at least a capacity to drain the old oil into; and a funnel or oil can spout to help pour fresh oil into the engine.

4   In addition, you should have plenty of clean rags and newspapers handy to mop up any spills. Access to the underside of the car is greatly improved if the car can be lifted on a hoist, driven onto ramps or supported by jack stands. Do not work under a car which is supported only by a bumper, hydraulic or scissors-type jack.

5   If this is your first oil change on the car, it is a good idea to crawl underneath and familiarize yourself with the locations of the oil drain plug and the oil filter. Since the engine and exhaust components will be warm during the actual work, it is best to figure out any potential problems before the car and its accessories are hot.

6   Allow the car to warm up to normal operating temperature. If the new oil or any tools are needed, use this warm-up time to gather everything necessary for the job. The correct type of oil to buy for your application can be found in *Recommended Lubricants Specifications* near the front of this Chapter.

7   With the engine oil warm (warm engine oil will drain better and more built-up sludge will be removed with the oil), raise the vehicle for access beneath. Make sure the car is firmly supported. If jack stands are used they should be placed towards the front of the frame rails which run the length of the car.

8   Move all necessary tools, rags and newspaper under the car. Position the drain pan under the drain plug. Keep in mind that the oil will initially flow from the pan with some force, so place the pan accordingly.

9   Being careful not to touch any of the hot exhaust pipe components, use the wrench to remove the drain plug near the bottom of the oil pan. Depending on how hot the oil has become, you may want to wear gloves while unscrewing the plug the final few turns.

10 Allow the old oil to drain into the pan. It may be necessary to move the pan further under the engine as the oil flow reduces to a trickle.

11 After all the oil has drained, clean the drain plug thoroughly with a clean rag. Small metal filings may cling to this plug which could immediately contaminate your new oil.

12 Clean the area around the drain plug opening and reinstall the drain plug. Tighten the plug securely with your wrench.

13 Move the drain pan in position under the oil filter.

14 Now use the filter wrench to loosen the oil filter. Chain or metal band-type filter wrenches may distort the filter canister, but don't worry too much about this as the filter will be discarded anyway.

15 Sometimes the oil filter is on so tight it cannot be loosened, or it is positioned in an area which is inaccessible with a filter wrench. As a last resort, you can punch a metal bar or long screwdriver directly through the **bottom** of the canister and use this as a T-bar to turn the filter. If this must be done, be prepared for oil to spurt out of the canister as it is punctured.

16 Completely unscrew the old filter. Be careful, it is full of oil. Empty the old oil inside the filter into the drain pan.

17 Compare the old filter with the new one to make sure they are of the same type.

18 Use a clean rag to remove all oil, dirt and sludge from the area where the oil filter mounts to the engine. Check the old filter to make sure the rubber gasket is not stuck to the engine mounting surface. If this gasket is stuck to the engine (use a flashlight if necessary) remove it.

19 Open one of the cans of new oil and fill the new filter with fresh oil. Also smear a light coat of this fresh oil onto the rubber gasket of the new oil filter.

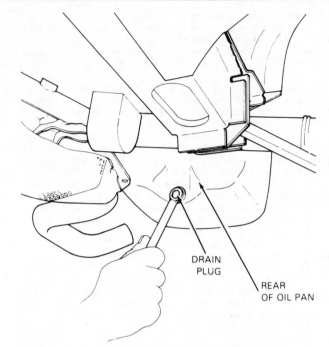

Fig. 1.11 Removing the oil drain plug (Sec 5)

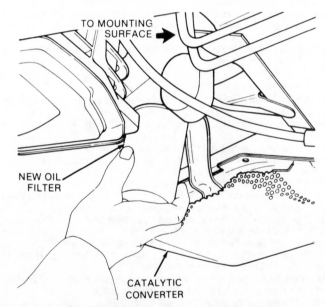

Fig. 1.12 Installing the oil filter (Sec 5)

20 Screw the new filter to the engine following the tightening directions printed on the filter canister or packing box. Most filter manufacturers recommend against using a filter wrench due to possible overtightening or damage to the canister.

21 Remove all tools, rags, etc. from under the car, being careful not to spill the oil in the drain pan. Lower the car off its support devices.

22 Move to the engine compartment and locate the oil filler cap on the engine.

23 If an oil can spout is used, push the spout into the top of the oil can and pour the fresh oil through the filler opening. A funnel placed into the opening may also be used.

24 Pour about 3 qts of fresh oil into the engine. Wait a few minutes to allow the oil to drain to the pan, then check the level on the oil dipstick (see Section 2 if necessary). If the oil level is at or near the lower 'Add' mark, start the engine and allow the new oil to circulate.

25 Run the engine for only about a minute and then shut it off. Immediately look under the car and check for leaks at the oil pan drain

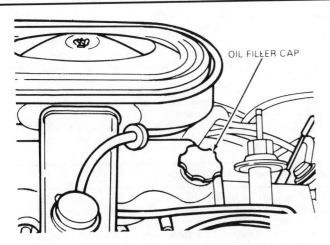

Fig. 1.13 Oil filler location (Sec 5)

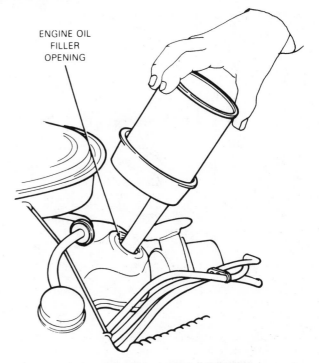

Fig. 1.14 Adding engine oil (Sec 5)

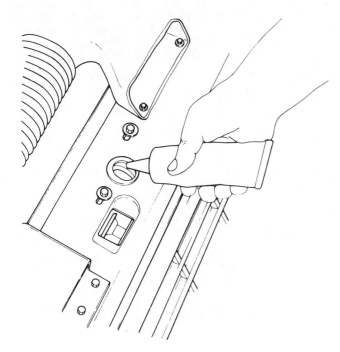

Fig. 1.15 Lubricating the hood latch (Sec 6)

Fig. 1.16 Lubricating the door weatherstripping (Sec 6)

plug and around the oil filter. If either is leaking, tighten with a bit more force.

26 With the new oil circulated and the filter now completely full, recheck the level on the dipstick and add enough oil to bring the level to the 'Full' mark on the dipstick.

27 During the first few trips after an oil change, make a point to check for leaks and also the oil level.

28 The old oil drained from the engine cannot be reused in its present state and should be disposed of. Oil reclamation centers, auto repair shops and gas stations will normally accept the oil which can be refined and used again. After the oil has cooled, it can be drained into a suitable container (capped plastic jugs, topped bottles, milk cartons, etc.) for transport to one of these disposal sites.

6 Chassis lubrication

1 There is no provision for lubrication of chassis or steering components on all models as they are 'lubed for life'. Only the rear wheel bearings (Chapter 11), clutch linkage (Chapter 8) and parking brake linkage (Chapter 9) require periodic lubrication.

2 The door, hood and liftgate hinges should be lubricated periodically with polythene grease.

3 Open the hood and smear a little grease on the hood latch mechanism. Have an assistant pull the release knob from inside the vehicle as you lubricate the cable at the latch.

4 Lubricate the door weatherstripping with silicone spray as this will reduce chafing and retard wear.

5 The key lock cylinders should be lubricated with spray-on graphite, available at auto parts stores.

Fig. 1.17 Spraying graphite into the lock cylinder (Sec 6)

7   Cooling system check

Caution: *The electric cooling fan can activate at any time, even when the ignition switch is in the Off position. Disconnect the fan motor or the battery negative cable when working in the vicinity of the fan.*

1   Many major engine failures can be attributed to a faulty cooling system. If equipped with an automatic transaxle the cooling system also plays an integral role in transaxle longevity.

2   The cooling system should be checked with the engine cold. Do this before the car is driven for the day or after it has been shut off for one or two hours.

3   Remove the radiator cap and thoroughly clean the cap (inside and out) with clean water. Also clean the filler neck on the radiator. All traces of corrosion should be removed.

4   Carefully check the upper and lower radiator hoses along with the smaller diameter heater hoses. Inspect their entire length, replacing any hose which is cracked, swollen or shows signs of deterioration. Cracks may become more apparent if the hose is squeezed.

5   Also check that all hose connections are tight. A leak in the cooling system will usually show up as white or rust colored deposits on the areas adjoining the leak.

6   Use compressed air or a soft brush to remove bugs, leaves, etc from the front of the radiator or air conditioning condenser. Be careful not to damage the delicate cooling fins, or cut yourself on the sharp fins.

7   Finally, have the cap and system tested for proper pressure. If you do not have a pressure tester, most gas stations and repair shops will do this for a minimal charge.

8   Exhaust system check

1   With the exhaust system cold (at least three hours after being driven), check the complete exhaust system from its starting point at the engine to the end of the tailpipe. This is best done on a hoist where full access is available.

2   Check the pipes and their connections for signs of leakage and/or corrosion indicating a potential failure. Check that all brackets and hangers are in good condition and are tight.

3   At the same time, inspect the underside of the body for holes, corrosion, open seams, etc which may allow exhaust gases to enter the trunk or passenger compartment. Seal all body openings with silicone or body putty.

4   Rattles and other driving noises can often be traced to the exhaust system, especially the mounts and hangers. Try to move the pipes, muffler and catalytic converter. If the components can come into contact with the body or driveline parts, secure the exhaust system with new mountings.

5   This is also an ideal time to check the running condition of the engine by inspecting the very end of the tailpipe. The exhaust deposits here are an indication of engine tune. If the pipe is black and sooty or bright white deposits are found here, the engine is in need of a tune-up including a thorough carburetor inspection and adjustment.

9   Suspension and steering check

1   Whenever the front of the car is raised for service it is a good idea to visually check the suspension and steering components for wear.

2   Indications of a fault in these systems are: excessive play in the steering wheel before the front wheels react; excessive sway around corners or body movement over rough roads; binding at some point as the steering wheel is turned.

3   Before the car is raised for inspection, test the shock absorbers by pushing downward to rock the car at each corner. If you push the car down and it does not come back to a level position within one or two bounces, the shocks are worn and need to be replaced. As this is done, check for squeaks and strange noises from the suspension components. Information on shock absorber and suspension components can be found in Chapter 11.

4   Now raise the front end of the car and support firmly by jack stands placed under the frame rails. Because of the work to be done, make sure the car cannot fall from the stands.

5   Check the front wheel hub nut for looseness and make sure that it is properly crimped in place.

6   Crawl under the car and check for loose bolts, broken or disconnected parts and deteriorated rubber bushings on all suspension and steering components. Look for grease or fluid leaking from around the steering box. Check the power steering hoses and their connections for leaks. Check the steering joints for wear.

7   Have an assistant turn the steering wheel from side to side and check the steering components for free movement, chafing or binding. If the steering does not react with the movement of the steering wheel, try to determine where the slack is located.

10   Fuel system check

1   There are certain precautions to take when inspecting or servicing the fuel system components. Work in a well ventilated area and do not allow open flames (cigarettes, appliance pilot lights, etc) to get near the work area. Mop up spills immediately and do not store fuel-soaked rags where they could ignite.

2   The fuel system is under some amount of pressure, so if any fuel lines are disconnected for servicing, be prepared to catch the fuel as it spurts out. Plug all disconnected fuel lines immediately after disconnection to prevent the tank from emptying itself.

3   The fuel system is most easily checked with the car raised on a hoist where the components under the car are readily visible and accessible.

4   If the smell of gasoline is noticed while driving, or after the car has sat in the sun, the system should be thoroughly inspected immediately.

5   Remove the gas filler cap and check for damage, corrosion and a proper sealing imprint on the gasket. Replace the cap with a new one if necessary.

6   With the car raised, inspect the gas tank and filler neck for punctures, cracks or any damage. The connections between the filler neck and the tank is especially critical. Sometimes a rubber filler neck will leak due to loose clamps or deteriorated rubber; problems a home mechanic can usually rectify.

7   Do not under any circumstances try to repair a fuel tank yourself (except rubber components) unless you have considerable experience. A welding torch or any open flame can easily cause the fuel vapors to explode if the proper precautions are not taken.

8   Carefully check all rubber hoses and metal lines leading away from the fuel tank. Check for loose connections, deteriorated hose, crimped lines or damage of any kind. Follow these lines up to the front of the car, carefully inspecting them all the way. Repair or replace damaged

sections as necessary.

9   If a fuel odor is still evident after the inspection, refer to Section 31 on the evaporative emissions system and Section 20 for carburetor adjustment.

11   Engine drivebelt check and adjustment

Caution: *The electric cooling fan can activate at any time, even when the ignition switch is in the Off position. Disconnect the fan motor or battery negative cable when working in the vicinity of the fan.*

1   The drivebelts, or V-belts as they are sometimes called, at the front of the engine play an important role in the overall operation of the car and its components. Due to their function and material make-up, the belts are prone to failure after a period of time and should be inspected and adjusted periodically to prevent major engine damage.

2   The number of belts used on a particular car depends on the accessories installed. Drivebelts are used to turn: the generator (alternator); AIR smog pump; power steering pump; water pump; fan; and air conditioning compressor. Depending on the pulley arrangement, a single belt may be used for more than one of these ancillary components.

3   With the engine off, open the hood and locate the various belts at the front of the engine. Using your fingers (and a flashlight if necessary), move along the belts checking for cracks or separation. Also check for fraying and for glazing which gives the belt a shiny appearance. Both sides of the belts should be inspected, which means you will have to twist the belt to check the underside.

4   The tension of each belt is checked by pushing on the belt at a distance halfway between the pulleys. Push firmly with your thumb and see how much the belt moves downward (deflects). A rule of thumb, so to speak, is that if the distance (pulley center to pulley center) is between 7 inches and 11 inches the belt should deflect $\frac{1}{4}$ inch. If the belt is longer and travels between pulleys spaced 12 inches to 16 inches apart, the belt should deflect $\frac{3}{8}$ in.

5   If it is found necessary to adjust the belt tension, either to make the belt tighter or looser, this is done by moving the belt-driven accessory on its bracket.

6   For each component there will be an adjustment or strap bolt and a pivot bolt. Both bolts must be loosened slightly to enable you to move the component.

7   After the two bolts have been loosened, move the component away from the engine (to tighten the belt) or toward the engine (to loosen the belt). Hold the accessory in this position and check the belt tension. If it is correct, tighten the two bolts until snug, then recheck the tension. If it is alright, fully tighten the two bolts.

8   It will often be necessary to use some sort of pry bar to move the accessory while the belt is adjusted. If this must be done to gain the proper leverage, be very careful not to damage the component being moved, or the part being pried against.

9   If equipped with power steering, the Thermactor air pump belt tension cannot be set until after the power steering belt has been set. A special Ford belt tension gauge is necessary to check these belts.

12   Air filter and crankcase emission filter replacement

1   At the specified intervals, the air filter and PV filter should be replaced with new ones. A thorough program of preventative maintenance would call for the two filters to be inspected periodically between changes.

2   The air filter is located inside the air cleaner housing on the top of the engine. To remove the filter, unscrew the wing nut at the top of the air cleaner and lift off the top plate.

3   While the top plate is off, be careful not to drop anything down into the carburetor.

4   Lift the air filter out of the housing.

5   To check the filter, hold it up to strong sunlight, or place a flashlight or droplight on the inside of the ring-shaped filter. If you can see light coming through the paper element, the filter is alright. Check all the way round the filter.

6   Wipe the inside of the air cleaner clean with a rag.

7   Place the old filter (if in good condition) or the new filter (if specified interval has elapsed) back into the air cleaner housing. Make sure it seats properly in the bottom of the housing.

8   Connect any disconnected vacuum hoses to the top plate and

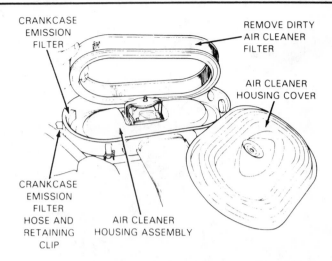

Fig. 1.18 Air cleaner element replacement (Sec 12)

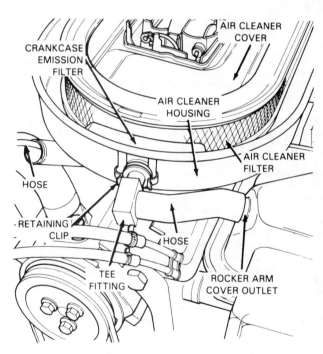

Fig. 1.19 Crankcase emission filter location (Sec 12)

reinstall the top plate with the wing nut.

9   The crankcase emission filter is also located inside the air cleaner housing. Remove the top plate as described and locate the filter on the side of the housing.

10   Pull the T-fitting filter nipple and hose away from the air cleaner housing.

11   Remove the metal locking clip which secures the filter holder to the air cleaner housing. Pliers can be used for this.

12   Remove the filter and plastic holder from the inside of the air cleaner.

13   Compare the new filter with the old one to make sure they are the same.

14   Place the new filter assembly into position and install the metal locking clip on the outside of the air cleaner.

15   Connect the crankcase emission hose and tighten the clamp around the end of the hose.

16   Reinstall the air cleaner top plate and any vacuum hoses which were disconnected.

17   For more information on these filters and the systems they are a part of, see Chapter 4 and Chapter 6.

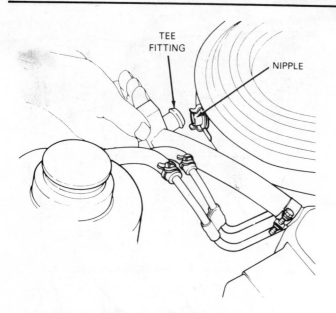

Fig. 1.20 Emission filter Tee fitting (Sec 12)

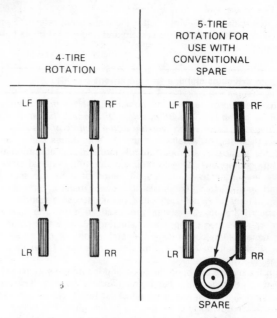

Fig. 1.21 Radial tire rotation diagram (Sec 14)

13 Clutch pedal free travel

There is no need for checking clutch pedal travel on these models because the clutch control system incorporates a self-adjuster device. Excessive clutch pedal effort, failure of the clutch to disengage or noise from the adjuster indicates faults in this device. Refer to Chapter 8 for further information on the clutch, adjuster and linkage.

14 Tire rotation

1   The tires should be rotated at the specified intervals and whenever uneven wear is noticed. Since the car will be raised and the tires removed anyway, this is a good time to check the brakes (Section 23) and/or repack the wheel bearings. Read over these Sections if this is to be done at the same time.

2   The location for each tire in the rotation sequence depends on the type of tire used on your car. Tire type can be determined by reading the raised printing on the sidewall of the tire. The accompanying figure shows the rotation sequence for each type of tire.

3   See the information in *Jacking and Towing* at the front of this manual for the proper procedures to follow in raising the car and changing a tire; however, if the brakes are to be checked do not apply the parking brake as stated. Make sure the tires are blocked to prevent the car from rolling.

4   Preferably, the entire car should be raised at the same time. This can be done on a hoist or by jacking up each corner of the car and then lowering the car onto jack stands placed under the frame rails. Always use four jack stands and make sure the car is firmly supported all around.

5   After rotation, check and adjust the tire pressures as necessary and be sure to check wheel nut tightness.

15 Thermo controlled air cleaner check

1   All models are equipped with a thermostatically controlled air cleaner which draws air to the carburetor from different locations depending upon engine temperature.

2   This is a simple visual check; however, if access is tight, a small mirror may have to be used.

3   Open the hood and find the vacuum flapper door on the air cleaner assembly. It will be located inside the long 'snorkel' of the metal air cleaner. Check that the flexible air hose(s) are securely attached and are not damaged.

4   If there is a flexible air duct attached to the end of the snorkel, leading to an area behind the grille, disconnect it at the snorkel. This will enable you to look through the end of the snorkel and see the flapper door inside.

5   The testing should preferably be done when the engine and outside air are cold. Start the engine and look through the snorkel at the flapper door which should move to a closed position. With the door closed, air cannot enter through the end of the snorkel, but rather air enters the air cleaner through the flexible duct attached to the exhaust manifold.

6   As the engine warms up to operating temperature, the door should open to allow air through the snorkel end. Depending on ambient temperature, this may take 10 to 15 minutes. To speed up this check you can reconnect the snorkel air duct, drive the car and then check that the door is fully open.

7   If the thermo controlled air cleaner is not operating properly, see Chapter 4 for more information.

16 Engine idle speed adjustment

1   Engine idle speed is the speed at which the engine operates when no accelerator pedal pressure is applied. This speed is critical to the performance of the engine itself, as well as many engine sub-systems.

2   A hand-held tachometer must be used when adjusting idle speed to get an accurate reading. The exact hook-up for these meters varies with the manufacturer, so follow the particular directions included.

3   Since the manufacturer used several different throttle linkages and positioners on these vehicles in the time period covered by this book, and each has its own peculiarities when setting idle speed, it would be impractical to cover all types in this Section. Chapter 4 contains information on each individual carburetor used. The carburetor used on your particular engine can be found in the Specifications Section of Chapter 4. However, all vehicles covered in this manual have an emissions decal in the engine compartment. The printed instructions for setting idle speed can be found on this decal, and should be followed since they are for your particular engine.

4   Basically, for most applications, the idle speed is set by turning an adjustment screw located at the side of the carburetor. This screw changes the linkage, in essence, depressing or letting up on your accelerator pedal. This screw may be on the linkage itself or may be part of the idle stop solenoid. Refer to the tune-up decal or Chapter 4.

5   Once you have found the idle screw, experiment with different length screwdrivers until the adjustments can be easily made, without coming into contact with hot or moving engine components.

6   Follow the instructions on the tune-up decal or in Chapter 4, which will probably include disconnecting certain vacuum or electrical connections. To plug a vacuum hose after disconnecting it, insert a properly-sized metal rod into the opening, or thoroughly wrap the open end with tape to prevent any vacuum loss through the hose.

7   If the air cleaner is removed, the vacuum hose to the snorkel should be plugged.
8   Make sure the parking brake is firmly set and the wheels blocked to prevent the car from rolling. This is especially true if the transaxle is to be in Drive, An assistant inside the car, pushing on the brake pedal is the safest method.
9   For all applications, the engine must be completely warmed-up to operating temperature, which will automatically render the choke fast idle inoperative.

17 Fuel filter replacement

1   The fuel filter is of the cylindrical screen type and is located inside the carburetor fuel inlet.
2   This job should be done with the engine cold (after sitting at least three hours). The necessary tools are open end wrenches to fit the fuel line nuts. Flare nut wrenches which wrap around the nut should be used if available. In addition you will need to gather together the replacement filter (make sure it is for your specific vehicle and engine), and clean rags.
3   Remove the air cleaner assembly. If vacuum hoses must be disconnected, make sure you note their positions and/or tag them to help during the reassembly process.
4   Now follow the fuel hose from the fuel pump to the point where it enters the carburetor.
5   Place some rags under the fuel inlet fittings to catch any fuel as the fittings are disconnected.
6   With the proper size wrench, hold the nut immediately next to the carburetor body. Now loosen the nut-fitting and the end of the metal fuel line. A flare nut wrench on this fitting will help prevent slipping and possible damage. However, an open-ended wrench should do the job. Make sure the larger nut next to the carburetor is held firmly while the fuel line is disconnected.
7   With the fuel line disconnected, move it slightly for better access to the inlet filter nut. Do not crimp the fuel line.
8   Now unscrew the fuel inlet filter nut which was previously held steady. Remove the filter from the carburetor.
9   Compare the old filter with the new one to make sure they are of the same length and design.
10 Start the new filter into the carburetor by hand and then fully tighten it to specification with the wrench.
11 Apply a coat of light oil to the fuel supply tube and nut and hand start the nut.
12 Hold the fuel inlet nut securely with a wrench while the fuel line is connected. Again, be careful not to cross-thread the connector. Tighten securely.
13 Plug the vacuum hose which leads to the air cleaner snorkel motor so the engine can be run.
14 Start the engine and check carefully for leaks. If the fuel line connector leaks, disconnect it using the above procedures and check for stripped or damaged threads. If the fuel line connector has stripped threads, remove the entire line and have a repair shop install a new fitting. If the threads look alright, purchase some thread sealing tape and tightly wrap the connector threads with the tape. Now reinstall and tighten securely. Inlet repair kits are available at most auto parts stores to overcome leaking at the fuel inlet filter nut.
16 Reinstall the air cleaner assembly, connecting all hoses to their original positions.

18 Ignition timing – adjustment

1   All vehicles are equipped with an emissions decal inside the engine compartment. The decal gives important ignition timing settings and procedures to be followed specific to that vehicle. If information on the tune-up decal supersedes the information given in this Section, the decal should be followed.
2   At the specified intervals, or when the distributor has been changed, the ignition timing must be checked and adjusted if necessary.
3   Before attempting to check the timing, make sure the idle speed is as specifired (Section 16).
4   Disconnect the vacuum hose from the distributor and plug the now-open end of the hose with a rubber plug, rod or bolt of the proper size. Make sure the idle speed remains correct; adjust as necessary.

FUEL FILTER
11/16"
MOTORCRAFT MODEL 740 CARBURETOR

Fig. 1.22 Fuel filter location (Sec 17)

5   Connect a timing light in accordance with the manufacturer's instructions. Generally, the light will be connected to power and ground sources and to the number 1 spark plug in some fashion. The number 1 spark plug is the first one on the right as you are facing the engine from the front.
6   Locate the numbered timing tag on the front cover of the engine, referring to the accompanying figure. It is just behind the lower crankshaft pulley. Clean it off with solvent if necessary to read the printing and small grooves.
7   Locate the notched groove across the crankshaft pulley. It may be necessary to have an assistant temporarily turn the ignition off and on in short bursts without starting the engine to bring this groove into a position where it can easily be cleaned and marked. Stay clear of all moving engine components if the engine is turned over in this manner.
8   Use white soap-stone, chalk or paint to mark the groove on the crankshaft pulley. Also put a mark on the timing tab in accordance with the number of degrees called for in the Specifications (Chapter 5) or on the tune-up decal inside the engine compartment. Each peak or notch on the timing tab represents 2°. The word 'Before' or the letter 'A' indicates advance and the letter 'O' indicates Top Dead Center (TDC). Thus if your vehicle specifications calls for 8° BTDC (Before Top Dead Center), you will make a mark on the timing tab 4 notches 'before' the 'O'.
9   Check that the wiring for the timing light is clear of all moving engine components, then start the engine.
10 Point the flashing timing light at the timing marks, again being careful not to come in contact with moving parts. The marks you made should appear stationary. If the marks are in alignment, the timing is correct. If the marks are not aligned, turn off the engine.
11 Loosen the locknut at the base of the distributor. Loosen the locknut only slightly, just enough to turn the distributor (See Chapter 5 for further details, if necessary).
12 Now restart the engine and turn the distributor until the timing marks coincide.
13 Shut off the engine and tighten the distributor locknut, being careful not to move the distributor.
14 Start the engine and recheck the timing to make sure the marks are still in alignment.
15 Disconnect the timing light, unplug the distributor vacuum hose and connect the hose to the distributor.
16 Drive the car and listen for 'pinging' noises. These will be most noticeable when the engine is hot and under load (climbing a hill, accelerating from a stop). If you hear engine pinging, the ignition timing is too far advanced (Before Top Dead Center). Reconnect the timing light and turn the distributor to move the mark 1° or 2° in the retard direction. Road test the car again for proper operation.
17 To keep 'pinging' at a minimum, yet still allow you to operate the car at the specified timing setting, it is advisable to use gasoline of the same octane at all times. Switching fuel brands and octane levels can decrease performance and economy, and possibly damage the engine.

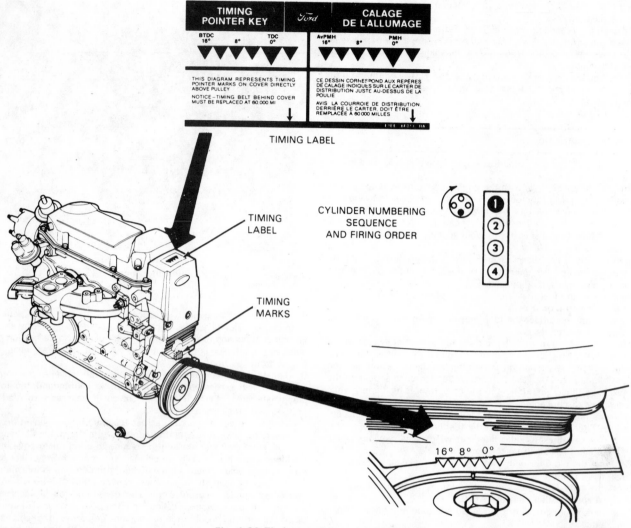

Fig. 1.23 Timing mark location (Sec 18)

19 Carburetor choke check

1   The choke only operates when the engine is cold, and thus this check can only be performed before the car has been started for the day.

2   Open the hood and remove the top plate of the air cleaner assembly. It is held in place by a wing nut at the center and four clips on the sides. If any vacuum hoses must be disconnected, make sure you tag the hoses for reinstallation to their original positions. Place the top plate and wing nut aside, out of the way of moving components.

3   Look at the top of the carburetor at the center of the air cleaner housing. You will notice a flat plate in each of the carburetor throats.

4   Have an assistant press the accelerator pedal to the floor. The plates should close fully. Start the engine while you observe the plates at the carburetor. Do not position your face directly over the carburetor, as the engine could backfire, causing serious burns. When the engine starts, the choke plates should open slightly.

5   Allow the engine to continue running at an idle speed. As the engine warms up to operating temperature, the plates should slowly open, allowing more cold air to enter through the top of the carburetor.

6   After a few minutes, the choke plates should be fully open to the vertical position.

7   You will notice that the engine speed corresponds with the plate opening. With the plate fully closed, the engine should run at a fast idle speed. As the plate opens, the engine speed will decrease.

8   If during the above checks a fault is detected, refer to Chapter 4 for specific information on adjusting and servicing the choke components.

20 Automatic transaxle throttle valve (TV) – adjustment

1   The throttle valve (TV) must be adjusted when called for in the maintenance schedule or when the transaxle shifts improperly. If automatic transaxle upshifts are soft or early or there is no kickdown action, the TV linkage is set too short. If the shifts are too harsh, the linkage is set too long.

2   After setting the proper curb idle (Chapter 4), turn the engine off and check that the carburetor throttle lever is against the top engine curb idle stop. The choke must be off and not in the fast idle cam position.

3   Set the coupling lever adjustment screw to its mid-range position. Make sure that the TV linkage shaft assembly is seated fully upward into the coupling lever.

4   At this point you will be working in the vicinity of the Exhaust Gas Recirculation (EGR) system. To avoid the possibility of burns, allow the EGR system to cool.

5   When it is safe to work near the EGR system, loosen the bolt on the sliding trunnion block of the TV control rod assembly one turn.

6   Inspect the rod for any corrosion which might impede its movement and clean it if necessary. Make sure that the trunnion blocks slide freely on the rod.

7   Push the transaxle TV control upward, using one finger as shown in Fig. 1.25, until the control lever is up against its internal stop. Maintain the pressure and tighten the trunnion bolt.

8   After adjustment, check that the carb throttle lever is against the hot engine idle stop. If it is not, repeat steps two through seven.

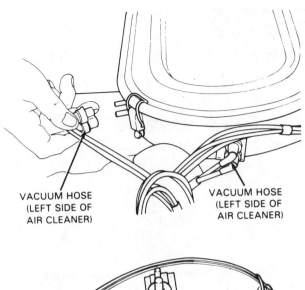

VACUUM HOSE
(LEFT SIDE OF
AIR CLEANER)

VACUUM HOSE
(LEFT SIDE OF
AIR CLEANER)

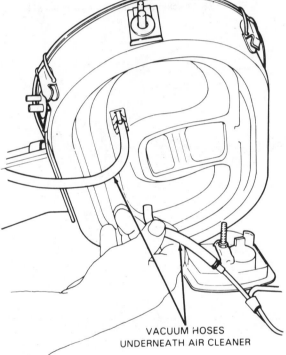

VACUUM HOSES
UNDERNEATH AIR CLEANER

Fig. 1.24 Air cleaner vacuum hose location and removal (Sec 19)

21 Spark plug replacement

1   The spark plugs are located on the side of the engine, facing the radiator grille. Before beginning work, disconnect the battery negative cable as the electric fan could activate at any time.

2   In most cases the tools necessary for a spark plug replacement job are: a plug wrench or spark plug socket which fits onto a ratchet wrench (this special socket will be insulated inside to protect the porcelain insulator) and a feeler gauge to check and adjust the spark plug gap. A special plug wire removal tool is available for separating the wire boot from the spark plug.

3   The best policy to follow when replacing the spark plugs is to purchase the new spark plugs beforehand, adjust them to the proper gap and then replace each plug one at a time. When buying the new spark plugs it is important that the correct plug is purchased for your specific engine. This information can be found on the tune-up decal located under the hood of your car or in the factory owner's manual. If differences exist between these sources, purchase the spark plug type specified on the tune-up decal as this information was printed for your specific engine.

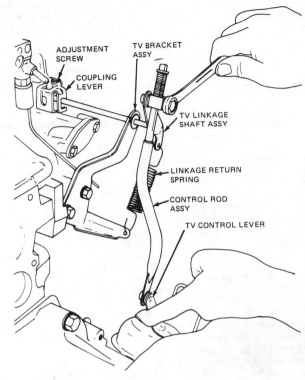

ADJUSTMENT
SCREW

TV BRACKET
ASSY

COUPLING
LEVER

TV LINKAGE
SHAFT ASSY

LINKAGE RETURN
SPRING

CONTROL ROD
ASSY

TV CONTROL LEVER

Fig. 1.25 Automatic transaxle throttle valve adjustment (Sec 20)

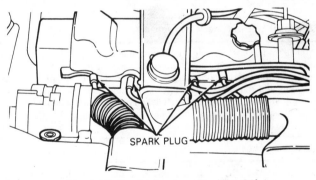

SPARK PLUG

Fig. 1.26 Spark plug location (Sec 21)

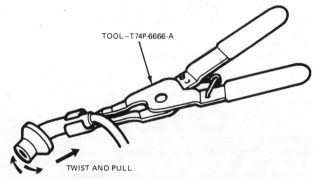

TOOL—T74P-6666-A

TWIST AND PULL

Fig. 1.27 Spark plug wire removal tool (Sec 21)

4   With the new spark plugs at hand, allow the engine to thoroughly cool before attempting the removal. During this cooling time, each of the new spark plugs can be inspected for defects and the gap can be checked.

5   The gap is checked by inserting the proper thickness gauge

between the electrodes at the tip of the plug. The gap between these electrodes should be the same as that given in the Specifications or on the tune-up decal. The wire should touch each of the electrodes. If the gap is incorrect, use the notched adjuster on the feeler gauge body to bend the curved side electrode slightly until the proper gap is achieved. Also at this time check for cracks in the spark plug body, indicating the spark plug should be replaced with a new one. If the side electrode is not exactly over the centre one, use the notched adjuster to align the two. If the spark plug is in good condition, the electrode can be cleaned and carefully filed flat with the proper file.

6   Cover the fenders of the car to prevent damage to exterior paint.
7   With the engine cool, remove the spark plug wire from one spark plug. Do this by grabbing the boot at one end of the wire, not the wire itself. Sometimes it is necessary to use a twisting motion while the boot and plug wire is pulled free (Fig. 1.30). Using the plug wire removal tool is the easiest and safest method.
8   If compressed air is available, use this to blow any dirt or foreign material away from the spark plug area. A common bicycle pump will also work. The idea here is to eliminate the possibility of material falling into the engine cylinder as the spark plug is replaced.
9   Now place the spark plug wrench or socket over the plug and remove it from the engine by turning in a counter-clockwise motion.
10   Compare the spark plug with those shown to get an indication of the overall running condition of the engine on page 105.
11   Insert one of the new plugs into the engine, tightening it as much as possible by hand. The spark plug should screw easily into the engine. If it doesn't, change the angle of the spark plug slightly, as chances are the threads are not matched (cross-threaded). **Note:** *Be extremely careful as these models have aluminum cylinder heads which can be easily damaged.*
14   Install the plug wire to the new spark plug, again using a twisting motion on the boot until it is firmly seated on the spark plug. Make sure wire is routed away from the hot exhaust manifold.
15   Follow the above procedures for the remaining spark plugs, replacing each one at a time to prevent mixing up the spark plug wires.

22   Wheel bearing check and repack

1   The front wheel bearings are adjusted and lubricated at the factory and normally need only be checked for looseness indicating bearing wear or improperly tightened hub nut. Refer to Chapter 11 for checking and maintenance of the front wheel bearings.
2   Adjustment, removal and installation and repacking procedures for the rear wheel bearings are also described in Chapter 11.

23   Brakes check

1   The brakes should be inspected every time the wheels are removed or whenever a fault is suspected. Indications of a potential braking system fault are: the car pulls to one side when brake pedal is depressed; noises coming from the brakes when they are applied; excessive brake pedal travel; pulsating pedal; and leakage of fluid, usually seen on the inside of the tire or wheel.

Disc brakes
2   Disc brakes can be visually checked without the need to remove any parts except the wheels.
3   Raise the vehicle and place securely on jack stands. Remove the front wheels. (See *Jacking and Towing* at the front of this manual if necessary).
4   Now visible is the disc brake caliper which contains the pads. There is an outer brake pad and an inner pad. Both should be inspected.
5   Inspect the pad thickness by looking at each end of the caliper and through the cut-out inspection hole in the caliper body. If the lining material is $\frac{1}{8}$ in or less in thickness, the pads should be replaced. Keep in mind that the lining material is riveted or bonded to a metal backing shoe and the metal portion is not included in this measuring.
6   Since it will be difficult, if not impossible, to measure the exact thickness of the remaining lining material, if you are in doubt as to the pad quality, remove the pads for further inspection or replacement. See Chapter 9 for disc brake pad replacement.
7   Before installing the wheels, check for any leakage around the brake hose connections leading to the caliper or damage (cracking,

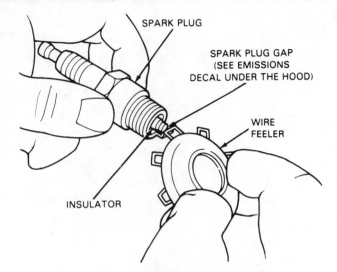

Fig. 1.28 Checking spark plug gap (Sec 21)

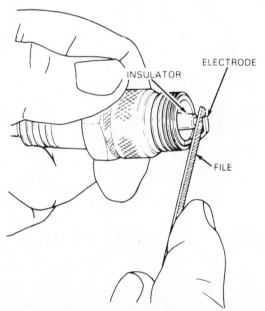

Fig. 1.29 Cleaning the spark plug electrode (Sec 21)

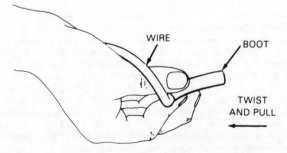

Fig. 1.30 Removing spark plug wire (Sec 21)

splitting etc.) to the brake hose. Replace the hose or fittings as necessary, referring to Chapter 9.
8   Also check the condition of the disc for scoring, gouging or burnt spots. If these conditions exist, the hub/rotor assembly should be removed for servicing (Chapter 9).

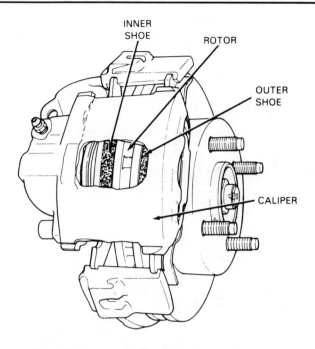

Fig. 1.31 Checking disc brake pad wear (Sec 23)

Drum brakes (rear)

9 Raise the vehicle and support firmly on jack stands. Block the front tires to prevent the car from rolling; however, do not apply the parking brake as this will lock the drums into place.

10 Remove the wheels, referring to *Jacking and Towing* at the front of this manual if necessary.

11 Mark the hub so it can be reinstalled in the same place. Use a scribe, chalk, etc. on drum and center hub and backing plate.

12 Pull the brake drum off the axle and brake assembly, referring to Chapter 9.

13 With the drum removed, carefully brush away any accumulations of dirt and dust. Do not blow this out with compressed air or in any similar fashion. Make an effort not to inhale this dust as it contains asbestos and is harmful to your health.

14 Observe the thickness of the lining material on both front and rear brake shoes. If the material has worn away to within $\frac{1}{8}$ in of the recessed rivets or metal backing, the shoes should be replaced. If the linings look worn, but you are unable to determine their exact thickness, compare them with a new set at the auto parts store. The shoes should also be replaced if they are cracked, glazed (shiny surface), or wet with brake fluid.

15 Check that all the brake assembly springs are connected and in good condition.

16 Check the brake components for any signs of fluid leakage. With your finger, carefully pry back the rubber cups on the wheel cylinder located at the top of the brake shoes. Any leakage is an indication that the wheel cylinders should be overhauled immediately (Chapter 9). Also check fluid hoses and connections for signs of leakage.

17 Wipe the inside of the drum with a clean rag, and denatured alcohol. Again, be careful not to breathe the dangerous asbestos dust.

18 Check the inside of the drum for cracks, scores, deep scratches or 'hard spots' which will appear as small discolorations. If these imperfections cannot be removed with fine emery cloth, the drum must be taken to a machine equipped to turn the drums.

19 If after the inspection process all parts are in good working condition, reinstall the brake drum. Install the wheel and lower the car to the ground.

Parking brake

20 The easiest way to check the operation of the parking brake is to park the car on a steep hill, with the parking brake set and the transmission in 'neutral'. If the parking brake cannot prevent the car from rolling, it is in need of adjustment (see Chapter 9).

24 Carburetor mounting torque

1 The carburetor is attached to the top of the intake manifold by two or four nuts. These fasteners can sometimes work loose through normal engine operation and cause a vacuum leak.

2 To properly tighten the carburetor mounting nuts, a torque wrench is necessary. If you do not own one, they can usually be rented on a daily basis.

3 Remove the air cleaner assembly, tagging each hose to be disconnected with a piece of numbered tape to make reassembly easier.

4 Locate the mounting nuts at the base of the carburetor. Decide what special tools or adaptors will be necessary, if any, to tighten the nuts with a properly sized socket and the torque wrench.

5 Tighten the nuts to specifications. Do not overtighten the nuts, as this may cause the threads to strip.

6 If you suspect a vacuum leak exists at the bottom of the carburetor, get a length of spare hose about the diameter of fuel hose. Start the engine and place one end of the hose next to your ear as you probe around the base of the carburetor with the other end. You will be able to hear a hissing sound if a leak exists. A soapy water solution brushed around the suspect area can also be used to pinpoint pressure leaks.

7 If, after the nuts are properly tightened, a vacuum leak still exists, the carburetor must be removed and a new gasket used. See Chapter 4 for more information.

8 After tightening nuts, reinstall the air cleaner, connecting all hoses to their original positions.

25 Spark plug wires check

1 The spark plug wires should be checked at the recommended intervals or whenever new spark plugs are installed.

2 The wires should be inspected one at a time to prevent mixing up the order which is essential for proper engine operation.

3 Disconnect the plug wire from the spark plug. A removal tool can be used for this, or you can grab the rubber boot, twist slightly and then pull the wires free. Do not pull on the wire itself, only on the rubber boot.

4 Inspect inside the boot for corrosion which will look like a white, crusty powder. Whenever a spark plug wire is removed, apply silicone grease to the inside of the boot to maintain conductivity of the ignition system.

5 Now push the wire and boot back onto the end of the spark plug. It should be a tight fit on the plug end. If not, remove the wire and use a pair of pliers to carefully crimp the metal connector inside the wire boot until the fit is secure.

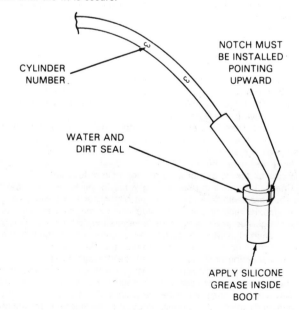

Fig. 1.32 Spark plug wire components (Sec 25)

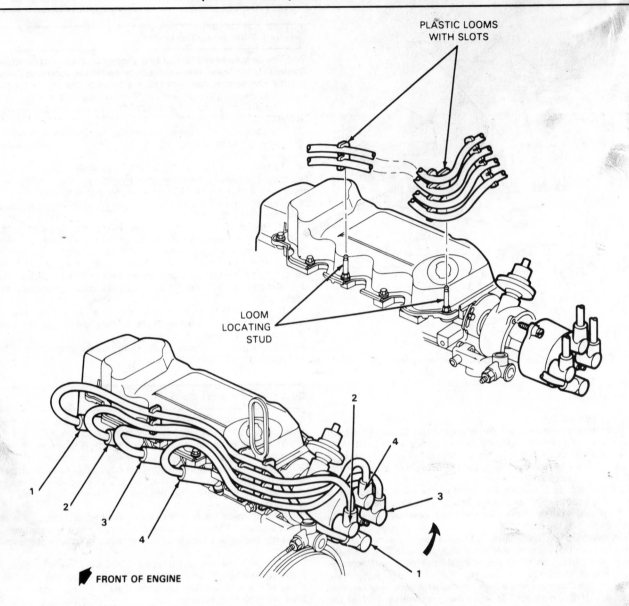

PLASTIC LOOMS
WITH SLOTS

LOOM
LOCATING
STUD

2

4

3

1

1

2

3

4

FRONT OF ENGINE

Fig. 1.33 Spark plug wire layout (Sec 25)

6   Now using a clean rag, clean the wire its entire length. Remove all built-up dirt and grease. As this is done, inspect for burns, cracks or any other form of damage. Bend the wires in several places to ensure the conductive inside wire has not hardened.

7   Disconnect the wire at the distributor (again, pulling and twisting only on the rubber boot). Check for corrosion and a tight fit in the same manner as the spark plug end. Again, apply silicone grease to the inside of the rubber boot.

8   Reinstall the wire boot onto the top of the distributor.

9   Check the remaining spark plug wires in the same way, making sure they are securely fastened at the distributor and spark plug.

10 A visual check of the spark plug wires can also be made. In a darkened garage (make sure there is ventilation), start the engine and observe each plug wire. Be careful not to come into contact with any moving engine parts. If there is a break or fault in the wire, you will be able to see arcing or a small spark at the damaged area.

11 If it is decided the spark plug wires are in need of replacement, purchase a new set for your specific engine model. Wire sets can be purchased which are pre-cut to the proper size and with the rubber boots already installed. Remove and replace each wire individually to prevent mix-ups in the firing sequence.

26 Windshield wiper blade element – removal and installation

1   The windshield wiper blade elements should be checked periodically for signs of cracking or deterioration. Two types of wiper blades are used, Trico and Tridon.

2   To gain access to the wiper blades, turn on the ignition switch and cycle the windshield wipers to a position on the windshield where the work can be performed. Turn off the ignition.

3   To remove either the Trico or Tridon blade, grasp either end of the blade frame and pull it away from the windshield, removing it by pulling the assembly from the pin.

Trico

4   To remove the element from the frame assembly, insert a screwdriver as shown in the figure and push down and in. This will release the blade element.

5   To install, slide the blade element into the frame assembly until all four tabs are locked.

Tridon

6   Locate the notch about one inch from the end of the plastic backing strip as shown in the accompanying figure.
7   Position the wiper blade assembly on a flat, non-slip surface with the notched end up.
8   Grasp the frame and push down so that the assembly is tightly bowed as shown in the figure. Grip the end of the backing strip firmly

and pull it up, twisting counterclockwise. This will pop the backing strip out of the retaining tab.

9   Pick up the wiper blade assembly, slide the backing strip down the frame until the next retaining tab and notch are aligned, twisting slightly until it pops out. Repeat until the blade element is detached.

10   Installation is the reverse of removal.

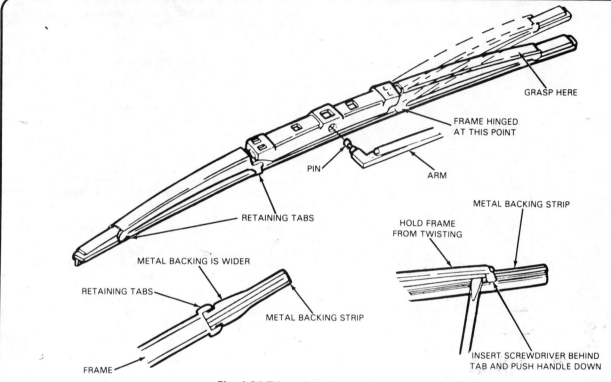

Fig. 1.34 Trico wiper blade replacement (Sec 26)

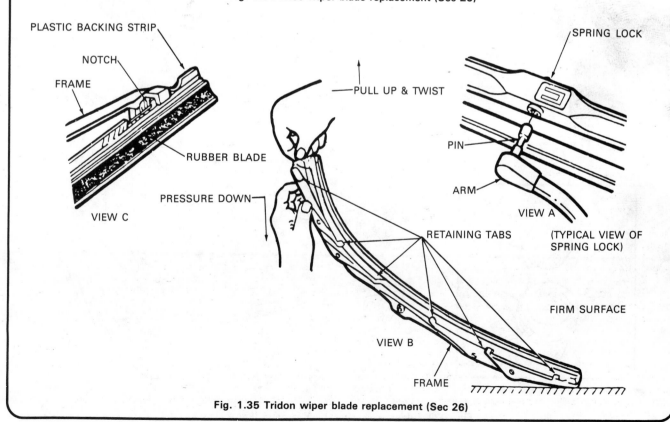

Fig. 1.35 Tridon wiper blade replacement (Sec 26)

27 Rear window washer fluid reservoir – checking

1   It is important that the rear window washer reservoir be checked periodically as it is easy for them to run dry because of their remote location.

2   The washer reservoir is located adjacent to the left taillight on 2-door models and the right taillight on 4-door models. Fill these reservoirs with the proper washer solution at the same time as the under-hood reservoir is checked.

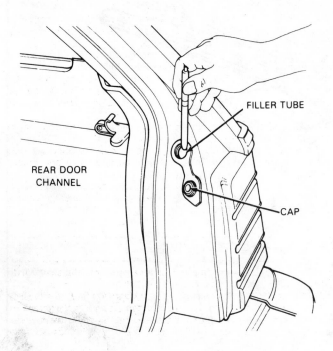

Fig. 1.36 4-door washer reservoir location (Sec 27)

28 Cooling system servicing (draining, flushing and refilling)

1   Periodically, the cooling system should be drained, flushed and refilled. This is to replenish the antifreeze mixture and prevent rust and corrosion which can impair the performance of the cooling system and ultimately cause engine damage.

2   At the same time the cooling system is serviced, all hoses and the fill cap should be inspected and replaced if faulty (see Section 7).

3   As antifreeze is a poisonous solution, take care not to spill any of the cooling mixture on the vehicle's paint or your own skin. If this happens, rinse immediately with plenty of clear water. Also, it is advisable to consult your local authorities about the dumping of antifreeze before draining the cooling system. In many areas reclamation centers have been set up to collect automobile oil and drained antifreeze/water mixtures rather than allowing these liquids to be added to the sewage and water facilities.

4   With the engine cold, remove the radiator pressure fill cap.

5   Move a large container under the radiator to catch the water/antifreeze mixture, as it is drained.

6   Drain the radiator. Most models are equipped with a drain plug at the bottom of the radiator which can be opened using a wrench to hold the fitting while the petcock is turned to the open position. If this drain has excessive corrosion and cannot be turned easily, or the radiator is not equipped with a drain, disconnect the lower radiator hose to allow the coolant to drain. Be careful that none of the solution is splashed on your skin or in your eyes.

7   Disconnect the coolant reservoir hose as shown, remove the reservoir and flush it with clean water.

8   Place a cold water hose (a common garden hose is fine) in the radiator filler neck at the top of the radiator and flush the system until the water runs clean at all drain points.

9   In severe cases of contamination or clogging of the radiator, remove it (see Chapter 3) and reverse flush it. This involves simply inserting the cold pressure hose in the bottom radiator outlet to allow the clear water to run against the normal flow, draining through the top. A radiator repair shop should be consulted if further cleaning or repair is necessary.

10   Where the coolant is regularly drained and the system refilled with the correct antifreeze/inhibitor mixture there should be no need to employ chemical cleaners or descalers.

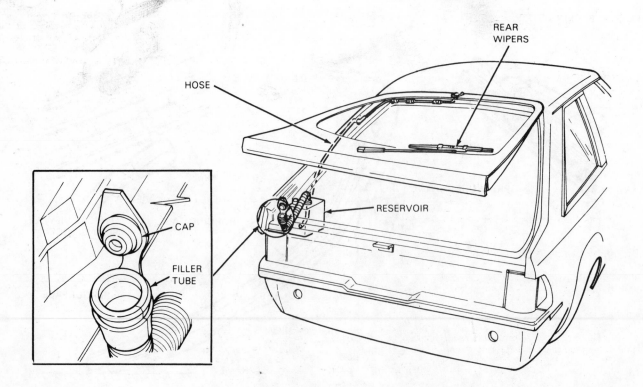

Fig. 1.37 2-door washer reservoir location (Sec 27)

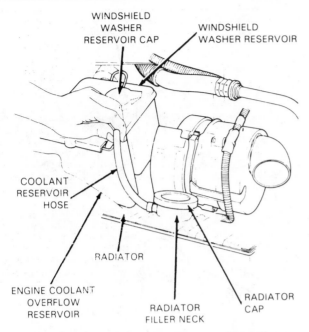

Fig. 1.38 Removing overflow hose (Sec 28)

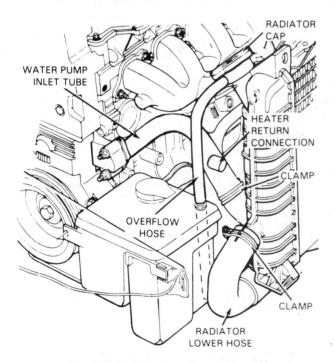

Fig. 1.39 Radiator hose layout (Sec 28)

11 Install the coolant reservoir, reconnect the hoses and replace the drain plug.
12 Fill the radiator to the base of the filler neck and then add more coolant to the expansion reservoir so that it reaches the 'FULL COLD' mark.
13 Run the engine until normal operating temperature is reached and with the engine idling, add coolant up to the correct level.
14 Always refill the system with a mixture of high quality antifreeze and water in the proportion called for on the antifreeze container or in your owner's manual. Chapter 3 also contains information on anti-freeze mixtures.
15 Keep a close watch on the coolant level and the various cooling hoses during the first few miles of driving. Tighten the hose clamps and/or add more coolant mixture as necessary.

29 Underhood hoses – checking and replacement

Caution: *Replacement of air conditioner hoses should be left to a dealer or a/c specialist who can de-pressurise the system and perform the work safely.*
1 The high temperature present under the hood can cause deteriora-tion of the numerous rubber and plastic hoses.
2 Periodic inspection should be made for cracking, loose clamps and leaking because some of the hoses are part of the emissions system and can affect the engine's running and idling.
3 Remove the air cleaner if necessary and trace the entire length of each hose. Squeeze the hose to check for cracks and look for swelling, discoloration and leaks.
4 If the vehicle has considerable mileage or one or more of the hoses is suspect, it is a good idea to replace all of the hoses at one time.
5 Measure the length and inside diameter of each hose and obtain and cut the replacement to size. As original equipment hose clamps are often good for only one or two uses, it is a good idea to replace them with screw-type clamps.
6 Replace each hose one at a time to eliminate the possibility of confusion. Hoses attached to the heater system, choke or ported vacuum switches contain radiator coolant so newspapers or rags should be kept handy to catch the spillage when they are discon-nected.
7 After installation, run the engine until up to operating temperature, shut it off and check for leaks. After the engine has cooled, re-tighten all of the screw-type clamps.

30 Battery – maintenance

1 All models are equipped with maintenance-free batteries which do not require the addition of water or electrolyte.
2 The top of the battery should be kept clean and free from dirt and moisture so that the battery does not become partially discharged by leakage through dampness and dirt. Clean the top of the battery with a baking soda and water solution, making sure that it does not enter the battery.
3 Once every three months, remove the battery and inspect the securing bolts, battery clamp bolts and leads for corrosion (white fluffy deposits which are brittle to the touch).
4 Clean the battery posts with a battery cleaning tool or wire brush.
5 Clean the battery cable terminals with a wire brush until the corrosion is removed and the metal in the terminal contact area is bright.
6 Apply grease or petroleum jelly around the base of the battery

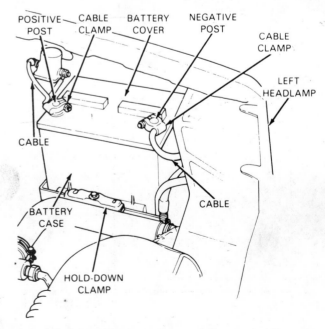

Fig. 1.40 Battery component layout (Sec 30)

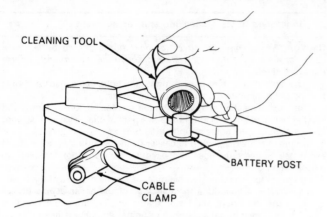

Fig. 1.41 Cleaning the battery post (Sec 30)

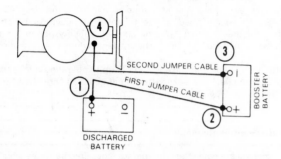

Fig. 1.43 Booster battery connection (Sec 31)

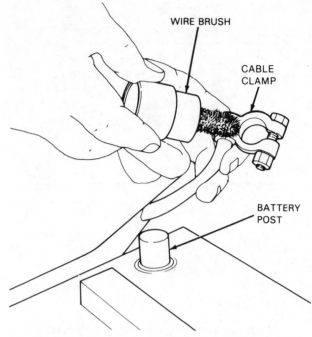

Fig. 1.42 Cleaning the battery terminal (Sec 30)

posts and install the battery cables (positive cable first) and tighten the terminal cable nuts securely.

7   If any doubt exists about the state of charge of the battery, it should be tested by a dealer or properly equipped shop.

31 Booster battery (jump) starting

1   Certain precautions are necessary prior to using a booster battery to 'jump' start the vehicle.

Before connecting the booster battery, make sure that the ignition switch is in the Off position.
The eyes should be shielded; safety goggles are a good idea.
Make sure that the booster battery source is 12 volt and not 24 volt, which could damage the starter.
The two vehicles must not touch each other.

2   Connect the end of one jumper cable to the positive (+) terminals of each battery.

3   Connect one end of the other jumper cable to the negative (-) terminal of the good battery. The other end of this cable should be connected to a good ground on the vehicle to be started, such as a bolt on the engine block.

4   Start the engine using the jumper battery and with the engine running at idle speed, disconnect the jumper cables in the reverse sequence to connection.

Chapter 2 Engine

Refer to Chapter 13 for information and specifications related to 1983 thru 1985 models

Contents

Specifications

Engine – general

Type .... Inline 4-cylinder

Displacement .... 1.3 or 1.6 liter

Bore and stroke
1.3L .... 3.15 in x 2.4 in (80 mm x 64.5 mm)
1.6L .... 3.15 in x 3.13 in (80 mm x 79.5 mm)

Firing order 1–3–4–2

Cylinder head and valve train

	In	(mm)
Valve guide bore diameter		
Intake	0.531 to 0.532	(13.481 to 13.519)
Exhaust	0.531 to 0.532	(13.481 to 13.519)
Valve seats		
Width-intake and exhaust	0.069 to 0.091	(1.75 to 2.32)
Angle	45°	
Runout (TIR)	0.003 max	(0.076)
Bore diameter (insert counterbore diameter)		
Intake	1.723 min	(43.763)
	1.724 max	(43.788)
Exhaust	1.428 min	(38.265)
	1.453 max	(38.288)
Gasket surface flatness	0.0016/1	(0.04/26)
	0.003/6	(0.08/156)
	0.059	(0.15) total
Valve stem-to-guide clearance		
Intake	0.0008 to 0.0027	(0.020 to 0.069)
Exhaust	0.0015 to 0.0032	(0.038 to 0.081)
Valve head diameter		
Intake	1.654	(42.0)
Exhaust	1.457	(37.0)
Valve face runout limit	0.002	(0.05)

Valve face angle .... | Intake 91° 25′ | Exhaust 91° 25′

Valve stem diameter (Standard)

	In	(mm)
Intake	.0.316	(8.034)
Exhaust	0.315	(8.008)
Oversize		
Intake	0.331	(8.414)
Exhaust	0.330	(8.388)
Oversize		
Intake	0.348	(8.834)
Exhaust	0.348	(8.828)

Valve springs

Compression pressure @ specified length

Loaded	180 lbs @ 1.09	(81.6 kg @ 27.71)
Unloaded	75 lbs @ 1.461	(34 kg @ 37.1)
Free length (approximate)	1.724	(43.79)
Assembled height	1.504 to 1.417	(38.19 to 35.99)
Service limit	10% pressure loss @ specified height	
Out-of-square limit	0.060	(1.53)

Rocker arm ratio .... | 1.65 : 1

Valve tappet, hydraulic

Diameter (standard)	0.874	(22.206)
Clearance to bore	0.0009 to 0.0026	(0.023 to 0.065)
Service limit	0.005	(0.127)
Collapsed tappet gap (nominal)		
Intake	0.059 to 0.194	(1.50 to 4.93)
Exhaust	0.059 to 0.194	(1.50 to 4.93)

Distributor shaft bearing bore diameter .... | 1.852 to 1.854 | (47.05 to 47.10)

Tappet bore diameter .... | 876 ± 0.0006 | (22.25 ± .015)

Camshaft bore inside diameter

No. 1	1.803 to 1.763	(45.808 to 44.783)
No. 2	1.774 to 1.773	(45.058 to 45.033)
No. 3	1.784 to 1.783	(45.308 to 45.283)
No. 4	1.794 to 1.793	(45.558 to 45.533)
No. 5	1.803 to 1.802	(45.808 to 45.783)

Camshaft

Lobe lift .... | 0.229 | (5.806)
Allowable lobe lift loss .... | 0.005 | (0.127)

Theoretical valve lift @ zero lash

Intake	0.376	(9.56)
Exhaust	0.375	(9.52)

End play .... | 0.0019 to 0.0059 | (0.050 to 150)
Service limit .... | 0.0078 | (0.20)

Journal-to-bearing clearance .... | 0.0009 to 0.0027 | (0.0023 to 0.068)

Journal diameter

No. 1	1.762 to 1.761	(44.76 to 44.74)
No. 2	1.772 to 1.771	(45.01 to 44.99)
No. 3	1.782 to 1.781	(45.26 to 45.25)
No. 4	1.792 to 1.798	(45.51 to 45.49)
No. 5	1.802 to 1.801	(45.76 to 45.74)
Runout limit	0.1	(2.54) (runout of center bearing relative to bearings No's. 1 & 5)
Out-of-round limit	0.008	(0.20)

Assembled gear face runout

Crankshaft	0.026	(0.65)
Camshaft	0.011	(0.275)

Cylinder block

	In	(mm)
Head gasket surface flatness	0.003 overall	(0.076)
	0.002/5.98	(0.05/1.152)

Cylinder bore

Diameter	3.15	(80)
Surface finish (RMS)	0.38 to 0.95	(9.652)
Out-of-round limit	0.0015	(0.04)
Out-of-round service limit	0.005	(0.127)
Taper service limit	0.01	(0.254)

Main bearing bore diameter	2.452 + 0.0005	(62.29 + 0.0142)
	− 0.0003	− 0.085)

Crankshaft and flywheel

Main bearing journal diameter	2.2834 to 2.2826	(58.0 to 57.98)
Out-of-round limit	0.0005	(0.013)
Taper limit	0.0003 per in	(0.008) per 25.4 mm
Journal runout limit	0.005	(0.13) (runout of bearings 2, 3 & 4 relative to bearings 1 & 5)

Thrust bearing journal

Length	1.135 to 1.136	(28.825 to 22.854)

Connecting rod journal

Diameter	1.886 to 1.885	(47.91 to 47.89)
Out-of-round limit	0.0005	(0.013)
Taper limit	0.0003 per in	(0.008) per 25.4 mm

Main bearing thrust face runout limit	0.001	(0.025)

Flywheel clutch face runout limit	0.007	(0.180)

Flywheel ring gear lateral runout

Standard transaxle	0.025	(0.64)
Automatic transaxle	0.005	(1.5)

Crankshaft endplay	0.004 to 0.008	(0.100 to 0.200)

Connecting rod bearings

Clearance to crankshaft		
Desired	0.0002 to 0.0003	(0.006 to 0.0064)
Allowable	0.0002 to 0.0025	(0.006 to 0.0064)
Bearing wall thickness (standard)	0.00016 to 0.0028	(0.004 to 0.072)

Main bearings

Clearance to crankshaft		
Desired	0.0008 to 0.0015	(0.020 to 0.028)
Allowable	0.0008 to 0.0026	(0.020 to 0.016)
Bearing wall thickness (standard)	0.0837 to 0.084	(2.128 to 2.138)

Connecting rod, piston and rings

Connecting rod

Piston pin bore diameter	0.8106 to 0.8114	(20.589 to 20.609)
Crankshaft bearing bore diameter	2.0035 to 2.0043	(50.89 to 50.91)
Out-of-round limit - piston pin bore	0.0004	(0.010)
Taper limit - piston pin bore	0.0004	(0.010)
Length (center-to-center) 1.6L	5.193 to 5.196	(131.905 to 131.975)
1.3L	4.285 to 4.288	(108.845 to 108.915)

Alignment (bore-to-bore max diff)

Twist	0.003/1.0	(0.076/25.4)
Bend	0.0015/1.0	(0.038/25.4)

Side clearance (assembled to crank)

Standard	0.004 to 0.011	(0.092 to 0.268)
Service limit	0.014	(0.356)

Piston diameter

Coded red	3.1466 to 3.1461	(79.925 to 79.910)
Coded blue	3.1478 to 3.1472	(79.955 to 79.940)
0.004 in (0.1 mm) oversize	3.1506 to 3.1500	(80.025 to 80.010)

Piston-to-bore clearance

	0.0008 to 0.0016	(0.020 to 0.040)

Pin bore diameter

	0.8122 to 0.8127	(20.630 to 20.642)

Ring groove width

Compression (top)	0.0653 to 0.0645	(1.660 to 1.640)
Compression (bottom)	0.0812 to 0.0802	(2.062 to 2.038)
Oil ring	0.1587 to 0.1578	(4.032 to 4.008)

Piston pin

Length	2.606 to 2.638	(66.2 to 67.0)
Standard diameter	0.8119 to 0.8124	(20.622 to 20.634)

Pin-to-piston clearance

	0.0002 to 0.0004	(0.005 to 0.011)

Pin-to-rod clearance

	Press fit - 8 kilonewton

Piston rings

Width

Compression (top)	0.0634 to 0.0621	(1.61 to 1.578)
Compression (bottom)	0.0786 to 0.078	(1.998 to 1.982)
Oil ring	Side seal (snug fit)	
Service limit side clearance	0.006	(0.15) max

Gap

Compression (top)	0.012 to 0.020	(0.30 to 0.50)
Compression (bottom)	0.012 to 0.020	(0.30 to 0.50)
Oil ring (steel rail)	0.016 to 0.055	(0.40 to 1.4)

Side clearance

1st ring	0.001 to 0.003	(0.030 to 0.082)
2nd ring	0.002 to 0.003	(0.049 to 0.084)

Lubrication system

Oil pump

Relief valve spring tension	0.921 (lbs at spec length)	(42.6 to 47.1 Newton @ 23.4)
Relief valve-to-bore clearance	0.0007 to 0.0031	(0.02 to 0.08)
Rotor outer race assembly end clearance (assembled)	0.0016 to 0.0025	(0.040 to 0.066)
Outer race-to-housing clearance (diametral)	0.0027 to 0.0055	(0.69 to 0.140)

Oil capacity w/filter

	4 US qts	(3.78L)

Torque specifications

	Ft-lb	Nm
Alternator bracket-to-block	30 to 40	40 to 54
Alternator pivot attaching nut	45 to 57	61 to 75
Alternator adjuster arm-to-block	30 to 40	40 to 54
Adjuster arm-to-alternator	24 to 34	33 to 46
Belt tensioner attaching bolt	17 to 20	23 to 27
Camshaft sprocket-to-cam	37 to 46	50 to 62
Camshaft thrust plate-to-head	7 to 11	10 to 15
Carburetor-to-manifold stud and nut	12 to 15	16 to 20
Connecting rod cap nut	19 to 25	26 to 34
Cylinder head-to-block		
Step 1	44	60
Step 2	½ turn from Step 1	
Step 3	½ turn from Step 2	
Crankshaft vent clamp attaching nut	1 to 2	1.25 to 2.25
Crankcase rear seal retainer	6 to 8	8 to 11
Crankshaft pulley nut	74 to 90	100 to 121
Distributor cap attaching screw	1 to 2	2 to 2.6
Distributor clamp-to-block	3 to 5	5 to 7
Exhaust manifold-to-block	15 to 20	21 to 26
EGR valve stud-to-spacer	12 to 15	16 to 20
EGR valve-to-spacer nut	13 to 19	18 to 26
Fan switch-to-water outlet housing	5 to 8	7 to 11
Fuel filter-to-carburetor	8 to 11	11 to 15
Fuel pump-to-head	14 to 21	19 to 29

	Ft-lb	Nm
Fuel line-to-filter	15 to 18	20 to 24
Fuel pump-to-line	15 to 18	20 to 24
Flywheel-to-crankshaft	59 to 69	80 to 94
Intake manifold stud-to-head	12 to 15	16 to 19
Intake manifold stud nut	12 to 16	16 to 20
Main bearing cap-to-block	67 to 80	90 to 108
Monolithic timing plug	15 to 25	20 to 34
Oil filter adaptor-to-block	21 to 26	28 to 35
Oil filter	12 to 16	16 to 21
Oil pan drain plug	16	22
Oil pan-to-block	6 to 8	8 to 11
Oil pump-to-block	6 to 8	8 to 11
Oil pump tube support-to-block	10 to 13	14 to 17
Oil gallery pipe plugs	8 to 12	11 to 16
Oil pick-up and screen-to-pump	6 to 8	8 to 11
Rocker arm stud-to-head	7 to 11	10 to 15
Rocker arm to-head-stud nut	15 to 19	21 to 25
Valve cover-to-head	6 to 8	8 to 11
Spark plug	17 to 23	23 to 31
Thermactor check valve attaching nut	6 to 10	8 to 13
Thermactor pump bracket-to-block	30 to 40	40 to 54
Thermactor pump pivot bolt	40 to 55	55 to 75
Thermactor pump adjuster arm-to-pump	40 to 55	55 to 75
Thermactor pump pulley-to-pump hub	13 to 18	17 to 24
Timing belt cover stud-to-block	7 to 9	9 to 11
Timing belt cover-to-block	5 to 7	7 to 9
Water drain plug	5 to 8	7 to 11
Water outlet housing	6 to 8	8 to 11
Water pump-to-block	5 to 8	7 to 11
Water pump inlet tube-to-water pump	4 to 5	5.5 to 7
Right engine support		
Mount-to-frame bolts	75 to 80	100 to 110
Insulator through-bolt	65 to 70	88 to 95
Support bracket nut	45 to 50	60 to 68
Left rear engine support		
Insulator attaching stud nut	75 to 80	100 to 110
Through-bolt nut	65 to 70	88 to 94
Left front engine support		
Through-bolt nut	65 to 70	88 to 95
Insulator attaching nuts	75 to 80	100 to 110

1 General information

The engine is of the overhead cam type with the valve gear operated by a camshaft which is mounted in five bearings directly in the aluminum cylinder head. The bearings have no inserts and if they are worn beyond specifications, the entire head must be replaced.

The camshaft is driven by a toothed belt which is driven by the crankshaft and also turns the water pump. Tension on the belt is maintained by a spring-loaded pulley. The camshaft drives rocker arms which in turn operate the hydraulic valve lifters.

The oil pump is mounted at the front end of the cylinder block and is driven directly by the crankshaft. The distributor is mounted horizontally at the rear of the block and is driven by a tang which fits in the end of the camshaft without the need for gears or a driveshaft.

The crankshaft is supported in the cylinder block by five main bearings with removable shells.

2 Operations possible without removing the engine from the vehicle

Timing belt – replacement
Camshaft oil seal – replacement
Camshaft – removal and installation
Cylinder head – removal and installation
Crankshaft front oil seal – replacement
Oil pan – removal and installation
Piston and connecting rods – removal and installation
Engine and transaxle supports – removal and installation
Intake manifold – removal and installation
Exhaust manifold – removal and installation

3 Operations possible only with the engine removed

Crankshaft main bearings – removal and installation
Crankshaft – removal and installation

4 Timing belt – removal, installation and adjustment

Note: *The manufacturer recommends that the engine drivebelt be replaced with a new one any time the tension is released or it is removed. This normally occurs when the water pump is removed or when timing belt replacement is called for in the maintenance schedule (Chapter 1).*

1 Disconnect the battery negative cable.
2 Remove the accessory drivebelts (Chapter 3).
3 Remove the timing belt cover.
4 Use a wrench on the crankshaft pulley bolt to rotate the engine until the timing mark on the camshaft pulley is aligned with the one on the cylinder head. Reinstall the front cover just long enough to check that the crankshaft pulley mark is aligned with the TDC mark on the cover (photos).
5 Remove the starter and lock the starter ring gear with a screwdriver. Remove the crankshaft pulley bolt (photo).
6 Loosen the belt tensioner bolts, pry the tensioner to one side and then re-tighten the bolts to hold it in position.
7 Remove the crankshaft pulley and the timing belt.
8 Starting at the crankshaft, install the new belt in a counterclockwise direction over the pulleys. Be sure to keep the belt span from the crankshaft to the camshaft tight while installing it over the remaining pulleys.
9 Loosen the belt tensioner attaching bolts so that the tensioner

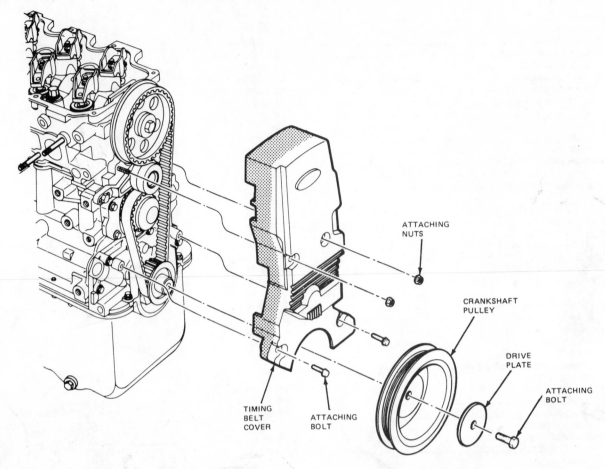

Fig. 2.1 Timing belt cover and pulley components (Sec 4)

4.4A Camshaft sprocket timing mark

4.4B Crankshaft sprocket timing marks

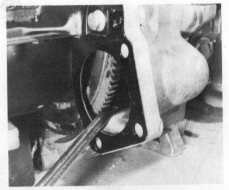

4.5 Locking flywheel starter ring gear

snaps into place against the belt. Do not tighten the tensioner bolts at this time.

10   Install the pulley and bolts and tighten to specification.

11   Rotate the crankshaft two revolutions and stop on the second revolution at the point where the crankshaft sprocket returns to the TDC position. Verify that the camshaft sprocket is also at TDC.

12   With an assistant holding a wrench on the crankshaft bolt so that it can't turn, tighten the crankshaft hex nut to specification as follows. Turn the camshaft counterclockwise until the specified torque value is reached. Hold this reading and tighten the belt tensioner attaching bolts to specification.

13   Install the timing belt cover.

14   Install and adjust the drivebelts (Chapter 3).

15   Reconnect the battery negative cable.

5   Camshaft oil seal – removal and installation

1   Disconnect the battery negative cable.

2   Remove the engine timing belt (Section 4).

3   Insert a suitable bar through the camshaft sprocket to lock it, remove the retaining bolt and withdraw the sprocket.

4   Using a suitable hooked tool, pry the oil seal out.

5   Apply a light coat of grease around the outer edge of the new seal. Place the seal in place and draw it into position, using the sprocket bolt and a suitable spacer piece such as a large socket.

6   Reinstall the sprocket and tighten the bolt to specification.

7   Install the timing belt and adjust the tension as described in Section 4.

8   Connect the battery negative cable.

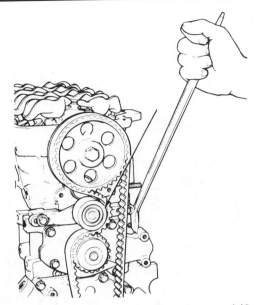

Fig. 2.2 Removing timing belt tension (at arrow) (Sec 4)

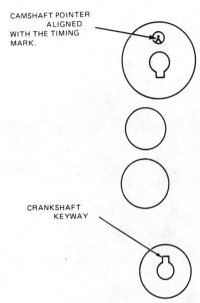

CAMSHAFT POINTER ALIGNED WITH THE TIMING MARK.

CRANKSHAFT KEYWAY

Fig. 2.3 The proper relationship of the upper and lower pulleys (Sec 4)

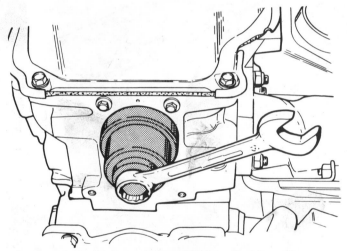

Fig. 2.4 Installing the camshaft oil seal (Sec 5)

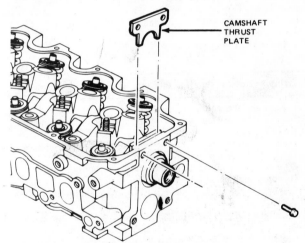

CAMSHAFT THRUST PLATE

Fig. 2.5 Camshaft thrust plate removal (Sec 6)

6 Camshaft – removal and installation

1 Disconnect the battery negative cable.

2 Disconnect the crankcase ventilation hose from the intake manifold and the rocker cover.

3 Extract the two larger screws from the lid of the air cleaner, raise the air cleaner, disconnect the hoses and remove the cleaner.

4 Disconnect the pipes. and remove the windshield washer fluid reservoir from the engine compartment.

5 Disconnect the HT leads from the spark plugs, then remove the distributor cap and secure it to the left-hand side of the engine compartment.

6 Unscrew the three bolts and withdraw the distributor from the cylinder head. Note that the distributor body is marked in relation to the cylinder head.

7 Unbolt and remove the fuel pump complete with coil spring.

8 Withdraw the insulating spacer and operating pushrod.

9 Unbolt the throttle cable bracket at the carburetor and then disconnect the cable by sliding back the spring clip.

10 Remove the rocker cover.

11 Unscrew the securing nuts and remove the rocker arms and guides. Keep the components in their originally installed sequence by marking them with a piece of numbered tape or by using a suitably sub-divided box.

12 Withdraw the hydraulic cam followers, again keeping them in their originally fitted sequence.

13 Slacken the alternator mounting and adjuster link bolts, push the alternator in towards the engine and slip the drivebelt from the pulleys.

14 Unbolt and remove the timing belt cover and turn the crankshaft to align the timing mark on the camshaft sprocket with the one on the cylinder head.

15 Loosen the bolts on the timing belt tensioner, lever the tensioner against the tension of its coil spring (if fitted) and retighten the bolts. With the belt now slack, slip it from the camshaft sprocket.

16 Pass a rod or large screwdriver through one of the holes in the camshaft sprocket to lock it and unscrew the sprocket bolt. Remove the sprocket.

17 Extract the two bolts and pull out the camshaft thrust plate.

18 Carefully withdraw the camshaft from the distributor end of the cylinder head (photo).

19 Refitting the camshaft is a reversal of removal, but observe the following points.

20 Lubricate the camshaft bearings before inserting the camshaft into the cylinder head.

21 It is recommended that a new oil seal is always fitted after the camshaft has been installed (see preceding Section). Apply thread locking compound to the sprocket bolt threads.

22 Fit and tension the timing belt as described in Section 4.

23 Oil the hydraulic cam followers with engine oil before inserting them into their original bores.

24 Replace the rocker arms and guides in their original sequence, use

6.18 When removing the camshaft, be careful not to contact the cylinder head

new nuts and tighten to the specified torque. It is essential that before each rocker arm is installed and its nut tightened, the respective cam follower is positioned at its lowest point (in contact with cam base circle). Turn the camshaft (by means of the crankshaft pulley bolt) as necessary to achieve this.

25 Use a new rocker cover gasket.

7 Cylinder head – removal and installation

1   Disconnect the battery negative cable.
2   Remove the air cleaner and detach the connecting hoses.
3   Drain the cooling system (Chapter 3).
4   Disconnect the coolant hoses from the thermostat housing.
5   Disconnect the coolant hoses from the automatic choke.
6   Disconnect the throttle cable from the carburetor.
7   Disconnect the fuel pipe from the fuel pump.
8   Disconnect the vacuum servo pipe (if so equipped) from the intake manifold.
9   Disconnect the leads from the coolant temperature sender, the ignition coil, and the anti-run-on solenoid valve at the carburetor.
10 Unbolt the exhaust downpipe from the manifold by unscrewing the flange bolts. Support the exhaust pipe by tying it up with wire.
11 Release the alternator mounting and adjuster link bolts, push the alternator in towards the engine and slip the drivebelt from the pulleys.
12 Unbolt and remove the timing belt cover.
13 Slacken the belt tensioner bolts, lever the tensioner to one side against the pressure of the coil spring (if fitted) and retighten the bolts.
14 With the timing belt now slack, slip it from the camshaft sprocket.
15 Disconnect the leads from the spark plugs and unscrew and remove the spark plugs.
16 Remove the rocker cover.
17 Unscrew the cylinder head bolts, progressively and in the reverse sequence to that given for tightening (Fig. 2.7). Discard the bolts, as new ones must be used at reassembly.
18 Remove the cylinder head complete with manifolds. Use the manifolds if necessary as levers to rock the head from the block. Do not attempt to tap the head sideways off the block as it is located on dowels, and do not attempt to lever between the head and the block or damage will result.
19 Before installing the cylinder head, make sure that the mating surfaces of head and block are perfectly clean with the head locating dowels in position. Clean the bolt holes free from oil. In extreme cases it is possible for oil left in the holes to crack the block.
20 Turn the crankshaft to position No.1 piston about 20 mm (0.8 in) before it reaches TDC.
21 Place a new gasket on the cylinder block and then locate the cylinder head on its dowels. The upper surface of the gasket is marked OBEN-TOP.
22 Install and tighten the cylinder head bolts, tightening them in four

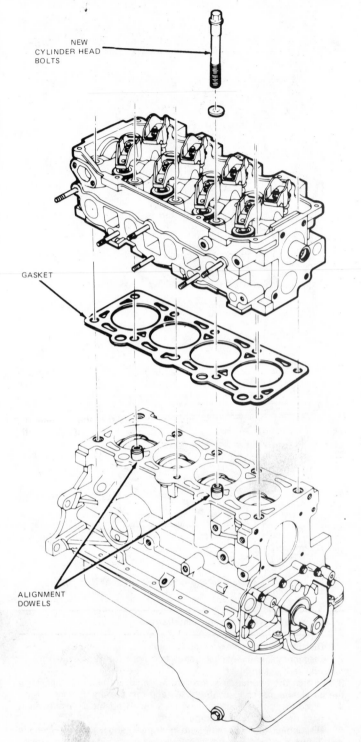

Fig. 2.6 Cylinder head removal and installation (Sec 7)

stages (see Specifications). After the first two stages, the bolt heads should be marked with a spot of quick-drying paint so that the paint spots all face the same direction. Now tighten the bolts (Step 1) through 90° (quarter turn) (Step 2), followed by a further 90° (Step 3). Tighten the bolts at each stage only in the sequence shown before going on to the next stage. If all the bolts have been tightened equally, the paint spots should now all be pointing in the same direction.
23 Fit the timing belt as described in Section 4.
24 Reinstallation and reconnection of all other components is a reversal of dismantling.
25 Refill the cooling system.

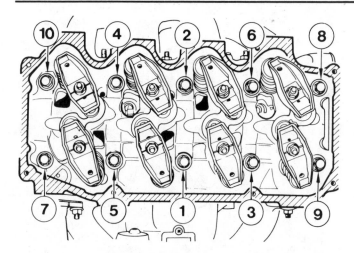

Fig. 2.7 Cylinder head bolt tightening and loosening sequence
(Secs 7, 13 and 16)

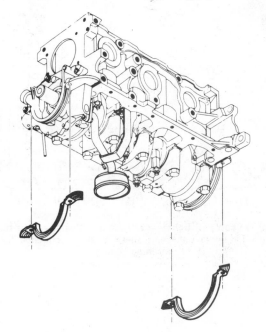

8 Crankshaft front oil seal – removal and installation

1 Disconnect the battery negative cable.
2 Release the alternator mounting and adjuster link bolts, push the alternator in towards the engine and slip the drivebelt from the pulleys.
3 Unbolt and remove the timing belt cover and by using a wrench or socket on the crankshaft pulley bolt, turn the crankshaft until the timing mark on the camshaft sprocket is in alignment with the mark on the cylinder head.
4 Unbolt and withdraw the starter motor so that the flywheel ring gear can be jammed with a cold chisel or other suitable device and the crankshaft pulley unbolted and removed.
5 Slacken the belt tensioner bolts, lever the tensioner to one side and retighten the bolts. With the belt slack, it can now be slipped from the sprockets. Before removing the belt note its original position on the sprockets (mark the teeth with quick-drying paint), also its direction of travel.
6 Pull off the crankshaft sprocket. If it is tight, use a two-legged extractor.
7 Remove the dished washer from the crankshaft, noting that the concave side is against the oil seal.
8 Using a suitably hooked tool, pry out the oil seal from the oil pump housing.
9 Grease the lips of the new seal and press it into position using the pulley bolt and a suitable distance piece made from a piece of tubing.
10 Install the thrust washer (concave side to oil seal), the belt sprocket and the pulley to the crankshaft.
11 Install and tension the timing belt by the method described in Section 25.
12 Install the timing belt cover.
13 Reinstall and tension the alternator drivebelt.
14 Remove the starter ring gear jamming device, reinstall the starter motor and reconnect the battery.

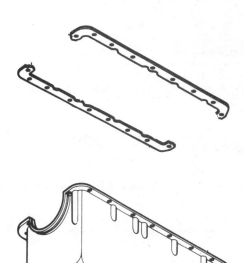

9 Oil pan – removal and installation

1 Disconnect the battery negative cable.
2 Drain the engine oil.
3 Unbolt and remove the starter motor.
4 Unbolt and remove the cover plate from the clutch housing.
5 Unscrew the plastic timing belt guard from the front end of the engine (two bolts).
6 Unscrew the sump securing bolts progressively and remove them.
7 Remove the sump and peel away the gaskets and sealing strips.
8 Make sure that the mating surfaces of the sump and block are clean, then fit new end sealing strips into their grooves and stick new side gaskets into position using thick grease. Press the front seal into the retainer and the rear seal into the oil pump slot. Apply adhesive to the oil pump flange and the mating surface of the pan gasket. The ends

Fig. 2.8 Oil pan installation (Sec 9)

of the side gaskets should overlap the seals.
9 Install the oil pan, taking care not to displace the gaskets and insert the securing bolts. Tighten the bolts in two stages to the final torque given in the Specifications. Install the timing belt guard.
10 Replace the cover plate to the flywheel housing.
11 Replace the starter motor.
12 Fill the engine with oil and reconnect the battery.

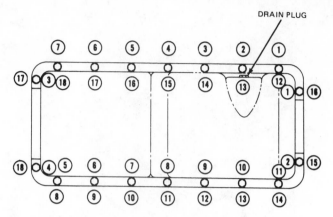

Fig. 2.9 Oil pan bolt tightening sequence. Use the inner number sequence for initial tightening and the outer sequence for final tightening (Sec 9)

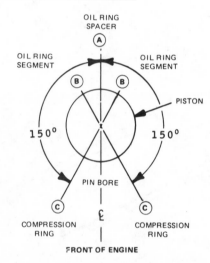

Fig. 2.11 Piston ring gap spacing diagram (Sec 10)

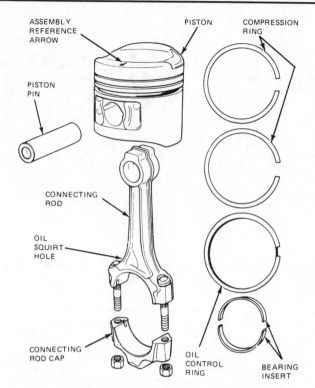

Fig. 2.10 Piston and connecting rod components (Sec 10)

10.13 Installing the piston with a ring compressor tool

10 Piston/connecting rods – removal and installation

1   Remove the oil pan as described in the preceding Section and the cylinder head as described in Section 7.
2   Check that the connecting rod and cap have adjacent numbers at their big-end to indicate their position in the cylinder block (No.1 nearest timing cover end of engine).
3   Bring the first piston to the lowest point of its throw by turning the crankshaft pulley bolt and then check if there is a wear ring at the top of the bore. If there is, it should be removed using a ridge reaming tool (refer to the beginning of this manual).
4   Unscrew the big-end bolts and remove them.
5   Tap off the cap. If the bearing shell is to be used again, make sure that it is retained with the cap. Note the two cap positioning roll pins.
6   Push the piston/rod out of the top of the block, again keeping the bearing shell with the rod if the shell is to be used again.
7   Repeat the removal operations on the remaining piston/rod assemblies.
8   Dismantling a piston/connectig rod is covered in Section 14.
9   To reinstall a piston/rod assembly, have the piston ring gaps staggered as shown in the diagram (Fig. 2.11). Oil the rings and apply a piston ring compressor. Compress the piston rings.
10 Oil the cylinder bores.
11 Wipe clean the bearing shell seat in the connecting rod and insert the shell.
12 Insert the piston/rod assembly into the cylinder bore until the base

of the piston ring compressor stands squarely on the top of the block.
13 Check that the directional arrow on the piston crown faces towards the timing cover end of the engine, then apply the wooden handle of a hammer to the piston crown. Strike the head of the hammer sharply to drive the piston into the cylinder bore and release the ring compressor (photo).
14 Oil the crankpin and draw the connecting rod down to engage with the crankshaft. Make sure the bearing shell is still in position.
15 Wipe the bearing shell seat in the big-end cap clean and insert the bearing shell.
16 Fit the cap, screw in the bolts and tighten them to the specified torque.
17 Repeat the operations on the remaining pistons/connecting rods.
18 Install the oil pan (Section 9) and the cylinder head (Section 7). Refill the engine with oil and coolant.

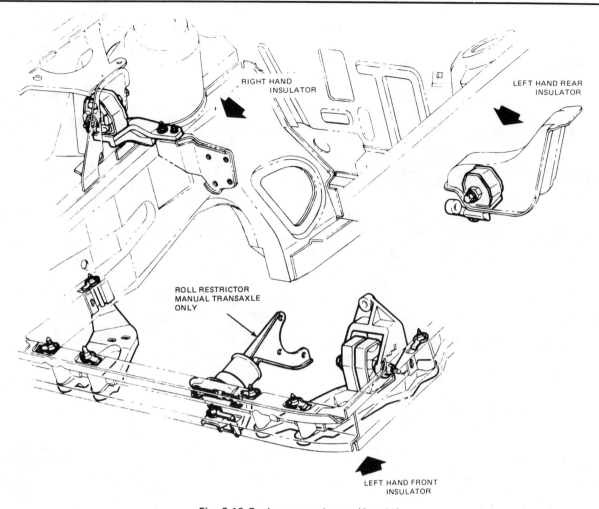

Fig. 2.12 Engine mount layout (Sec 11)

11 Engine supports and insulators – removal and installation

1   The engine supports and insulators can be removed if the weight of the engine/transaxle unit is taken off them.

Right insulator

2   Raise the engine one inch by using a jack and block of wood under the oil pan.
3   Remove the support bracket attaching nut and lower the vehicle until the support bracket is almost touching the fender apron.
4   Remove the insulator through-bolt and nut and work the insulator out of the vehicle.
5   Install the new insulator (insulator stud pointing down) by working it into position and inserting the through-bolt. The insulator must be installed with the word 'Front' facing the transaxle bracket (Fig. 2.15).
6   Raise the engine and install the support bracket attaching nut.
7   Lower the engine, install the through-bolt nut and tighten to specification.

Left rear insulator

8   Raise the vehicle and support the transaxle with a jack and a block of wood.
9   Remove the insulator stud nut and move the engine about ½ in toward the right side of the vehicle.
10 Remove the through-bolt and nut and remove the insulator from the mounting bracket.
11 Install the insulator stud through the transaxle mounting bracket and install the stud nut.
12 Install the through-bolt to the transaxle bracket and tighten to specification.

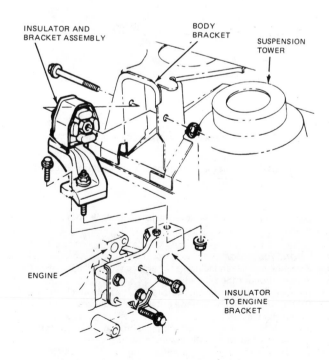

Fig. 2.13 Right engine mount and insulator (Sec 11)

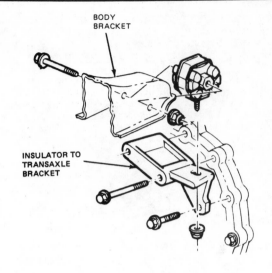

MANUAL TRANSAXLE

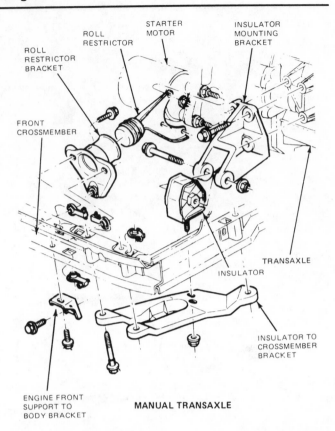

MANUAL TRANSAXLE

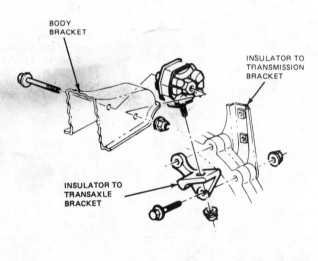

AUTOMATIC TRANSAXLE

Fig. 2.14 Left rear engine mount and insulator (Sec 11)

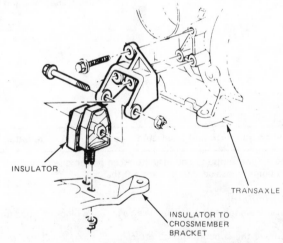

AUTOMATIC TRANSMISSION

Fig. 2.15 Left front engine mount and insulator (Sec 11)

13 Lower the vehicle and remove the jack and block from beneath the transaxle.

Left front insulator

14 Raise the vehicle and support the engine with a block of wood and a jack placed under the oil pan.
15 Remove the two insulators to support bracket attaching nuts.
16 Remove the through-bolt and nut and raise the engine sufficiently to remove the insulator.
17 To install, place the insulator in position into the support bracket and tighten the nut to specification.
18 Install the through-bolt and nut and tighten to specification.
19 Place the insulator against the support bracket and install the nuts, tightening to specification.
20 Lower the vehicle.

12 Engine – removal

1   Remove the hood as described in Chapter 12.
2   Remove the air cleaner assembly, duct and heat tube.
3   Remove the alternator air intake tube (if equipped).
4   Disconnect the battery negative cable.
5   Drain the engine coolant into a suitable container.
6   Remove the ignition coil secondary wire.
7   Remove the alternator drivebelts and mounting bolts and position the alternator out of the way.
8   Remove the Thermactor air supply hose at the Thermactor and remove the pump.

9 Disconnect the heater hose and upper and lower radiator hoses. On automatic transaxle models, disconnect the oil cooler lines at the radiator.
10 Disconnect the radiator cooling fan and remove the fan shroud.
11 Remove the radiator (Chapter 3).
12 Disconnect the heater hose at the metal tube.
13 Disconnect any remaining vacuum hoses, fuel lines and electrical connections which would interfere with engine removal.
14 On power brake equipped models, disconnect the vacuum line at the engine.
15 On automatic transaxle equipped models, disconnect the kick-down rod at the carburetor.
16 Disconnect the Thermactor valve vacuum hose.
17 Disconnect the accelerator at the carburetor and remove the mounting bracket.
18 Disconnect the vapor canister hose.
19 Raise the vehicle.
20 Remove the heater supply tubes and clamps.
21 Disconnect the battery cable from the starter motor and remove the brace at the front of the motor.
22 On manual transaxle models, remove the roll restricter.
23 Remove the starter motor.
24 Disconnect the exhaust pipe at the manifold.
25 Remove the transaxle support bracket at the front of the inspection cover and remove the cover.
26 Remove the crankshaft pulley.
27 On automatic transaxle vehicles, remove the nuts attaching the torque converter to the flywheel.
28 On manual transaxle vehicles, remove the lower timing belt cover bolts.
29 Remove the lower attaching bolts for the converter housing (automatic) or flywheel housing (manual).
30 Remove the coolant bypass hose from the intake manifold and disconnect the battery negative cable at the cylinder block.
31 Remove the right engine mount insulator-to-engine attaching bolt (Section 11).
32 Lower the vehicle and attach lifting brackets to the engine. Remove the rear, top Thermactor pump bracket and this can be used as an attaching point for one lifting bracket.
33 Connect a suitable hoisting device to the engine and lift sufficiently so that engine mount through-bolt can be removed from the insulator. Remove the insulator bracket.
34 On manual transaxle models, remove the timing belt cover.
35 Support the weight of the transaxle with a jack.
36 Remove the remaining transaxle attaching bolts.
37 Lift the engine from the vehicle, making sure that it is lifted vertically to provide enough clearance. Lower the engine to the floor or workbench and support it so that it cannot roll over.

13 Engine – complete dismantling

1 The need for dismantling will have been dictated by wear or noise in most cases. Although there is no reason why only partial dismantling cannot be carried out to replace such items as the oil pump or crankshaft rear oil seal, when the main bearings or big-end bearings have been knocking and especially if the vehicle has covered high mileage, then it is recommended that a complete strip-down be carried out and every engine component examined as described in Section 14.
2 Position the engine so that it is upright and safely chocked on a bench or other convenient working surface. If the exterior of the engine is very dirty it should be cleaned before dismantling, using a suitable solvent and a stiff brush or a water-soluble solvent.
3 Remove the alternator, the mounting bracket and exhaust heat shield, and the adjuster link.
4 Disconnect the heater hose from the coolant pump.
5 Drain the engine oil and remove the filter.
6 Jam the flywheel starter ring gear to prevent the crankshaft turning and unscrew the crankshaft pulley bolt. Remove the pulley.
7 Unbolt and remove the timing belt cover.
8 Slacken the two bolts on the timing belt tensioner, lever the tensioner against its spring pressure and tighten the bolts to lock it in position.
9 With the belt now slack, note its running direction and mark the mating belt and sprocket teeth with a spot of quick-drying paint. This is not necessary if the belt is being replaced.

10 Disconnect the spark plug leads and remove the distributor cap complete with HT leads.
11 Unscrew and remove the spark plugs.
12 Disconnect the crankcase ventilation hose from its connector on the crankcase.
13 Remove the rocker cover.
14 Unscrew the cylinder head bolts in the reverse order to tightening and discard them. New bolts must be used at reassembly.
15 Remove the cylinder head complete with manifolds.
16 Turn the engine on its side. Do not invert it as sludge in the oil pan may enter the oilways. Remove the oil pan bolts, withdraw the pan and peel off the gaskets and sealing strips.
17 Remove the bolts from the clutch pressure plate in a progressive manner until the pressure of the assembly is relieved and then remove the cover, taking care not to allow the driven plate (friction disc) to fall to the floor.
18 Unbolt and remove the flywheel. The bolt holes are offset so it will only fit one way.
19 Remove the engine adaptor plate.
20 Unbolt and remove the crankshaft rear oil seal retainer.
21 Unbolt and remove the timing belt tensioner and take out the coil spring.
22 Unbolt and remove the coolant pump.
23 Remove the belt sprocket from the crankshaft using the hands or if tight, a two-legged puller. Take off the thrust washer.
24 Unbolt the oil pump and pick-up tube and remove them as in assembly.
25 Unscrew and remove the oil pressure switch.
26 Turn the crankshaft so that all the pistons are half-way down the bores, and feel if a wear ridge exists at the top of the bores. Remove any ridge, using a ridge reamer tool.
27 Inspect the big-end and main bearing caps for markings. The main bearings should be marked 1 to 5 with a directional arrow pointing to the timing end. The big-end caps and connecting rods should have adjacent matching members towards the oil filter side of the engine. Number 1 is at the timing end of the engine. Make your own marks if necessary.
28 Unscrew the bolts from the first big-end cap and remove the cap. The cap is located on two roll pins, so if the cap requires tapping off make sure that it is not tapped in a sideways direction.
29 Retain the bearing shell with the cap if the shell is to be used again.
30 Push the piston/connecting rod out of the top of the cylinder block, again retaining the bearing shell with the rod if the shell is to be used again.
31 Remove the remaining pistons/rods in a similar way.
32 Remove the main bearing caps, keeping the shells with their respective caps if the shells are to be used again. Lift out the crankshaft.
33 Take out the bearing shells from the crankcase, noting the semi-circular thrust washers on either side of the centre bearing. Keep the shells identified as to position in the crankcase if they are to be used again.
34 Pry down the spring arms of the crankcase ventilation baffle and remove it from inside the crankcase just below the ventilation hose connection.
35 The engine is now completely dismantled and each component should be examined as described in the following Section before reassembling.

14 Engine – inspection and overhaul

1 Clean all components, using the proper solvent. The crankshaft should be wiped clean and the passages cleaned out with a suitable brush.
2 Measure and compare each component to Specifications, as this is the only way to determine if wear has occurred. Never assume that a component is unworn because it looks alright. Always replace any doubtful component with a new one.

Crankshaft, main and connecting rod bearings

3 The need for new main bearings or the regrinding of the crankshaft will be determined by the presence of knocking, low oil pressure denoted by the oil pressure light staying on, or the engine having high mileage.

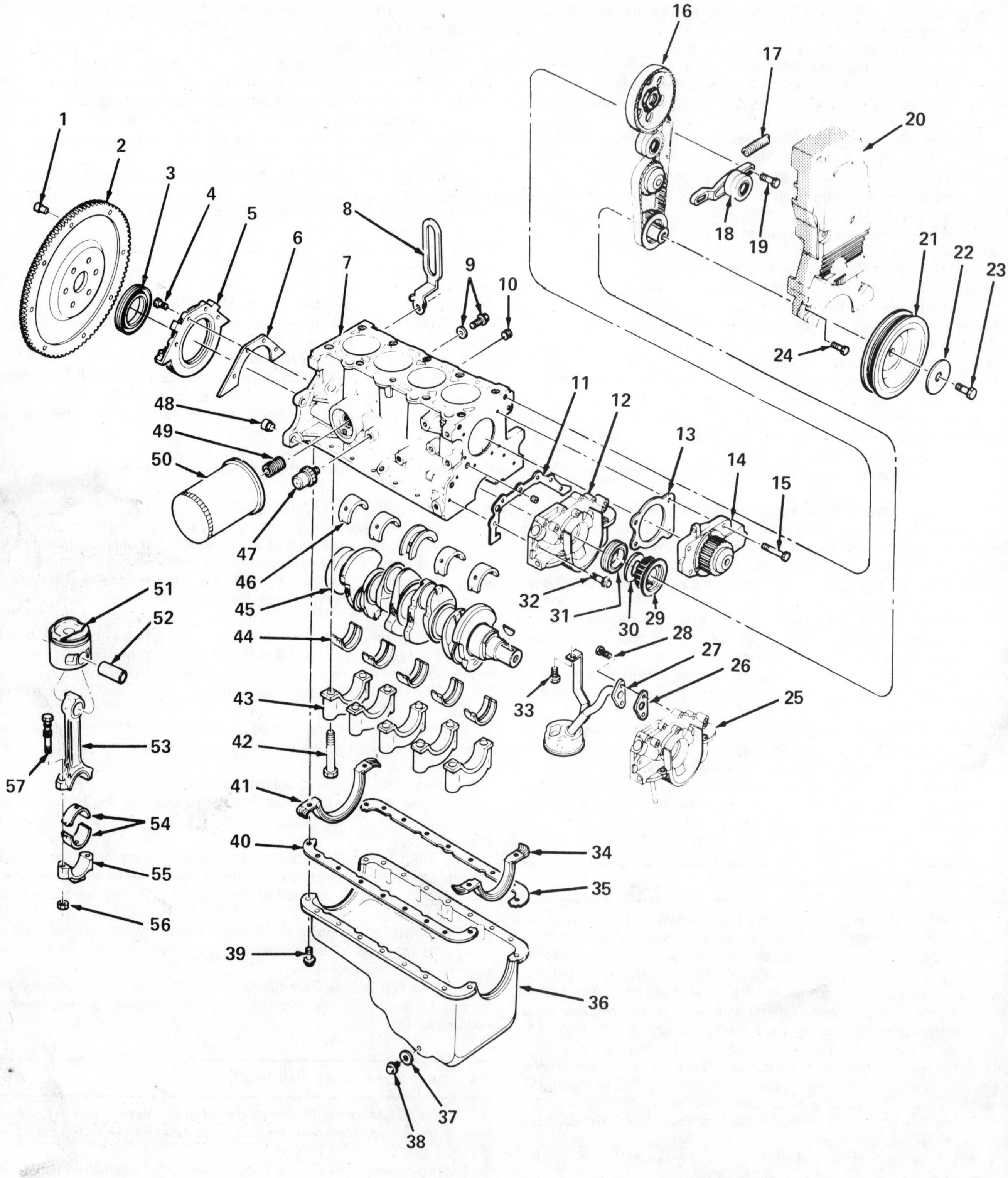

Fig. 2.16 Exploded view of the engine cylinder block and components (Secs 13 and 14)

4   The crankshaft journals and crankpins should be checked for out-of-round (ovality) and taper, using a micrometer. The crankshaft can be taken to an engine builder or mechanic to have these measurements taken. If any of these measurements are out of Specification, have the crankshaft reground. The engine rebuilder generally supplies the necessary undersize bearings.

5   A simple way to check the crankshaft main and rod bearing journals for wear and taper is to use Plastigage. Place a piece of Plastigage across the full width of the bearing surface, about $\frac{1}{4}$ in off center and install the bearing cap. Tighten the cap to specification and then remove it. Measure the width of the Plastigage at its widest point to obtain the minimum bearing clearance and the narrowest point for the maximum clearance, using the supplied gauge. The difference between these two measurements equals the taper. Be sure that the crankshaft is not rotated while the Plastigage is in place and remove all traces of Plastigage from the journal after measurement.

6   The bearings should be replaced with new ones even if the crankshaft is in good condition unless the vehicle has very few miles on it. Check the bearing surfaces for wear and scoring.

Cylinder bores, pistons and connecting rods

7   Cylinder bore wear will be evidenced by smoke from the exhaust, excessive oil consumption and fouling of the spark plugs.

8   The cylinder bore should be measured for wear, taper and out-of-round. To determine taper, measure about an inch into the bore at the top and bottom with a cylinder bore gauge. The difference between the two measurements is the taper. Take measurements all of the way around the bore to determine ovality. A rebore and oversized pistons will be necessary if the cylinder measurements are out of specification.

9   If new pistons are needed, the job should be left to your dealer or a machine shop because of the special tools needed.

10 The piston rings can be removed using a piston ring expanding tool (refer to the front of this manual). Clean the piston ring grooves with suitable tool and check that the oil ring slots and holes are open. Remove carbon and varnish deposits from the piston using the proper solvent and inspect for cracks and signs of detonation or pre-ignition.

11 Prior to installation, check the piston rings for proper end and side clearance. Insert a feeler gauge at the top of the ring groove and measure the side clearance. Push the ring to the bottom of its travel in the bore and measure the end gap. Insert the ring into its groove in the piston and measure the side clearance with a feeler gauge. Ring end gap clearance can be adjusted by lightly filing the ring end.

12 Install the rings, using a suitable tool (refer to the beginning of this manual), taking care to avoid damaging the molybdenum coating on the top rings.

13 Prior to installation of the piston, the cylinder bore should be honed using the cylinder hone shown at the beginning of the manual.

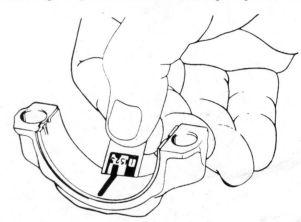

Fig. 2.17 Measuring Plastigage (Sec 14)

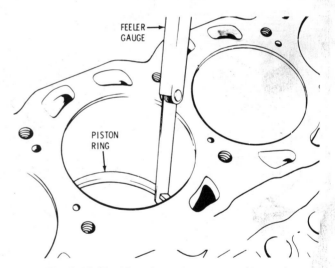

Fig. 2.18 Checking piston ring end gap (Sec 14)

1   Pressure plate alignment dowel
2   Flywheel
3   Crankshaft rear seal
4   Retainer bolt
5   Seal retainer
6   Retainer gasket
7   Cylinder block
8   Engine lifting eye
9   Monolithic timing plug and gasket
10 Coolant drain plug
11 Oil pump gasket
12 Oil pump
13 Water pump gasket
14 Water pump
15 Water pump bolt
16 Timing belt – installed view
17 Tensioner spring
18 Tensioner bracket and idler
19 Tensioner bolt
20 Timing belt cover
21 Crankshaft pulley
22 Pulley bolt washer
23 Pulley bolt
24 Cover bolt
25 Crankshaft hub
26 Oil pump
27 Pick-up tube gasket
28 Pick-up bolt
29 Crankshaft sprocket
30 Timing belt guide
31 Crankshaft front seal
32 Oil pump bolt
33 Brace bolt
34 Pan front seal
35 Pan side gasket
36 Oil pan
37 Drain plug seal
38 Oil pan drain plug
39 Pan bolt
40 Pan side gasket
41 Pan rear seal
42 Cap bolt
43 Main bearing caps
44 Lower main bearing inserts
45 Crankshaft
46 Upper main bearing inserts
47 Oil pressure sending unit
48 Transmission alignment dowel
49 Oil filter adapter
50 Oil filter
51 Piston
52 Piston pin
53 Connecting rod
54 Connecting rod bearings
55 Connecting rod cap
56 Cap nut
57 Cap bolt

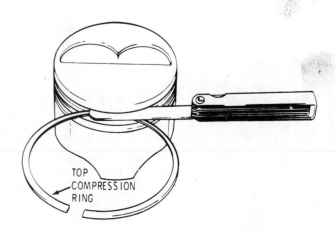

Fig. 2.19 Checking piston ring side clearance (Sec 14)

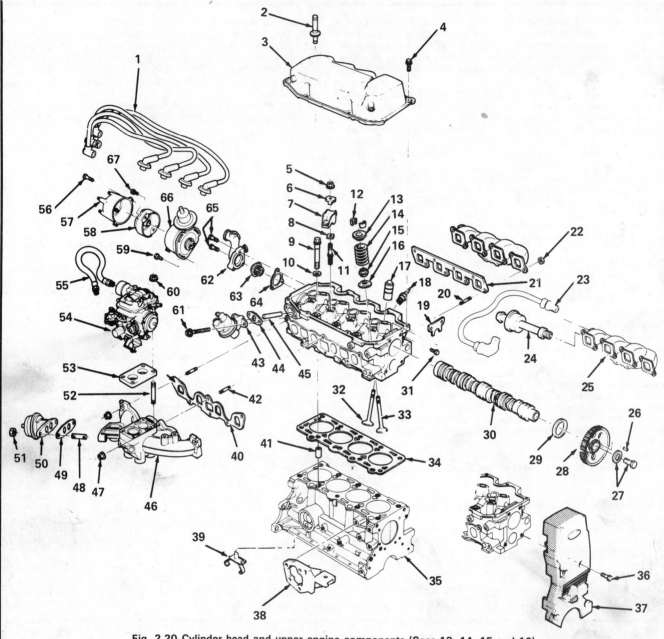

Fig. 2.20 Cylinder head and upper engine components (Secs 13, 14, 15 and 16)

1 Spark plug cable set
2 Cover bolt and stud
3 Rocker arm cover
4 Cover screw
5 Fulcrum nut
6 Rocker arm fulcrum
7 Rocker arm
8 Fulcrum washer
9 Cylinder head bolt
10 Cylinder head bolt washer
11 Fulcrum stud
12 Valve spring retainer keys
13 Valve spring retainer
14 Valve spring
15 Valve stem seal
16 Valve spring seat
17 Hydraulic tappet

18 Spark plug
19 Camshaft thrust plate
20 Manifold stud
21 Exhaust manifold gasket
22 Manifold nut
23 EGR tube
24 Air injection check valve
25 Exhaust manifold
26 Cam sprocket shaft key
27 Sprocket bolt and washer
28 Camshaft sprocket
29 Camshaft seal
30 Camshaft
31 Thrust plate bolt
32 Intake valve
33 Exhaust valve
34 Cylinder head gasket

35 Cylinder block
36 Cover bolts and nuts
37 Timing belt cover
38 Engine mount
39 Crankcase ventilation baffle
40 Intake manifold gasket
41 Cylinder head alignment dowel
42 Manifold stud
43 Fuel pump
44 Fuel pump gasket
45 Fuel pump push rod
46 Intake manifold
47 Manifold nut
48 Valve stud
49 EGR valve gasket
50 EGR valve

51 Valve nut
52 Carburetor stud
53 Carburetor mounting gasket
54 Carburetor
55 Fuel line
56 Cap screw
57 Distributor cap
58 Rotor
59 Distributor bolt
60 Carburetor nut
61 Pump bolt
62 Thermostat housing
63 Thermostat
64 Housing gasket
65 Housing bolt
66 Distributor
67 Rotor screw

Timing sprockets and belt

14 Inspect the teeth of the timing sprockets for wear and check that the tension idler pulley turns freely and is not loose or grooved. Replace any idler puller that is suspect.

15 Replace the timing belt and the tensioner idler spring.

Flywheel

16 Inspect the surface of the manual transaxle flywheel for scoring and cracks. If not scored beyond specification, the flywheel can be machined so that the friction surface is flat, otherwise it must be replaced. Check the automatic transaxle flywheel for cracks. Inspect the flywheel starter ring gear for worn or broken teeth and if replacement is necessary, have the job done by a properly equipped shop.

Oil pump

17 Clean the oil pump in the proper solvent and inspect it for wear, grooving or scoring of the mating surface and the rotor for nicks or burrs. Check the gears for damage, wear or looseness. Use a feeler gauge to check if gear-to-housing clearances are within specification. Check the relief spring for free movement and to see if it is collapsed or worn. The oil pump cannot be rebuilt and a suspect unit should be replaced with a new one.

Oil seals and gaskets

18 Replace the oil seals in the oil pump and the crankshaft rear oil seal retainer. After the camshaft has been installed, replace the camshaft oil seal.

19 Replace all gaskets and oil seals which have been removed during engine disassembly.

Crankcase

20 Clean out the oil passages with a piece of wire, suitable brush or compressed air. Flush out the coolant passages with water under pressure. Inspect the crankcase and block for stripped threads in bolt holes and replace any freeze plugs which are leaking or rusting.

Camshaft and bearings

21 Inspect the camshaft gear and lobes for damage and wear. Some models are equipped with oversize camshaft bearing surfaces and this will be marked on the cylinder head and as shown on the camshaft itself.

22 Check the bearing internal diameters against those in the Specifications with a micrometer. If these are worn beyond specification, the cylinder head will have to be replaced.

23 Temporarily install the camshaft and thrust plate and check the camshaft endfloat. If out of specification, install a new thrust plate.

Valve lifters

24 It is seldom that the hydraulic type valve lifters (tappets) wear in their cylinder head bores. If the bores are worn then a new cylinder head is called for. Some models have oversized tappets and this will be noted by a stamping on the cylinder head.

25 If the cam lobe contact surface shows signs of a depression or groove, replace them with new ones.

26 The valve lifter can be dismantled for replacement of individual components after extracting the circlip, but after high mileage it is probably better to replace the follower complete. After reassembly of a valve lifter, do not attempt to fill it with oil but just smear the parts with a little oil during assembly.

Cylinder head and rocker arms

27 The usual reason for dismantling the cylinder head is to remove the carbon deposits and to grind in the valves. Reference should therefore be made to the next Section in addition to the dismantling operations described here.

28 Remove the intake and exhaust manifolds and their gaskets, also the thermostat housing (Chapter 3).

29 Unscrew the nuts from the rocker arms and discard the nuts. New ones must be fitted at reassembly.

30 Remove the rocker arms and the hydraulic cam followers, keeping them in their originally fitted sequence. Keep the rocker guide and spacer plates in order.

31 The camshaft need not be withdrawn but if it is wished to do so, first remove the thrust plate and take the camshaft out from the rear of the cylinder head.

32 The valve springs should now be compressed. A standard type of compressor will normally do the job, but a forked tool can be purchased or made up to engage on the rocker stud using a nut and distance piece to compress it.

33 Compress the valve spring and extract the split collets. Do not overcompress the spring, or the valve stem may bend. If it is found when screwing down the compressor tool that the spring retainer does not release from the collets, remove the compressor and place a piece of tubing on the retainer so that it does not impinge on the collets and place a small block of wood under the head of the valve. With the cylinder head resting flat down on the bench, strike the end of the tubing a sharp blow with a hammer. Refit the compressor and compress the spring.

34 Extract the split collets and then gently release the compressor and remove it.

35 Remove the valve spring retainer, the spring and the valve stem oil seal. Withdraw the valve.

36 Valve removal should start with No.1 valve (nearest timing cover end). Keep the valves and their components in their originally installed order by placing them in a piece of card which has holes punched in it and numbered 1 to 8.

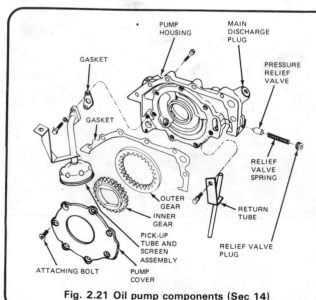

Fig. 2.21 Oil pump components (Sec 14)

Fig. 2.22 Oversize camshaft marking location (Sec 14)

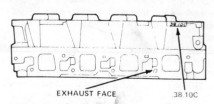

Fig. 2.23 Oversize tappets are stamped on the exhaust face and oversize camshafts on the upper edge of the cylinder head (Sec 14)

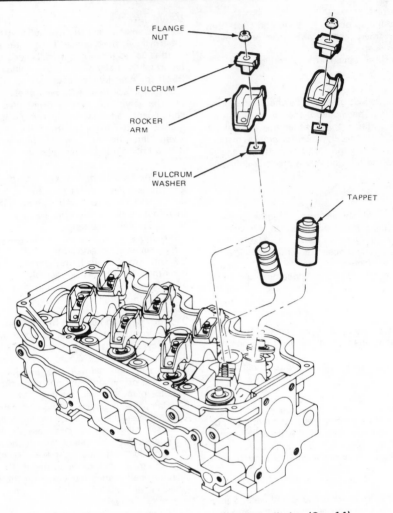

Fig. 2.24 Valve rocker arm and tappet installation (Sec 14)

37 To check for wear in the valve guides, place each valve in turn in its guide so that approximately one third of its length enters the guide. Rock the valve from side to side. If any more than the slightest movement is possible, the guides will have to be reamed (working from the valve seat end) and oversize stemmed valves fitted. If you do not have the necessary reamer, leave this work to your Ford dealer or machine shop.

38 Examine the valve seats. Normally the seats do not deteriorate, but the valve heads are more likely to burn away. If the seats require recutting, use a standard cutter, available from most accessory or tool stores.

39 Replacement of any valve seat which is cracked or beyond recutting is definitely a job for your dealer or engine rebuilder.

40 If the rocker arm studs must be removed for any reason, a special procedure is necessary. Warm the upper ends of the studs with a blow torch flame (**not** a welder) before unscrewing them. Clean out the cylinder head threads with an M10 tap and clean the threads of oil or grease. Discard the old studs and fit new ones, which will be coated with adhesive compound on their threaded portion. Screw in the studs without pausing, otherwise the adhesive will start to set and prevent the stud seating.

41 If the cylinder head mating surface is suspected of being distorted, it can be checked and surface ground by your dealer or machine shop. Distortion is possible with this type of light alloy head if the bolt tightening method is not followed exactly, or if severe overheating has taken place.

42 Check the rocker arm contact surfaces for wear. Replace the valve springs if they have been in service for 80 000 km (50 000 miles) or more.

43 Commence reassembly of the cylinder head by fitting new valve

14.43 Installing a valve stem oil seal using a socket

stem oil seals (photo).

44 Oil the No.1 valve stem and insert the valve into its guide.

45 Fit the valve spring (closer coils to cylinder head), then the spring retainer.

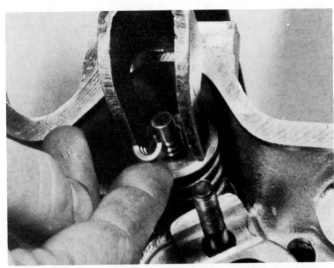

14.46 Make sure that the valve retainer collet is securely seated in valve stem grooves

46 Compress the spring and engage the split collets in the cut-out in the valve stem. Hold them in position while the compressor is gently released and removed (photo).

47 Repeat the operations on the remaining valves, making sure that each valve is returned to its original guide or a new valve has been fitted, into the seat into which it was ground.

48 Once all the valves have been fitted, support the ends of the cylinder head on two wooden blocks and strike the end of each valve stem with a plastic or copper-faced hammer, just a light blow to settle the components.

49 Fit the camshaft (if removed) and a new oil seal as described in Section 5.

50 Smear the hydraulic lifters with engine oil and insert them into their original bores.

51 Fit the rocker arms with their guides and spacer plates, use new nuts and tighten to the specified torque. It is important that each rocker arm is installed only when its particular cam follower is at its lowest point (in contact with the cam base circle).

52 Reinstall the exhaust and intake manifolds and the thermostat housing, using all new gaskets.

15 Cylinder head – cleaning and inspection

1 Because the cylinder head is an aluminum casting, extreme care must be taken during removal, installation and cleaning.

2 Carefully remove any carbon deposits from the combustion chamber with a scraper and wire brush, leaving the valves in place to protect the valve seats. **Note:** *Be careful not to damage the gasket surface.*

3 After the valves are removed, clean the valve guide bores and all bolt holes, using a thin brush and solvent.

4 Check the head for flatness by placing a straight edge diagonally across it and using a straight edge to determine if warpage is within specifications (Fig. 2.25).

5 Inspect the valve seats and measure the width (Fig. 2.26).

6 Remove the carbon deposit from the valves with a wire brush and a suitable solvent and inspect for bent stems and burning or pitting.

16 Engine – reassembly

1 With everything clean and parts replaced where necessary, begin reassembly by inserting the ventilation baffle into the crankcase. Make sure that the spring arms engage securely.

2 Insert the bearing half shells into their seats in the crankcase, making sure that the seats are perfectly clean.

3 Stick the semi-circular thrust washers on either side of the center bearing with thick grease. Make sure that the oil channels face outwards (photo).

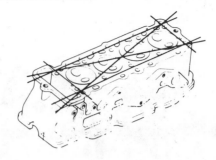

Fig. 2.25 Cylinder head warpage check (Sec 15)

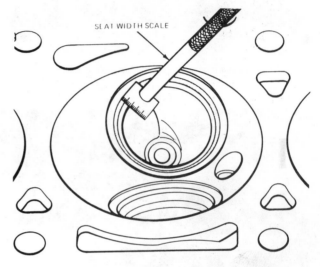

SEAT WIDTH SCALE

Fig. 2.26 Measuring valve seat width (Sec 15)

4 Oil the bearing shells and carefully lower the crankshaft into position (photo).

5 Insert the bearing shells into the main bearing caps, making sure that their seats are perfectly clean. Oil the bearings and install the caps to their correct numbered location and with the directional arrow pointing towards the timing belt end of the engine.

6 Tighten the main bearing cap bolts to the specified torque.

7 Check the crankshaft endfloat. Ideally, a dial gauge should be

16.3 Inserting the crankshaft thrust washer

16.4 Lubricate the bearings prior to installing the crankshaft

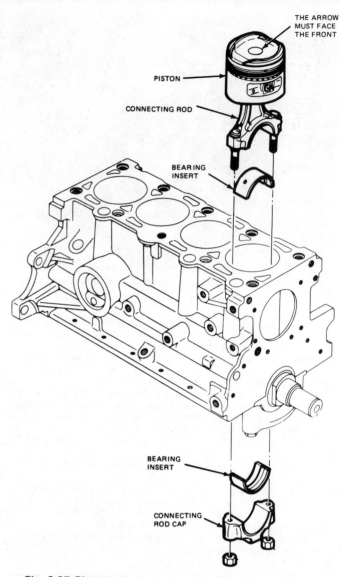

Fig. 2.27 Piston and connecting rod assembly installation
(Sec 16)

16.7 Checking the crankshaft endfloat with a feeler gauge

16.11 Wrap tape around the front end of the crankshaft to prevent
damage to the oil pump seal during installation

used, but feeler blades are an alternative if inserted between the face
of the thrust washer and the machined surface of the crankshaft
balance web, having first pried the crankshaft in one direction and then
the other (photo). Provided the thrust washers at the center bearing
have been replaced, the endfloat should be within specified tolerance.
If it is not, oversize thrust washers are available (see Specifications).
8   The pistons/connecting rods should now be installed. The arrow
on the top of the piston must face forward and the cylinder bore
number on the connecting rod face and cap must face the exhaust
manifold side.
9   Oil the cylinder bores and install the pistons/connecting rods as
described in Section 10.
10 Fit the oil pressure switch and tighten to the specified torque.
11 Before fitting the oil pump, action must be taken to prevent
damage to the pump oil seal from the step on the front end of the
crankshaft. First remove the Woodruff key and then build up the front
end of the crankshaft using adhesive tape to form a smooth inclined
surface to permit the pump seal to slide over the step without its lip
turning back or the seal spring being displaced during installation
(photo).
12 If the oil pump is new, pour some oil into it before installation in
order to prime it and rotate its driving gear a few turns (photo).
13 Align the pump gear flats with those on the crankshaft and install
the oil pump complete with new gasket. Tighten the bolts to the
specified torque.

16.12 Prime the oil pump prior to installation

16.15A Installing oil pump pick-up tube

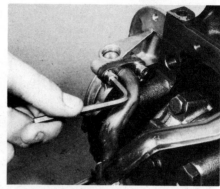
16.15B Use an Allen wrench to tighten the oil pick-up tube bolt

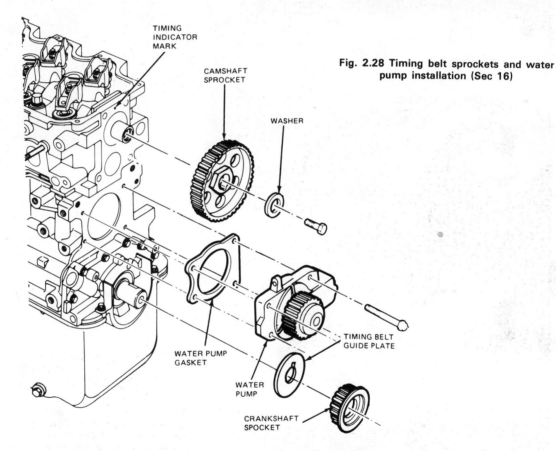

Fig. 2.28 Timing belt sprockets and water pump installation (Sec 16)

14 Remove the adhesive tape and tap the Woodruff key into its groove.

15 Bolt the oil pump pick-up tube into position (photos).

16 To the front end of the crankshaft, fit the thrust washer (belt guide) so that its concave side is towards the pump.

17 Fit the crankshaft belt sprocket. If it is tight, draw it into position using the pulley bolt and a distance piece. Make sure that the belt retaining flange on the sprocket is towards the front of the crankshaft and the nose of the shaft has been smeared with a little grease before fitting.

18 Install the coolant pump using a new gasket and tightening the bolts to the specified torque.

19 Fit the timing belt tensioner and its coil spring (where fitted). Lever the tensioner fully against spring pressure and temporarily tighten the bolts.

20 Using a new gasket, bolt on the rear oil seal retainer, which will have been fitted with a new oil seal and the seal lips greased.

21 Engage the engine adaptor plate on its locating dowels and then install the flywheel. It will only go on in one position as it has offset holes. Insert new bolts and tighten to the specified torque.

22 Install the clutch (Chapter 8).

23 With the engine resting on its side (not inverted unless you are quite sure that the pistons are not projecting from the block), fit the sump, gaskets and sealing strips as described in Section 7.

24 Fit the cylinder head as described in Section 7, using new bolts. Refit the manifolds and timing probe.

25 Install and tension the timing belt as described in Section 4.

26 Using a new gasket, fit the rocker cover, on models without a gasket, apply a $\frac{5}{32}$ in (3.8 mm) bead of silicone sealant to the valve cover flange.

27 Reconnect the crankcase ventilation hoses and EGR supply hose between the rocker cover and the crankcase.

28 Screw in a new set of spark plugs, correctly gapped, and tighten to the specified torque **Note:** *If the specified torque is exceeded, the plugs may be impossible to remove.*

29 Fit the timing belt cover.

30 Fit the crankshaft pulley and tighten the bolt to the specified torque while the flywheel ring gear is locked to prevent it turning.

31 Smear the sealing ring of a new oil filter with a little grease, and screw it into position using hand pressure only.

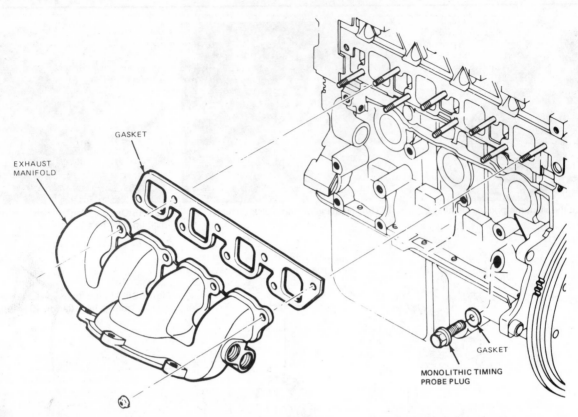

GASKET

EXHAUST
MANIFOLD

GASKET

MONOLITHIC TIMING
PROBE PLUG

Fig. 2.29 Exhaust manifold and monolithic timing probe installation (Secs 16 and 19)

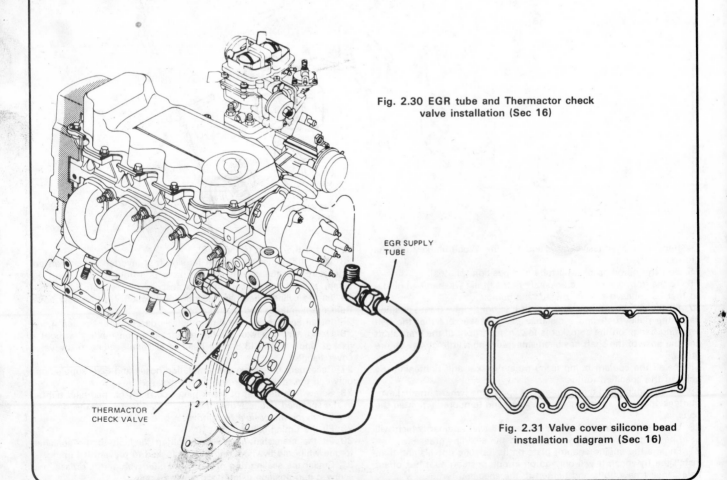

Fig. 2.30 EGR tube and Thermactor check
valve installation (Sec 16)

EGR SUPPLY
TUBE

THERMACTOR
CHECK VALVE

Fig. 2.31 Valve cover silicone bead
installation diagram (Sec 16)

32 Install the engine mounting brackets, if removed.
33 Replace the ancillaries. The alternator bracket and alternator (Chapter 10), the fuel pump (Chapter 4), the thermostat housing (Chapter 3), and the distributor (Chapter 5).
34 Fit the distributor cap and reconnect the HT leads.
35 Check the tightness of the oil drain plug and insert the dipstick.

17 Engine – installation

1   Lower the engine into the engine compartment, taking care not to not contact the fender or cowl.
2   Connect the engine to the transaxle. On manual transaxle models, engage the input shaft to the clutch disc (Chapter 8). On automatic transaxle models, engage the torque converter studs to the flywheel. On all models, engage the alignment dowels on the rear of the engine to the transaxle housing. Install the converter or clutch housing upper attaching bolts and remove the jack supporting the transaxle.
3   Place the right engine mount insulator attaching bracket in position on the engine and install the attaching bolts (Section 11). Install the through-bolt and lower bracket nut. Do not tighten the nut to specification at this time.
4   Remove the lifting device and brackets.
5   Connect the electrical connectors and automatic transaxle kick-down rod.
6   Connect the vacuum hoses, vapor canister hose and Thermactor valve vacuum line.
7   Connect the heater hoses, fuel pump lines and power brake vacuum hose.
8   Install the accelerator cable and brackets and connect the cable to the carburetor.
9   On manual transaxle models, connect the coolant bypass hose.
10 Install the radiator and connect the lower coolant hose and the automatic transaxle lower cooler line and bracket.
11 Connect the battery negative cable to the engine block.
12 Install the radiator cooling fan and shroud assembly and the upper radiator hose. Connect the fan electrical connector.
13 Raise the vehicle and tighten the engine mount through-bolt nut

to specification at this time.
14 On automatic transaxle equipped models, install the torque converter-to-flywheel attaching nuts.
15 Install the crankshaft pulley and converter or clutch housing lower bolts and cover.
16 Install the support bracket and starter motor and connect the battery negative cable. Install the brace to the front of the starter motor.
17 Connect the exhaust inlet pipe and, on manual transaxle models, the roll restricter.
18 Lower the vehicle and install the timing belt cover (manual transaxle models).
19 Install the Thermactor pump, supply hose and the alternator. Install the drivebelts and adjust to specification (Chapter 3).
20 Connect the battery and install the alternator air intake (if equipped).
21 Fill the cooling system to the proper level with the specified coolant (Chapter 1).
22 Fill the crankcase with the proper amount and grade of oil (Chapter 1).
23 Install the hood (Chapter 12).
24 Start the engine and check for leaking coolant, oil or fuel.
25 Install the air cleaner assembly, intake duct and heat tube. Check that all vacuum lines are installed securely.
26 Check and adjust if necessary, the curb idle speed (Chapters 4 and 5).

18 Intake manifold – removal and installation

1   Disconnect the battery negative cable.
2   Drain the cooling system partially and disconnect the heater hoses.
3   Remove the air cleaner assembly and disconnect and label any vacuum hoses which would interfere with removal.
4   Disconnect the carburetor bowl vent, choke cap and idle fuel solenoid wires.
5   Remove the EGR supply tube (Chapter 6).

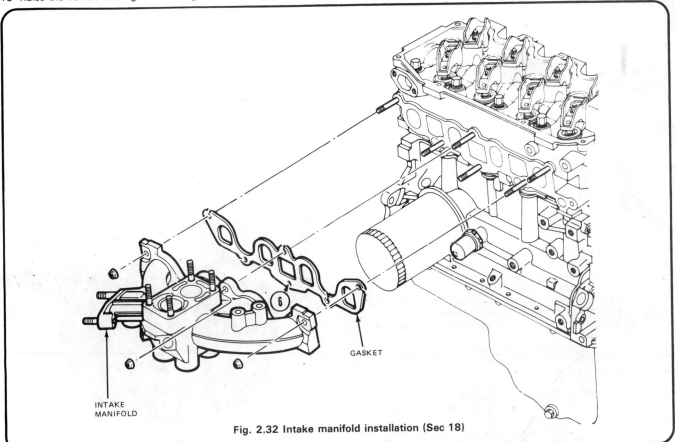

INTAKE MANIFOLD

GASKET

Fig. 2.32 Intake manifold installation (Sec 18)

6   Raise the vehicle and support it securely.
7   Remove and label the ported vacuum switch connectors.
8   Remove the bottom three intake manifold nuts.
9   Lower the vehicle and disconnect the fuel line from the filter and the return line from the carburetor.
10 Disconnect the accelerator cable, speed control cable (if equipped) and throttle valve linkage (automatic transaxle). Remove the cable bracket bolts.
11 Remove the fuel pump (Chapter 4).
12 Remove the remaining attaching nuts and the intake manifold. Be careful not to damage the intake manifold gasket surfaces.
13 With the gasket surfaces of the manifold and cylinder head free of old gasket material, install gasket, place the manifold in position and install the retaining nuts, tightening to specification.
14 Install the fuel pump.
15 Install the Thermactor pump, bracket, hoses and drivebelt.
16 Connect any throttle cables and brackets which were removed.
17 Connect the fuel lines.
18 Raise the vehicle and support it securely.
19 Connect the ported vacuum switch and the heater hoses.
20 Connect the wires to the choke cap, bowl vent and idle fuel solenoid.
21 Reconnect any vacuum hoses which were removed and install the

20 Oil pump – removal and installation

1   Remove the timing belt cover, timing chain and pulleys (Section 4).
2   Remove the water pump (Section 3) and oil pan (Section 9).
3   Remove the oil pump and support brace attaching bolts and remove the oil pump (Fig. 2.33).
4   Installation is the reverse of removal and a new crankshaft front oil seal must be installed (Section 8).

21 Hydraulic valve lifter clearance – checking

1   The valve stem-to-rocker arm clearance must be within specification with the valve lifter completely collapsed.
2   To check the clearance, crank the engine with the ignition off until the number one piston is at Top Dead Center (TDC) on the compression stroke. With the spark plug removed and your finger over the hole, the compression can be felt.
3   Mark the crankshaft pulley with chalk or white paint at TDC (position 1 in Fig. 2.34) and 180 degrees opposite (position 2 in the Figure).

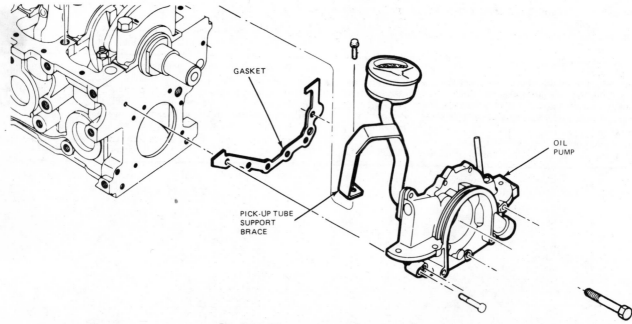

Fig. 2.33 Oil pump installation (Sec 20)

air cleaner assembly.
22 Fill the cooling system with the specified coolant.
23 Connect the battery negative cable.

19 Exhaust manifold – removal and installation

1   Disconnect the battery negative cable.
2   Remove the air cleaner assembly and alternator air inlet tubes.
3   Remove the hot air tube and shroud assembly.
4   Disconnect the exhaust gas oxygen sensor and EGR supply tube at the exhaust manifold.
5   Unbolt the exhaust pipe from the manifold.
6   Remove the attaching nuts and remove the manifold. It may be necessary to rock the manifold up and down to break it loose from the cylinder head. Do not attempt to use a screwdriver or pry bar to pry on the manifold as this could damage the gasket surfaces (Fig. 2.29).
7   To install, place the manifold and gasket in position, install the attaching nuts and tighten to specification.
8   Reinstall the removed components and connect the battery negative cable.

Fig. 2.34 Marking the crankshaft pulley (Sec 21)

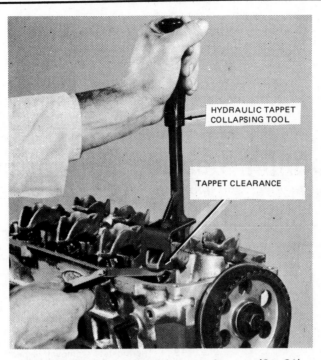

Fig. 2.35 Checking collapsed tappet clearance (Sec 21)

4   The hydraulic lifter should be slowly bled down until it is completely collapsed as described in Steps 5, 6 and 7. The following should be checked against specifications for wear:

   a)   Fulcrum
   b)   Hydraulic lifter
   c)   Cam lobe

5   With the crankshaft pulley in position 1 (TDC), check the following valves:
   No. 1 intake   No. 1 exhaust
   No. 2 intake

6   Rotate the crankshaft pulley to position 2 and check the following valves:
   No. 3 intake   No. 3 exhaust

7   Rotate the pulley 180 degrees and back to position 1 and check the following valves:
   No. 4 intake   No. 4 exhaust
   No. 2 exhaust

8   If any components are out of specification, they must be replaced to bring the valve gear back into proper relationship.

Chapter 3 Cooling, heating and air conditioning

Refer to Chapter 13 for specifications and information related to 1983 thru 1985 models

Contents

Specifications

System type	Pressurized, assisted by a belt-driven water pump and electric fan
Thermostat type	Wax pellet
Radiator	Corrugated fin, copper/brass or aluminum construction with removable plastic tanks, crossflow type
Radiator pressure text	16 to 18 psi
Radiator cap operating pressure	16 psi
Electric fan operating temperatures	Fan cuts in at 221°F (105°C) and runs until temperature drops to 201°F (87°C)
Water pump type	Belt-driven impeller

Cooling system capacities*

	US qts
1.3L engine	7.4
1.6L engine	8.0

Approximate, consult owners manual for actual capacity

Coolant type	50/50 mix of non-phosphate ethylene glycol base anti-freeze

Drivebelt tension (measured with Ford tension gauge)

$\frac{1}{4}$-in V-belt

New (A)	50 to 80 lbs
Used (B)	40 to 60 lbs
Allowable	30 lbs

4K V-ribbed

New (A)	90 to 120 lbs
Used (B)	90 to 110 lbs
Allowable	60 lbs

5K V-ribbed

New (A)	110 to 140 lbs
Used (B)	110 to 130 lbs
Allowable	75 lbs

(A) A new belt is one which has been used for less than one revolution of the pulley

(B) A used belt is one which has been used for ten minutes of operation

Torque specifications

	Ft-lb	Nm
Water pump	5 to 7	7 to 10
Thermostat housing	12 to 15	16 to 20
Radiator shroud-to-radiator	7 to 8	9 to 11
Fan motor-to-shroud	4 to 5	5 to 6
Radiator-to-front body panel	5 to 7	7 to 9
Water pump inlet tube-to-water pump	4 to 5	5 to 6
Water pump inlet tube-to-cylinder block	30 to 40	40 to 55
Fan-to-motor	1 to 2	3 to 4
Alternator and air pump adjusting arm bolt	24 to 40	33 to 54
Alternator pivot bolt	45 to 57	61 to 77
Air pump pivot bolt	40 to 55	55 to 75
Water pump pulley-to-hub	6 to 8	8 to 11
Alternator bracket-to-cylinder block	29 to 31	40 to 42
Air pump bracket-to-cylinder head or block	25 to 29	34 to 39
Alternator adjusting arm-to-air pump bracket	15 to 18	21 to 25
Air pump-to-bracket	32 to 37	44 to 51
Air pump pulley-to-air pump	6 to 8	8 to 11
Oil cooler nuts	9 to 11	12 to 15
Left vent duct-to-cowl nuts	6 to 9	8 to 12
Heater case-to-dash panel	3 to 7	4 to 9

1 General information

Caution: *Whenever working in the vicinity of the fan, always make sure that the ignition is turned off as the fan could activate automatically.*

The cooling system on all models consists of a crossflow-type radiator, an electrically-driven fan mounted in a radiator shroud, a thermostat and a water pump.

Coolant is circulated through the radiator tubes and is cooled by air passing through the cooling fins. The coolant is circulated by a pump mounted on the front of the engine and driven by the engine timing belt.

A thermostat allows the engine to warm up by remaining closed until the coolant in the radiator, heater, intake manifold and cylinder head is at operating temperature. The thermostat then opens, allowing

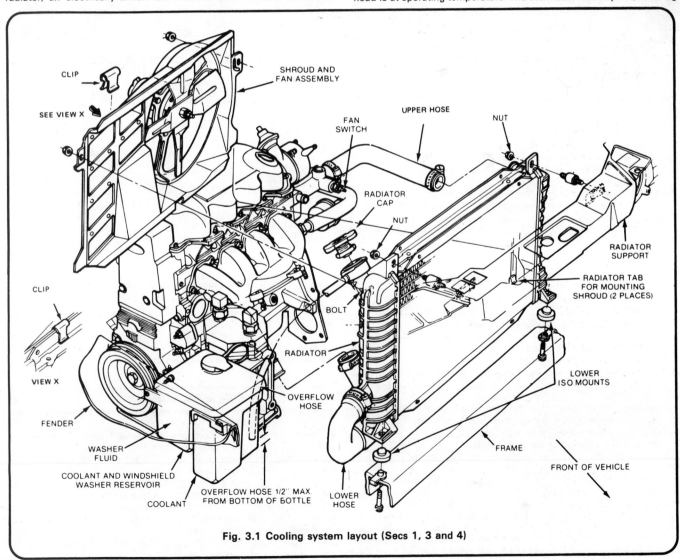

Fig. 3.1 Cooling system layout (Secs 1, 3 and 4)

full circulation of coolant throughout the cooling system.

A thermal switch in the thermostat housing activates the electric fan when a certain temperature is reached so that it will aid in drawing air through the radiator. On air conditioned models the fan operates whenever the air conditioning is turned on.

All models are equipped with a coolant expansion reservoir which also incorporates a windshield washer reservoir (see Chapter 1). As the radiator coolant expands, a pressure relief valve in the radiator cap allows the coolant to flow through the overflow hose into the reservoir. When the system cools and contracts, there is a pressure drop and the coolant is drawn back into the radiator. The reservoir level is not an indicator of radiator coolant level; the radiator itself should be checked for this.

The heating system operates by directing air through the heater core mounted in the dash, to the interior of the vehicle by a system of ducts. Temperature is controlled by mixing heated air with fresh air and by a system of flapper doors in the ducts and a heater motor.

Some models are equipped with an integral-type air conditioner/heater system which consists of an evaporator core and ducts in the dash and a compressor in the engine compartment.

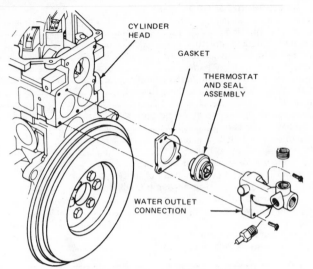

Fig. 3.2 Thermostat installation (Sec 2)

2 Thermostat – removal, inspection and installation

1   The most common symptom of thermostat failure is poor heater performance and/or failure of the vehicle to reach operating temperature. This is caused by the thermostat's staying in the open position.

2   Disconnect the battery negative cable and the fan wiring connector at the thermostat housing.

3   Place a suitable container under the radiator and attach a piece of $\frac{7}{16}$-in ID (10 mm) tubing to the petcock to aid draining. Remove the radiator cap and drain the radiator to below the level of the thermostat.

4   Remove the top radiator hose at the radiator, unbolt the thermostat housing and lift the assembly from the engine. Remove the thermostat from the housing by rotating it in a counterclockwise direction and lifting it out.

5   Hold the thermostat up to the light and if there is any leakage of light around the valve, replace the thermostat with a new one. Inspect the gasket and gasket area of the housing to make sure that the gasket is seated securely.

6   Inspect the thermostat housing and if the cup and ball is not pressed into the bleed hole, the housing must be replaced.

7   Clean the thermostat housing and make sure that the gasket mating surfaces are free of nicks.

8   Insert the thermostat into the housing, compress the gasket and rotate the thermostat clockwise to lock it in place. The thermostat locking tabs must be 90° from the heater hose inlet.

9   Using a new gasket, reinstall the thermostat and housing to the engine.

10 Install the radiator hose, refill the radiator to the proper level with the specified coolant and install the radiator cap.

11 Reconnect the battery negative cable and the fan wiring connector.

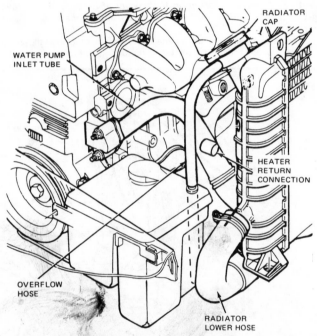

Fig. 3.3 Water inlet tube and heater return connection (Sec 3)

3 Water pump – removal and installation

1   Disconnect the battery negative cable.

2   Drain the cooling system (Chapter 1).

3   Remove the engine accessory drivebelts (Section 7).

4   Remove the engine front timing belt cover and set the number one cylinder at TDC.

5   Referring to Chapter 1 as necessary, loosen the timing belt tensioner bolts and fasten the tensioner out of the way to the left. Remove the timing belt and camshaft sprocket.

6   Remove the timing belt cover rear stud.

7   Disconnect the heater hose at the water pump and the inlet tube, referring to Figs. 3.3 and 3.4.

8   Remove the water pump bolts and water pump assembly.

9   Inspect the gasket mating surfaces of the water pump and cylinder block and make sure that they are clean and free from nicks.

10 Coat a new gasket on both sides with water resistant sealer and place it on the water pump. Coat the water pump bolts with sealer and install the water pump, tightening the bolts to specification. Rotate the water pump to make sure that the impeller turns freely.

11 Reconnect the heater return tube and water inlet pipe and install the timing cover stud.

12 Referring to Chapter 1, reinstall the timing belt and sprockets and adjust to the proper tension.

13 Reconnect the battery negative cable.

4 Radiator – removal and installation

1   Disconnect the battery negative cable.

2   Drain the radiator as described in Chapter 1. Attaching a piece of $\frac{7}{16}$ in ID (10 mm) tubing to the petcock tube will make the job easier.

3   Remove the alternator air tube (if equipped) and carburetor air intake from the radiator support.

4   From the upper end of the fan shroud, remove the two nuts and the clip attaching it to the radiator. Disconnect the fan and remove the shroud as shown in the accompanying figure.

5   Disconnect the upper and lower radiator hoses at the engine and the overflow hose at the radiator.

6   On automatic transaxle models, disconnect the oil cooler hoses, cap the tubes and plug the hoses.

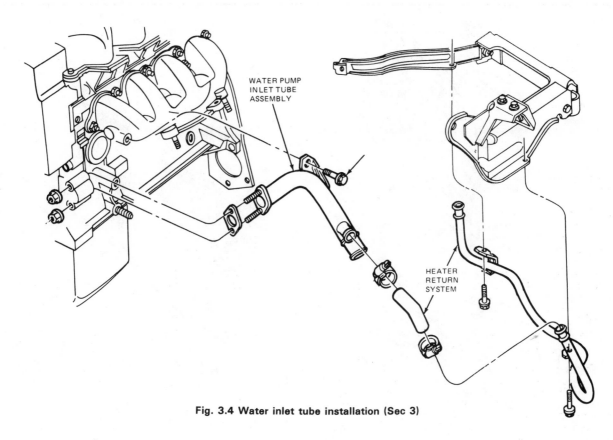

Fig. 3.4 Water inlet tube installation (Sec 3)

WATER PUMP INLET TUBE ASSEMBLY

HEATER RETURN SYSTEM

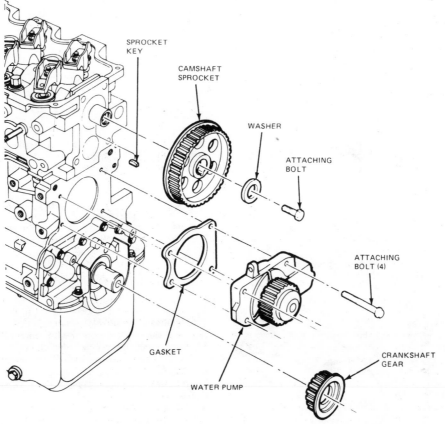

SPROCKET KEY

CAMSHAFT SPROCKET

WASHER

ATTACHING BOLT

ATTACHING BOLT (4)

GASKET

WATER PUMP

CRANKSHAFT GEAR

Fig. 3.5 Water pump installation (Sec 3)

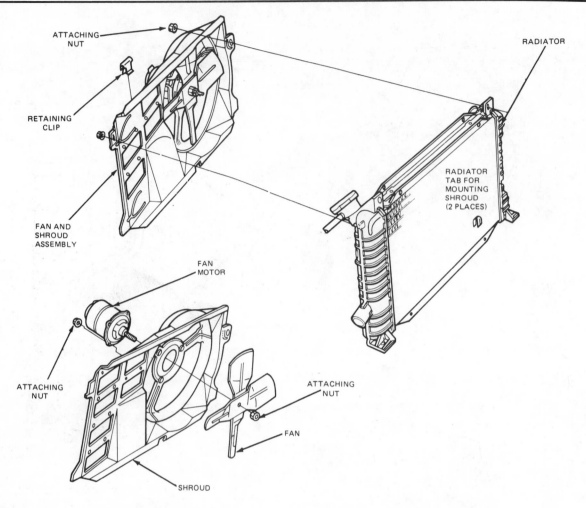

Fig. 3.6 Fan shroud and motor installation (Secs 4 and 9)

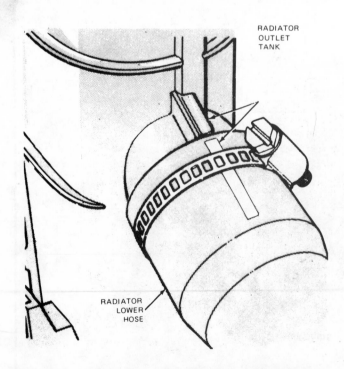

Fig. 3.7 Lower radiator hose alignment mark (Sec 4)

7   Remove the two nuts attaching the top of the radiator to the support and, tipping it rearward for clearance of the mounting stud, remove it from the vehicle. If the lower rubber mounts have come out with the radiator, return them to their proper location.

8   To install, check to make sure that the rubber mounts are in place and the lower radiator hose is installed properly with the white mark on the hose aligned with the outlet tank rib as shown in Fig. 3.7.

9   Place the lower end of the radiator in position in the rubber mounts and the mounting studs on the radiator support through the holes at the top. Install the retaining nuts and tighten to specification.

10 Connect the lower radiator hose to the engine and the oil cooler hoses (if equipped) to the radiator.

11 Place the fan shroud on the lower radiator mounting bosses and install the upper bolts and retaining nuts and the retaining clip.

12 Connect the cooling fan wires and the radiator hose overflow tube.

13 Reinstall the alternator air tubes (if equipped) and carburetor air intake tube to the radiator support.

14 Refill the cooling system with the specified coolant.

15 Connect the battery negative cable.

5   Radiator core and tanks – disassembly, inspection and reassembly

1   These vehicles differ from normal design in that the radiator tanks are of molded plastic and can be removed from and reinstalled to the radiator core.

2   Remove the radiator (Section 4).

3   Insert a screwdriver between the tank and the end of the heater tab and pry the tab away from the tank edge, working all the way

around the tank as shown in Fig. 3.8.

4   Remove the tanks and carefully set the core aside. **Note**: *Be extremely careful as the core is very fragile.*

5   Inspect each tank for cracks, damage to the mounting brackets, fan shroud bosses or gasket sealing surface. If there is any doubt about the condition of a tank, replace it with a new one. These are available from your dealer, as are the O-ring gaskets needed for reassembly. Take any part to be replaced with you to the dealer so you can obtain a duplicate replacement.

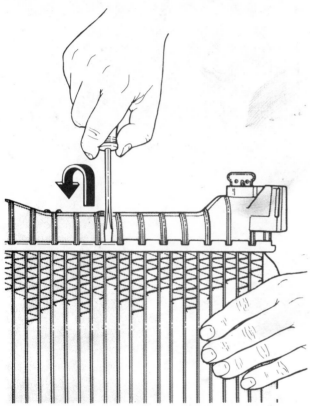

Fig. 3.8 Bending tabs away from the radiator tank (Sec 5)

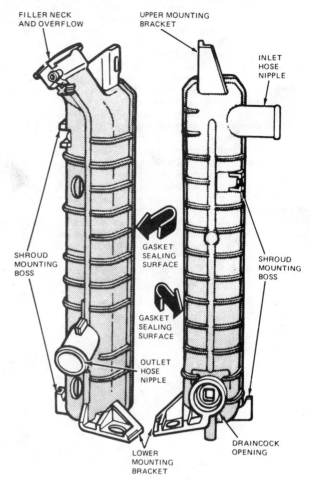

Fig. 3.9 Radiator tank components (Sec 5)

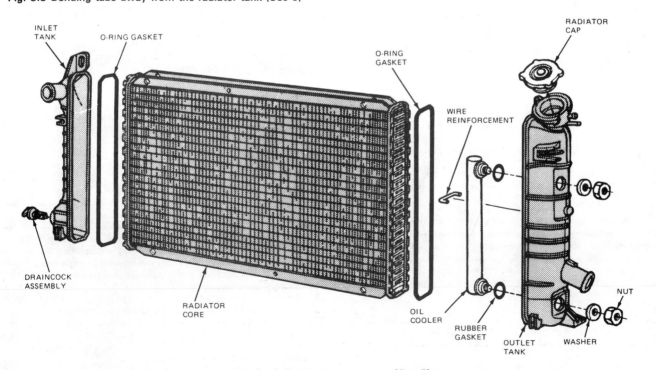

Fig. 3.10 Radiator components (Sec 5)

6   Carefully inspect the radiator core for cracks or splits in the tubes or fins, corrosion, deposits in the tubes or damage to the O-ring gasket surface. Some of these conditions can be corrected by a radiator shop for less than the cost of a new core. If the core is beyond repair it may be wise to obtain a completely new radiator assembly rather than try to reinstall the old tanks to a new core.

7   On automatic transaxle models, remove the oil cooler tube and inspect it for cracks or leaks. If it is to be replaced, transfer the inlet and outlet rubber gasket to the new tube.

8   Lubricate the new O-ring gaskets with anti-freeze solution and install it to the radiator core header tank as shown in Fig. 3.11.

9   Make sure that the outlet tank wire reinforcement is in place and install the tank carefully to the core.

10 Carefully install the radiator end tank to the core, taking care not to scratch the sealing surface of the tank.

11 Check to make sure that the tanks are properly in place and install two $\frac{3}{4}$-inch pipe clamps, taking care not to tighten them more than $\frac{1}{4}$ turn, just enough to compress the O-ring (Fig. 3.12).

12 With the pipe clamps holding the tanks in place, initially squeeze the header tubes against the tanks, using pliers (Fig. 3.13).

13 A tool for the final squeezing of the header tabs can be made using suitable locking pliers. Insert the shank of an $\frac{11}{32}$-in drill bit into the jaws of the pliers and then turn the adjustment screw and then the lock nut

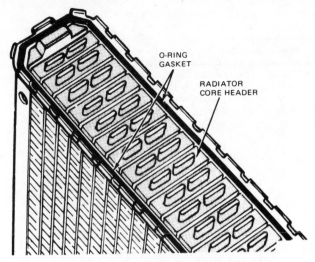

Fig. 3.11 O-ring gasket installation (Sec 5)

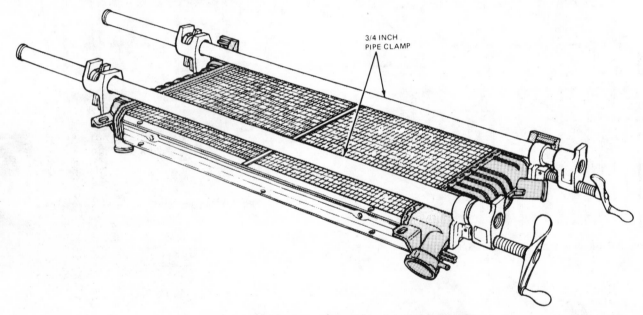

Fig. 3.12 Installing radiator tanks with pipe clamp (Sec 5)

to hold that dimension (Fig. 3.14).

14 With the locking pliers adjusted to the $\frac{11}{32}$-in dimension, squeeze all of the accessible header tabs down against the lip of the tank base (Fig. 3.15).

15 Remove the pipe clamps and squeeze down any tabs which were not accessible.

16 Install steel crimp rings over each side of the core header and initially bend them back at a 45° angle with standard pliers as shown in Fig. 3.16.

17 Following the procedure used in step 13, adjust the locking pliers to a $\frac{3}{8}$-in jaw opening, using the shank of a drill bit.

18 With the locking pliers adjusted to a $\frac{3}{8}$-in jaw opening, squeeze the steel crimp ring tabs against the header tabs (Fig. 3.17).

19 At this point it is a good idea to have the radiator pressure tested at a radiator shop as it is a simple matter to correct any minor leaks by squeezing the steel crimp rings in the area of the leak.

20 Reinstall the radiator (Section 4).

6   Radiator draincock – removal and installation

1   Remove the radiator (Section 4).

2   Remove the draincock stem by turning it counterclockwise and

withdrawing it from the radiator (Fig. 3.18).

3   Squeeze the draincock body sides together with needle nosed pliers and remove the draincock from the radiator.

4   To install, insert the draincock into the radiator inlet tank until it locks in place.

5   Install the draincock stem.

6   Install the radiator.

7   Drivebelts – inspection and replacement

1   All models are equipped with four-rib or five-rib K-section belts as well as conventional $\frac{1}{4}$-in V belts. Maintaining proper tension on these belts so that accessories they drive will operate properly is critical. The belts should be inspected periodically for wear, cuts and contamination as well as for proper tension.

2   To replace a drivebelt, loosen the adjustment bolts and push the pivoting components away from the belt until the belt can be removed. Do not pry on the pulley to remove the belt as this could cause nicks or gouges which could damage the new belt.

3   Install the new belt and hold tension on it while tightening the adjustment bolts.

4   Check the belt tension as described in Section 8.

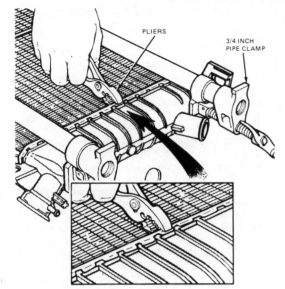

Fig. 3.13 Squeezing heater tabs against the tank with pliers
(Sec 5)

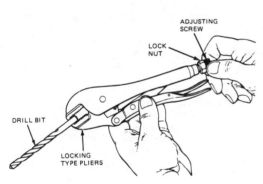

Fig. 3.14 Adjusting locking plier jaws to specified opening (Sec 5)

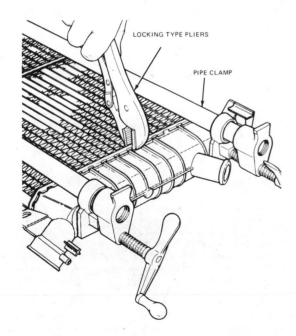

Fig. 3.15 Squeezing header tabs with the adjusted locking pliers
(Sec 5)

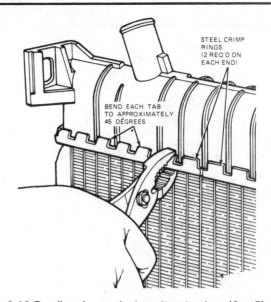

Fig. 3.16 Bending the steel crimp rings in place (Sec 5)

Fig. 3.17 Squeezing the steel crimp rings with locking pliers
(Sec 5)

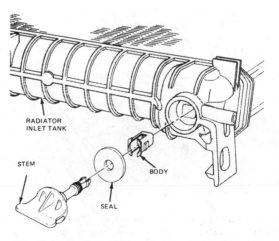

Fig. 3.18 Radiator draincock installation (Sec 6)

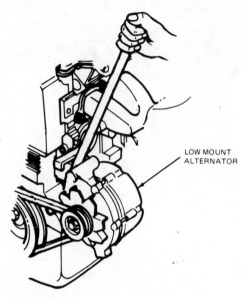

Fig. 3.19 Adjusting low mount alternator belt tension (Sec 8)

8 Drivebelts – tensioning

1　The $\frac{1}{4}$-in V belts can be checked for proper tension either with a tension gauge or by the deflection method described in Chapter 1.
2　The restricted room in the engine compartment and the construction of the K-section belt required that tension be checked only with a tension gauge.

Low-mount alternator (without power steering or air conditioning)

3　Place the tension gauge on the belt and loosen the adjustment and pivot bolts.
4　Insert a pry bar between the alternator and bracket and apply pressure to the housing of the alternator until the proper tension is reached (Fig. 3.19).
5　Hold the tension on the alternator and tighten the adjustment and pivot bolts to specification.
6　Recheck and retighten as necessary.

Low-mount Thermactor air pump (without power steering)

7　Install the tension gauge and loosen the adjustment and pivot bolts.
8　Grasp the pry area of the pump with locking pliers or open-end wrench and pull the pump away from the engine (Fig. 3.20).
9　When the tension is to specification, tighten the adjustment and pivot bolts.

Power steering pump (without air conditioning)

10　Referring to Fig. 3.21, loosen the adjustment and pivot bolts from above (Step 1).
11　From underneath the vehicle, install the tension gauge and loosen one pump adjusting bolt (Step 2 in the Figure).
12　Apply tension to the drivebelt with a $\frac{1}{2}$-inch drive socket handle in the hole in the adjusting bracket until the specified tension is reached and then tighten the adjusting bolt (Step 3 in the Figure).
13　From above the engine, tighten the adjustment and pivot bolts to specification. Recheck the tension and remove the tension gauge.

High-mount Thermactor air pump

14　Loosen the pivot bolt and adjustment bolt and pull upward on the pump (Fig. 3.22).
15　The V belt tension can be checked with either the tension gauge or the deflection method.

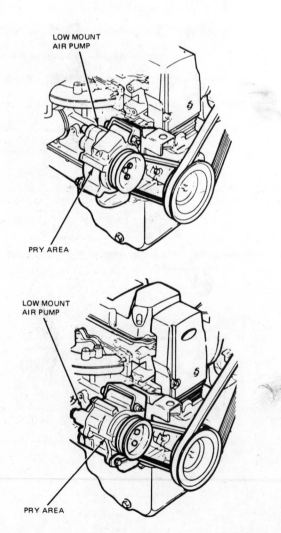

Fig. 3.20 Pry areas on the two types of Thermactor air pumps (Sec 8)

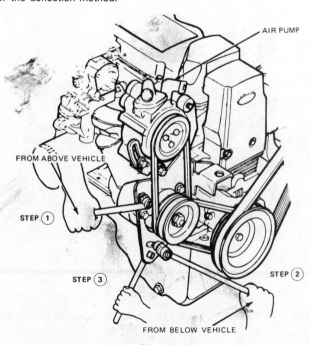

Fig. 3.21 Power steering pump belt adjustment procedure (Sec 8)

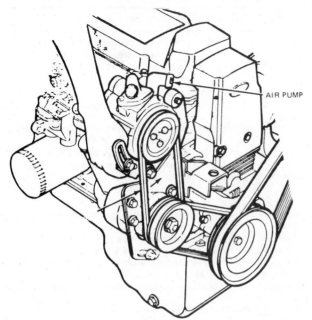

AIR PUMP

Fig. 3.22 High mount Thermactor air pump V-belt adjustment (Sec 8)

16 Tighten the adjustment and pivot bolts to specification.

High-mount alternator (without air conditioning)

17 Loosen the pivot and adjustment bolts (View A in Fig. 3.23).
18 Install the belt tension gauge (View C).
19 Remove the alternator fan shield, using a screwdriver blade (View A).
20 Install the tensioning tool (View B) underneath the alternator housing through-bolt (View C).
21 Insert a $\frac{1}{2}$-inch ratchet into the tensioning tool to use as a pry bar and move the alternator towards the engine to achieve the proper tension (View C).
22 After adjustment, tighten the adjusting bolt to specification, followed by the pivot bolt.
23 Remove the tensioning tool and reinstall the alternator fan shield clip.

9 Electric fan – removal and installation

1 Disconnect the battery negative cable.
2 At the fan motor, disconnect the wiring connector.
3 Disconnect the wire loom from the shroud by pushing down on the two lock fingers and then pulling the connector from the end of the motor.
4 Remove the two nuts which retain the motor and shroud and lift the motor and shroud assembly from the engine compartment.
5 Remove the nut retaining the fan to the motor shaft and remove the fan. The retaining nut has a left-hand thread.
6 Remove the three attaching nuts and remove the motor from the shroud.
7 To install, place the fan motor in the shroud and install the retaining nuts.
8 Install the fan to the motor shaft and install the retaining nut (turning it counterclockwise).
9 Place the fan motor and shroud assembly in the vehicle and install the retaining nuts.
10 Install the motor wire loom and connect the wiring connector to the motor, making sure the lock fingers snap in place.
11 Connect the battery negative cable.

10 Heater control – removal and installation

1 Remove the center finish panel from the instrument panel by removing the two screws and unsnapping it.
2 Remove the control assembly attaching screws and disconnect the control cables.
3 Withdraw the assembly from the instrument panel and disconnect the electrical connectors.
4 Disconnect the lever arms from the control cables and the function and temperature control end retainers.
5 If a new control assembly is being installed, transfer the necessary components from the old assembly.
6 To install, connect the cable end retainers and connect the function and temperature controls (Figs. 3.25 and 3.26).
7 Connect the wiring connectors.
8 Place the control assembly in the instrument panel and install the attaching screws.
9 Preset the control cable self-adjusting clip (Section 11).
10 Connect the function and temperature cables to the heater case.
11 Install the instrument panel center finish panel.

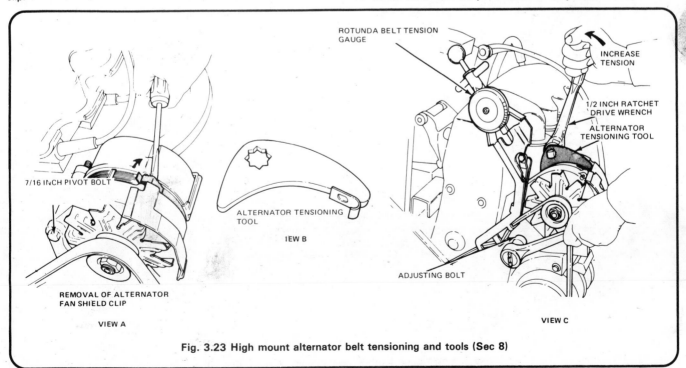

ROTUNDA BELT TENSION GAUGE

INCREASE TENSION

1/2 INCH RATCHET DRIVE WRENCH

ALTERNATOR TENSIONING TOOL

7/16 INCH PIVOT BOLT

ALTERNATOR TENSIONING TOOL

IEW B

ADJUSTING BOLT

REMOVAL OF ALTERNATOR FAN SHIELD CLIP

VIEW A

VIEW C

Fig. 3.23 High mount alternator belt tensioning and tools (Sec 8)

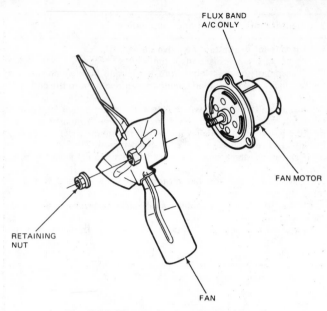

Fig. 3.24 Electric fan installation (Sec 9)

11 Heater control cable – adjustment

1   The function and temperature control cables are self-adjusting in operation but if replaced, they must be preset so that they won't kink. The adjustment can be made before or after installation.

Adjustment before installation

2   Insert a small screwdriver blade into the wire end loop at the crank arm end of the cable (Fig. 3.27).
3   Slide the self-adjusting clip down the wire with a pair of pliers until it is about one inch from the end as shown in the figure.
4   Install the appropriate cable assembly, as shown in the figure.
5   Push the control to the top of the slot to position the self-adjusting clip. Check for proper operation.

Adjustment after installation

6   Move the temperature lever to Cool or the function lever to the Off position.
7   With the crank arm held firmly in position, insert the blade of a small screwdriver in the wire lip and pull the cable through the self-adjusting clip until there is approximately one inch of space between it and the loop (Fig. 3.27).
8   Push the control lever to the top of the slot to position the self-adjusting clip.
9   Check for proper operation.

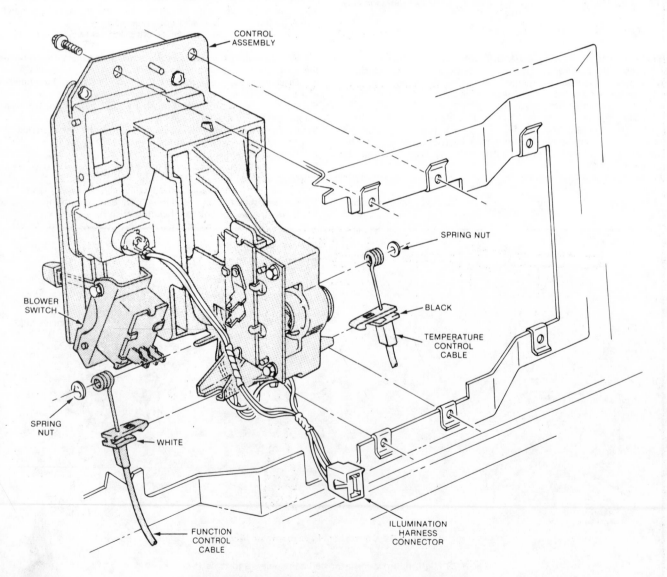

Fig. 3.25 Heater control assembly installation (Sec 10)

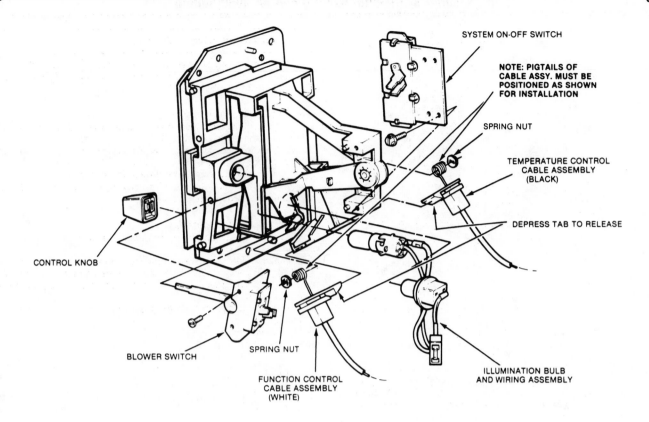

Fig. 3.26 Control assembly components (Secs 10 and 11)

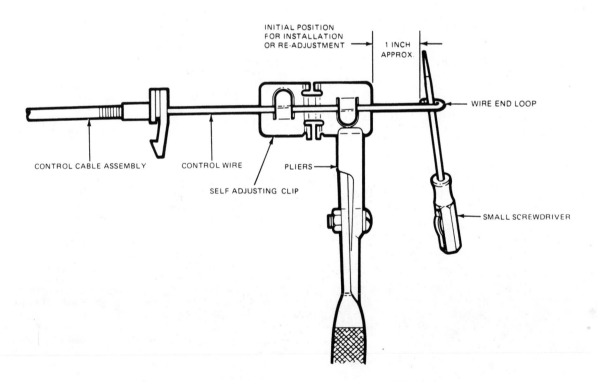

Fig. 3.27 Control cable adjustment (Sec 11)

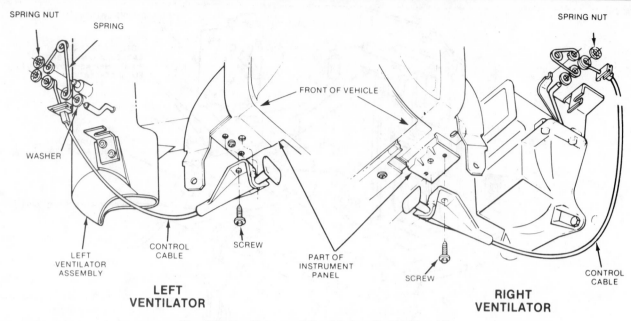

Fig. 3.28 Ventilator control cable installation (Sec 12)

12 Left ventilator cable – removal and installation

1   Remove the two retaining screws which attach the control cable assembly to the instrument panel lower edge (Fig. 3.28).
2   Remove the spring cap nut securing the cable to the door crank arm.
3   Unsnap the control cable housing end retainer from the bracket and remove the cable assembly.
4   To install, line up the cable housing and retainer grooves with the ventilator cable bracket assembly and slide the retainer into the slot

until it locks (Fig. 3.29).
5   Install the cable loop on the ventilator door arm.
6   Place the control cable knob housing in position on the lower edge of the instrument panel and align it with the tab hole. Install the retaining screws.
7   Check for proper operation.

13 Left ventilator assembly – removal and installation

1   Remove the screws attaching the ventilator assembly control to the instrument panel and the screws retaining the left ventilator assembly to the cowl panel and remove the ventilator assembly as shown in the figure.
2   Disconnect the ventilator door crank arm and remove the cable end loop.
3   Disengage the cable end retainer and slide the retainer off the bracket.
4   To install, engage the ventilator control retainer to the door crank arm.
5   Connect the cable to the left ventilator assembly bracket.
6   Place the ventilator assembly in position and install the three retaining nuts.
7   Install the control cable housing tab to the instrument panel tab slot and install the retaining screws.
8   Check for proper operation.

14 Left ventilator door – removal and installation

1   Remove the left ventilator assembly (Section 13).
2   Remove the door retaining screw (Fig. 3.31).
3   Remove the door by sliding it off the crank arm loop.
4   To install, place the door crank arm in place, slide it into the top of the ventilator housing and position the door mounting bracket pocket over the crank arm shaft loop and install the retaining screw.
5   Install the left ventilator assembly.

15 Right ventilator assembly – removal and installation

1981 models

1   Remove the glove compartment door and hinge (Chapter 12).
2   Remove the two screws retaining the control cable to the instrument panel and remove the cable assembly.
3   Pull the right register duct from the instrument panel.
4   Remove the ventilator grille from the assembly.

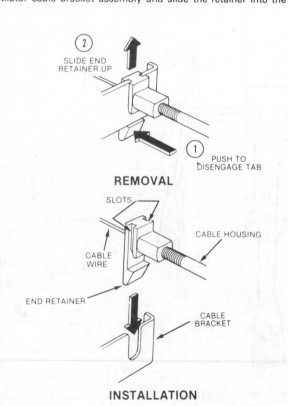

Fig. 3.29 Control cable end retainer removal and installation (Secs 12 and 13)

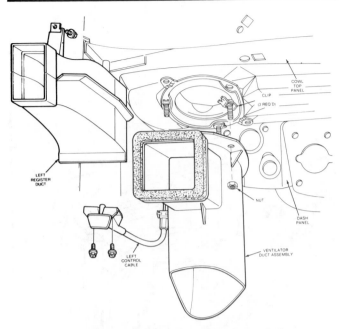

Fig. 3.30 Left ventilator and register installation
(Secs 13, 14 and 17)

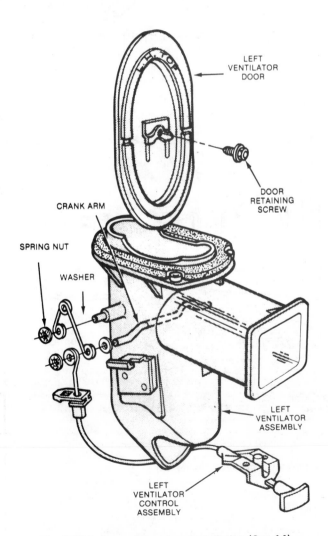

Fig. 3.31 Left ventilator door installation (Sec 14)

5   Remove the retaining screws and remove the ventilator (Fig. 3.32).
6   Disengage the ventilator door crank arm from the cable end loop and remove the control cable.
7   To install, connect the ventilator door crank to the control cable.
8   Install the control cable housing retainer to the cable bracket.
9   Install the grille and retaining clip on the ventilator.
10 Place the register duct in position between the register opening and the ventilator assembly.
11 Install the glove compartment door and hinge.
12 Install the register duct retaining screw.
13 Install the control cable to the instrument panel lower edge.
14 Check for proper operation.

1982 models

15 Remove the glove compartment door and hinge (Chapter 12).
16 Remove the six screws which retain the ventilator duct to the blower housing and remove the ventilator (Fig. 3.33).
17 Place the ventilator in position on the heater blower case and install the retaining screws.
18 Install the glove compartment door and hinge.
19 Check the ventilator for proper operation.

16 Right ventilator door – removal and installation

1   Remove the right ventilator assembly (Section 15).

1981 models

2   Disengage the ventilator grille from the mounting pins on the side of the ventilator and remove the grille.
3   Remove the retaining screw and remove the door from the crank arm shaft.
4   To install, place the door in the ventilator and install the retaining screw.

1982 models

5   Use a screwdriver to disengage the door from the shaft and remove the door.
6   To install, place the door to the ventilator on the crank arm shaft and push until it locks in place.
7   On all models, cycle the door to check for proper operation and reinstall the vent assembly if removed.

17 Register ducts and vents – removal and installation

1   To gain access on some models, it will be necessary to remove the instrument panel as described in Chapter 12.
2   Remove the register or vent duct retaining screws and remove the duct or vent (Fig. 3.34).
3   Prior to installation, make sure that the duct's retainers shown in the figure are in place.
4   Place the duct or vent in position and push it into position and then install the retaining screw.
5   Install the instrument panel.

18 Register louver – removal and installation

1   Insert the blade of a screwdriver or pocket knife under the louver retaining tab and pry the tab towards the louver until it clears the hole (Fig. 3.35).
2   Pull the end of the register assembly out so that the assembly cannot return to the hole. Repeat this process at the other end and then pull the louver from the opening.
3   To install, place the louver in the opening and press it into place. The pivots at either end of the louver assembly are different so make sure that the louver is installed in the original position.

19 Heater core – removal and installation

1   Drain the cooling system into a suitable container.
2   Disconnect the heater hoses at the heater core and plug the core

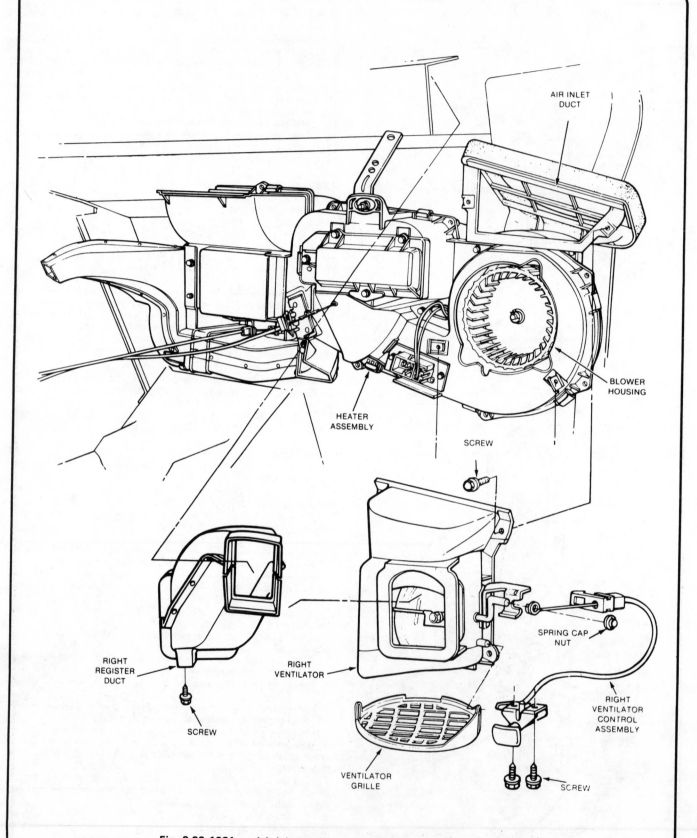

AIR INLET
DUCT

BLOWER
HOUSING

HEATER
ASSEMBLY

SCREW

RIGHT
REGISTER
DUCT

RIGHT
VENTILATOR

SPRING CAP
NUT

RIGHT
VENTILATOR
CONTROL
ASSEMBLY

SCREW

VENTILATOR
GRILLE

SCREW

Fig. 3.32 1981 model right ventilator and register duct (Secs 15 and 16)

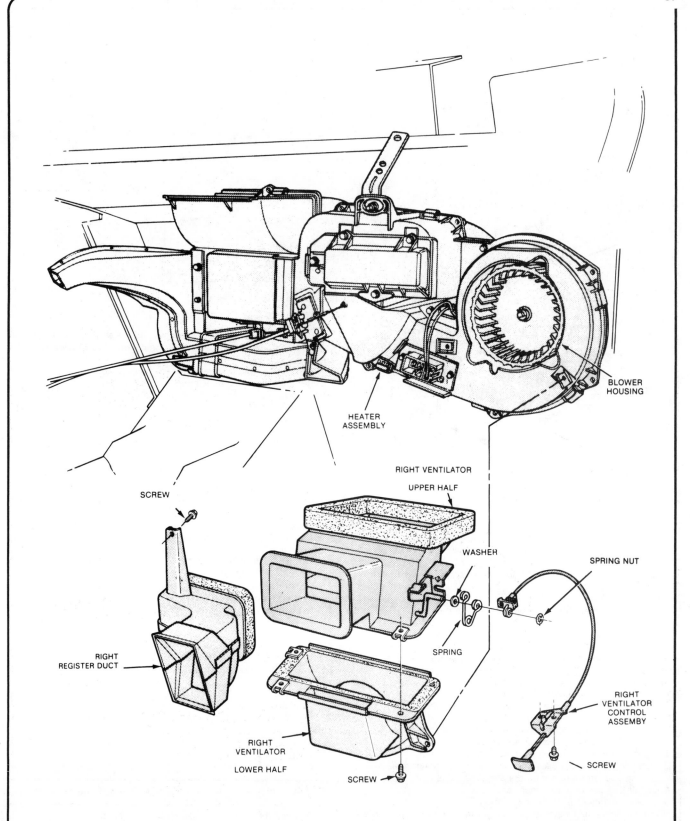

Fig. 3.33 Right register and ventilator duct installation (1982 models) (Secs 14, 15 and 16)

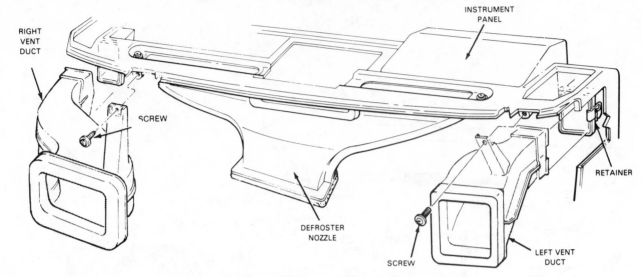

Fig. 3.34 Register duct and ventilator installation (Sec 17)

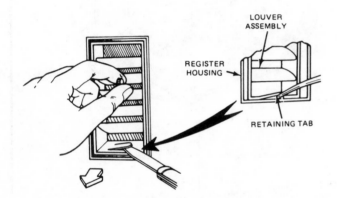

Fig. 3.35 Register louver removal (Sec 18)

tubes so that coolant cannot spill in the passenger compartment.
3   Remove the glove compartment door, liner and lower reinforcement (Chapter 12).
4   Place the temperature control in the Warm position.
5   Remove the heater core cover.
6   From inside the engine compartment, loosen the two nuts which hold the heater case assembly to the dash panel. Loosen the heater core by pushing the core tubes inward, toward the passenger compartment.
7   From inside the vehicle, withdraw the heater core through the glove compartment opening (Fig. 3.36).
8   To install, place the core to the case opening, with the core tubes at the top.
9   Install the heater core by sliding it into the heater case opening.
10 Install the heater core cover and screws.
11 Tighten the two heater core-to-dash panel nuts.
12 Connect the heater hoses and clamps to the heater core.
13 Fill the cooling system with the specified coolant.
14 Install the glove compartment assembly.
15 Check the heater for proper operation.
16 After running the vehicle at operating temperature, allow it to cool and check the coolant level to make sure that it is at the proper level.

20 Heater case – removal and installation

1   Disconnect the battery negative cable.
2   Drain the cooling system.
3   Disconnect the heater hoses at the heater core tubes and plug the tubes.

4   Remove the steering column cover, lower shroud and disconnect the column bracket so that the steering column can be lowered to the seat.
5   Remove the radio covers and speakers (Chapter 10).
6   Remove the instrument panel center bracket.
7   Disconnect the ventilator control handles.
8   Disconnect the speedometer cable at the transaxle (Chapter 8).
9   Disconnect the heater blower resistor wiring harness and (if equipped) the right door courtesy light switch at the A pillar.
10 Disconnect the function and temperature control cables at the heater case (Section 10).
11 Remove the instrument panel and center brace and pull the panel toward the rear to gain access to the heater case.
12 Remove the heater case top support-to-heater case nut.
13 In the engine compartment, remove the two nuts securing the heater case to the dash (Fig. 3.37).
14 Loosen the insulation around the air inlet opening of the top of the control panel and remove the heater case by withdrawing it from the dash panel.
15 To install, place the heater core assembly in position to the dash panel and cowl top plate and install the retaining nut.
16 Install the two nuts in the engine compartment which attach the heater case to the dash.
17 Reposition the insulation around the air inlet.
18 Install the instrument panel top cowl center brace.
19 Install the instrument panel (Chapter 12).
20 Connect the temperature and function cables to the self-adjusting clip (Section 11) and heater case (Section 10).
21 Connect the door courtesy light (if equipped) and blower resistor wiring.
22 Connect the ventilator controls.
23 Install the radio speakers and covers.
24 Install the steering column and shrouds and connect the speedometer cable.
25 Connect the heater hoses to the core and refill the cooling system.
26 Connect the battery negative cable.

21 Heater blower motor and wheel – removal and installation

1   Remove the right ventilator assembly (Section 15).
2   Remove the hub clamp from the blower motor hub and withdraw the wheel assembly.
3   Remove the blower motor attaching screws inside the blower housing, withdraw the motor and disconnect the motor wires.
4   To install the motor, connect the wiring, position the motor and install the retaining screws.
5   To install the blower wheel, align the flat on the wheel hub with the flat on the motor shaft and install a new hub clamp.
6   Install the right ventilator assembly and test for proper operation.

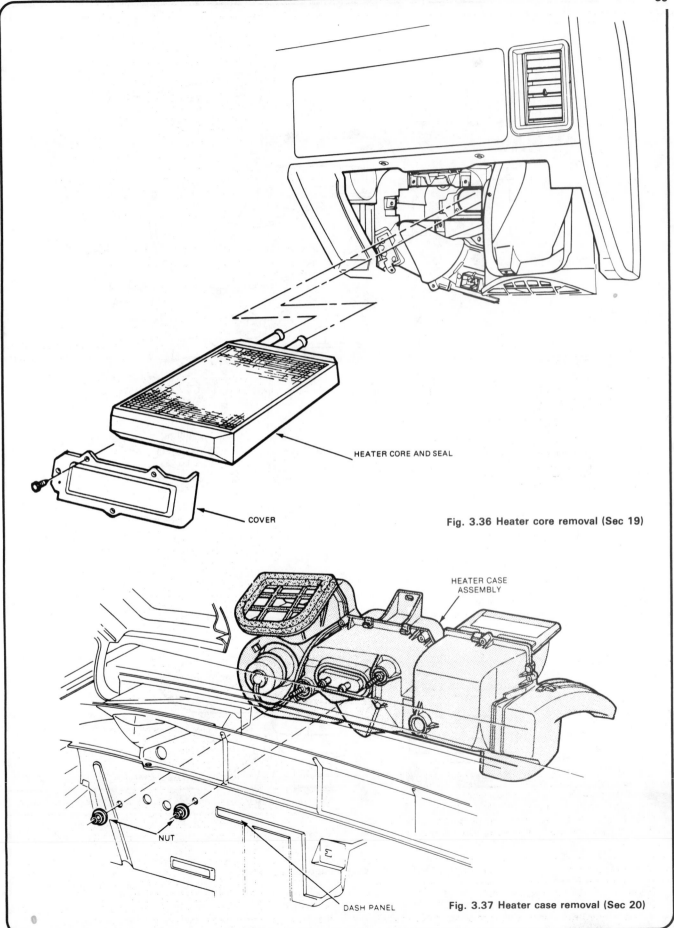

HEATER CORE AND SEAL

COVER

Fig. 3.36 Heater core removal (Sec 19)

HEATER CASE
ASSEMBLY

NUT

DASH PANEL

Fig. 3.37 Heater case removal (Sec 20)

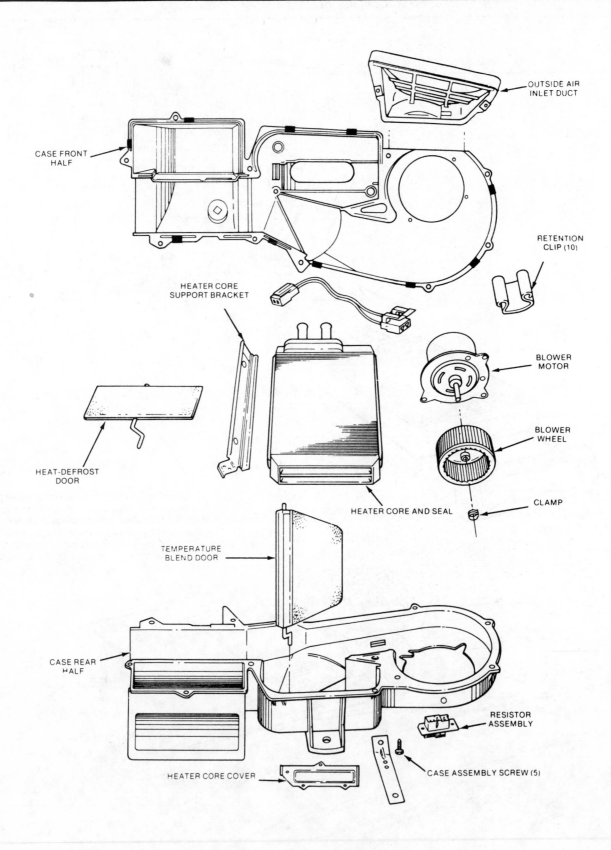

CASE FRONT HALF

OUTSIDE AIR INLET DUCT

RETENTION CLIP (10)

HEATER CORE SUPPORT BRACKET

BLOWER MOTOR

HEAT-DEFROST DOOR

BLOWER WHEEL

HEATER CORE AND SEAL

CLAMP

TEMPERATURE BLEND DOOR

CASE REAR HALF

RESISTOR ASSEMBLY

HEATER CORE COVER

CASE ASSEMBLY SCREW (5)

Fig. 3.38 Heater case components (Sec 20)

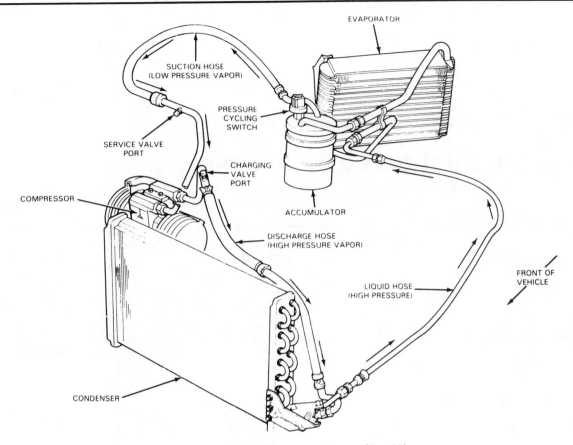

EVAPORATOR

SUCTION HOSE
(LOW PRESSURE VAPOR)

PRESSURE
CYCLING
SWITCH

SERVICE VALVE
PORT

CHARGING
VALVE
PORT

COMPRESSOR

ACCUMULATOR

DISCHARGE HOSE
(HIGH PRESSURE VAPOR)

FRONT OF
VEHICLE

LIQUID HOSE
(HIGH PRESSURE)

CONDENSER

Fig. 3.39 Air conditioner components (Sec 22)

22 Air conditioning system – general information

The air conditioning system consists of a condenser mounted in front of the radiator, an evaporator, a suction accumulator, an evaporator mounted in the dash panel, a compressor to transfer the refrigerant through the system and associated hoses.

The temperature in the passenger compartment is lowered by transferring the heat to the refrigerant in the evaporator, passing the refrigerant through a suction accumulator and then to the condenser.

Maintenance is confined to keeping the system properly charged with refrigerant, the compressor drivebelt tensioned properly and making sure the condenser is free of leaves or accumulations of dirt or debris. The system is under considerable pressure and any work should be left to a properly equipped shop.

Chapter 4 Fuel and exhaust systems

Refer to Chapter 13 for specifications and information related to 1983 thru 1985 models

Contents

Specifications

General

Fuel tank capacity (approximate)
1.3L manual transaxle	9.0 US gallons
1.6L manual transaxle	10.0 US gallons
All automatic transaxle	11.3 US gallons

Fuel pump static pressure*
1981	4.0 to 6.0 psi
1982	4.5 to 6.5 psi

*With engine at curb idle, transaxle in neutral, new fuel filter and the fuel tank return line pinched off.

Carburetor
Type	Motorcraft model 740 2-V
Curb idle speed	See Emissions decal
Fast idle speed	See Emissions decal
Dry float clearance	0.246 in ± 0.010 in (6.25 mm ± .25 mm)
Wide open throttle (WOT) cutout switch adjustment	
Pin-to-arm overlap	0.120 in (3 mm)
Lever-to-switch gap	0.120 in (3 mm)

Torque specifications
	Ft-lb	Nm
Carburetor-to-intake manifold	12 to 15	16 to 20
Carburetor air horn-to-main body	14 (In-lb)	1.6
Choke diaphragm cover screws	5 (In-lb)	.56
Choke housing screws	1.5	2.0
Carburetor diaphragm cover screws	10.6 (In-lb)	1.2
Choke cap retainer screws	5.3 (In-lb)	.6
Solenoids-to-carburetor	3.0	4.0
Carburetor main jet and well assemblies	5.3 (In-lb)	.6
Power valve cover screws	7.1 (In-lb)	.8
Fuel filter	6.6	9.04
Kicker attaching screws	1.5	2.0
Fuel inlet seat	15 (In-lb)	1.7
Carburetor stud-to-air cleaner	5 to 7	7 to 10
Air cleaner duct shroud-to-intake manifold	10 to 15	14 to 20
Air cleaner wing nut	2 to 3	3 to 4
Throttle cable mounting bracket	10 to 15	14 to 20
Throttle pedal pivot bolt	6 to 9	8 to 12
Exhaust pipe U-bolt	40 to 55	54 to 74
Catalytic converter inlet bolt	20 to 29	29 to 40

1 General information

The fuel system consists of a rear-mounted fuel tank, a fuel pump operated by the engine camshaft which draws the fuel to the carburetor and associated lines and filters.

The exhaust system is composed of pipes, a muffler, a catalytic converter and heat shields for carrying the exhaust gases from the engine to the rear of the vehicle.

The catalytic converter requires the use of unleaded fuel.

2 U.S. Federal regulations – emission controls

The fuel system is designed so that the car will comply with all US Federal regulations covering emission hydrocarbons and carbon monoxide. To achieve this, the ignition system must be accurately set using the proper equipment. Proper ignition timing is a must before attempting any other emission-related adjustments. The information in this Chapter is given to assist the reader to clean and/or replace certain components before taking the vehicle to the local Ford dealer or repair shop for final adjustments. Failure to do this could mean that the car will not comply with the regulations.

3 Thermostatic air cleaner and duct system – general information

The air cleaner contains a replaceable filter element and is retained to the carburetor by a wing nut.

An additional feature of the air cleaner is the control system for the intake air which ensures that fuel atomization within the carburetor takes place using air that is the proper temperature. This is achieved by a duct system which draws in either fresh air or pre-heated air from a heat shroud around the engine exhaust manifold.

When the engine is cold, heated air is directed from the exhaust manifold into the air cleaner and, as the engine warms up, cold air is progressively mixed with this warm air to maintain the proper air temperature for proper fuel atomization. At high ambient temperature the hot air intake is closed off completely.

The mixing of the air is regulated by a vacuum-operated motor in the air cleaner duct, which is controlled by a bi-metal temperature sensor and a cold weater modulator valve.

The air filter element and crankcase emission filter are located in the air cleaner assembly and must be replaced periodically according to the maintenance schedule, as described in Chapter 1.

4 Air cleaner duct and valve – testing

1   Check the air cleaner assembly for proper installation and make sure that the vacuum hoses are correctly installed.
2   Push on the duct door to make sure that it isn't sticking or binding.
3   Start the engine and allow it to reach operating temperature. The duct door should open. If it doesn't and it isn't stuck or binding, replace it.
4   With the engine off, disconnect the vacuum motor.
5   Referring to the beginning of this manual, install a vacuum pump to the motor connection tube and apply and hold 16 inches of vacuum.
6   The duct door should stay closed for 60 seconds. If it doesn't, replace the duct and valve assembly.
7   Reconnect any hoses which were removed.

5 Fuel pump – general information

The fuel pump is bolted to the cylinder head and actuated by a lobe on the camshaft via a pushrod. It is a sealed unit which must be replaced if a fault develops.

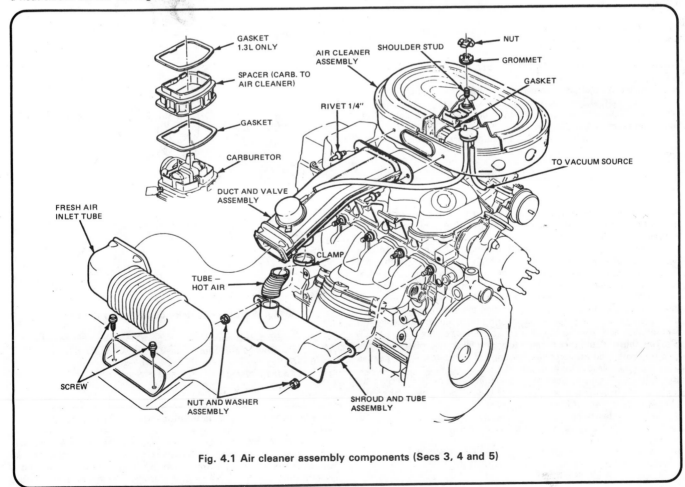

Fig. 4.1 Air cleaner assembly components (Secs 3, 4 and 5)

6 Fuel pump – testing

1   The simplest test for determining if a fuel pump is at fault is to disconnect the outlet hose and route it into a suitable transparent container.
2   Disconnect the ignition coil wire so the engine can be cranked with the starter motor without starting.
3   Turn the engine over with the starter and observe the fuel pump outlet hose. If it is not exhibiting definite spurts of fuel, the pump should be replaced with a new one.

7 Fuel pump – removal and installation

1   Using two suitable wrenches, loosen the fuel line nut at the fuel pump outlet.
2   Loosen both fuel pump mounting nuts two turns.
3   Turn the engine over by intermittently engaging the starter to

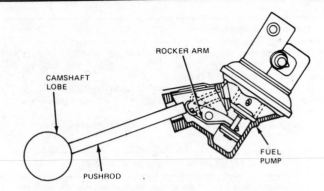

Fig. 4.2 Fuel pump actuation (Sec 5)

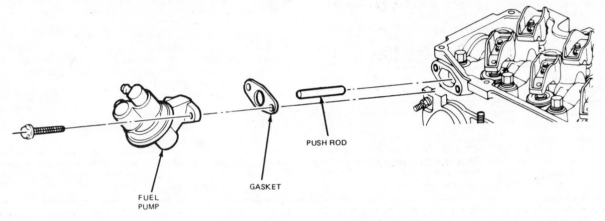

Fig. 4.3 Fuel pump installation (Secs 5 and 7)

determine the camshaft lobe's low point so that the pushrod will not be against the fuel pump lever.
4   Remove the fuel lines from the fuel pump inlet and outlet.
5   Unbolt the fuel pump and remove it, leaving the pushrod in place.
6   Using a new gasket, install the fuel pump and tighten the mounting bolts to specification.
7   Connect the fuel lines, run the engine for two minutes and check for leaks.

8 Electric choke – description and testing

1   The electrically-operated choke located in the carburetor has a heating element to aid in faster choke release and help reduce emissions during warmup.
2   The choke consists of a bi-metal thermostatic coil mounted to a heat conductive post. The electric heating element heats the coil which expands, opening the choke plate. Initial opening (pulldown) of the choke plate is controlled by a vacuum diaphragm and spring.
3   Check all of the carburetor nuts for tightness. Make sure that linkages work freely and hose connections are secure.
4   With the air cleaner lid removed, bring the engine up to operating temperature and observe that the choke plate operates.
5   The choke plates should open fully. If they do not, disconnect the electric choke lead at the choke cap and connect a test light in series with the choke lead wire and ground.
6   If the light glows, the choke cap unit is faulty and should be replaced with a new one. If the light does not glow, either the alternator or the stator lead are defective.
7   With any faults corrected and the choke plates open, hold the throttle at $\frac{1}{4}$ to $\frac{1}{2}$ open and close the throttle plates and then release them.
8   The plates should rotate to the fully open position. If they do not, check and clean the choke system to correct the fault.
9   Replace the air cleaner lid.

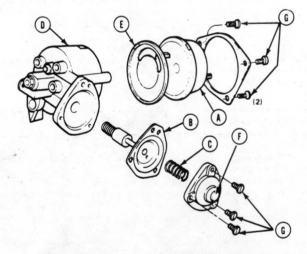

Fig. 4.4 Electric choke components (Sec 8)

A Heating element
B Pulldown diaphragm
C Spring
D Choke housing
E Choke housing shield
F Choke housing adjusting plug seal
G Screws

9 Motorcraft 740 2-V carburetor – general information

The Motorcraft 740 carburetor incorporates five metering systems: idle, main metering, acceleration, power enrichment and choke to achieve smooth performance at all driving speeds. The choke system (Section 8) is used for cold starting. The idle system provides

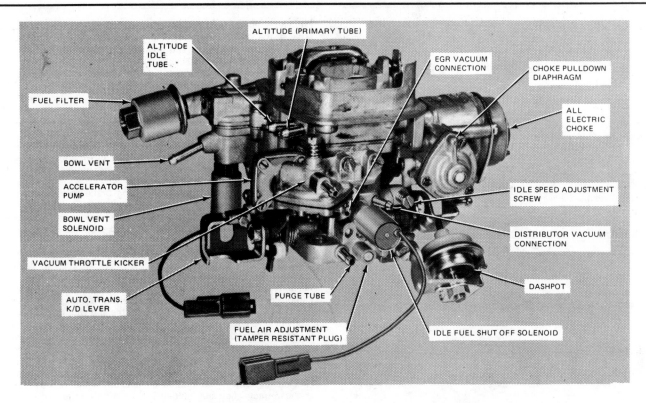

Fig. 4.5 Motorcraft 740 2-V carburetor components (Secs 9 and 12)

the proper air/fuel mixture for idling and low speed driving, while the main metering system takes over during normal driving.

The mechanically-operated accelerating system uses a diaphragm-type pump to provide fuel for initial stages of acceleration. A manifold vacuum operated power valve in the power enrichment system enhances performance during moderate to heavy acceleration.

The vacuum ports for the distributor and EGR system are located in the primary venturi area of the carburetor.

A variety of throttle positioners and vacuum kickers are used to modify throttle opening and closing thus regulating engine speed for purposes of lowering emissions or operating accessories.

10 Fast and curb idle speed – setting

1 Connect a tachometer.
2 With the engine in Neutral or Park, run the engine until it is up to operating temperature.
3 Locate the air supply valve and trace the vacuum line. If the line connects to the carburetor, disconnect it at the air supply valve and

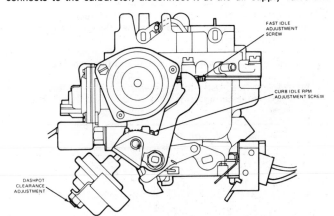

Fig. 4.6 Curb and fast idle speed adjustment (Sec 10)

plug it. Install a bypass hose between the intake manifold and the connection on the control valve.
4 Place the fast idle cam on the second adjustment stop (Fig. 4.6).

Fast idle
5 Prior to checking the fast idle, disconnect the EGR valve vacuum hose and plug it.
6 Start the engine and run it until the cooling fan cuts in. Check the fast idle speed against the specification on the emissions decal. To adjust, loosen the lock nut on the fast idle screw, adjust as necessary and re-tighten. The cooling fan must be on throughout this procedure.
7 Unplug the vacuum hose and reconnect it to the EGR valve.

Curb idle
8 To check the curb idle, perform Steps 1 through 5, then depress the throttle slightly so that the fast idle cam can rotate. With the transmission in the specified gear (emissions decal), check the curb idle rpm against the specification on the decal and adjust the curb idle screw as necessary.
9 Check and adjust the dashpot (if equipped) clearance.
10 If equipped with automatic transaxle, the throttle linkage (Chapter 7) must be adjusted if the curb idle is increased more than 100 rpm.
11 Turn off the engine and remove the bypass hose from the air valve and reinstall all vacuum hoses which might have been removed.

11 Air conditioner or throttle kicker speed – adjustment

1 Connect a tachometer.
2 Start the engine and bring it up to operating temperature.
3 If there is a vacuum hose between the carburetor and air supply valve, disconnect the hose and plug it. Install a hose between the intake manifold and the air supply valve bypass connection.
4 If equipped with air conditioning, set the selector at maximum cooling with the blower switch on high and disconnect the compressor clutch wire. If equipped with kicker only, disconnect and plug the vacuum hose and install a hose between the intake manifold and kicker.
5 Run the engine until the cooling fan cuts in, place the transaxle in

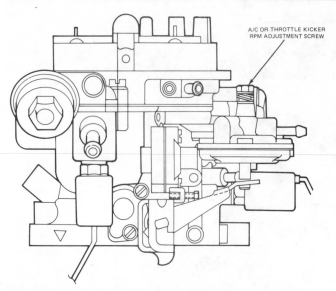

Fig. 4.7 Air conditioner or vacuum throttle kicker speed setting (Sec 11)

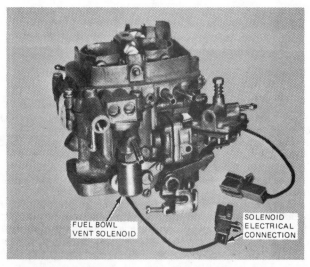

Fig. 4.8 Fuel bowl vent, solenoid and connector (Sec 12)

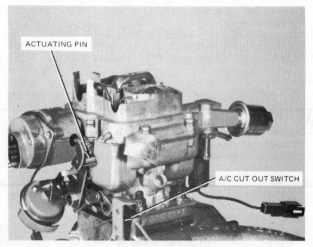

Fig. 4.9 Wide open throttle (WOT) cut-out switch location (Sec 13)

the gear specified on the emissions decal and check the engine speed against the specifications on the decal. The fan must be running throughout the procedure and adjustments are made by turning the adjustment screw (Fig. 4.7).

6   Turn off the engine, remove the tachometer and any bypass hoses from the kicker and air supply valve and reconnect any hoses which were removed.

12 Carburetor fuel bowl vent – testing

1   Fuel vapors are passed from the fuel bowl vent to the carbon canister during normal operation and strong gasoline odors are an indication of a fault in the vent system.
2   Block the wheels, apply the parking brake and remove the air cleaner assembly.
3   Disconnect the bowl vent-to-canister hose at the canister and inspect the vent solenoid for damage and proper electrical connections.
4   Attach a rubber squeeze-type bulb to the canister end of the vent hose.
5   With the ignition off and the choke plates open, squeeze the bulb which will force air into the fuel bowl vent. If fuel is forced through the carburetor metering system, the bowl vent is working properly. If it is not, start the engine, run it for two minutes and shut it off. Repeat the test.
6   If fuel is still not evident in the metering system, remove the carburetor air horn (Section 16) and check the condition of the bowl vent plunger seal and the valve seats. If there are any burrs on the valves or seats, correct the condition. The bowl vent seals can be checked by turning the ignition on and off. If the vent plunger and spring retract when the ignition is turned on and extend when it is turned off, the vent seals are faulty.
7   Squeeze the bulb and force air into the vent system with the ignition in the 'on' position. If the pressure builds up (resistance is felt when the bulb is squeezed rapidly), the vent system is working properly.
8   If the pressure does not build up, remove the bulb, reinstall the air cleaner and all hoses, start the engine and run it for 15 seconds at approximately 2500 rpm and shut it off.
9   Disconnect the solenoid electrical lead and connect it to one lead of a test light. Connect the other test light lead to ground.
10 Turn the ignition switch on. If the test lamp does not glow, either the battery is dead or the solenoid electrical lead has an open circuit. Correct any fault and repeat the test in Step 5.
11 If the test lamp glows, the solenoid electrical system is good. Repeat Step 6; if the bowl vent plunger and spring do not extend or retract with the ignition in either the 'on' or 'off' positions, replace the solenoid, plunger, seal and plunger spring.
12 Reinstall the air horn, reinstall the squeeze bulb and perform the test in step five to verify that the system is working properly.
13 After testing, make sure that the air cleaner assembly and all hoses are installed properly.

13 Wide open throttle (WOT) cut-out switch – adjustment

1   The air conditioner cut-out switch must have proper overlap of the actuating pin and switch activating arm when the throttle linkage is in the wide open position.
2   The measurements should be taken of both the pin and arm overlap and the gap between the switch and fast idle lever to make sure that they are to specification (Fig. 4.10).
3   Adjustments are made to the switch position by bending the switch support bracket outward.

14 Dry fuel float – adjustment

1   Remove the air horn assembly (Section 16).
2   Place the air horn upside down at a 45° angle with the float tank lightly resting on the inlet needle (Fig. 4.11).
3   Measure the clearance at the extreme end of the float with a suitable gauge such as the proper size drill bit.
4   Remove the float and adjust to specification by bending the float adjustment tang (Fig. 4.12).

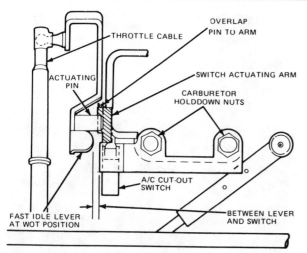

Fig. 4.10 Wide open throttle cut-out switch adjustment (Sec 13)

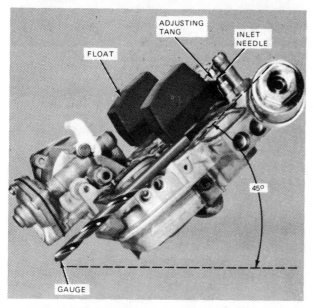

Fig. 4.11 Checking dry float adjustment (Sec 14)

Fig. 4.12 Float lever adjustment tang (Sec 14)

15 Carburetor – removal and installation

1   Remove the air cleaner assembly and disconnect the throttle cable and (if equipped) the speed control cable.
2   Disconnect the tag all vacuum hoses, fuel lines and vacuum throttle kickers.
3   Disconnect the idle bowl vent solenoid wires and choke cap wire.
4   On automatic transaxle equipped vehicles, remove the throttle valve (TV) linkage.
5   Remove the carburetor mounting nuts with a suitable cranked wrench.
6   Clean all gasket surfaces and inspect for nicks and gouges.
7   Install the gasket, place the carburetor on the spacer, install the mounting nuts and alternately to specification.
8   Install the TV linkage (automatic transaxle models) and adjust (Chapter 7).
9   Connect the choke cap and solenoid wires.
10   Connect all fuel and vacuum lines.
11   Install the throttle cable and (if equipped) speed control cable.
12   Start the engine and check all vacuum lines and linkages for leaks and proper operation.
13   Install the air cleaner assembly.
14   Check and adjust if necessary, the curb and fast idle speed (Section 10).

16 Carburetor – disassembly

Note: *Refer to Figure 4.22 for component numbering.*

Air horn
1   Remove the carburetor (Section 15).
2   Remove the fuel filter (20).
3   Remove the six air horn screws (14) and washer (Fig. 4.13).
4   Lift the air horn assembly and gasket (18) from the carburetor and turn it over (Fig. 4.14).
5   Remove the float hinge pin (16), float (17), inlet needle, seat and gasket assembly (19).
6   Remove the air horn gasket (18).
7   Remove the fuel return line check valve and fitting (21).

Choke
8   Remove the two choke retaining rivets (9) by the following procedure. If the rivet mandrel is below the rivet head thickness, drive it downward with a suitable punch and drill out the remainder of the head with a $\frac{1}{8}$-in drill. Remove any remaining rivet debris with a $\frac{1}{8}$-in punch to preserve the rivet hole dimension. Remove the retaining screw.
9   Remove the retaining ring (11), choke cover assembly (12) and dirt shield (13).

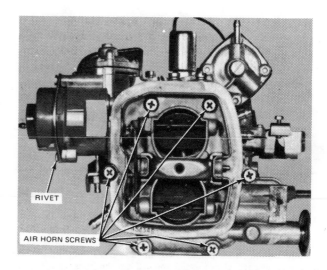

Fig. 4.13 Air horn installation (Sec 16)

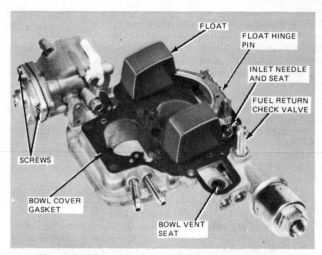

Fig. 4.14 Air horn assembly components (Sec 16)

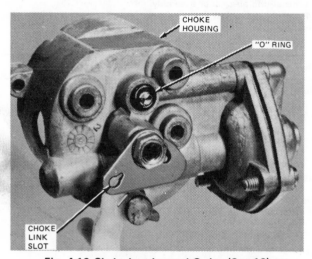

Fig. 4.16 Choke housing and O-ring (Sec 16)

Fig. 4.18 Accelerator pump retaining cover screws (Sec 16)

Fig. 4.15 Choke housing retaining screws (Sec 16)

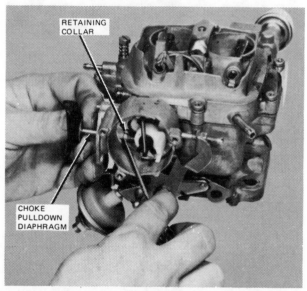

Fig. 4.17 Removing choke housing pulldown diaphragm (Sec 16)

and slide the shaft and lever outward.
15 Pull outward on the choke pulldown diaphragm assembly (30) until the shaft is against the plastic retaining collar. Press on the plastic clip and slide the assembly out (Fig. 4.17).

Accelerator pump
16 If equipped, remove the vacuum throttle kicker.
17 Remove the accelerator pin screws (47), cover (46), diaphragm (47) and return spring (Fig. 4.18).
18 Remove the accelerator pump nozzle (57), using needle nose pliers (Fig. 4.19).

Main body
Note: Refer to Figs. 4.21 and 4.22.
19 Using a suitable tool such as Ford tool T81P-95-9510-A, remove the idle fuel shut-off solenoid (7) and washer (8).
20 Remove the bowl vent solenoid assembly (39), $\frac{5}{8}$-in hex nut and washer (40).

10 Remove the choke cover retaining screw (Fig. 4.15).
11 Slide the housing away and disconnect the choke link. Remove the O-ring from the housing (Fig. 4.16).
12 Remove the choke pulldown cover (27) and spring (29).
13 Disconnect the choke assist spring from the housing (23).
14 Remove the choke bi-metal shaft nut, lock washer and choke lever

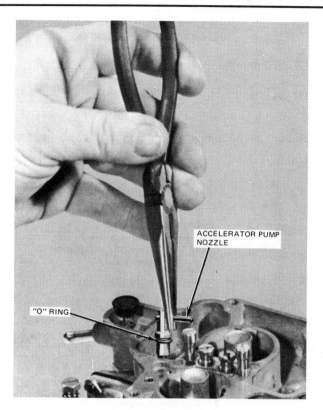

Fig. 4.19 Accelerator pump removal (Sec 16)

21 Remove the power valve screws (41), cover (42), spring (43) and diaphragm (44).

22 If equipped, remove the dashpot and vacuum throttle kicker.

23 Remove the idle mixture plugs (59 and 60) by the following procedure. Punch a hole through both plugs with a suitable punch and a $\frac{3}{32}$-in drill. Using a plug removal tool, pull the plugs out.

24 Count and record the number of turns necessary to lightly seat the idle mixture adjustment needle. Remove the needle screw (61) and O-ring (62).

25 Noting which is the primary and which is the secondary, remove the primary and secondary fuel discharge nozzle (Fig. 4.20).

26 Remove the primary (49) and secondary (53) idle jets and jet holders and identify them by number (Fig. 4.20).

27 Remove and identify the high speed air bleeds (51 and 53) and main well air tubes (52 and 56) (Fig. 4.23).

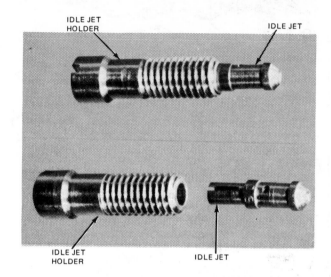

Fig. 4.20 Idle jets and holders (Sec 16)

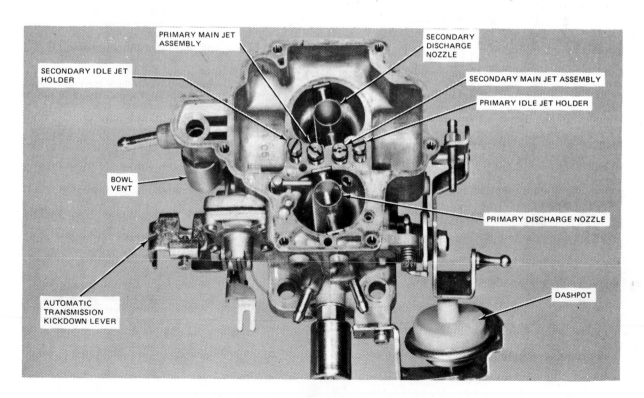

Fig. 4.21 Carburetor main body (Sec 16)

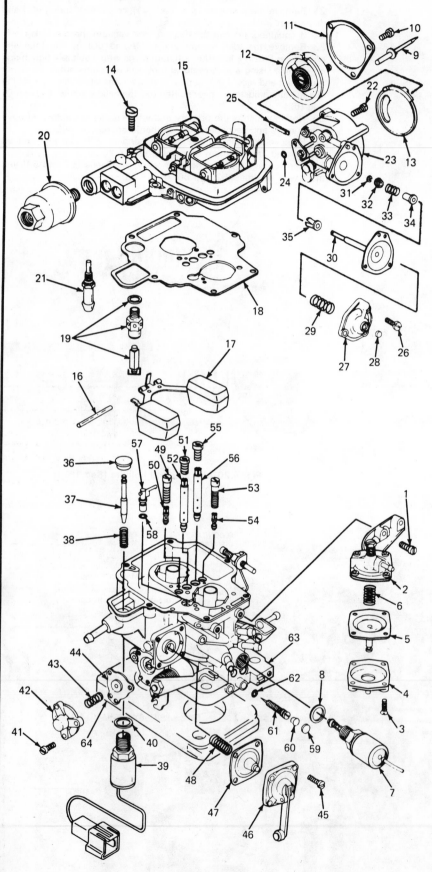

Fig. 4.22 Exploded view of Motorcraft 740 carburetor (Secs 16 and 17)

1 Throttle kicker screw and lock washer
2 Throttle kicker assembly
3 Cover screws (4)
4 Diaphragm cover
5 Throttle kicker diaphragm assembly
6 Diaphragm spring
7 Idle shutoff diaphragm
8 Solenoid gasket
9 Choke cover retaining rivet (2)
10 Choke cover retaining screw (1)
11 Choke cover retaining ring
12 Choke cover assembly
13 Choke housing dirt shield
14 Air horn screw and lock washer (6)
15 Air horn assembly
16 Float pin
17 Float and lever assembly
18 Air horn gasket
19 Needle, seat and gasket assembly
20 Fuel inlet filter
21 Fuel return check valve
22 Choke housing assembly screw (3)
23 Choke housing assembly
24 Choke housing O-ring
25 Choke link seal retainer
26 Cover screw (3)
27 Diaphragm cover
28 Plastic adjusting screw plug
29 Diaphragm spring
30 Choke pulldown diaphragm assembly
31 Bushing retainer E-clip
32 Small bumper spring bushing
33 Bumper spring
34 Large bumper spring bushing
35 Guide bushing
36 Bowl vent seal
37 Bowl vent seal plunger
38 Seal plunger spring
39 Bowl vent solenoid
40 Bowl vent solenoid gasket
41 Cover screw (3)
42 Power enrichment valve cover
43 Power enrichment valve diaphragm
44 Enrichment valve diaphragm assembly
45 Cover screw (4)
46 Pump diaphragm cover
47 Accelerator pump diaphragm assembly
48 Diaphragm return spring
49 Primary jet holder
50 Primary idle jet
51 Primary air bleed
52 Primary main well tube
53 Secondary idle jet holder
54 Secondary idle jet
55 Secondary air bleed
56 Secondary main well tube
57 Accelerator pump discharge nozzle assembly
58 Pump nozzle O-ring
59 Idle fuel mixture needle plug
60 Plastic fuel mixture needle plug
61 Idle mixture adjustment needle
62 Idle mixture adjustment needle O-ring
63 Main body assembly
64 Spacer and gasket assembly

Fig. 4.23 High speed air bleeds, main well air tubes and main jets (Secs 16 and 17)

17 Carburetor – reassembly

Note: *Refer to Figure 4.22 for component numbering.*

Main body

1   Install the high-speed air bleeds (51) and well tubes (52), main jets (56), tightening to specification (Fig. 4.23).
2   Install the idle jet holders (49 and 53) and idle jets (50 and 54) (Fig. 4.20).
3   Install the primary and secondary fuel ducting nozzles, idle mixture screw (61) and O-ring (62) and plugs (59 and 60) (Fig. 4.21).
4   Install (if equipped) the vacuum throttle kicker and dashpot.
5   Install the power valve diaphragm (44), spring (43), cover (42) and screws.
6   Install the fuel bowl vent solenoid (39) and washer (40) and the shut-off solenoid (7) and washer (8).

Accelerator pump

7   Lubricate and install the O-ring (58) onto the accelerator pump nozzle (57) and install the nozzle (Fig. 4.19).
8   Install the accelerator pump return spring (48), diaphragm (47), pump cover (46) and cover screws (45), tightening to specification.

Choke

9   When installing the diaphragm assembly (30), make sure that the plastic is held in place and install the spring (33), pulldown cover (27) and screws (Fig. 4.17).
10 Install the O-ring (24) and housing assembly (23) and connect it with a choke link (22). Install the screws and tighten to specification (Fig. 4.16).
11 Install the choke housing shield (13), choke unit (12) and retaining ring (11), as follows. Assemble the choke cap spacer and cap after engaging the bi-metal loop on the choke housing shaft lever and align the index tab. Install the choke cap retainer over the cap, using the screw to loosely hold the assembly in place. Use the two rivets $\frac{1}{2}$ in long, $\frac{1}{8}$ in diameter, with a $\frac{1}{2}$ in diameter head) to align the assembly. Install the rivets lightly to hold the assembly in place and then reposition the rivet gun on the rivet mandrel and fully install the rivets until the mandrell breaks off. Repeat for the second rivet and then tighten the securing screw to specification.

Air horn assembly

12 Install the fuel return line and check the valve and fitting assembly (21).
13 Install the air horn gasket (18).
14 Install the inlet needle seat and gasket assembly (19) and tighten to specification.
15 Install the inlet needle, float (16) and hinge pin (17), opening the throttle for clearing the fast idle lever.
16 Install the bowl cover (15) and tighten the screws (14) to specification.
17 Install a new fuel filter (20) and tighten to specification.
18 Install the carburetor (Section 15).

18 Fuel tank – removal and installation

1   Remove any fuel from the tank by siphoning or pumping.
Caution: *Do not use your mouth to start a siphoning action.*
2   Disconnect all hoses and electrical connections at the fuel tank.
3   Remove the front bolts attaching the tank retaining straps to the vehicle. With the help of an assistant, lower the tank and remove it.
4   If the tank is steam cleaned, the vapor separator assembly must be replaced with a new one.
5   Installation is the reverse of removal and new retaining strap bolts must be used.

19 Throttle cable – removal and installation

1   Remove the air cleaner assembly.
2   Remove the snap-in nylon bushing fron the pedal arm.
3   From inside the passenger compartment, depress the snap-in tabs and push out on the throttle cable to remove it from the dash.

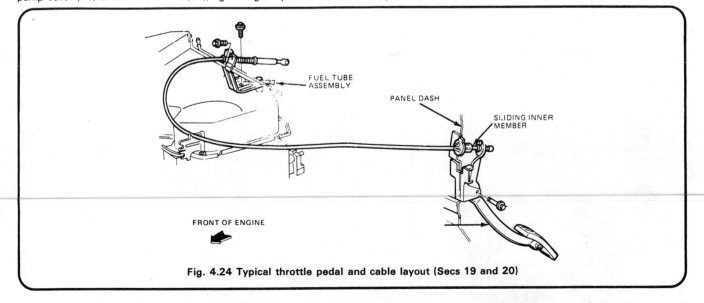

Fig. 4.24 Typical throttle pedal and cable layout (Secs 19 and 20)

4   On automatic transaxle models, remove the throttle cable from the ignition wire retainer.

5   Disconnect the cable from the carburetor lever, by inserting a screwdriver between the cable and the lever and twisting it.

6   Remove the cable housing-to-engine mounting bracket attaching screw and remove the cable from the bracket slot.

7   Remove the speed control cable (if equipped).

8   To install, insert the pedal end of the throttle cable through the dash, snapping it into the dash panel. Make sure the cable cover is in place.

9   Place the cable housing in position in the engine mount bracket and install the fuel line attaching clip and the retaining screw.

10   Install the speed control cable (if equipped).

11   Connect the throttle cable to the carburetor throttle lever and on automatic transaxle models, snap the cable into the pedal into the ignition wire retainer.

12   Remove the throttle cable protective cover and snap the nylon cable bushing fully into position.

13   Check for smooth operation and reinstall the air cleaner assembly.

20   Throttle pedal – removal and installation

1   Pry the nylon bushing from the throttle pedal arm.

2   Remove the attaching pivot bolt from the pedal assembly and bracket and remove the throttle pedal assembly (Fig. 4.24).

3   To install, insert the pivot bolt and tighten to specification.

4   Check to make sure that all carpeting and sound insulation is in proper position so as not to impede throttle operation.

5   Snap the nylon bushing into the throttle pedal arm and check the pedal assembly for proper operation.

21   Exhaust system – removal and installation

1   Allow the exhaust system to cool for at least one hour prior to beginning work. Raise the vehicle and support it securely.

2   Remove the U-bolt assembly and rubber insulators, disconnect the muffler from the catalytic converter and remove the muffler by sliding it toward the rear.

3   Disconnect the flange fasteners from the catalytic converter inlet pipe and remove the converter.

4   To install, line up the flanges on the converter and inlet pipe and, using new gaskets, loosely install the attaching bolts.

5   Slide the muffler assembly onto the converter outlet, engaging the muffler slot with the converter tab.

6   Install the rubber insulators on the hangers and install the U-bolt and tighten to specification.

7   From the front of the exhaust system, align the components and tighten the inlet bolts to specification.

8   Check the system for leaks and lower the vehicle.

Chapter 5 Engine electrical systems

Refer to Chapter 13 for specifications and information related to 1981 thru 1985 models

Contents

Specifications

Ignition

Spark plugs .... Refer to Emissions decal for your particular vehicle

Timing mark location .... Front of timing belt cover directly behind the crankshaft pulley

Firing order .... 1 – 3 – 4 – 2

Direction of distributor rotation .... Counterclockwise

Charging

Alternator type .... Rear terminal

Field current amps (@ 12V) 4.25

Brush length
Standard .... 0.480 in (12.19 mm)
Service limit .... 0.250 in (6.35 mm)

Slip ring minimum diameter .... 1.22 in (31 mm)

Starter motor

Brush length .... 0.45 in (11.4 mm)

Brush spring tension .... 80 oz (22 Nm)

Commutator runout limit .... 0.005 in (0.127 mm)

Maximum starting circuit voltage drop 0.5V

Torque specifications

	Ft-lb	Nm
Alternator mounting bolts		
Bracket-to-block	30 to 40	40 to 54
Pivot	45 to 60	61 to 81
Adjuster arm-to-block	30 to 40	40 to 55
Adjuster arm-to-alternator	24 to 34	33 to 46
Alternator through-bolts	3 to 4	4 to 6
Alternator pulley nut	60 to 100	82 to 135
Distributor hold down	4 to 5	5 to 7
Distributor diaphragm retaining screws	2 to 3	3 to 4
Distributor cap hold down bolts	1 to 2	2 to 3
Distributor rotor hold down screws	2 to 3	3 to 4
Spark plugs	17 to 22	20 to 30
TFI module attaching screws	9 to 16 (In-lb)	1 to 2

1   General information

The engine electrical system is composed of a battery, a charging system, starter and ignition system.

The charging system consists of the alternator, voltage regulator and battery. The starting system is operated by electrical power from the battery by way of a starter relay which activates the starter motor. The ignition system includes the distributor, ignition wires and spark plugs.

2   Battery – removal and installation

1   The battery is located at the left front corner (driver's side) of the engine compartment and held in place by clamps at the base.
2   Hydrogen gas is produced by the battery and open flames or lighted cigarettes should be kept away from the battery at all times.
3   Always disconnect the negative (-) battery cable first, followed by the positive (+) cable.
4   After the cables are disconnected, unbolt the battery retaining clamp.
5   When removing the battery, use a battery lifting device or pick it up by the corners because the molded plastic case can distort, forcing electrolyte and/or fumes out the vents.
6   Installation is the reverse of removal. Be careful not to overtighten the securing clamp bolt as this may damage the battery case.

3   Alternator – general information

The alternator is operated by a drivebelt turned by the crankshaft pulley. The rotor turns inside the stator which produces an alternating electric current. This is converted to direct current by diodes. The current is adjusted to battery charging needs by an electronic voltage regulator.

4   Alternator – maintenance

The alternator requires very little maintenance because the only components subject to wear are the brushes and bearings.

The bearings are sealed for life and the brushes should be inspected for wear after about 75 000 miles (120 000 km) and checked for wear against specifications.

Regular maintenance consists of cleaning the alternator of grease and dirt, checking the electrical connections for tightness and adjusting the drivebelt for proper tension.

5   Alternator – special procedure

Note: *Whenever the electrical system of the car is being attended to, and external means of starting the engine is used, there are certain precautions that must be taken, otherwise serious and expensive damage to the alternator can result.*
1   Always make sure that the negative terminal of the battery is grounded. If the terminal connections are accidentally reversed or if the battery has been reverse charged the alternator diodes will be damaged.

2   The output terminal of the alternator marked 'BAT' or 'B+' must never be grounded but should always be connected directly to the positive terminal of the battery.
3   Whenever the alternator is to be removed or when disconnecting the terminals of the alternator circuit, always disconnect the battery, ground terminal first.
4   The alternator must never be operated without the battery to alternator cable connected.
5   If the battery is to be charged by external means always disconnect both the battery cables before the external charger is connected.
6   Should it be necessary to use a booster charger or booster battery to start the engine always double check that the negative cable is connected to negative terminal and the positive cable to positive terminal.

6   Alternator – removal and installation

1   Disconnect the battery negative cable.
2   Loosen the alternator adjusting bolt.
3   Loosen the alternator pivot bolt.
4   Disconnect the electrical connections.
5   Support the alternator while removing the drivebelt adjusting and pivot bolts.
6   Lift the alternator away from the vehicle.
7   Installation is the reverse of removal. Tighten the bolts to specifications.
8   Adjust the drivebelts to specification (Chapter 3).

7   Alternator – fault diagnosis and repair

1   Due to the special training and equipment necessary to test or service the alternator it is recommended that if a fault is suspected, the vehicle should be taken to a dealer or a shop with the proper equipment. Because of this the home mechanic should limit maintenance to checking connections and the inspection and replacement of the brushes.
2   The ammeter (ALT) gauge or alternator warning lamp on the instrument panel indicates the charge or discharge (D) current passing into or out of the battery. With the electrical equipment switched on and the engine idling the gauge needle may show a discharge condition. At fast idle or at normal driving speeds the needle should stay on the 'charge' side of the gauge, with the charged state of the battery determining just how far over.
3   If the gauge does not show a charge or (if equipped) the alternator lamp is on, there is a fault in the system. Before inspecting the brushes or replacing the alternator, the battery conditions, belt tension and electrical cable connections should be checked.

8   Alternator brushes – removal, inspection and installation

1   Remove the alternator as described in Section 8.
2   On air conditioned models, remove the air intake shroud (Section 11). Scribe a line across the length of the alternator housing to ensure correct reassembly.
3   Remove the housing through-bolts and the nuts and insulators from the rear housing. Make a careful note of all insulator locations.
4   Withdraw the rear housing section from the stator, rotor and front

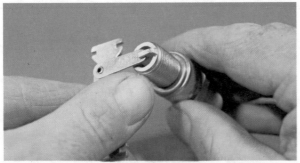

Measuring plug gap. A feeler gauge of the correct size (see ignition system specifications) should have a slight 'drag' when slid between the electrodes. Adjust gap if necessary

Adjusting plug gap. The plug gap is adjusted by bending the ground electrode inwards, or outwards, as necessary until the correct clearance is obtained. Note the use of the correct tool

Normal. Gray brown deposits, lightly coated core nose. Gap increasing by around 0.001 in (0.025 mm) per 1000 miles (1600 km). Plugs ideally suited to engine, and engine in good condition

Carbon fouling. Dry, black, sooty deposits. Will cause weak spark and eventually misfire. Fault: over-rich fuel mixture. Check: carburetor mixture settings, float level and jet sizes; choke operation and cleanliness of air filter. Plugs can be re-used after cleaning

Oil fouling. Wet, oily deposits. Will cause weak spark and eventually misfire. Fault: worn bores/piston rings or valve guides; sometimes occurs (temporarily) during running-in period. Plugs can be re-used after thorough cleaning

Overheating. Electrodes have glazed appearance, core nose very white – few deposits. Fault: plug overheating. Check: plug value, ignition timing, fuel octane rating (too low) and fuel mixture (too weak). Discard plugs and cure fault immediately

Electrode damage. Electrodes burned away; core nose has burned, glazed appearance. Fault: pre-ignition. Check: as for 'Overheating' but may be more severe. Discard plugs and remedy fault before piston or valve damage occurs

Split core nose (may appear initially as a crack). Damage is self-evident, but cracks will only show after cleaning. Fault: pre-ignition or wrong gap-setting technique. Check: ignition timing, cooling system, fuel octane rating (too low) and fuel mixture (too weak). Discard plugs, rectify fault immediately

housing assembly.

5   Remove the brushes and springs from the brush holder assembly which is located inside the rear housing.

6   Check the length of the brushes against the wear dimension given in Specifications at the beginning of the Chapter and replace with new ones if necessary.

7   Install the springs and brushes into the holder assembly and retain them in place by inserting a piece of stiff wire through the rear housing and brush terminal insulator. Make sure that enough wire protrudes through the rear of the housing so that it may be withdrawn at a later stage (Fig. 5.1).

8   Install the rear housing rotor and front housing assembly to the stator, making sure that the scribed marks are aligned.

9   Install the housing through-bolts and rear end insulators and nuts but do not tighten at this time.

10 Carefully extract the piece of wire from the rear housing and check that the brushes are seated on the slip ring. Tighten the through-bolts and rear housing nuts.

11 Install the alternator as described in Section 6.

9   Alternator air intake shroud and fan shield – removal and installation

1   An air intake and fan shroud assembly is installed on air conditioned models to aid in alternator cooling.

2   Disconnect the air intake tube from the shroud housing.

3   Remove the retaining clip and nut and remove the shroud (Fig. 5.2).

4   Remove the fan shield and nut assembly.

5   Installation is the reverse of removal.

10 Alternator voltage regulator – general information

Alternator voltage output is controlled by a transistor regulator which is set at the factory.

Special equipment is necessary to check for faults and this should be left to your dealer or a qualified shop or garage. If the voltage regulator is suspected of a fault, it must be replaced with a unit of the

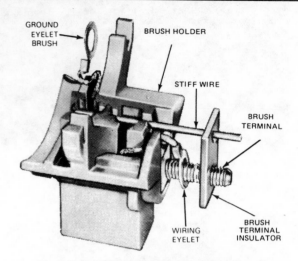

Fig. 5.1 Retracting alternator brushes (Sec 8)

same model and type. Regulators vary greatly in design and a unit of similar appearance can have different properties internally which could lead to electrical system damage.

Make sure that the ignition switch is off when removing or installing a voltage regulator to avoid damage to the new unit.

11 Starting system – general information

The starter motor system consists of a motor with an integral positive engagement drive, the battery, a remote control starter switch, a neutral start switch on some models, the starter relay and the necessary wiring.

When the ignition switch is turned to the Start position, the starter relay is energized through the starter control circuit. The relay then connects the battery to the starter motor.

Cars equipped with an *automatic transaxle* have a neutral start

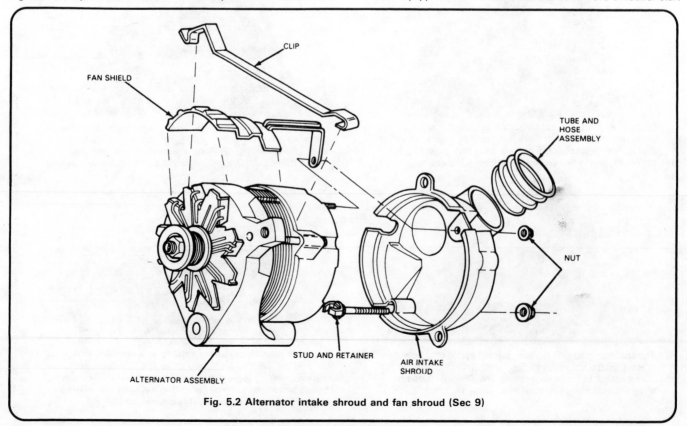

Fig. 5.2 Alternator intake shroud and fan shroud (Sec 9)

switch in the starter control circuit which prevents operation of the starter if the selector lever is not in the N or P positions.

With the starter in its rest position, one of the field coils is connected directly to ground through a set of contacts. When the starter is first connected to the battery, a large current flows through the grounded field coil and operates a movable pole shoe. The pole shoe is attached to the starter drive plunger lever and so the drive is engaged with the ring gear on the flywheel.

When the movable pole shoe is fully seated, it opens the field coil grounding contacts and the starter is in normal operational condition.

A special holding coil is used to maintain the movable pole shoe in the fully seated position while the starter is turning the engine.

12 Starter motor – testing on engine

1   If the starter motor fails to operate, then check the condition of the battery by turning on the headlights. If they glow brightly for several seconds and then gradually dim, the battery is in a discharged condition.

2   If the headlights continue to glow brightly and it is obvious that the battery is in good condition, check the tightness of the battery leads and all cables relative to the starting system. If possible, check the wiring with a voltmeter or test light for breaks or short circuits.

3   Check that there is current at the relay when the ignition switch is operated. If there is, then the relay should be suspect.

4   If there is no current at the relay, then suspect the ignition switch. On models with automatic transaxle check the Neutral start switch.

5   Should the above checks prove negative then the starter motor brushes probably need replacement or at the worst there is an internal fault in the motor.

13 Starter motor – removal and installation

1   Disconnect the battery negative cable.
2   Raise the vehicle and support it securely.
3   Disconnect the starter cable from the starter.
4   On vehicles equipped with manual transaxles, remove the three

nuts retaining the roll restrictor brace to the starter studs at the transaxle and remove the brace. On automatic transaxle models, remove the two nuts attaching the hose bracket to the starter studs and remove it.

5   Remove the rear starter support bracket (two nuts). Remove the retaining nut at the rear of the starter stud through-bolt and withdraw the bracket.

6   On manual transaxle vehicles, remove the three mounting studs and remove the starter. On automatic transaxle models, remove the two starter studs and then the starter mounting bolt, followed by the starter assembly.

7   To install, place the starter on the transaxle housing, install the studs or bolts and tighten them to specification.

8   On manual transaxle models, install the roll restricter brace on the starter mounting studs and install the three nuts. On automatic transaxle vehicles, install the hose bracket and nuts.

9   Install the rear starter support bracket and connect the starter cable.

10   Lower the vehicle and connect the battery negative cable.

14 Ignition system – general information

The ignition system consists of a solid state distributor, ignition coil and/or ignition module, spark plug wires and special 14 mm long reach spark plugs.

The distributor is mounted horizontally and driven directly by a tang in the distributor shaft inserted into the end of the camshaft. The shaft turns a stator which provides an electric signal which causes the ignition module to turn on and off, thus generating the high voltage sent to the spark plugs. Centrifugal and vacuum advance mechanisms in the distributor vary the spark timing to conform to engine speed.

Some models are equipped with Thick Film Integrated (TFI) ignitions which use a different design ignition module.

Because the system requires a high-voltage spark, high-tension spark plug wires and a plug boot design to seal the spark plug cavity against moisture are used. A special deep reach 14 mm spark plug with a screw-on type gasket is used to provide a better seal.

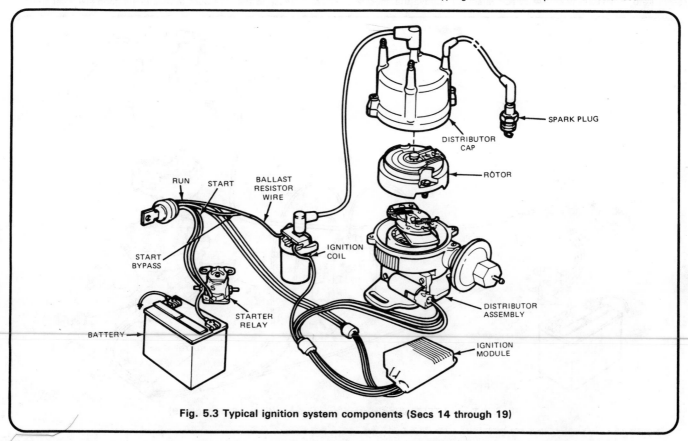

Fig. 5.3 Typical ignition system components (Secs 14 through 19)

15 Distributor – removal, inspection and installation

1   Disconnect the wiring connector and vacuum hose from the distributor.
2   Use a screwdriver to loosen the distributor cap retaining screws, remove the distributor and place it out of the way with the wires attached.
3   Remove the two hold-down screws and remove the distributor rotor. On some models the hold-down screws have a special head which requires the use of Ford tool T82L-12270-A or equivalent.
4   Remove the distributor hold-down bolts. Some models use the special bolt requiring the special tool here also. Lift the distributor away from the cylinder head.
5   Turn the distributor shaft to make sure that it rotates freely and check that the O-ring and drive coupling spring are present and in good position.
6   To install, position the distributor in the cylinder head and insert the offset drive coupling tang into the slot in the end of the camshaft.
7   Install the distributor hold-down bolt, tightening until the distributor can barely be rotated.
8   Install the rotor and tighten the screws to specification.
9   Connect the wiring harness connector.
10 Install the distributor cap and tighten the hold-down screws or bolts to specification. Make sure that the spark plug wires are properly seated in the cap.
11 Check the ignition timing as described in Chapter 1, adjusting as necessary.
12 Tighten the distributor hold-down bolts or screws to specification and install the diaphragm vacuum hose.

16 Thick Film Integrated (TFI) ignition module – removal and installation

1   Remove the distributor cap and place it out of the way with the wires still attached.
2   Remove the TFI harness connector (Fig. 5.4).
3   Referring to Section 15, remove the distributor from the engine, using Ford tool T82L-12270-A (or equivalent) to remove the special

hold-down bolts.
4   Place the distributor on a working surface and remove the two TFI module retaining screws.
5   Disengage the module terminals from the connector in the distributor by pulling the right side down the mounting flange and then upward. Remove the TFI module.
6   Prior to installation, apply an approximately $\frac{1}{2}$-in coat of silicone grease to the module base plate.
7   Position the TFI module on the distributor mounting flange, carefully move it towards the distributor bowl and securely engage the three connector pins.
8   Install the TFI module retaining screws and tighten to specification.
9   Install the distributor cap and check that the ignition wires are securely seated.
10 Install the TFI harness connector.
11 Check the ignition timing as described in Chapter 1, adjusting as necessary.

17 Distributor cap and rotor – removal, inspection and installation

1   After loosening the hold-down screws, lift the distributor cap directly upward to avoid damaging the rotor blade and spring.
2   Loosen the rotor hold-down studs and remove the rotor by lifting straight off the distributor advance weight plate.
3   Prior to installing a new rotor, the brass electrode surface should be coated with a $\frac{1}{32}$-in layer of silicone grease on all sides outward from the plastic to and including the outer edge. When reinstalling the used rotor, do not disturb the existing silicone grease or reapply more. The silicone darkens with age and appears to be a deposit on the cap and rotor but this is normal. Inspect the cap and rotor for cracks and burns and for damage to the cap contacts or carbon button and damage to the rotor blade or spring. Replace any questionable components with new ones.
4   Install the rotor and hold-down screw1s, tightening to specification.
5   Install the distributor cap and screws, tightening to specification. When installing the spark plug wires to a new cap, apply a coat of silicone grease to the wire boot to maintain a good electrical contact.

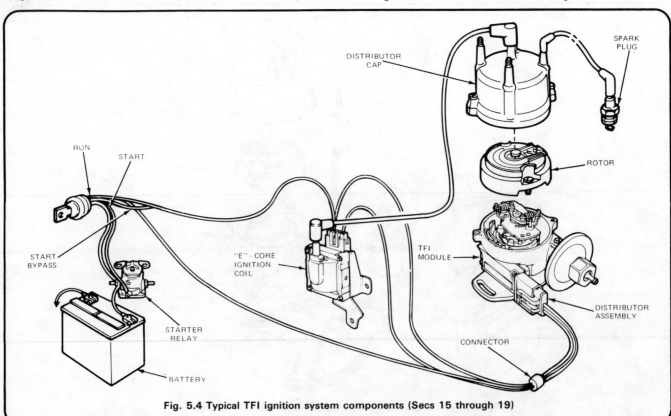

Fig. 5.4 Typical TFI ignition system components (Secs 15 through 19)

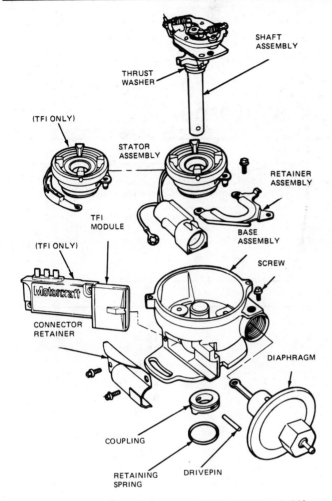

Fig. 5.5 Distributor components (Secs 16 through 19)

Labels in figure:
SHAFT ASSEMBLY
THRUST WASHER
(TFI ONLY)
STATOR ASSEMBLY
RETAINER ASSEMBLY
TFI MODULE
BASE ASSEMBLY
(TFI ONLY)
SCREW
CONNECTOR RETAINER
DIAPHRAGM
COUPLING
RETAINING SPRING
DRIVEPIN

18 Vacuum advance diaphragm – removal, inspection and installation

1   Remove the distributor cap and rotor (Section 17) and disconnect the vacuum hose.
2   Remove the distributor (Section 15).
3   Remove the diaphragm retaining screw (Fig. 5.5).
4   Remove the diaphragm assembly partly away from the housing until it just clears the distributor base.
5   Disengage the rod from the stator pivot pin by tilting the diaphragm assembly. Remove the diaphragm assembly.
6   Inspect the O-ring for cracks or tears, replacing any worn or damaged parts with new ones.
7   Line up the diaphragm casting with the screw hole in the distributor base.
8   Position the stator pin by rotating the stator assembly in a clockwise direction.
9   Insert the diaphragm assembly rod end into the distributor base and engage the rod to the stator pin by tilting the assembly.
10 Seat the diaphragm assembly into the distributor base so that the threaded holes in the diaphragm and distributor are lined up.
11 Install the diaphragm retaining screw and tighten to specification.
12 Install the diaphragm vacuum hose.
13 Install the distributor (Section 15).
14 Install the distributor rotor and cap (Section 17).

19 Distributor assembly – dismantling, inspection and reassembly

1   Remove the distributor cap (Section 17).
2   Remove the distributor (Section 15), and place it on a workbench.
3   Remove the distributor rotor (Section 17).
4   Use a small screwdriver or an icepick to carefully remove the drive coupling spring (Fig. 5.5).
5   If possible, use compressed air to blow away any dust and oil from the drive end of the shaft.
6   Mark the drive coupling and shaft with a dab of paint and make a note of the orientation for ease of reassembly. Align the drive pin with the slot in the base.
7   Have an assistant hold the distributor steady in a fixture such as a vise and use a $\frac{1}{8}$-in drift to drive the pin from the shaft. Remove the drive coupling.
8   Inspect the end of the shaft for burrs prior to removal, especially in the area of the drive pin hole. Remove any burrs with a fine file or emery cloth.
9   Remove the shaft assembly by gently pulling upward on the shaft plate.
10 Hold the shaft in your hand and move the shaft plate to check for free movement of the advance mechanism. It should advance easily and then spring back when released. If there is any binding, replace the distributor assembly with a new one.
11 Remove the two screws which retain the stator connector to the distributor bowl.
12 On TFI-equipped models, remove the connector from the top of the TFI models.
13 Remove the three stator assembly retaining screws and carefully remove the stator.
14 Remove the stator retainer from the stator assembly.
15 Inspect the stator bumper for excessive wear and the diaphragm O-ring for cracks or tears, replacing with new components as needed.
16 Inspect the distributor bore bushing for wear or heat damage. If the bushing is damaged, the distributor assembly must be replaced with a new one.
17 Inspect the shaft oil seal for cuts or tears, replacing the distributor with a new one if the seal is damaged.
18 Check the oil seal retaining spring for kinks or breaks and the distributor base O-ring for cuts, replacing as necessary.
19 Inspect the distributor casting for wear or cracks. If any damage is found, replace the distributor assembly.
20 To assemble the stator retainer assembly to the stator, slide the stator bumper into the groove at the bottom, with the horseshoe-shaped opening at the diaphragm rod pivot pin.
21 Plug the connector into the TFI module (if equipped).
22 With the stator assembly placed over the distributor bore bushing and diaphragm pivot pin in front of the mounting hole, align the stator retaining plate with the holes in the base, using a small screwdriver. If properly assembled, the assembly should rotate freely.
23 Install the screws retaining the connector to the distributor base and tighten to specification.
24 Route the two stator wires behind the connector wire guard so that they are not twisted.
25 Install the vacuum advance diaphragm assembly.
26 Lightly lubricate the distributor shaft with 10 W oil.
27 Insert the shaft assembly into and through the distributor base bushing, install the drive coupling over the shaft and align the paint marks made during disassembly.
28 Place the pin into the drive coupling and shaft and with the help of an assistant holding the assembly steady on a firm surface, drive the pin in place until the end is flush with the step in the drive coupling.
29 Check for free movement of the coupling on the pin and make sure the pin does not protrude above the step in either direction.
30 Make sure that the distributor shaft turns freely and install the spring in the drive coupling groove.
31 Install the distributor in the cylinder head (Section 15).
32 Install the distributor cap and rotor.

Chapter 6 Emissions control systems

Contents

Specifications

Torque specifications

	ft-lb	Nm
EGR valve stud-to-spacer	12 to 15	16 to 20
EGR valve-to-spacer	13 to 19	18 to 26
Thermactor check valve attaching nut	6 to 10	8 to 13
Thermactor pump bracket-to-block	30 to 40	40 to 54
Thermactor pump pivot bolt	40 to 55	55 to 75
Thermactor pump adjuster arm-to-pump	40 to 55	55 to 75
Thermactor pump pulley-to-pump hub	13 to 18	17 to 24

1 General information

In order to meet US Federal anti-pollution laws, vehicles are equipped with a variety of emissions control systems, depending on the model and the state in which it was sold.

Since the emissions systems control so many of the engine's functions, drivability and fuel consumption as well as conformance to the law can be affected should any faults develop. Therefore, it is very important that the emissions systems be kept operating at peak efficiency.

This Chapter will describe all of the systems which may be installed in order to cover all models.

The emission label located under the hood contains information important to properly maintaining the emissions control systems as well as for keeping the vehicle correctly tuned.

2 Positive Crankcase Ventilation system – description and maintenance

The PCV system consists of the crankcase emissions filter and associated hoses. The system operates by drawing vapors from the crankcase into the air cleaner and then back into the carburetor.

Maintenance consists of periodically removing the hoses, checking them for obstructions and replacing the emissions filter. Emissions filter replacement is described in Chapter 1.

3 Evaporative Emission Control (EEC) – description and maintenance

The EEC system is designed to limit the emission of fuel vapors to the atmosphere. It consists of the fuel tank, pressure and vacuum sensitive fuel filler cap, a restrictor bleed orifice, charcoal canister and associated connecting hoses.

When the fuel tank is filled, vapors are discharged to the atmosphere through the filler tube and the space between the inner fuel filler tube and the outer neck. With this system, when fuel covers the filler control tube, vapors can no longer escape because a vapor

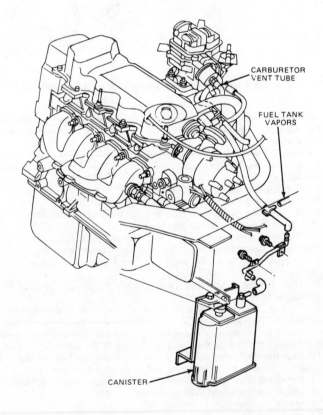

CARBURETOR VENT TUBE

FUEL TANK VAPORS

CANISTER

FRONT OF VEHICLE

Fig. 6.1 Evaporative emissions control system layout (Sec 3)

lock is created by the orifice.

When thermal expansion occurs in the fuel tank, vapor is forced through the orifice and is drawn into the carburetor as soon as the engine is started.

Some models incorporate a fuel bowl vent valve to direct vapors which collect in the carburetor back into the charcoal canister when the engine is off.

Maintenance consists of inspecting the system for leaks and checking the purge valve of the canister for proper operation.

4 Exhaust Gas Recirculation (EGR) system – general information

The EGR system is designed to re-introduce small amounts of exhaust gas into the combustion cycle to reduce the generation of oxide of nitrogen (NOx). The amount of gas re-introduced is governed by engine temperature and vacuum.

The EGR valve is a vacuum-operated unit installed in the intake manifold adjacent to the carburetor. When it is open it allows gasses to enter the manifold.

Some models also use a Wide Open Throttle (WOT) valve which closes the EGR valve when the throttle is at or near wide-open throttle.

5 EGR valve – removal, inspection and installation

1   The most common problems involved with the EGR valve are indicated by detonation, surge or hesitation, rough idling and loss of power. For the home mechanic, the best way to determine if the EGR valve is at fault is to remove and inspect it.
2   Disconnect all vacuum hoses, the air inlet and hot air tube from the air cleaner and remove the air cleaner assembly.
3   Remove the carburetor and gasket (Chapter 4).
4   Disconnect the EGR valve vacuum hose.
5   Unbolt and remove the EGR valve (Fig. 6.2).
6   Cycle the EGR valve fully by pushing it with your finger. If the valve sticks or does not operate smoothly, clean or replace the valve with a new unit. Inspect the gasket for signs that exhaust gas has leaked past it.
7   Inspect and clean the EGR passage (Section 6).
8   Install the EGR valve and a new gasket, tightening the retaining nuts to specifications.
9   Reinstall the carburetor and air cleaner assembly.
10 Some models are equipped with an Inferred Mileage Sensor

(IMS), which must be replaced with a new one or the EGR warning lamp on the dash will remain lit. The IMS module is a blue plastic box with a three-pin connector which is located behind the glove box. Remove the attaching screws, unplug and remove the module and install a new one.
9   Start the engine and check the curb idle speed (Chapter 4), adjusting as necessary.

6 EGR passage – inspection and cleaning

1   Remove the carburetor (Chapter 4) and EGR valve (Section 5).
2   Place a clean, lint-free rag in the intake manifold opening to prevent foreign matter from entering through the EGR passage.
3   Inspect the passage for carbon deposits, using a flashlight and a mirror.
4   Clean the passage, using spray carburetor cleaner and a small screwdriver or scraper. Finish the cleaning job with a bottle brush.
5   Use a vacuum cleaner to remove any remaining loose carbon particles, from the EGR and intake manifold passages. Clean and inspect the EGR and carburetor mounting surfaces.
6   Remove the cloth and inspect the EGR passage to make sure that it is free of carbon or other foreign material. Check that the small hole above the EGR passage is not obstructed.
7   Reinstall the carburetor and EGR valve.

7 Thermactor exhaust control system – description and maintenance

The Thermactor system reduces hydrocarbon (HC) and carbon monoxide (CO) content of the exhaust gasses by continuing the oxidation of the unburned gases after they leave the combustion chamber. This is accomplished by mixing air with the hot exhaust gasses, promoting further reduction of the concentration of pollutants.

The Thermactor air pump draws air into an impeller-type centrifugal fan and exhausts it into the exhaust manifold through a vacuum-controlled air bypass valve and check valve. During deceleration, when there is a high level of intake manifold vacuum, the diaphragm check valve operates to shut off the Thermactor air by venting it to the atmosphere. The air supply check valve is a one-way type which allows Thermactor air to pass to the exhaust manifold but will not allow exhaust gasses to flow in the reverse direction.

There is little the home mechanic can do in the way of maintenance of the Thermactor system without special equipment other than checking the tension and condition of the drivebelt and the security and condition of the hose connections.

8 Wide Open Throttle (WOT) valve – description and testing

1   When the throttle is at or near the wide open position, the high vacuum signal present operates the WOT valve and vents EGR vacuum to the atmosphere. Reduced power at wide open throttle is a symptom of a fault in the WOT valve and that it is not venting properly.
2   To check the WOT valve, warm up the engine to operating temperature and set the throttle at the kickdown step on the carburetor (Chapter 4).
3   To the EGR side of the WOT valve, connect a vacuum gauge and make a note of the reading.
4   Connect a vacuum pump to the carburetor venturi and apply six inches of vacuum.
5   If the vacuum reading drops to zero, the valve is faulty and should be replaced with a new unit.
6   Remove the vacuum gauge and pump and reconnect all vacuum hoses.

9 Dashpot – description and testing

1   During deceleration, the dashpot slows the closing of the throttle plates to aid in the control of hydrocarbon emissions. As the throttle opens, the spring extends the dashpot plunger. When it closes, the throttle lever puts pressure on the plunger, slowly forcing the air out of the dashpot chamber, returning the throttle plates slowly to idle.

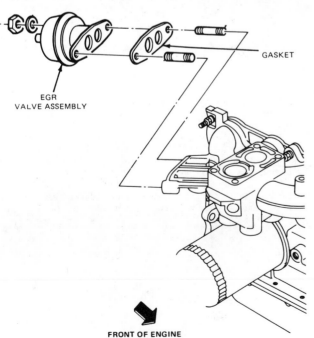

GASKET

EGR VALVE ASSEMBLY

FRONT OF ENGINE

Fig. 6.2 EGR valve and gasket installation (Secs 5 and 6)

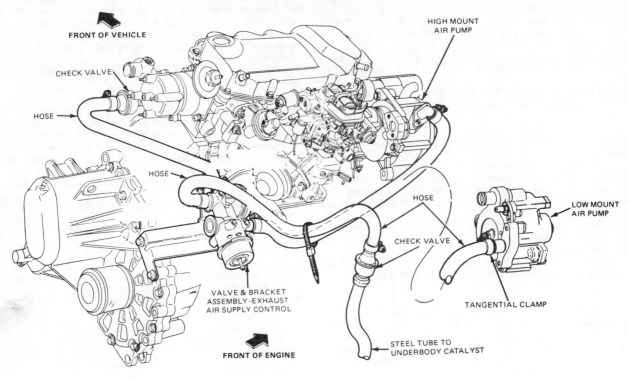

Fig. 6.3 Typical Thermactor system layout (Sec 7)

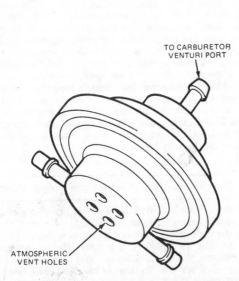

Fig. 6.4 Wide Open Throttle valve (Sec 8)

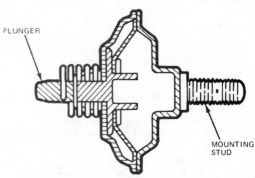

Fig. 6.5 Dashpot components (Sec 9)

10 Catalytic converter – general information

The catalytic converter is located upstream of the exhaust muffler. The converter consists of a ceramic honeycomb-like core housed in a stainless steel pipe. The core is coated with a platinum and paladium catalyst which converts unburned carbon monoxide and hydrocarbons into carbon dioxide and water by a chemical reaction.

No special maintenance of the converter is required, but it can be damaged by the use of leaded fuels, engine misfire, excessive richness of the carburetor mixture, incorrect operation of the Thermactor system or running out of gasoline.

2   To test the dashpot, push the plunger slowly in, to collapse it. If the plunger moves in easily, or is hard to push in to the bottomed position, replace it with a new unit.

Chapter 7A Manual transaxle

Refer to Chapter 13 for specifications related to 1983 thru 1985 models

Contents

Specifications

Transaxle type .... 4-speed, synchromesh on all forward gears

Oil capacity .... 5.0 US pts

Oil type .... Type 'F' automatic transmission fluid

Torque specifications

	ft-lb	Nm
Filler plug	9 to 14	12 to 20
Control arm balljoint-to-steering knuckle	37 to 44	50 to 60
Stabilizer-to-control arm	59 to 73	80 to 99
Transaxle-to-engine bolts	28 to 31	38 to 42
Transaxle case-to-clutch housing	13 to 17	18 to 23
Shift lever-to-control arm screw	15 to 20	20 to 27
Shift lever-to-housing assembly screw	3 to 7	4 to 9
Shift control selector plate	6 to 8	8 to 11
Shift fork interlock sleeve pin	12 to 15	16 to 20
Back-up lamp switch	14 to 18	19 to 24

1 General information

All manual models are equipped with a 4-speed transaxle assembly which incorporates a differential assembly and is mounted in-line with the engine. Drive from the engine passes through the transaxle gears and then to the differential gears which drive the axleshafts which are mounted behind and parallel to the engine (Fig. 7.1).

All forward gears are synchromesh and the floor-mounted shift linkage operates the transaxle internal shift assembly through a shift lever and stabilizer.

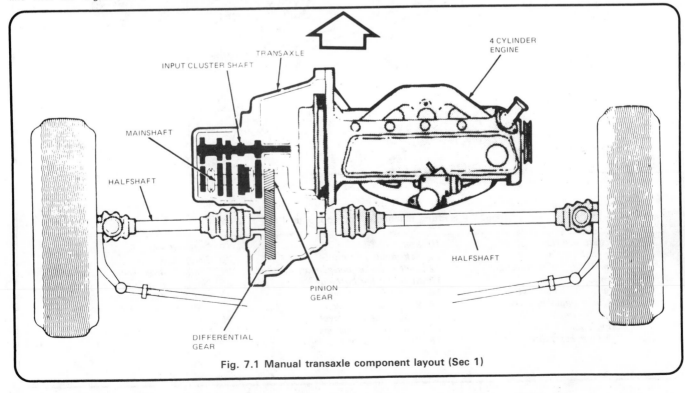

Fig. 7.1 Manual transaxle component layout (Sec 1)

2   Shift lever assembly – removal and installation

1   Loosen the locking nut and remove the gearshift knob.
2   Release the snaps on the shift lever boot by pulling outward on the assembly. Slide the boot from the shift lever.

3   Remove the four shift lever-to-mounting bracket retaining bolts. Lift the lever assembly upward through the tunnel opening (Fig. 7.2).
4   Raise the vehicle and support it securely.
5   Unbolt the shifter stabilizer bar from the transaxle (Fig. 7.3).
6   Disconnect the bias spring at the shift rod, loosen the shift rod clamp nut and remove the clamp and clamp assembly.

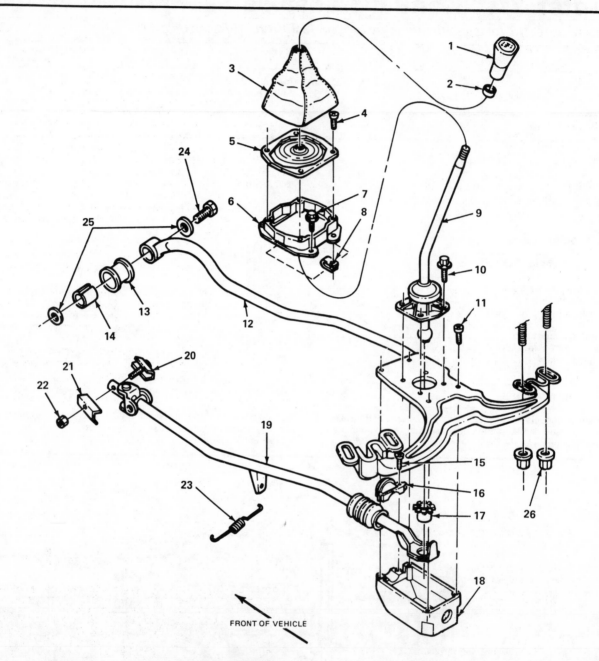

FRONT OF VEHICLE

Fig. 7.2 Shifting mechanism components (Secs 1, 2 and 3)

1 Gearshift lever knob	10 Bolt
2 Shift knob locking nut	11 Self-tapping screw
3 Upper shifting boot assembly	12 Shift stabilizer bar support assembly
4 Screw	13 Stabilizer bar bushing
5 Lower shifting boot assembly	14 Gearshift rod sleeve
6 Shift boot retaining assembly	15 Self-tapping screw
7 Shift boot retaining bolt	16 Control selector cover
8 Spring nut	17 Anti-vibration bushing
9 Shift lever assembly	18 Control selector housing

19 Shift rod and clevis assembly
20 Clamp assembly
21 Gearshift lever clamp (2 required)
22 Clamp assembly nut
23 Gearshift tube retaining spring
24 Stabilizer bar attaching bolt
25 Flat washer
26 Nut and washer assembly

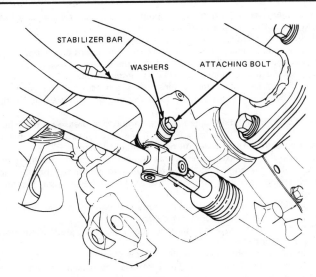

Fig. 7.3 Shifting mechanism stabilizer bar attachment (Secs 2 and 3)

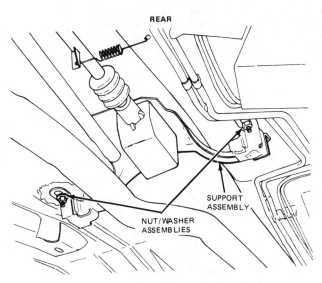

Fig. 7.4 Shift support assembly (Sec 2)

7 Remove the four shifter support nut and washer assemblies.

8 Lower the exhaust system (if necessary) and remove the shifter support assembly from the vehicle underside (Fig. 7.4).

9 Remove the selector housing from the shift rod assembly.

10 Remove the selector cover from the housing.

11 Remove the shift rod and clevis assembly from the selector housing.

12 Remove the stabilizer bar bushing by pushing the metal sleeve out of the center and then grasping it with a pair of pliers and withdrawing it.

13 Inspect the bushing for wear and if it appears serviceable, lubricate it and the metal sleeve with chassis grease. Install the bushing and then insert the metal sleeve into the bushing so that it is centered.

14 Install the shift rod and clevis assembly in the selector housing.

15 Install the selector cover and install the housing to the support assembly.

16 Place the support assembly in position underneath the vehicle and loosely install the attaching bolts.

17 Install the shift rod over the transaxle input shaft and rotate the rod so that the holes in the shaft are aligned with the shift rod universal joints. Install the bolt and clamp assembly, tightening to specification.

18 Align the stabilizer bar bushing with the boss on the transaxle case and install the bolt and two washers, one on each side of the bushing.

19 Tighten the support assembly nuts to specification.

20 Install the bias spring to the shift rod.

21 Lower the vehicle.

22 From inside the vehicle, lower the shift assembly into position with the lower plastic pivot ball inserted into the round socket on the end of the shift rod.

23 Install the four retaining screws and tighten to specification.

24 Depress the clutch and move the shift lever into all four gears to check for proper operation and tightness of all fasteners.

25 Install the shift boot assemblies.

26 Install the shift knob and tighten the lock nut.

3 Manual transaxle – removal and installation

1 Disconnect the battery negative cable.

2 Remove the top transaxle-to-engine mounting bolts.

3 Disconnect the clutch cable by pulling the end forward and releasing it from the clutch arm.

4 Remove the clutch cable casing from the top of the transaxle case.

5 Raise the vehicle and support it securely.

6 Unbolt the brake hose clips from the suspension strut brackets.

7 Remove and discard the bolt securing the lower control arm balljoint to the steering knuckle.

8 When disengaging the steering knuckle, the pry bar must not contact the balljoint boot or lower arm. Pull back on the plastic brake shield to provide clearance, insert a suitable pry bar and disengage the steering knuckle (Fig. 7.5).

9 Prior to removing the halfshaft from the transaxle, obtain some rags and a suitable container to catch the resulting transaxle fluid leakage. Insert a suitable pry bar and gently pry the inboard end of the halfshaft from the transaxle, taing care not to damage the oil seal (Fig. 7.6).

10 Swing the steering knuckle and shaft away from the transaxle.

11 Wire the axle out of the way, in a horizontal position so that the constant velocity joint won't be damaged.

12 Repeat the procedure in steps 7 through 11 on the left side axleshaft and steering knuckle. If the axleshaft does not pull out easily,

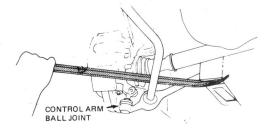

Fig. 7.5 Disengaging the control arm and steering knuckle (Sec 3)

Fig. 7.6 Prying the halfshaft from the transaxle (Sec 3)

a suitable size bar can be inserted through from the opposite side of the transaxle to drive it out.

13 Insert suitable plugs in the differential seals to protect the seals and keep the differential gears from shifting.

14 Remove and discard the front stabilizer bar nuts and disconnect the bar at the control arms (Fig. 7.7).

15 Remove and discard the stabilizer bar mounting bracket bolts and remove the brackets (Fig. 7.2).

16 Loosen the knurled retaining rings and disconnect the speedometer cable.

17 Use a small screwdriver to disconnect the backup lamp connector.

18 Remove the engine roll restrictor-to-starter bracket nuts.

19 Remove the roll restrictor and starter stud bolts.

20 Remove the stiffener brace attaching bolts at the bottom of the clutch housing.

21 Disconnect the shift mechanism crossover spring and remove the bolts attaching the shifter assembly stabilizer bar to the transaxle and remove the shifting mechanism.

22 Place a jack under the transaxle and loosen the rear mount stud nut (Fig. 7.9).

23 Loosen the two upper rear mounting bolts and remove the bolt from the bottom of the mount (Fig. 7.10).

24 Unbolt the transaxle from the transaxle case.

25 Lower the transaxle until it clears the rear mount and support the engine with a block of wood and a jack under the oil pan.

26 Remove the remaining transaxle-to-engine bolts.

27 Using gloves to protect against the sharp edges of the transaxle case, move the transaxle away from the engine and lower it to the floor.

28 Prior to installation, smear a small amount of grease on the input shaft splines and the guide sleeves. If the clutch has been removed, make sure that it has been properly centered (Chapter 8).

29 Raise the transaxle with the jack and with the help of an assistant, engage it to the engine so that the input shaft is inserted through the clutch splines and the unit is sitting on the clutch housing locating dowels.

30 Install the transaxle attaching bolts and tighten to specification.

31 Reconnect the speedometer cable.

32 Install the transaxle mounting bolts and mounting stud and tighten to specification.

33 Install and tighten to specification the front transaxle nuts.

34 Connect the backup lamp and remove the jack from under the transaxle.

35 Install and tighten to specification the stiffener brace attaching bolts.

36 Place the engine rear cover plate over the starter and install the stud bolts, tightening to specification.

37 Install the engine roll restrictor and bolts.

38 Install the shifting mechanism and stabilizer and bolts, tightening to specification. Install the crossover spring.

39 Install a new spring clip to the grooves in the inner ends of the halfshaft splines, being careful not to expand or stretch them.

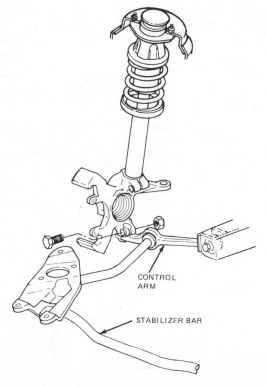

Fig. 7.7 Front stabilizer bar and control arm components (Sec 3)

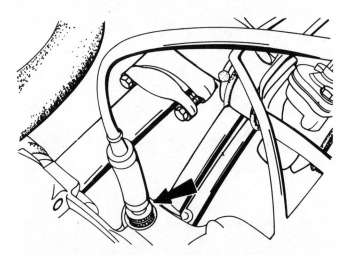

Fig. 7.8 Speedometer cable retaining ring (arrow) (Sec 3)

Fig. 7.9 Loosening the rear transmission mount stud nut (Sec 3)

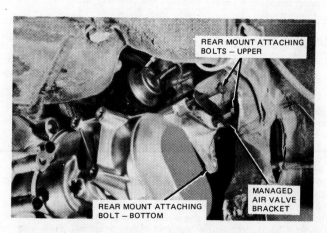

Fig. 7.10 Rear transmission mount bolt location (Sec 3)

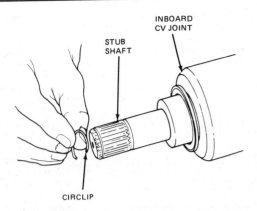

Fig. 7.11 Installing the spring clip to the halfshaft (Sec 3)

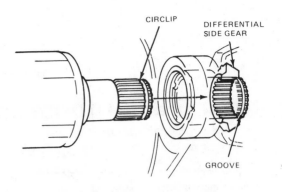

Fig. 7.12 Halfshaft-to-transaxle installation (Sec 3)

40 Insert the shafts fully into the transaxle, being careful not to damage the oil seals, until the spring clip is felt to seat in the differential side gear (Fig. 7.12).
41 Assemble the lower balljoints to the steering knuckles.
42 Install the new nuts and bolts and tighten to specification.
43 Reinstall the brake line retaining clips.
44 Install the stabilizer bar to the control arm with new bolts, but do not tighten the bolts at this time.
45 Install the stabilizer mounting brackets using new bolts and tighten to specification. Tighten the stabilizer bar-to-control arm bolts at this time.
46 Fill the transaxle to the bottom of the filler plug hole with the specified lubricant.
47 Lower the vehicle and reconnect the clutch cable.

48 Install the two transaxle-to-engine mounting bolts and tighten to specification.
49 Reconnect the battery negative cable and cycle the clutch pedal several times to check for proper operation and adjustment.

4 Manual transaxle service

Because of the special tools and techniques required in the overhauling and disassembly of the transaxle, it is recommended that this be left to a dealer or a properly-equipped shop.

The shifting linkage has been designed with no provision for adjustment. Service consists of replacing worn components and periodic inspection for loose bolts or fasteners.

Chapter 7B Automatic transaxle

Refer to Chapter 13 for specifications related to 1983 thru 1985 models

Contents

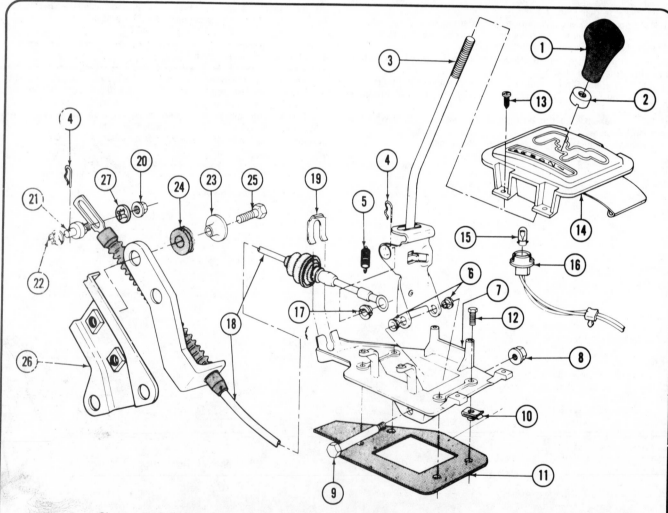

Chapter 7.13 Exploded view of the automatic transaxle shift mechanism (Secs 6, 7, 8 and 9)

1 Shift knob	8 Nut	16 Bulb harness	22 Shift rod clevis bushing
2 Shift lever ball lock nut	9 Bolt	17 Shift lever cable housing	23 Control cable bracket spacer
3 Control lever and adaptor assembly	10 Spring nut	18 Cable and bracket assembly	24 Control cable bracket insulator
4 Retaining pin	11 Selector housing seal	19 Hand brake cable spring lock clip	25 Hex head bolt
5 Parking gear lockout return spring	12 Hex head bolt	20 Nut and washer	26 Control cable bracket retainer
6 Shift lever shaft bushing	13 Screw	21 Shift connecting rod adjusting stud	27 Push-on nut
7 Control selector housing	14 Bezel		
	15 Illumination bulb		

Specifications

Transaxle type	3-speed, fully automatic, floor-mounted shifter
Fluid capacity	9.8 US qts
Fluid type	DEXRON II or equivalent

Torque specifications

	Ft-lb	Nm
Shift lever-to-housing	3 to 7	4 to 9
Shift lever-to-control cable retaining nut	10 to 15	14 to 20
Control cable bracket	15 to 25	20 to 34
Control cable retaining nut	10 to 14	14 to 19
Pivot bolt	13 to 20	18 to 27
Neutral start switch-to-case	7 to 9	9 to 12
Oil pan-to-case bolts	15 to 19	20 to 26

---

5 General information

The automatic transaxle combines a 3-speed automatic transmission and differential assembly into one unit. Power from the engine passes through the transmission to the differential and then to the halfshafts and front wheels.

All models feature a transaxle oil cooler with the cooler element located in the radiator.

Due to the complexity of the automatic transaxle unit, it is recommended that any major fault diagnosis or repair be left to a dealer or properly-equipped transmission shop. This Chapter will cover information useful to the owner in routine maintenance.

6 Shift lever and housing assembly – removal and installation

Note: *Refer to the component numbering in Figure 7.13.*

1   Remove the lock nut (2) and knob (1) and remove the console or consolette as described in Chapter 12.
2   Remove the bezel assembly screws (13).
3   Lift the bezel (14) sufficiently to allow the indicator bulb harness (16) to be disconnected and then remove the bezel.
4   Remove the cable retaining clip (19).
5   From the lever and housing assembly (7), remove the retaining pin (4) and slide out the control cable assembly (18) and bushing (17).
6   Remove the four retaining bolts (12) and remove the lever and housing assembly.
7   Place the lever and housing assembly (7) in position in the floor pan and tighten the bolts to specification.
8   Install the cable (18) and bushing (17) on the control assembly attaching shaft.
9   Install the cable retainer pin (4).
10 Install the cable assembly to the housing with the retaining clip (19).
11 With the indicator in Park or Drive, install the bezel (14) on the lever assembly, connect the illumination bulb harness and install the screws (13).
12 Install the console, shift knob (1) and lock nut (2).
13 Adjust the shift linkage as described in Section 10 and check for proper operation.

7 Shift control cable and bracket assembly – removal and installation

Note: *Refer to component numbering in Figure 7.13.*

1   Remove the shift knob, console, bezel and control cable clip and pin as described in Section 6.
2   Push the rubber grommet towards the engine compartment and disengage it from the floor pan.
3   Raise the vehicle and support it securely.
4   Remove the nut and cable (18 and 20) from the transaxle shift lever.
5   Remove the bracket bolts (25) and remove the cable.
6   To install, insert the rounded end of the cable through the floor pan.

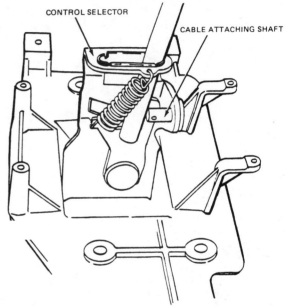

Fig. 7.14 Control assembly cable installation (Sec 6)

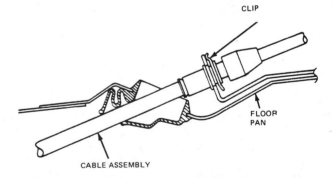

Fig. 7.15 Control cable floor pan installation (Sec 7)

7   Push the cable rubber boot into the opening in the body panel (Fig. 7.15).
8   Lower the vehicle.
9   Install the cable assembly (18) into the selector housing (7) and retain it with the clip (19).
10 Install the control cable assembly (18) and bushing (17) on the selector lever shaft and secure it with the pin (4).
11 Install the bezel (14), console (12) and shift knob (1).
12 Place the selector in the Drive position and hold it in place while installing the other end of the control cable.
13 Raise the vehicle and support it securely.

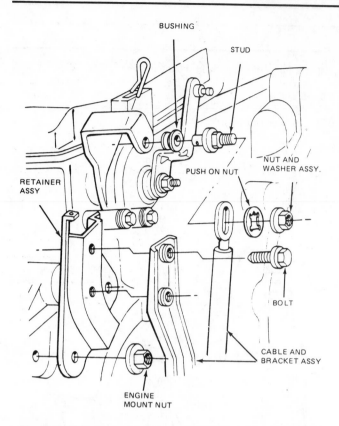

BUSHING

STUD

NUT AND
WASHER ASSY.

PUSH ON NUT

RETAINER
ASSY

BOLT

CABLE AND
BRACKET ASSY

ENGINE
MOUNT NUT

Fig. 7.16 Shift control cable and bracket installation (Sec 7)

14 Place the control cable bracket on the retainer bracket, install the bolts (25) and tighten to specification (Fig. 7.16).
15 Move the shift lever into the second Drive detent forward from the rearmost position.
16 Install the cable end onto the transaxle lever stud, aligning the flats on the stud with the slot in the end of the cable and start the nut (20) (Fig. 7.16).
17 Check that the selector lever has not moved into the Drive detent and then tighten the nut to specification.
18 Lower the vehicle and check for proper operation of the linkage and Neutral start switch.

8 Control cable retainer bracket – removal and installation

Note: *Refer to component numbering in Figure 7.13.*
1 Raise the vehicle and support it securely.

2 Remove the cable bracket securing bolts (25).
3 Place a jack under the engine to support it.
4 Remove the screw retaining the air pump hose to the retainer bracket.
5 Remove the two nuts attaching the retainer bracket assembly (26) to the engine mount bracket, leaving the two bolts in place.
6 Remove the bracket assembly.
7 To install, position the bracket assembly (26) on the engine mount bolts and install the two nuts.
8 Place the cable assembly bracket on the retainer bracket, install the two bolts (25) and tighten to specification.
9 Install the clip and hoses in the bracket and tighten the retaining screw.
10 Remove the jack, lower the vehicle and check the shift mechanisms for proper operation.

9 Neutral start switch – removal, adjustment and installation

1 Disconnect the battery negative cable.
2 Remove the rear managed air supply hoses and disconnect the vacuum hoses from the air valve.
3 Remove the screw retaining the air valve supply hose band to the shift control bracket.
4 Remove the air cleaner assembly.
5 Disconnect the Neutral start switch connector.
6 Remove the two attaching bolts and remove the Neutral start switch.
7 To install, position the switch on the manual shaft and loosely install the attaching bolts.
8 Use a No 43 (0.089 in) drill to set the switch by inserting it in the hole provided.
9 Tighten the attaching bolts to specification and then remove the drill bit.
10 Reconnect the Neutral start switch connector.
11 Install the screw which retains the managed air valve supply hose band to the shift control bracket.
12 Connect the two rear air valve hoses and all vacuum hoses to the valve itself.
13 Install the air cleaner assembly and reconnect the battery cable.
14 Check the engine to make sure that it starts in both Neutral and Park.

10 Shift control linkage – adjustment

1 Raise the vehicle and support it securely.
2 Place the shift selector in the rearward Drive position and hold it in place throughout the adjustment procedure.
3 From underneath the vehicle, loosen the nut retaining the manual lever to the control cable.
4 Move the shift selector forward to the second detent from the rearmost position and tighten the attaching nut to specification.
5 Lower the vehicle and check the operation of the shifter and Neutral start switch.

Chapter 8 Driveline

Contents

Specifications

Clutch Type .... Single dry plate-type with diaphragm-type spring pressure plate

Diameter .... 8.0 in (200 mm)

Constant Velocity (CV) joint lubricant type .... Ford D8RZ-19590-A or equivalent

Torque specifications

	Ft-lb	Nm
Clutch housing-to-engine bolt	28 to 38	38 to 52
Pressure plate-to-flywheel bolt	12 to 24	17 to 32
Clutch release arm bolt	12 to 24	17 to 32
Front hub nut	180 to 200	244 to 271
Outer CV joint center screw	120	163
Lower ball joint nut	37 to 44	50 to 60
Brake hose clip	7 to 8	11 to 12
Wheel lug nuts	80 to 105	108 to 142
Clutch pedal assembly-to-brake support	15 to 25	20 to 34
Clutch stop mounting bracket-to-pedal assembly bolt	15 to 25	20 to 34

1 General information

The clutch disc is held in place against the flywheel by the pressure plate springs. During disengagement such as during gear shifting, the clutch pedal is depressed which operates a cable and pulls on the release lever so that the release bearing pushes on the pressure plate springs, disengaging the clutch.

The clutch control assembly incorporates a spring-loaded pawl and quadrant device which compensates for clutch face wear so that clutch pedal free-play never needs adjustment.

Power from the engine is passed through the transaxle to the front wheels by two unequal length halfshafts. The halfshafts are comprised of three sections: the inner splined ends which are held in the differential gears by spring clips, two constant velocity (CV) joints and the outer splined end which is secured to the hub with a staked nut. The CV joints are internally splined and contain ball bearings because they operate at various lengths and angles as the halfshafts move through their range of travel. The CV joints are lubricated for life and protected by rubber boots which must be inspected periodically for cracks, tears and signs of leakage which could lead to damage and failure of the halfshaft.

2 Clutch pedal and self-adjustment mechanism – removal and installation

1 Prop the clutch pedal up so that the self-adjusting clutch pawl is free of the adjuster mechanism (Fig. 8.1).
2 Disconnect the clutch cable from the clutch release lever in the engine compartment by unhooking it with a pair of pliers.
3 Remove any under-dash air ducts which could interfere with clutch pedal removal.
4 Remove the clutch shield from the clutch pedal assembly.
5 Release the pawl by lifting upwards on the clutch pedal, rotating the quadrant forward and then unhooking the clutch cable (Section 3). The gear quadrant should not be allowed to snap back, but should swing back.
6 Remove the cable by pulling it through the recess between the clutch pedal and gear quadrant. Disconnect the cable from the rubber isolator on the pedal stop bracket.
7 Remove the gear quadrant tension spring and unbolt and remove the pedal pivot bolt.
8 Remove the washers, bushings, pivot pin, tension spring and adjuster pawl.
9 Prior to installation, lubricate the quadrant pivot, bore, pivot pin and spacers with light engine oil.
10 Install the pawl, spring, pivot pin and retaining clip into the clutch pedal.
11 Install the gear quadrant to the clutch pedal and rotate it so that the pawl is on the quadrant face.
12 Install the pivot bushings and sleeve to the clutch pedal (Fig. 8.2).
13 Install the tension spring to the pedal recess.
14 Place the clutch pedal stop mounting bracket and spring washer in position on the pedal assembly, install the through-bolt and nut and tighten to specification. Make sure that the spring washer is not trapped under the pivot pin and allows proper movement.
15 Install the clutch cable (Section 3).
16 Install the clutch pedal shield.
17 Secure the clutch pedal with a piece of wire so that it is in its uppermost position and the pawl is disengaged from the quadrant.
18 Install the clutch cable to the release lever.
19 Remove the wire from the clutch pedal and adjust by cycling the pedal fully several times.

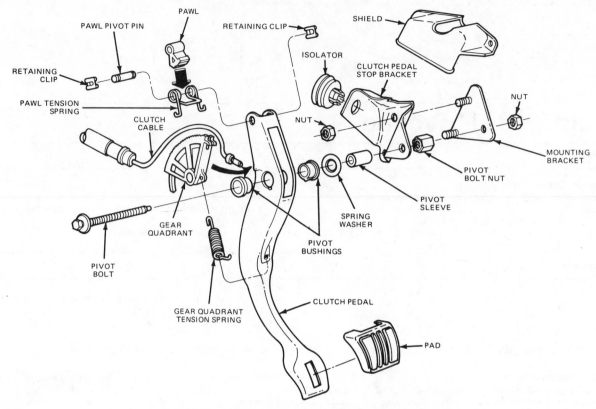

Fig. 8.1 Clutch pedal and adjuster components (Secs 2 and 3)

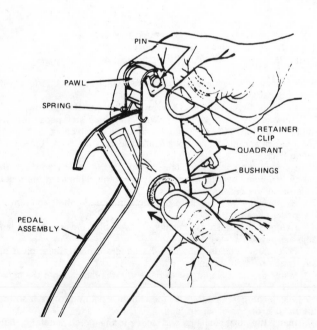

Fig. 8.2 Pivot bushing installation (Sec 2)

3   Clutch cable – removal and installation

1   Prop the clutch pedal in its upward most position so that the adjuster pawl is clear of the quadrant.
2   In the engine compartment, disconnect the cable from the release lever with a pair of pliers.
3   Remove the clutch pedal assembly shield (Fig. 8.1).

4   Pull up on the clutch pedal to release self-adjuster pawl, rotate the quadrant forward and disconnect the cable from the quadrant. The quadrant should swing backward, not snap back which could damage it.
5   Remove the cable by pulling it out through the opening between the pedal and quadrant, into the engine compartment.
6   To install, insert the cable through the dash panel and grommet from the engine compartment side (Fig. 8.3).
7   Insert the cable through the stop bracket isolator and into the opening between the pedal and quadrant.
8   Install the clutch pedal assembly shield.
9   With the pedal secure in its upward most position (held by an assistant or piece of wire), attach the cable to the clutch release lever.
10 Adjust the clutch self-adjusting mechanism by depressing the pedal fully several times.

4   Clutch – removal, inspection and installation

1   Remove the transmission as described in Chapter 7A.
2   Loosen the six pressure plate bolts gradually and evenly so as not to distort the pressure plate cover. Mark the location of the cover on the flywheel for ease of reinstallation (Fig. 8.4).
3   Remove the pressure plate from the locating dowels while supporting the clutch disc (photo).
4   Inspect the clutch disc lining for wear, cracking or signs of oil which is an indication of a leaking engine or transaxle oil seal leak. Because of the difficulty and expense involved in this job, the clutch disc should be replaced with a new unit unless it is in virtually new condition.
5   Inspect the clutch pressure plate face for wear or scoring and the fingers bends, twisting or cracks. Replace the pressure plate if any of these conditions are present.
6   Inspect the friction surface of the flywheel for scoring, grooves or cracking. The flywheel can either be resurfaced or replaced, depending on the degree of damage.
7   Inspect the release bearing for signs of wear on its contact surfaces. Hold the bearing in your fingers and rotate it to make sure that it turns easily. Again, it is better to replace any suspect

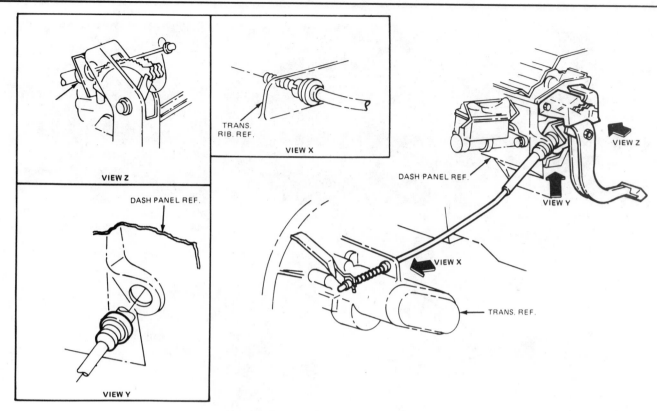

Fig. 8.3 Clutch cable installation (Sec 3)

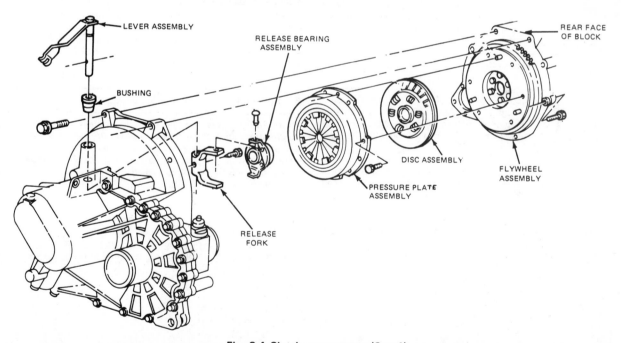

Fig. 8.4 Clutch components (Sec 4)

components rather than take a chance that they are alright and have to go to the expense of replacement later on.

8 Prior to installation, inspect the flywheel, clutch disc and pressure plate and make sure they are free of oil or grease.

9 Place the disc in position with the proper side toward the flywheel. The disc is stamped 'flywheel side' (photo).

10 Position the pressure plate on the flywheel dowels and install but do not tighten the securing bolts.

11 The clutch must be aligned with the input shaft, using an alignment tool available from a dealer or automotive parts store.

12 With the disc in place, alternately tighten the pressure plate bolts to specification (photo).

13 Remove the alignment tool.

14 Prior to installation, lubricate the splines of the input shaft, the release bearing hub, the clutch lever end and bushing bore lightly with grease. Lubricate also to within 0.025 in (6.3 mm) of the rear shoulder of the transaxle extension and the clutch lever bores (Fig. 8.5).

15 Install the release bearing to the fork, retaining it with the pin (photo).

16 Install the engine as described in Chapter 7A.

4.3 Support the clutch disc during cover plate removal

4.9 Clutch disc flywheel side marking (arrows)

4.12 With the clutch disc aligned with the tool, tighten the pressure plate bolts

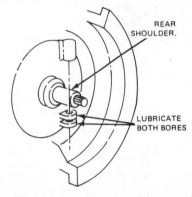

Fig. 8.5 Clutch housing transaxle extension and clutch lever bore lubrication (Sec 4)

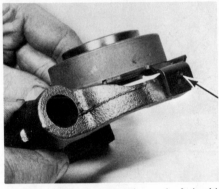

4.15 Install the release bearing to the fork with the retaining pin (arrow)

5   The front hub is staked in place and this should be checked periodically for looseness (Section 6).

5   Halfshaft and constant velocity (CV) joints – inspection and fault diagnosis

1   A clicking during turns is a symptom of a fault in the outboard constant velocity joint (CV) joint. Inspect the CV joint boot for damage.
2   All CV joint boots should be periodically inspected for cuts, damage or signs that the grease has leaked which could lead to joint damage.
3   Vibration during acceleration is a sign of a worn or damaged inboard or outboard CV joint or a sticking inboard joint. Vibration at steady driving speeds is associated with out-of-round or unbalanced tires and not the halfshafts or CV joints. **Note:** *The manufacturer recommends that the front tires not be 'spin balanced' on the vehicle because of the possibility of CV joint damage.*
4   The area around the differential oil seal where the halfshaft enters the transaxle should be checked for leaks.

6   Halfshaft – removal and installation

Note: *Prior to beginning this operation, obtain a new hub and lower control arm bolt and nut for each side of the vehicle to be worked on.*
1   Block the wheels securely, set the parking brake, place the transaxle in first gear (manual) or Park (automatic) and loosen the front wheel hub nut. This nut is staked in place and must be loosened without unstaking (Fig. 8.6).
2   Raise the vehicle and support it securely.
3   Remove the front wheel and then remove the hub nut and washer. Discard the nut and retain the washer for re-use.
4   Unbolt the brake hose routing clip at the front suspension strut.
5   Remove the steering knuckle attaching nut and use a suitable drift to drive out the bolt. Discard the nut and bolt (Fig. 8.7).

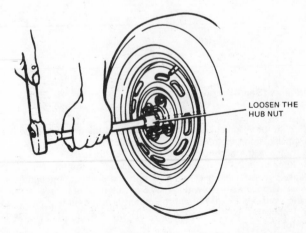

Fig. 8.6 Loosening the front hub nut (Sec 6)

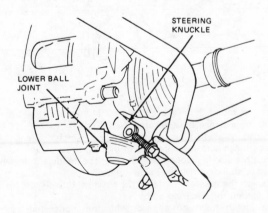

Fig. 8.7 Removing the lower balljoint bolt (Sec 6)

6 Use a pry bar to remove the steering knuckle, taking care to not contact the bushing pocket or balljoint boot (Fig. 8.8).

7 On automatic transaxle models, the right halfshaft must be removed first. A suitable bar is then inserted through the transaxle to push out the left halfshaft. On all models if both halfshafts are to be removed, suitable sized wood or plastic dowels must be inserted into the differential gears to keep them from falling out of alignment.

8 Disconnect the halfshaft from the transaxle housing by inserting a pry bar between the case and the shaft, taking care not to damage the differential dust deflector, CV joint or boot (Fig. 8.9).

9 Wire the shaft out of the way in a horizontal position, so as not to damage the CV joint (Fig. 8.10).

10 Disconnect the outboard CV joint from the hub, using a suitable puller (Fig. 8.11).

11 Remove the halfshaft from the vehicle.

12 Install a new spring clip into the groove on the inboard CV joint splined hub by starting one end in the groove and working it around the shaft (Fig. 8.12).

13 Align the splines of the inner end of the shaft with those in the differential gears and carefully insert the shaft until the spring clip is felt to seat in the differential (Fig. 8.13).

14 Insert the outboard CV joint stub shaft into the hub as far as it will go. Install a wheeler puller, oil the center thread to make sure of a true reading, and use a torque wrench to tighten the shafts center screw to specification (Fig. 8.14).

15 Install the control arm to the steering knuckle, using a new nut and bolt.

16 Install the brake hose routing clip to the suspension strut.

17 Install the front wheels and lower the vehicle.

18 Install a new hub nut and the washer and tighten to specification.

19 Stake the hub nut into the groove in the spindle using a suitable rounded punch or chisel. Do not use a sharpened chisel as it could split the nut. A staking tool can be made from a chisel by rounding the radius across the end to 0.6 in (1.5 mm) (Figs. 8.15 and 8.16).

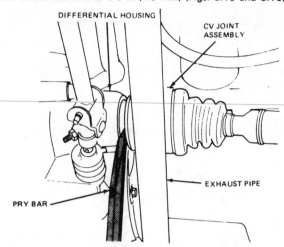

Fig. 8.9 Removing the halfshaft from the transaxle (Sec 6)

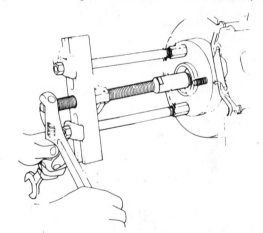

Fig. 8.11 Disconnecting the outboard CV joint with a wheel puller (Sec 6)

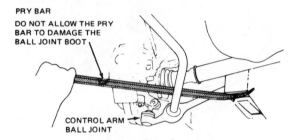

Fig. 8.8 Balljoint removal (Sec 6)

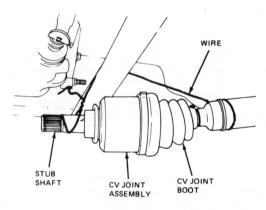

Fig. 8.10 Supporting the halfshaft with wire (Sec 6)

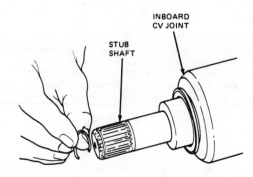

Fig. 8.12 Installing the spring clip to the axle groove (Sec 6)

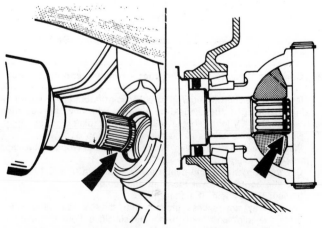

Fig. 8.13 Installing the axle into the transaxle (left) and with the spring clip properly engaged in the differential gear (right) (Sec 6)

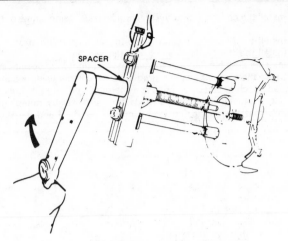

Fig. 8.14 Installing the outer CV joint (Sec 6)

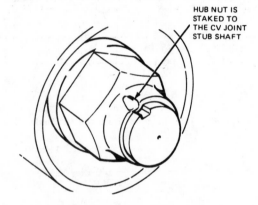

Fig. 8.16 Properly staked hub nut (sec 6)

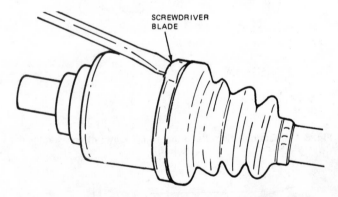

Fig. 8.18 Releasing air trapped in the boot (Sec 7)

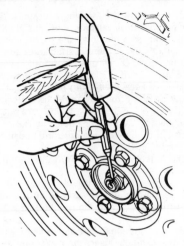

Fig. 8.15 Staking the hub nut into place (Sec 6)

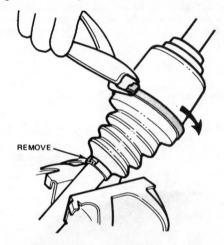

Fig. 8.17 CV joint boot clamp removal (Sec 7)

8   Install the boot over the CV joint and into the grooves provided.
9   The boot protects the CV joint by being sealed air tight so check to make sure that no air is trapped inside the boot. If air is trapped, use a screwdriver blade to allow the excess air to escape (Fig. 8.18).
10   The outer edges of the boot must not have indentations or dimples as this could lead to chafing and eventually a hole. Grasp the outer circumference of the boot and pull outward to pop out any indentations.
11   Install the clamps, taking care not to overtighten and cut the boot.
12   Reinstall the halfshaft (Section 6).

7   Constant Velocity (CV) joint boot – removal and installation

1   If after inspection (Section 5), the CV joint boots are found to be leaking or damaged, they should be replaced with new ones as soon as possible. The CV joints should be inspected at this time (Section 8).
2   Remove the halfshafts as described in Section 6.
3   Place the halfshaft in a vise, using two pieces of wood or jaw caps to protect the shaft from damage.
4   Cut the boot clamp and peel it away as shown (Fig. 8.17).
5   Roll the boot back over the shaft and remove.
6   Inspect the CV joint (Section 8).
7   Wipe away any excess grease from the CV joint and shaft. Lubricate the joint and boot, using the specified Ford Lubricant or equivalent. The inboard CV joint requires one packet of grease each for the joint and boot. The ouboard joint should be filled with $1\frac{1}{3}$ packets of grease with the remaining $\frac{2}{3}$ packet going into the boot.

8   Constant Velocity (CV) joint – inspection

1   Test drive the vehicle to determine if any of the faults described in Section 5 are present. The most common symptoms, vibration on acceleration and a clicking noise during turns are caused by premature wear of the CV joint due to the grease leaking out through a tear in the boot.
2   Raise the vehicle and support it securely.
3   Inspect the boots for cuts or looseness and the area around the CV joints for signs of lubricant leakage.
4   If a damaged boot is found, remove it, take a sample of grease from inside the CV joint and rub it between your fingers. If a grittiness is felt, the grease is contaminated and the CV joint will probably exhibit accelerated wear.
5   If the CV joint is determined to be alright, grease the joint and install a new boot (Section 7).
6   Should one or more CV joints be found to be contaminated or excessively loose or worn, an overhaul of the halfshaft will be necessary. Due to the special tools and techniques required, this should be left to a dealer or qualified shop.

Chapter 9 Braking system

Refer to Chapter 13 for specifications related to 1983 thru 1985 models

Contents

Specifications

General

Brake fluid type .... DOT type 3

Pedal free height
Power .... 7.3 in to 8.2 in
Non-power .... 9.0 in to 10.2 in

Pedal travel
Power .... 2.8 in
Non-power .... 3.3 in

Drum brakes
Drum diameter
2-door .... 7.0 in (180 mm)
4-door and wagon .... 8.0 in (203 mm)

Out-of-round limit .... 0.005 in (0.127 mm)

Drum-to-lining clearance .... 0.0008 in (0.020 mm)

Lining wear limits
7-in (lining surface-to-shoe) .... 0.060 in (1.5 mm)
8-in (lining surface-to-rivet head) .... $\frac{1}{32}$ in (0.79 mm)

Wheel cylinder bore diameter .... 0.811 in (20.6 mm)

Service limit (incl. honing) .... 0.887 in (21.36 mm)

Disc brakes
Lining thickness .... 0.48 in (12.16 mm)

Service limit .... 0.0125 in (0.3175 mm)

Disc thickness
Standard .... 0.945 in (24.0 mm)
Service .... 0.940 in (23.88 mm)
Allowable variation .... 0.0004 in (0.01 mm)

Runout limit .... 0.002 in (0.005 mm)

Caliper maximum bore diameter .... 2.125 in (54 mm)

Master cylinder bore diameter .... 0.828 in (21 mm)

Torque specifications

	Ft-lb	Nm
Brake booster-to-dash panel	13 to 25	18 to 33
Brake hose-to-caliper	20 to 30	28 to 40
Brake pedal pivot shaft nut	15 to 25	21 to 33
Caliper bleed screw	6 to 15	8 to 20
Caliper locating pins	18 to 24	24 to 34
Master cylinder mounting nuts	13 to 25	18 to 33
Parking brake control bolts	13 to 20	17 to 28
Rear brake backing plate-to-spindle	29 to 47	40 to 65
Pressure differential valve bracket bolt	7 to 11	10 to 14
Wheel cylinder bleed screw	8 to 15	10 to 20

1 General information

All models are equipped with disc-type front and self-adjusting drum-type rear hydraulically-operated brakes. Front brakes are of the sliding pin design featuring special bolts which both retain the caliper to the steering knuckle and locate it during movement.

The rear drum brakes are either seven or eight inches in diameter, depending on model. Two-door models use the seven-inch brakes while all others use eight-inch. The two brakes differ somewhat in design and require different overhaul procedures.

Some models are equipped with power-assisted brakes and all models have a cable-actuated parking brake which operates the rear brakes only.

2 Hydraulic brake system bleeding

1   All air must be removed from the hydraulic fluid in the braking system in order to maintain proper operation. On power brake models, apply the brakes with the engine off several times to remove the vacuum reserve.

2   Clean the area around the top of the master cylinder and remove the cap. Keep the master cylinder filled with the specified grade of brake fluid during the bleeding operation.

3   Obtain a clean jar and a piece of rubber tubing which will fit snugly over the bleed screw. Pour a sufficient amount of brake fluid in the jar to cover the end of the tubing. Place the other end of the tubing over the bleed screw fitting on the wheel to be bled. The dual diagonal brake system used on these models links opposite corners of the vehicles so the system must be bled in the following sequence: right rear, left front, left rear, right front brake. **Note:** *Always bleed the brake component with the longest line first.*

4   Remove the rubber dust cap from the bleeder screw, place a suitable end wrench on the bleeder fitting and install the rubber tubing around the fitting. Have an assistant slowly push down on the brake pedal as you release the bleed screw by turning the wrench approximately $\frac{3}{4}$ turn. Repeat this operation until no air bubbles are released into the brake fluid in the jar.

5   Repeat the bleeding operation on the other three wheels and with the bleed screws closed, have the assistant apply the brakes several times to make sure the pedal is firm. During this operation, check to make certain that all brake pads and shoe assemblies are in proper position.

6   Install the rubber bleeder screw dust caps and check that the master cylinder is filled to within $\frac{1}{4}$ inch of the top edges.

7   Install the master cylinder gasket and cover.

3 Pressure differential valve – centralization

1   After any repair or bleed operation it is possible that the dual brake warning light will come on due to the pressure differential valve remaining in an off-center position.

2   To centralize the valve, first turn the ignition switch to the On or Acc position.

3   Depress the brake pedal several times and the piston will center itself again causing the warning light to go out.

4   Turn the ignition off.

4 Flexible hoses – inspection, removal and replacement

1   Inspect the condition of the flexible hydraulic hoses leading to

each of the front disc brake calipers and the one at the front of the rear axle. If they are swollen, damaged or chafed, they must be replaced.

2   Wipe the top of the brake master cylinder reservoir and unscrew the cap. Place a piece of polythene sheet over the top of the reservoir and replace the cap. This is to stop hydraulic fluid siphoning out during subsequent operations.

3   To remove a flexible hose wipe the union and any supports free from dust and undo the union nuts from the metal pipe ends.

4   Undo and remove the lock nuts and washers securing each flexible hose end to the support and lift away the flexible hose.

5   Replacement is the reverse sequence to removal. It will be necessary to bleed the brake hydraulic system as described in Section 2. If one hose has been removed it is only necessary to bleed either the front or rear brake hydraulic system.

5 Disc brake caliper and pad – removal and installation

1   The brake pads should be replaced when the friction surface is worn to within 0.125 in (0.3175 mm) of the pad backing plate.

2   Remove the master cylinder cap and remove sufficient fluid so that the reservoirs are half full.

3   Raise the vehicle and support it securely.

4   Remove the front wheels.

5   Apply upward pressure on the caliper anti-rattle spring and then unsnap the spring fingers (photo).

6   Use a Torx-type tool or $\frac{3}{8}$ in Allen head wrench to loosen the caliper locating pin so that it can be backed out but not removed (photo). Remove the pin only if new bushings are to be installed as pin installation can be difficult.

7   Lift the caliper from the steering knuckle (photo).

8   Remove the inner brake pad from the caliper (photo).

9   Support the caliper out of the way with a piece of wire so that the brake hose is not kinked or stretched. If the caliper is to be removed, disconnect and plug the brake hose.

10 Remove the outboard brake pad (photo).

11 Prior to installing the news brake pads, the caliper piston must be compressed so that the new thicker pads will fit over the disc during installation. Use a C-clamp and a block of wood measuring approximately $2\frac{3}{4}$ in x 1 in x $\frac{3}{4}$ in to push the piston squarely back into its bore.

12 Inspect the area around the outboard pad contact area and remove any rust build-up.

13 Install the inboard pad to the caliper, making sure that the clips fit snugly to preclude any possibility of rattles during operation.

14 Install the outboard shoe and hold it in place as the caliper is rotated forward into position.

15 Insert the locater pins and hand start them, making sure that the plastic sleeves are in position in the rubber insulators. Tighten the pins to specification.

16 Install the anti-rattle spring.

17 If the brake line has been removed, unplug and reinstall it, tightening to specification.

18 Fill the master cylinder to the specified level, bleed the brakes (Section 2) and centralize the pressure differential valve (Section 3).

19 Reinstall the front wheels and lower the vehicle.

20 Pump the brakes several times to position the new pads and test drive the vehicle.

6 Brake disc – inspection, removal and installation

1   Raise the front of the vehicle and remove the front wheels.

2   Inspect the surface of the brake disc. If there is scoring, cracking

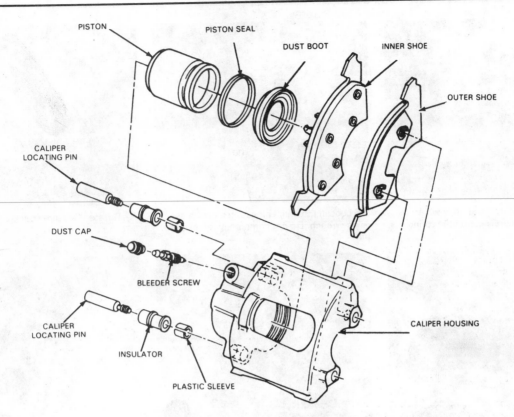

Fig. 9.1 Disc brake components (Secs 5, 6 and 7)

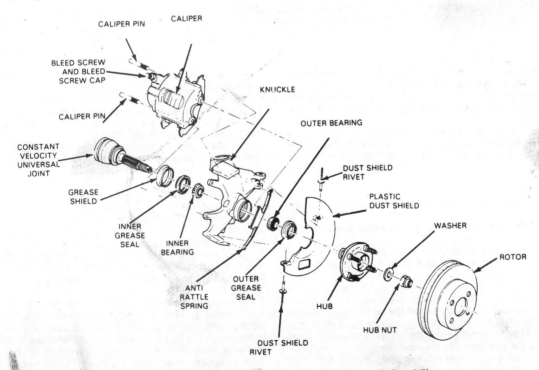

Fig. 9.2 Exploded view of front hub and brake (Secs 5, 6 and 7)

or deep grooving, the disc must be refaced or replaced with a new one. The refacing operation must not reduce the thickness below the minimums in the Specifications section.

3   The disc can be checked for distortion by using a dial gauge or a feeler gauge inserted between its face and a fixed point as the disc is rotated. This will determine runout and if the disc exceeds the limits in specification, replace it with a new unit.

4   Remove the caliper (Section 5).

5   Remove the disc by grasping it firmly and pulling it from the hub studs.

6   Clean the new disc thoroughly with carburetor cleaner to remove the protective coating.

7   Install the disc to the hub and reinstall the caliper.

8   Install the front wheels and lower the vehicle.

5.5 Release the anti-rattle springs while keeping an upward pressure on the spring

5.6 Loosen the caliper locating pin with an Allen wrench. Do not completely remove the pin

5.7 Rotate the caliper backwards to remove it

5.8 Remove the inboard pad by unsnapping it from the piston

5.10 Remove the outboard pad by lifting it from the steering knuckle notches

8.1 Using a mirror to check the brake shoe lining wear

7 Caliper – removal, overhaul and installation

1   Loosen the wheel bolts, raise the front of the vehicle and remove the wheel.
2   Disconnect the brake flexible hose from the caliper. This can be carried out in one of two ways. Either disconnect the flexible hose from the rigid hydraulic pipeline at the support bracket by unscrewing the union or, once the caliper is detached, hold the end fitting of the hose in an open-ended wrench and unscrew the caliper from the hose. Do not allow the hose to twist.
3   Unscrew and partially remove the two caliper mounting bolts and remove the caliper.
4   Brush away all external dirt and pull off the piston dust-excluding cover.
5   Apply air pressure to the fluid inlet hole and eject the piston. Only low air pressure is needed for this, such as is produced by a foot-operated tire pump.
6   Using a sharp pointed instrument, pick out the piston seal from the groove in the cylinder bore. Do not scratch the surface of the bore.
7   Examine the surfaces of the piston and the cylinder bore. If they are scored or show evidence of metal-to-metal rubbing, then a new piston housing will be required. Where the components are in good condition, discard the seal and obtain a repair kit.
8   Wash the internal components in clean brake hydraulic fluid or methylated spirit only, nothing else.
9   Using the fingers, manipulate the new seal into its groove in the cylinder bore.
10   Dip the piston in clean hydraulic fluid and insert it squarely into its bore.
11   Connect the rubber dust excluder between the piston and the piston housing and then depress the piston fully.
12   Install the caliper by reversing the removal operations. Tighten the mounting bolts to the specified torque.
13   Bleed the brake hydraulic circuit (see Section 2).

8 Rear drum brakes – inspection

1   The brake shoes can be inspected for wear by removing the rubber inspection plug in the backing plate and using a mirror to see if the linings are worn beyond specification (photo).
2   To further inspect the drum brakes, raise the rear of the vehicle and support it securely. Remove the grease cap, cotter pin, nut lock, adjusting nut, flat washer and outer bearing and remove the drum and hub (Fig. 9.3).
3   If the drum will not come off easily, use either of the following procedures.
4   On 7-inch brakes (2-door models), remove the inspection plug and use a screwdriver to apply side pressure to the adjuster pivot, releasing the brake adjustment pressure (Fig. 9.4).
5   On 8-inch brakes (all models except 2-door), remove the bracket which retains the brake line to the axle, remove the inspection plug and use a screwdriver and brake adjustment tool to back the adjuster off (Fig. 9.5).
6   Clean the brake of dust and debris, making sure not to breathe the dust. Inspect the brakes for leaking wheel cylinders, worn linings and loose or bent retaining springs. Always replace brake shoes in axle sets of four, even if only one side is worn or damaged. If the shoes have absorbed brake fluid or oil, do not attempt to clean them. Replace them with new units. Check the drum friction surface for excessive grooving or scoring and make sure that the drum is not worn beyond specification. Replace any worn or damaged drum with a new one.
7   Reinstall the drum and hub and adjust the hub nut as described in Chapter 11.

9 Rear drum brake shoes (7-inch) – removal and installation

1   Raise the rear of the vehicle and support it securely.
2   Remove the wheel and hub assembly (Section 8).

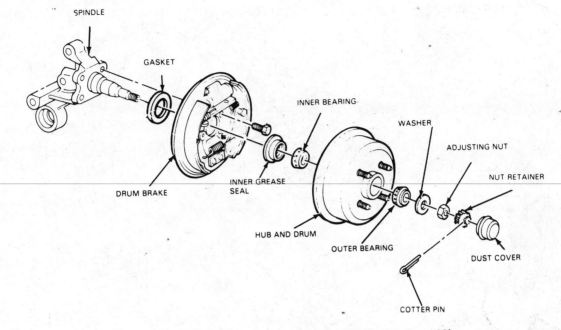

Fig. 9.3 Rear drum brake, hub and spindle layout (Secs 8, 9 and 12)

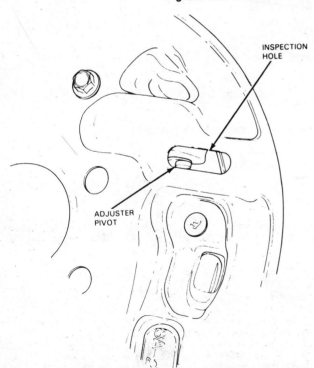

Fig. 9.4 Releasing the adjuster (7-in brake) (Sec 8)

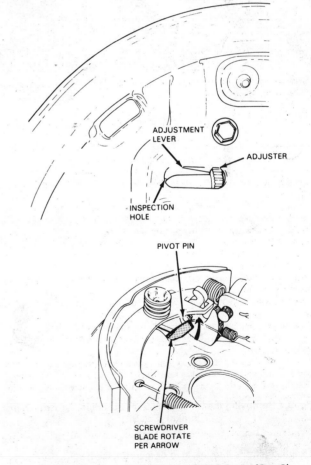

Fig. 9.5 Backing off adjuster on 8-inch brake (Sec 8)

3   On both brake shoes, compress the hold-down spring, rotate the washer and remove the pin (Fig. 9.6).
4   Lift the complete brake shoe and adjuster assembly off the backing plate.
5   Disconnect the parking brake cable from the lever.
6   Remove the lower retracting spring from the brake shoes.
7   Rotate the shoe over the adjusting strut until the retracting spring is slack and then disengage the leading shoe (Fig. 9.7).
8   Pivot the strut downward and away from the trailing shoe until the spring tension is relaxed and then disengage the shoe (Fig. 9.8).
9   To disassemble the adjuster, pull the quadrant away from the knurled pin in the strut, rotate it toward the quadrant until the teeth are disengaged, release the spring and slide the quadrant out (Fig. 9.9).
10   Remove the horseshoe clip and spring washer from the pin on the

trailing brake shoe and disconnect the parking brake lever.
11   Prior to installation, apply a light coating of white high temperature grease to all points on the backing plate where it contacts the shoes. Also, lightly lubricate the adjuster strut-to-quadrant contact surfaces.
12   Install the adjuster quadrant pin into the slot in the strut so that

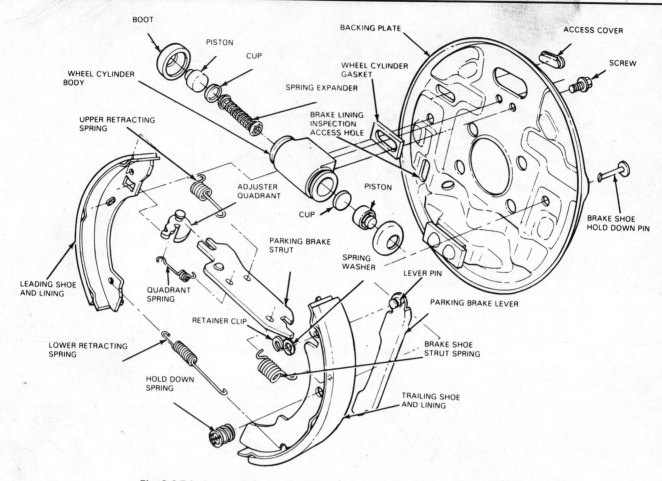

Fig. 9.6 7-inch drum brake components (2-door models) (Secs 8, 9, 11 and 12)

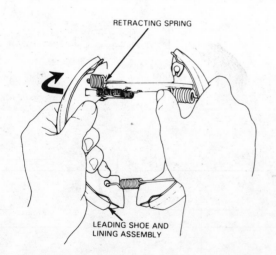

Fig. 9.7 Removing the brake shoe from the adjusting strut (7-in brake) (Sec 9)

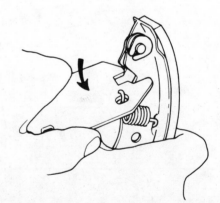

Fig. 9.8 Removing the adjuster strut from the trailing shoe (7-in brake) (Sec 9)

the knurled pin fits into the third or fourth notch (Fig. 9.10).
13 Install the adjuster spring.
14 Install the trailing brake shoe to the parking brake lever and crimp the clip retaining the lever.
15 Pivot the adjuster strut into place on the trailing shoe and install the attaching spring. The end of the spring must be flat against the shoe web and parallel to the strut.
16 Install the lower retracting spring between the leading and trailing shoes.

17 Install the retracting spring for the adjuster and strut to both parts and then pivot the leading shoe over the quadrant and into position.
18 To fit the shoe and strut assembly over the anchor plate and wheel cylinder piston inserts, expand the assembly, taking care not to damage the wheel cylinder rubber boots.
19 Connect the parking brake lever to the cable.
20 Install the hold-down pins, springs and washers to retain the shoes.
21 Install the hub and drum assembly and adjust the wheel bearings as described in Chapter 11.
22 Install the wheels and lower the vehicle.
23 Drive the vehicle in reverse and apply the brakes several times to actuate the automatic brake adjuster mechanism.

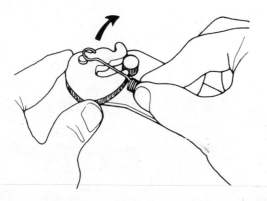

Fig. 9.9 Removing the adjuster quadrant (7-in brake) (Sec 9)

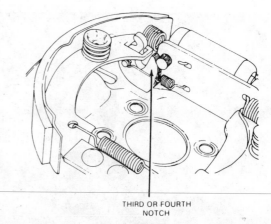

THIRD OR FOURTH
NOTCH

Fig. 9.10 Adjuster quadrant installation (7-in brake) (Sec 9)

10 Rear drum brake shoes (8-inch) – removal and installation

1   Raise the vehicle and support it securely.
2   Remove the hub and drum assembly (Section 8).
3   Remove the hold-down springs, pins and washers from both shoes (photo).
4   Lift the entire shoe and adjuster assembly from the backing plate (Fig. 9.12).
5   Disconnect the parking brake cable from the lever.
6   Separate the shoes and disengage the adjuster mechanism by removing the retracting springs.
7   Remove the parking brake lever from the trailing shoe by removing the retaining clip and washer and then sliding the lever off the pin on the shoe.
8   Prior to installation, lightly lubricate all points on the backing plate where the shoes make contact with white high temperature grease.
9   Lubricate the adjuster screw threads and the socket end of the adjuster screw. Install the stainless steel washer over the adjusting screw end, install the socket and turn the adjusting pivot nut to the limit of the threads and then back it off $\frac{1}{2}$ turn.
10 Install the parking brake lever to the trailing shoe assembly, crimping the clip securely.
11 Connect the parking brake cable to the lever.

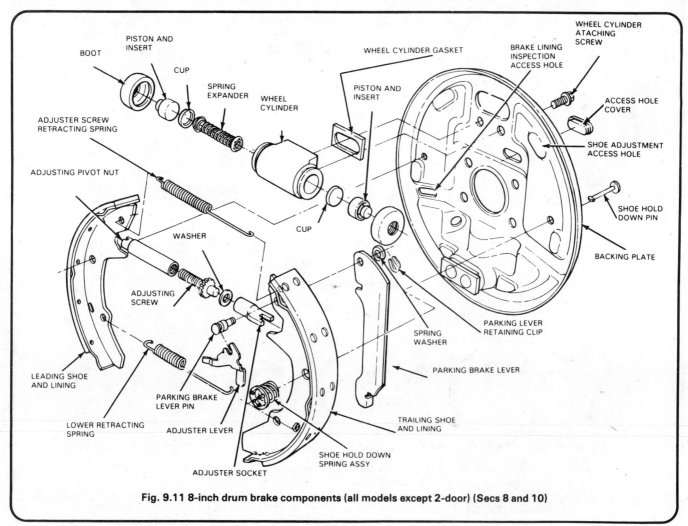

Fig. 9.11 8-inch drum brake components (all models except 2-door) (Secs 8 and 10)

10.3 Remove the hold-down spring washers by compressing the spring and aligning the slot with the tab on the end of the pin

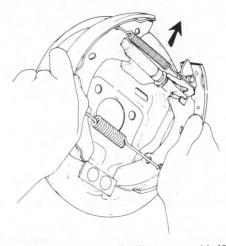

Fig. 9.12 Removing the shoe and adjuster assembly (8-in brake) (Sec 10)

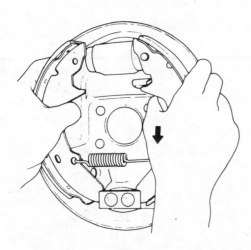

Fig. 9.13 Installing the brake shoe assembly to the backing plate (8-in brake) (Sec 10)

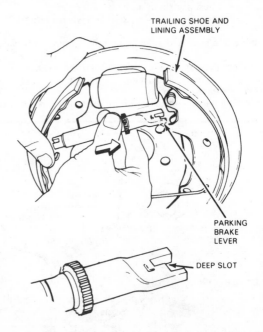

TRAILING SHOE AND LINING ASSEMBLY

PARKING BRAKE LEVER

DEEP SLOT

Fig. 9.14 Brake adjuster installation (8-in brake) (Sec 10)

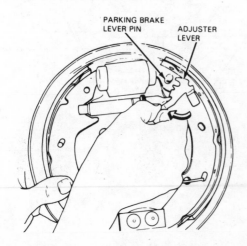

PARKING BRAKE LEVER PIN

ADJUSTER LEVER

Fig. 9.15 Installing the adjuster lever to the parking brake lever pin (8-in brake) (Sec 10)

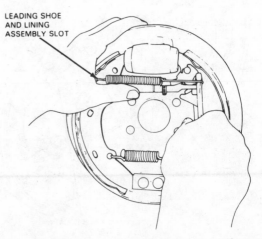

LEADING SHOE AND LINING ASSEMBLY SLOT

Fig. 9.16 Upper retracting spring installation (8-in brake) (Sec 10)

12 Connect the lower retracting spring and install the shoe assembly to the backing plate. Stretch the retracting spring as the assembly is installed downward (Fig. 9.13).

13 Insert the adjuster screw assembly between the slots in the leading and trailing shoes with the adjuster socket end slot fitting into the trailing shoe and parking brake lever. The adjuster socket blades are marked R and L and the letters must be installed in the upright position, facing the wheel cylinder and on the correct side so that the deeper slots will fit into the parking brake lever (Fig. 9.14).

14 Install the adjuster lever into the parking brake lever pin groove and trailing shoe web (Fig. 9.15).

15 Connect the upper retracting spring to the leading shoe and use a suitable spring tool to stretch the other end of the spring to install it into the notch on the adjuster lever (Fig. 9.16).

16 Install the hold-down pins, springs and washers.

17 Install the hub and drum assembly and adjust the bearings as described in Chapter 11.

18 Install the wheels, lower the vehicle and apply the brakes several times as you drive the vehicle in reverse to actuate the self-adjuster mechanism.

11 Rear wheel cylinder – removal, overhaul and installation

Caution: *Brake fluid is corrosive to paint and certain metals. Take special care in its handling during the following procedures.*

1 Remove the rear brake shoes as described in the preceding Section 5.

2 Disconnect the fluid pipeline from the wheel cylinder and cap the end of the pipe to prevent loss of fluid. A bleed screw rubber dust cap is useful for this.

3 Unscrew the two bolts which hold the wheel cylinder to the brake backplate and remove the cylinder with sealing gasket.

4 Clean away external dirt and then pull off the dust-excluding boots.

5 The pistons will probably shake out. If they do not, apply air pressure (from a tire pump) at the fluid inlet hole to eject them.

6 Examine the surfaces of the pistons and the cylinder bores for scoring or metal-to-metal rubbing areas. If evident, replace the complete cylinder assembly.

7 Where the components are in good condition, discard the rubber seals and dust excluders and obtain a repair kit.

8 Any cleaning should be done using denatured alcohol.

9 Reassemble by dipping the first piston in clean brake fluid and inserting it into the cylinder. Fit a dust excluder to it.

10 From the opposite end of the cylinder body, insert a new seal, spring, a second new seal, the second piston and the remaining dust excluder. Use only the fingers to manipulate the seals into position and make quite sure that the lips of the seals are installed in the proper direction.

11 Bolt the wheel cylinder to the backplate, reconnect the fluid line and replace the shoes.

12 Install the brake drum and wheel and lower the vehicle to the floor.

13 Bleed the hydraulic circuit (Section 2).

12 Brake drum – inspection and replacement

1 Whenever a brake drum is removed, brush out dust from it, taking care not to inhale it as it contains asbestos and is injurious to health.

2 Examine the internal friction surface of the drum. If deeply scored, or so worn that the drum has become pocketed to the width of the shoes, then the drums must be replaced with new ones.

3 Regrinding is not recommended as the internal diameter will no longer be compatible with the shoe lining contact diameter.

13 Master cylinder – removal, overhaul and installation

Caution: Brake fluid is corrosive to paint and certain metals. Take special care in its handling during the following procedures.

1 Syphon out as much fluid as possible from the master cylinder reservoir using an old battery hydrometer or a poultry baster. Do not drip the fluid onto the paintwork or it will act as an effective paint stripper.

2 Disconnect the pipelines from the master cylinder by unscrewing the unions.

3 Disconnect the leads from the level warning switch in the reservoir cap (if equipped). Remove the cap.

4 Working inside the vehicle, remove the spring clip which retains the pushrod to the pedal arm.

5 Working within the engine compartment, unbolt the master cylinder from the firewall and remove it.

6 Clean away external dirt and then detach the fluid reservoir by tilting it sideways and gently pulling. Remove the two rubber seals.

7 Secure the master cylinder carefully in a vise fitted with jaw protectors.

8 Unscrew and remove the piston stop bolt.

9 Pull the dust excluder back from around the pushrod and using snap-ring pliers, extract the snap-ring which is now exposed (Fig. 9.18).

10 Remove the pushrod, dust excluder and washer.

11 Withdraw the primary piston assembly, which will already have been partially ejected.

12 Tap the end of the master cylinder on a block of wood and eject the secondary piston assembly.

13 Examine the piston and cylinder bore surfaces for scoring or signs of metal-to-metal rubbing. A grooved or scored cylinder should be replaced with a complete new master cylinder assembly. Some models are equipped with aluminum master cylinders which are identifiable by their unpainted areas being anodized clear, red, orange or green. If the anodizing in the bore shows any wear or scoring beyond being a somewhat lighter color, replace the master cylinder with a new unit.

14 Where the components are in good condition, dismantle the primary piston by unscrewing the screw and removing the sleeve. Remove the spring, retainer, seal and the shim. Pry the second seal from the piston.

15 Dismantle the secondary piston in a similar way.

16 Discard all seals and obtain a repair kit.

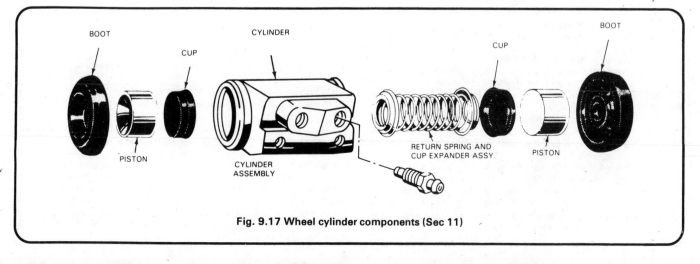

Fig. 9.17 Wheel cylinder components (Sec 11)

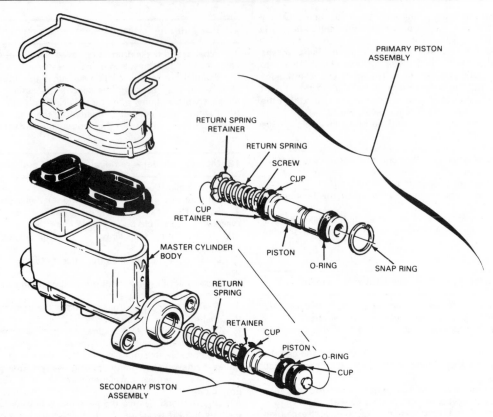

Fig. 9.18 Master cylinder components (Sec 13)

17 Cleaning of components should be done in brake fluid or methylated spirit only – nothing else.
18 Using the new seals from the repair kit, assemble the pistons, making sure that the seal lips are the correct way round.
19 Dip the piston assemblies in clean brake fluid and enter them into the cylinder bore.
20 Fit the pushrod complete with new dust excluder and secure with a new clip.
21 Engage the dust excluder with the master cylinder.
22 Depress the pushrod and screw in the stop bolt.
23 Locate the two rubber seals and push the fluid reservoir into position.
24 It is recommended that a small quantity of fluid is now poured into the reservoir and the pushrod operated several times to prime the unit.
25 Install the master cylinder by reversing the removal operations.
26 Bleed the complete hydraulic system on completion of the work (see Section 2).

14 Brake pedal – removal and installation

1 Disconnect the battery negative cable.
2 Disconnect the pushrod and slide the stoplight switch along the brake pedal pin far enough to clear the pin. Slide the switch upward and out and then remove the switch bushing.
3 In the engine compartment, loosen the master cylinder nuts and slide the pushrod and nylon washer off the pedal pin.
4 Remove the lock nut and the pivot bolt, pedal, spacer and bushing from the pedal support.
5 Prior to installation, lubricate the bushing and spacer in the pedal hub with 10W30 engine oil.
6 Place the brake pedal in the support, install the pivot bolt and nut and tighten to specification.
7 Install the nylon washer, speed control adaptor (if equipped) and black stoplight switch bushing onto the pedal pin.
8 Place the stoplight switch in position so that it straddles the pushrod with the slot on the pedal pin and outer frame just clearing the pin.
9 Slide the assembly inward and install the nylon washer and retainer.

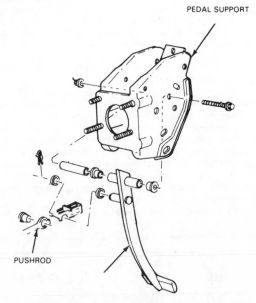

Fig. 9.19 Brake pedal installation (Sec 14)

10 Tighten the master cylinder nuts to specification.
11 Reconnect the stoplight switch and battery negative cable.

15 Brake pedal free height and travel measurement

1 If brake pedal travel is not within specifications, one or more faults in the brake system could be present. On power brake equipped models all measurements should be taken with the engine running.
2 Measure and record the distance from the sheet metal of the floorboard to the top center of the brake pedal pad. This measurement (A in Fig. 9.20) is the pedal free height and should be checked against the Specifications section.

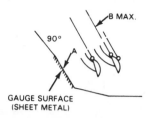

Fig. 9.20 Brake pedal free height (A) and travel (B) measurements (Sec 15)

3 Have an assistant depress the brake pedal with approximately 25 lbs pressure and measure the distance from the pedal and the floor. The difference between this and the free pedal height is the pedal travel (B in the figure) which should be checked against specifications.
4 If pedal travel is beyond specification, adjust the drum brakes by making several stops in Reverse which will actuate the automatic adjuster mechanism.
5 If brake adjustment does not bring the pedal travel within specification, remove the rear drums and inspect the brakes and adjuster mechanisms (Section 8), replacing any worn parts.
6 If travel is still excessive, bleed the braking system as described in Section 2.

16 Parking brake control assembly – removal and installation

1 Pull the assembly into the seventh notch position, remove the adjusting nut and return the handle to the released position.
2 Remove the two control assembly-to-floor pan bolts, lift the assembly and disconnect the brake light and ground wire (Fig. 9.21).
3 Remove the control assembly.
4 To install, position the adjusting rod into the assembly clevis and place the control assembly on the floor pan.
5 Install the ground wire to the forward attaching screw.
6 Install the assembly attaching bolts and tighten to specification.
7 Connect the brake light to the assembly and adjust the parking brake (Section 17).

17 Parking brake – adjustment

1 Prior to adjustment, apply approximately 100 lbs pressure to the brake pedal three times. On power brake equipped models, the engine must be running during this operation.
2 With the transaxle in Neutral, raise the vehicle and support it securely.
3 With the control in the 12th notch (two notches from full application), loosen the adjusting nut just sufficiently to eliminate rear brake drag with the control fully released.
4 Lower the vehicle and check the parking brake for proper operation.

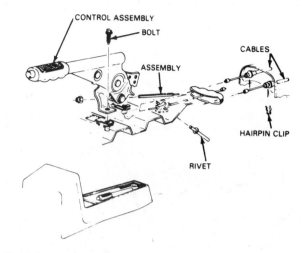

Fig. 9.21 Parking brake control assembly components (Sec 16)

18 Parking brake cables – replacement

Primary cable
1 Raise the vehicle and support it securely.
2 Extract the spring clip and clevis pin and disconnect the primary cable from the equaliser.
3 Working inside the vehicle, disconnect the cable from the parking brake control lever, again by removal of clip and pin. Drift out the cable guide to the rear and withdraw the cable through the floor pan.
4 Installation is a reversal of removal. Adjust the parking brake if necessary as described in Section 17.

Secondary cable
5 Unlock the adjuster nut from its sleeve by prying their shoulders apart.
6 Slacken the parking brake cable by turning the adjuster nut.
7 Release the cable connector from its body guide by extracting the spring clip and passing the inner cable through the slit in the guide.
8 Now disconnect the cable from its body guide on the right-hand side of the vehicle.
9 Separate the cable assembly/equaliser from the primary cable by extracting the spring clip and clevis pin.
10 Release the cable from the body guides.
11 Remove the rear wheels and the brake drums (Section 8).
12 Release the shoe hold-down spring so that the shoe can be swivelled and the parking brake lever unclipped from the relay lever.
13 Remove the cable ends through the brake backplate and withdraw the complete cable assembly from the vehicle.
14 Installation is a reversal of removal. Grease the cable groove in the equalizer and adjust the parking brake as described in Section 17.

Chapter 10 Chassis electrical system

Refer to Chapter 13 for specifications and information related to 1983 thru 1985 models

Contents

Specifications

Lamp	**Bulb number**
Front parking and turn signal	1157
Headlamp	H6054
Backup	1168
Rear license plate	168
Rear parking, stop and side marker	1157
Cargo and dome	906
Dome/map	906/1816
Engine compartment	906
PRNDL shift selector	1445
Heater	161
Air conditioner control	1892

1 General description

The electrical system is of the 12 volt negative ground type.

Power for the lighting system and all electrical accessories is supplied by a lead/acid-type battery which is charged by an alternator. Circuits are protected from overload by a system of fuses and fuse links.

This Chapter covers repair and service procedures for various lighting and electrical components not associated with the engine. Information on the battery, alternator, voltage regulator and starter motor can be found in Chapter 5.

Note: *Whenever the electrical system is worked on, the negative battery cable should be disconnected to prevent electrical shorts and/or fires.*

2 Fuses

The electrical circuits of the car are protected by a combination of fuses, circuit breakers and fusible links.

The fuse panel or fuse box is located in most models underneath the dashboard, on the left side of the vehicle. It is easily accessible for fuse inspection or replacement without completely removing the box from its mountings.

Each of the fuses is designed to protect a specific circuit, and the various circuits are identified on the fuse panel itself.

If an electrical component has failed, your first check should be the fuse. A fuse which has 'blown' can be readily identified by inspecting the element inside of the glass tube. If this metal element is broken, the fuse is inoperable and must be replaced with a new one.

When removing and installing fuses it is important that metal objects are not used to pry the fuse in or out of the holder. Plastic fuse pullers are available for this purpose.

It is also important that the correct fuse be installed. The different electrical circuits need varying amounts of protection, indicated by the amperage rating on the fuse.

Caution: *At no time should the fuse be bypassed by using metal or foil. Serious damage to the electrical system could result.*

If the replacement fuse immediately fails do not replace again until the cause of the problem is isolated and corrected. In most cases this will be a short circuit in the wiring system caused by a broken or deteriorated wire.

3 Fuse links

1   In addition to fuses, the wiring system incorporates fuse links for overload protection. These links are used in circuits which are not ordinarily fused.

2   Fuse links are several wire gauges smaller than the circuit they are incorporated into. The fuse links are green or black and have a molded color identification tag. The tag color identifications are as follows:

Green – 14 gauge
Orange – 16 gauge
Yellow – 17 gauge
Red – 18 gauge
Blue – 20 gauge

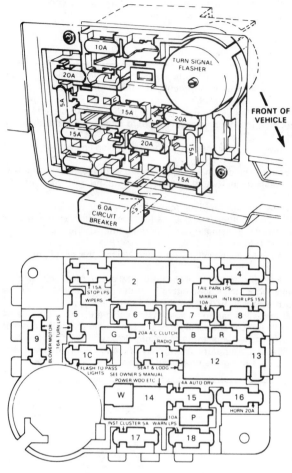

Fig. 10.1 Fuse and circuit breaker panel (Sec 2)

1 Stop lamps, hazard warning lamps 15 amp fuse
2 Windshield wiper, washer pump, interval wiper
   6 amp circuit breaker
3 Not used
4 Tail, parking, side marker lamps, instrument cluster
   illumination lamp, license lamp 15 amp fuse standard,
   10 amp fuse console
5 Turn signal, back-up lamps 15 amp fuse
6 Air conditioner clutch, heated rear window relay,
   liftgate release, speed control module, rear wiper/washer,
   digital clock display module, air conditioner throttle
   positioner 20 amp fuse
7 Not used
8 Courtesy lamps, key warning buzzer, clock 15 amp fuse
9 Air conditioner blower motor - 30 amp fuse
   Heater blower motor - 15 amp fuse
10 Flash-to-pass, 20 amp fuse
11 Radio, tape player, premium sound with one amplifier,
   15 amp fuse
12 Not used
13 Instrument cluster illumination, radio, climate control,
   clock, ash tray, diagnostic module 5 amp fuse
14 Not used
15 Not used
16 Horn, front cigar lighter, 20 amp fuse
17 Not used
18 Warning indicator lamps, low fuel module, auto lamp
   system, dual timer buzzer, tachometer 10 amp fuse

3 Fuse links cannot be repaired. A new fuse link of the same gauge,
length and insulation must be used to replace a blown link. This
process is as follows:
4 Disconnect the battery ground cable.
5 Disconnect the fuse link or fuse link eyelet terminal from the

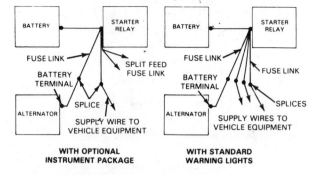

Fig. 10.2 Fuse link locations (Sec 3)

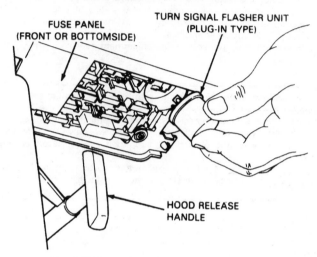

Fig. 10.3 Turn signal flasher location (Sec 4)

battery terminal of the starter relay.
6 Determine which circuit is damaged and the cause of the overload.
7 Cut the damaged fuse link from the circuit and discard it. Strip the
insulation from the circuit wire back from the cut approximately $\frac{1}{2}$ inch.
8 Determine the proper replacement fuse link and crimp it into place
in the wiring circuit. It may be necessary to cut one or both eyelets off
the fuse link when reinstalling.
9 Use a resin core solder at each end of the new link to obtain a
good solder joint.
10 Use plenty of electrical tape around the soldered joint. No exposed
wiring should show.
11 Connect a fuse link at the starter solenoid. Connect the battery
ground cable. Test the circuit for proper operation.

4 Turn signal and hazard flasher – removal and installation

1 The turn signal and emergency flasher units are located directly
opposite one another on the top and bottom of the fuse panel. While
similar in appearance, the two units are not interchangeable. The turn
signal flasher is color coded blue while the emergency flasher is
aluminum colored.
2 To remove the flasher unit, grasp it securely and pull outward to
unplug it.
3 To install, align the flasher unit contact prongs and the fuse panel
slots and press into place.

5 Horn – fault testing

1 If horn proves inoperable, the first check should be the fuse. A
blown fuse can be readily identified at the fuse panel in the left side of
the instrument panel.
2 If the fuse is in good condition, disconnect the electrical lead at the
horn. Run jumper wires from the battery positive and negative
terminals to the horn terminals (Fig. 10.4).

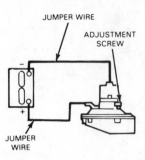

Fig. 10.4 Horn test connection (Sec 5)

3　If the horn does not work and there is no evidence of spark at the battery terminal, turn the adjusting screw $\frac{1}{4}$ to $\frac{3}{8}$ of a turn counter-clockwise, making sure to secure the adjustment screw by clinching the housing extension with pliers.

4　If the horn does not sound after adjustment, replace it with a new unit.

6　Headlight sealed beam unit – removal and installation

1　Remove the headlamp screws, door and retaining ring. Make sure that the *retaining* screws and not the *adjustment* screws are removed.

2　Pull the headlight forward and support it as you disconnect the wiring plug.

3　Install the plug to the new headlight and position it by locating the glass tabs at the back in the slots in the receptacle.

4　Install the headlight retaining ring, screws and door.

5　Check the headlight alignment.

7　Headlight – alignment

1　It is always advisable to have the headlights aligned on proper optical beam setting equipment but if this is not available the following procedure may be used.

2　Position the car on level ground 10 feet (3.048 meters) in front of a dark wall or board. The wall or board must be at right-angles to the center-line of the car.

3　Draw a vertical line on the board or wall in line with the center-line of the car.

4　Bounce the car on its suspension to ensure correct settlement and then measure the height between the ground and the centre of the headlights.

5　Draw a horizontal line across the board or wall at this measured height. On this horizontal line mark a cross on either side of the vertical center-line, the distance between the center of the light unit and the center of the car.

6　Remove the headlight rims and switch the headlights onto full beam.

7　By careful adjusting of the horizontal and vertical adjusting screws on each light, align the centers of each beam onto the crosses which were previously marked on the horizontal line.

8　Bounce the car on its suspension again and check that the beams return to the correct position. At the same time check the operation of the dipswitch. Replace the headlight rims.

9　This is a temporary, emergency operation until the headlights can be adjusted using the proper equipment.

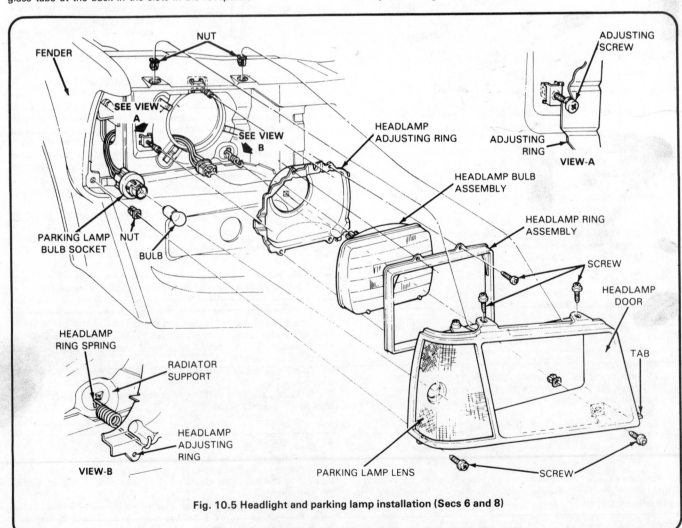

Fig. 10.5 Headlight and parking lamp installation (Secs 6 and 8)

8 Bulb replacement – front end

Parking lamp

1   Remove the headlight door and parking lamp lens assembly (Fig. 10.5).
2   Turn the parking lamp bulb socket counterclockwise and remove from the headlight door.
3   Push the bulb inward, turn it counterclockwise and remove.
4   To install, line up the retainer pins, insert the bulb into the socket and press inward as you turn clockwise to lock it in position.
5   Install the headlight door.

Side marker lamp

6   From inside the engine compartment, twist the bulb socket and remove it from the fender (photo).
7   Press the bulb inward and turn it counterclockwise to remove it.
8   Install a new bulb to the socket and then install the socket to the fender.

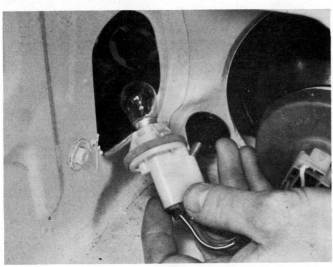

8.6 The front side marker lamp socket is accessible through the fender from the engine compartment

9 Bulb replacement – rear end

2-door and station wagon models

1   The various rear lamp bulbs are accessible from inside the rear compartment. It may be necessary to remove trim panels to reach the lamp.
2   Remove the bulb socket by turning it counterclockwise to its stop and withdraw the bulb.
3   To install, line up the retainer pins, insert the bulb and rotate it clockwise to lock it.
4   Reinstall any trim panels which were removed.

4-door models

5   Remove the rear lamp housing and screws and pull the lens assembly outward.
6   Rotate the bulb socket counterclockwise and remove it.
7   Replace the bulb as described in Sections 2 and 3.
8   Reinstall the lens assembly.

License plate bulb (all models)

9   Remove the lamp attaching screws and push in on the socket to remove it from the lamp assembly.
10 Remove the bulb from the socket by pushing in and turning it counterclockwise.
11 Install the new bulb to the socket and then install the socket to the lamp.
12 Install the lamp assembly.

Back-up lamp

13 On 2-door and 5-door models, the backup lamp bulb is replaced using the same procedure described in steps 2 and 3.
14 On 4-door models, remove the backup lamp lens bottom screw and remove the lamp assembly.
15 Pull the socket from the assembly, replace the bulb and reinstall the socket.
16 Install the lamp assembly.

10 Interior lamps – bulb replacement

Dome lamp

1   Grasp the dome lamp lens and pull downward on the right side of the assembly to remove it.
2   Spread the assembly apart and remove the bulb.
3   Replace the bulb, slide the socket into place and push the lamp assembly back into position.
4   On the optional combination dome/map lamp, the dome lens is removed by pressing inward on the sides. The map lamp bulb is removed by unscrewing the lens.

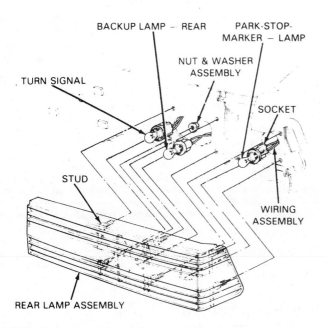

Fig. 10.6 Rear lamp bulb location (2-door models) (Sec 9)

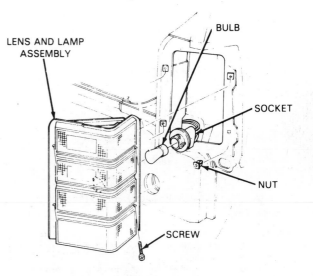

Fig. 10.7 Taillight bulb installation (Sec 9)

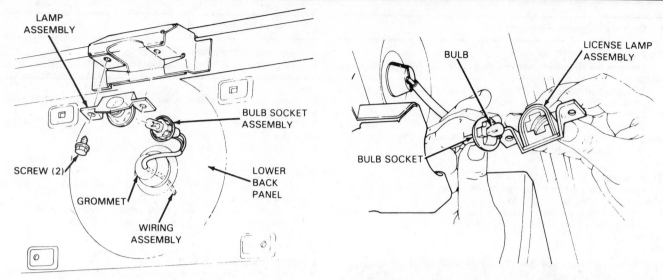

Fig. 10.8 Rear license plate lamp removal (2-door and wagon) (Sec 9)

Fig. 10.9 License lamp bulb removal (2-door and wagon) (Sec 9)

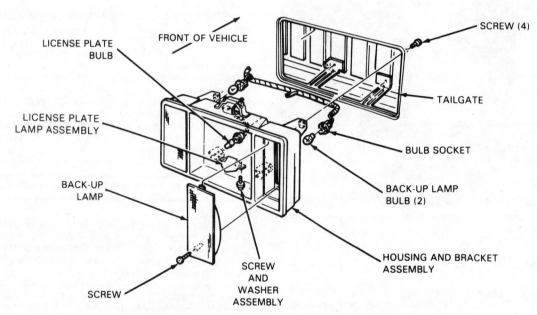

Fig. 10.10 Backup and license lamp layout (4-door) (Sec 9)

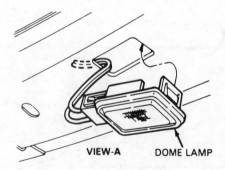

Fig. 10.11 Dome lamp removal (Sec 10)

Cargo lamp

5   The rear cargo area lamp on the 4-door models is the same design as the standard dome lamp.

6   On 2-door and 5-door models the lamp is removed by pulling down on the top.

Transaxle selector control lamp bulb

7   On floor-mounted controls, remove the screw retaining the console cover and remove the cover.

8   Remove the selector cover and dial indicator.

9   Lift the cover assembly off and turn the bulb socket counterclockwise to remove it.

10   Replace the bulb and reinstall the selector cover.

11   On console mounted selectors, remove the finish panel and quadrant bezel and place the selector lever in its first position. Remove the lamp socket and bulb.

12   Replace the bulb and reinstall socket, finish panel and quadrant bezel.

Glove compartment lamp

13   Grasp the bulb with your thumb and forefinger and pull it out of the lock striker assembly.

---

11   Bulb replacement – instrument panel

1   The instrument panel cluster panel must be removed to gain

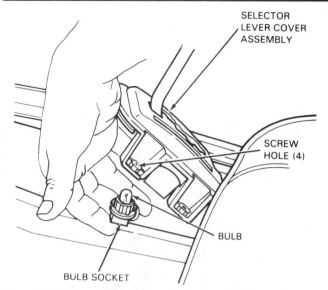

Fig. 10.12 Transaxle selector control lamp bulb replacement (Sec 10)

access to the instrument panel bulbs (Section 14).

2 Some instrument panel bulb replacement requires the removal of the printed circuit (Section 15).

12 Headlight switch – removal and installation

1 Disconnect the battery negative cable.

2 Pull the control knob to the On position.

3 Reach under the instrument panel and press the release button on the switch. With the release button pushed in, pull the control knob out of the switch (Fig. 10.13).

4 Unscrew the bezel nut which retains the switch to the instrument panel.

5 Detach the switch, disconnect the electrical connector and remove the switch.

6 To reinstall, connect the electrical plug to the connector, place the switch in position on the instrument panel and install the bezel nut.

7 Insert the knob and shaft into the switch, rotating it slightly until a click is heard.

8 Connect the battery ground cable and check the switch for proper operation.

13 Windshield wiper switch – removal and installation

1 Disconnect the battery negative cable.

2 Remove the steering column shrouds and unplug the electrical connector.

3 Peel the foam shield back to gain access to the hex-headed retaining screws. Remove the screws and lift off the switch.

4 To install, place the switch in position, install the screws and reinstall the foam shield.

5 Plug in the electrical connector and install the steering column shrouds.

6 Reconnect the battery negative cable.

14 Instrument cluster – removal and installation

1 Disconnect the battery negative cable.

2 Remove the steering column shrouds.

3 Remove the finish panel.

4 Remove the instrument cluster retaining screws (Fig. 10.14).

5 Disconnect the speedometer cable by reaching under the dash and pressing on the flat plastic cable quick-disconnect.

6 Lift the cluster away from the instrument panel, unplug the instrument cluster connector and remove the cluster from the vehicle.

7 Installation is the reverse of removal.

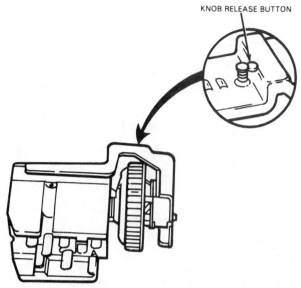

Fig. 10.13 Headlight switch release knob location (Sec 12)

15 Instrument printed circuit – removal and installation

1 The printed circuit that comprises the 'wiring' of the instrument panel should be handled as little as possible to avoid damage to the circuit sheet.

2 Disconnect the battery negative cable.

3 Remove the instrument cluster as described in Section 14.

4 Unsnap the printed circuit from the instrument voltage regulator.

5 Remove the illumination and indicator assemblies.

6 Remove the screws retaining the cluster resistor and remove the resistor.

7 Remove the fuel gauge attaching nuts and remove the printed circuit.

8 To install, place the printed circuit over the backplate locating pins.

9 Install the illumination and indicator assemblies and fuel gauge attaching nuts.

10 Install the instrument cluster resistor.

11 Place the instrument voltage regulator in position, install the attaching screw and snap the printed circuit to the regulator.

12 Install the instrument cluster as described in Section 14.

13 Connect the battery negative cable.

16 Speedometer cable – removal and installation

1 Disconnect the cable at the speedometer head.

2 From the upper end of the cable casing, pull out the speedometer core. Speed sensor equipped vehicles have an upper and a lower cable.

3 If the speedometer core is broken, it will be necessary to unbolt the lower end of the cable casing at the transaxle and remove the broken piece of core from the casing.

4 To install, insert the core into the speedometer casing from the speedometer head end.

5 Connect the speedometer casing to the head and (if removed) install the hex nut to the casing at the transaxle.

17 Speedometer head – removal and installation

Note: *US Federal law requires that the odometer in any replacement speedometer must register the same mileage as that on the removed speedometer.*

1 Disconnect the battery negative cable.

2 Disconnect the speedometer cable and remove the instrument cluster (Section 14).

3 Remove the lens assembly from the cluster.

4 Remove the gauge assembly, followed by the speedometer head assembly, from the cluster backplate.

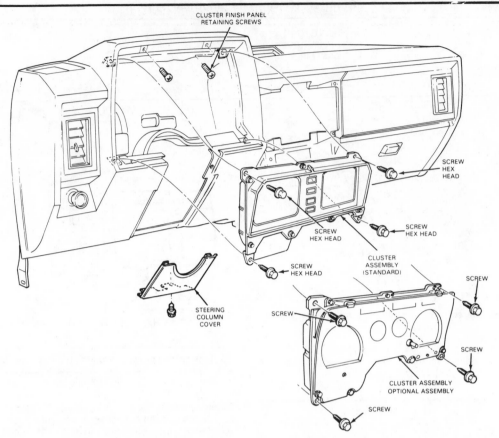

Fig. 10.14 Instrument cluster installation (Sec 14)

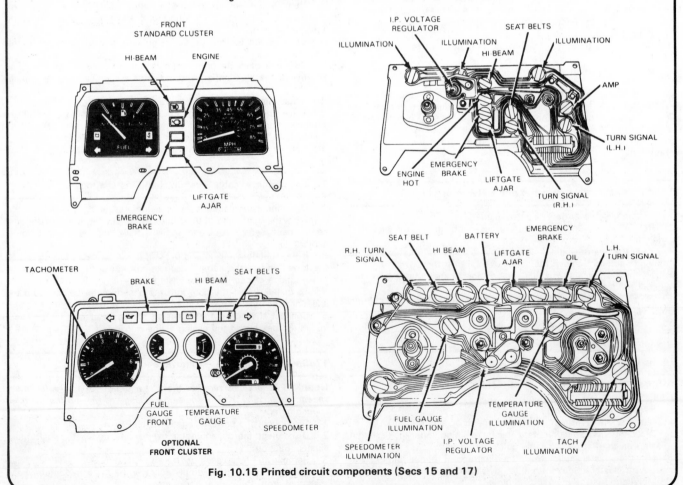

Fig. 10.15 Printed circuit components (Secs 15 and 17)

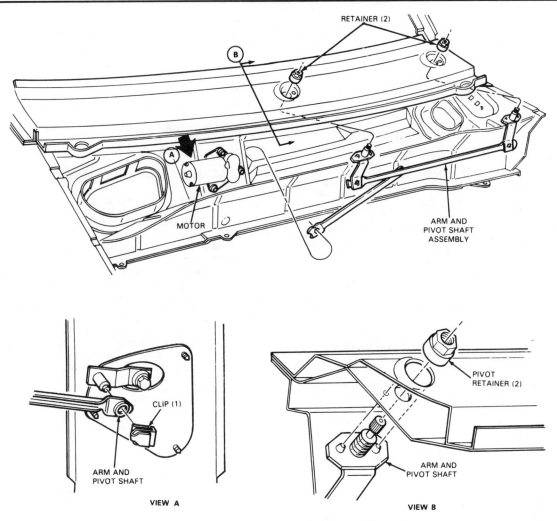

Fig. 10.16 Wiper motor and linkage layout (Sec 18)

5   Install the speedometer head onto the cluster backplate followed by the gauge assembly.
6   Install the cluster lens assembly.
7   Reinstall the instrument cluster.
8   Reconnect the battery negative cable.

18 Windshield wiper motor – removal and installation

1   Disconnect the battery negative cable.
2   In the engine compartment, remove the water shield cover from the passenger side of the cowl.
3   Disconnect the wiper motor electrical connector.
4   Disconnect the clip on the wiper operating arm.
5   Remove the three screws attaching the motor to the bracket (Fig. 10.16).
6   Disconnect the wiper arm from the motor, remove the three bolts and withdraw the motor from the bracket.
7   Installation is the reverse of removal.

19 Windshield washer assembly – removal and installation

1   Use a small screwdriver to unlock the tabs and disconnect the electrical connector. Remove the retaining screws and lift the washer reservoir and motor assembly from the vehicle (Fig. 10.17).
2   Drain the reservoir by disconnecting the hose with a small screwdriver.
3   Pry out the retaining ring which holds the motor in the reservoir.
4   Grasp one wall around the electrical terminals with a pair of pliers and pull the motor, seal and impeller assembly out. If the impeller and

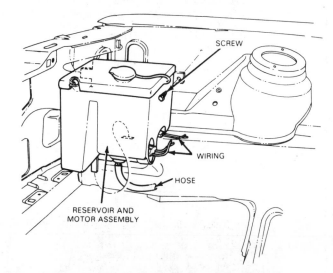

Fig. 10.17 Windshield washer layout (Sec 19)

seal become separated they can be reassembled. Inspect the reservoir for foreign matter before installing the old motor in a new reservoir.
5   Prior to installation, lubricate the outside of the seal with powdered graphite for ease of assembly (Fig. 10.18).
6   Position the small projection on the motor end cap with the slot in the reservoir and assemble so that the seal seats against the bottom of the motor cavity.

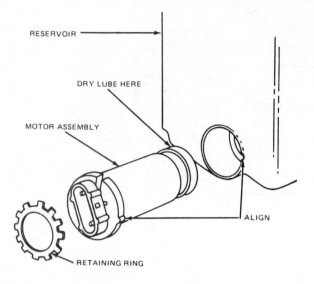

RESERVOIR

DRY LUBE HERE

MOTOR ASSEMBLY

ALIGN

RETAINING RING

Fig. 10.18 Windshield washer motor installation (Sec 19)

7   Use a 1 inch twelve-point socket to hand press the retaining ring against the motor end plate.
8   Fill the reservoir and check for leaks.
9   The cowl mounted nozzle jets can be adjusted for the proper spray pattern by carefully bending them with needle-nosed pliers, taking care not to crimp them.

20 Rear window wiper motor – removal and installation

1   Disconnect the battery negative cable and remove the wiper arm and blade assembly.
2   Remove the pivot shaft nut, spacer and seals.
3   On 2-door models, remove the inner trim panel. On 4-door models, remove the license plate housing and disconnect the lamp wiring.
4   On 2-door models, remove the three retaining screws attaching the motor and bracket, disconnect the wiring connector and remove the entire assembly. On 4-door models, remove the motor and bracket retaining screws, disconnect the motor and remove it.
5   Installation is the reverse of removal.

21 Rear washer reservoir and pump motor – removal and installation

1   On 4-door models, remove the right quarter trim panel. On 2-door and wagon models, remove the left quarter trim panel.
2   Remove the retaining screws and remove the reservoir.
3   Disconnect the supply hose, nozzle hose and electrical connector from the reservoir.
4   Pry the motor assembly out of the reservoir with a small screw driver and remove the screen and seal.
5   Flush the reservoir out with clean water and inspect for any foreign matter.
6   Prior to installation, lubricate the outside of the motor seal with powdered graphite.
7   Install the screen and then push the motor seal fully into the cavity.
8   Line up the motor with the cavity and insert it, using only hand pressure.
9   Reconnect the supply hose, nozzle hose and electrical connector and install the reservoir.
10 Fill the reservoir and install the trim panel.

22 Radio or tape player – removal and installation

1   Disconnect the battery negative cable.
2   Remove the air conditioning floor duct (if equipped).
3   Disconnect the leads to the speaker, antenna and power source.
4   Remove the control knobs and control shaft nuts, washers and discs.
5   Remove the ash tray.
6   Slide the radio forward while tipping the rear downward and then remove from the instrument panel.
7   Install the rear support and slide the unit into the instrument panel.
8   Install the control shaft nuts, washers and discs.
9   Install the ash tray.
10 Connect the power, speaker and antenna leads.
11 Reinstall the air conditioning floor duct (if removed) and install the control knobs.
12 Connect the battery negative cable and check for proper operation.

23 Stoplight switch – removal and installation

Standard brakes
1   Disconnect the wiring harness at the switch, first lifting the locking tab.

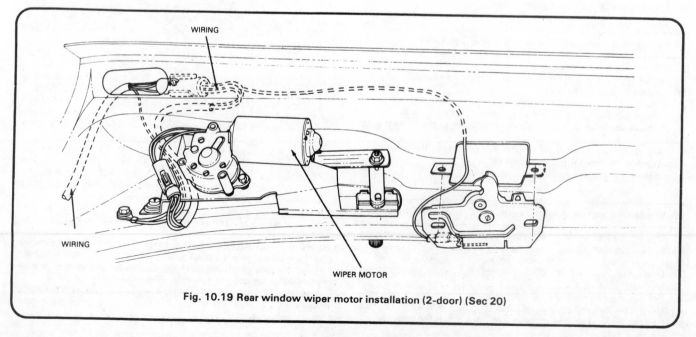

WIRING

WIRING

WIPER MOTOR

Fig. 10.19 Rear window wiper motor installation (2-door) (Sec 20)

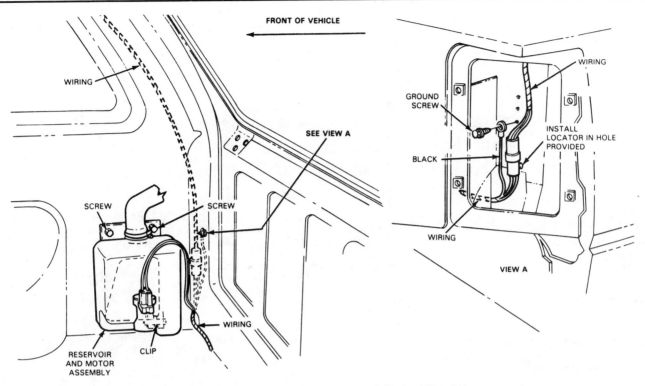

Fig. 10.20 Rear window washer reservoir (4-door) (Sec 21)

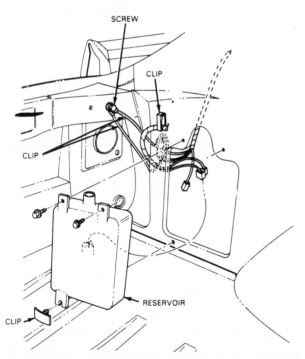

Fig. 10.21 2-door and wagon rear washer installation (Sec 21)

2   Remove the hairpin retainer and slide the switch, pushrod, nylon washer and black bushing away from the pedal and remove the switch.
3   To install, place the switch with the U-shaped side nearest the pedal and directly over or under the pin. The black bushing must be in the pushrod eyelet with the washer face on the side closest to the retaining pin.
4   Slide the switch up or down so that the master cylinder pushrod and black bushing are trapped and then push the switch firmly downward.
5   Install the plastic washer and hairpin retainer.
6   Connect the wiring connector.

Power brakes
7   Disconnect the battery negative cable and the switch wiring connector.
8   Remove the hairpin retainer and slide the switch sufficiently to clear the pin so that the switch can be removed (Fig. 10.23).
9   To install, place the switch so that it straddles the pushrod with its slot on the pedal pin and the outer frame hole just clear of the pin.
10 Slide the switch downward onto the pin and pushrod and then inward toward the brake pedal arm.
11 Install the nylon washer and hairpin retainer.
12 Connect the switch connector and battery negative cable.

24 Grid-type heated rear window defogger – testing and repair

1   The rear window defogger consists of a rear window with a number of horizontal elements that are baked onto the glass.
2   Small breaks in the element system can be successfully repaired without removing the rear window.
3   To test the grids for proper operation, start the engine and turn on the system.
4   Use a strong light inside the vehicle to visually inspect the wire grid from the outside. A broken wire will appear as a brown spot.
5   From inside the car, use a 12-volt DC voltmeter and contact the broad reddish brown strips on the back window. The meter reading should be 10 to 13 volts. A lower voltage reading indicates a loose connection on the ground side of the glass.
6   Make a good ground contact with the meter's negative lead.
7   Touch each grid line at its midpoint with the positive lead. The reading should be approximately 6 volts, indicating the line is good.
8   No reading indicates that the line is broken between the midpoint of the line and the side.
9   A reading of 12 volts means that the circuit is broken between the midpoint and passenger side or the grounding pigtail on the passenger side of the glass is loose.
10 Once the area needing repair is determined, it is recommended that a grid repair kit be obtained from a dealer.
11 Clean the area to be repaired with alcohol to remove dirt, grease or other foreign material.
12 With the area clean and dry, mark the spot to be repaired on the outside of the glass.
13 Shake the bottle of grid repair compound for at least one minute

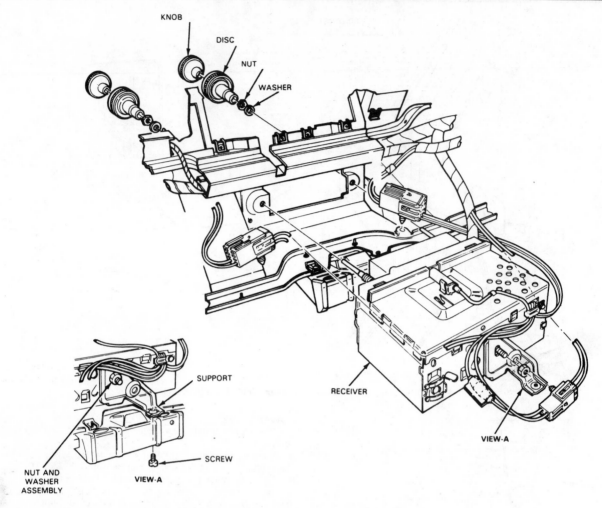

Fig. 10.22 Radio or tape player installation (Sec 22)

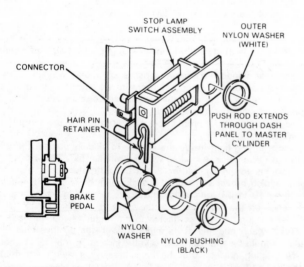

Fig. 10.23 Stoplight switch installation (Sec 23)

and shake it frequently during use. The compound and the glass must be at room temperature.

14 Mask the area above and below the break with electrical tape so that the gap is the same as the width of the grid.

15 Apply several smooth continuous strokes of the coating, using the brush applicator cap. The repair coating should extend $\frac{1}{4}$ in on both sides of the break (Fig. 10.24).

16 Allow the repair to dry for at least 3 minutes and remove the tape. The repair can be energized within 3 minutes. Optimum hardness occurs after 24 hours.

25 Digital clock – setting

1 After power to the clock has been cut off and returned, the clock will display all zeros and will have to be reset.

Time

2 To reset the time, turn the ignition switch to the Accessories or On position and pull out the Time button (Fig. 10.25).

3 Use a ballpoint pen or similar instrument to push the recessed button (1 in the figure) in to advance the hours. Make sure to note whether an A (AM) or P (PM) appears as this affects the date portion of the clock.

4 With the hours set, push in the minutes button (2 in the figure) and advance the minutes.

5 With the proper time displayed, push the Time button to start the clock.

Date

6 With the set and the ignition switch still in the Accessories or On position, pull out the Date button (Fig. 10.25).

7 Push the recessed button (1 in the Figure) in to advance the month.

8 After setting the month, push in the second recessed button (2 in the Figure) to advance the date.

9 With the proper month and date displayed, push the Date button back in.

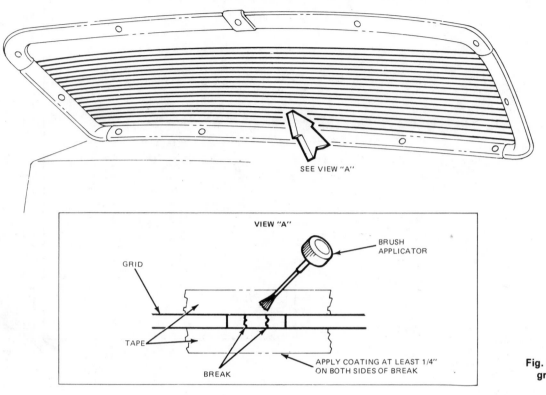

Fig. 10.24 Rear window grid repair (Sec 24)

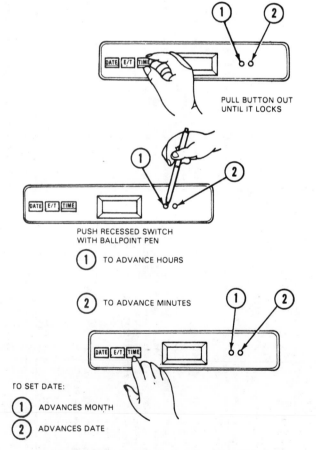

Fig. 10.25 Digital clock resetting (Sec 25)

Elapsed time

10 Pull out on the E/T button which will zero the E/T time. It may be necessary to first push the button in to unlock it.

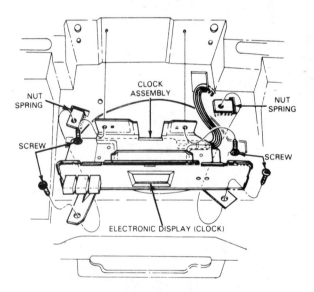

Fig. 10.26 Digital clock removal or installation (Sec 26)

11 Push the E/T button in to display elapsed time and then push it again for time of day. The elapsed time will display the minutes and seconds for 60 seconds and will then revert to displaying the hours and minutes.

26 Digital clock – removal and installation

1 Disconnect the battery negative cable.
2 Remove the radio speaker and grille.
3 Remove the three retaining screws, remove the clock and disconnect the wiring connector.
4 To install, position the clock, install the retaining screws and plug in the wiring connector.
5 Reconnect the battery negative cable.
6 Reset the clock (Section 25).

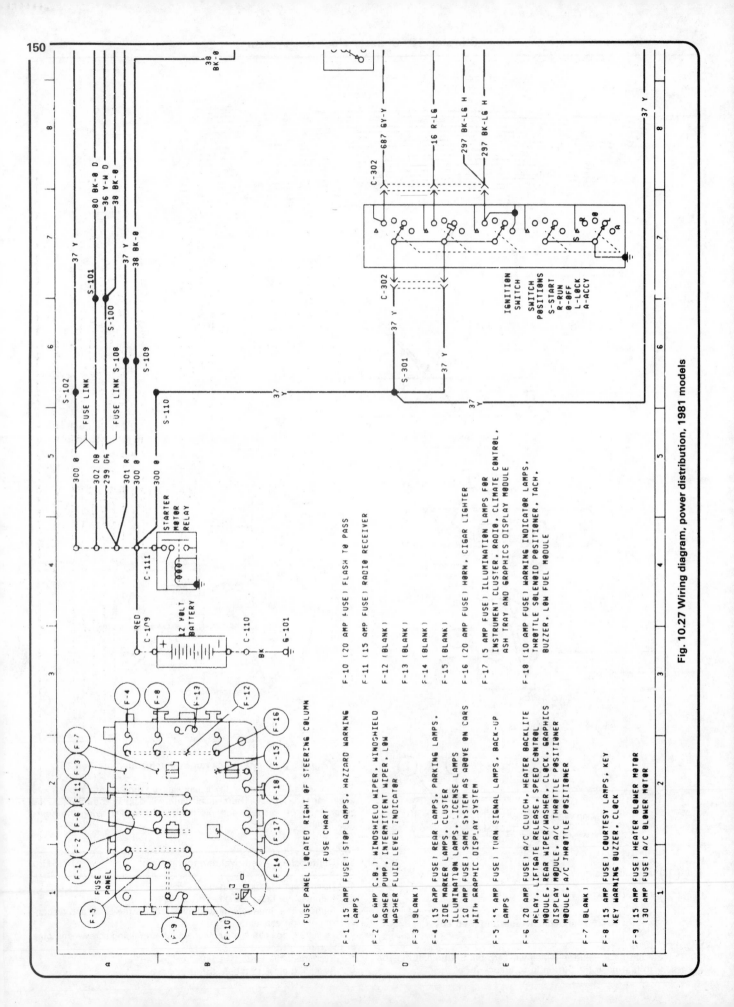

Fig. 10.27 Wiring diagram, power distribution, 1981 models

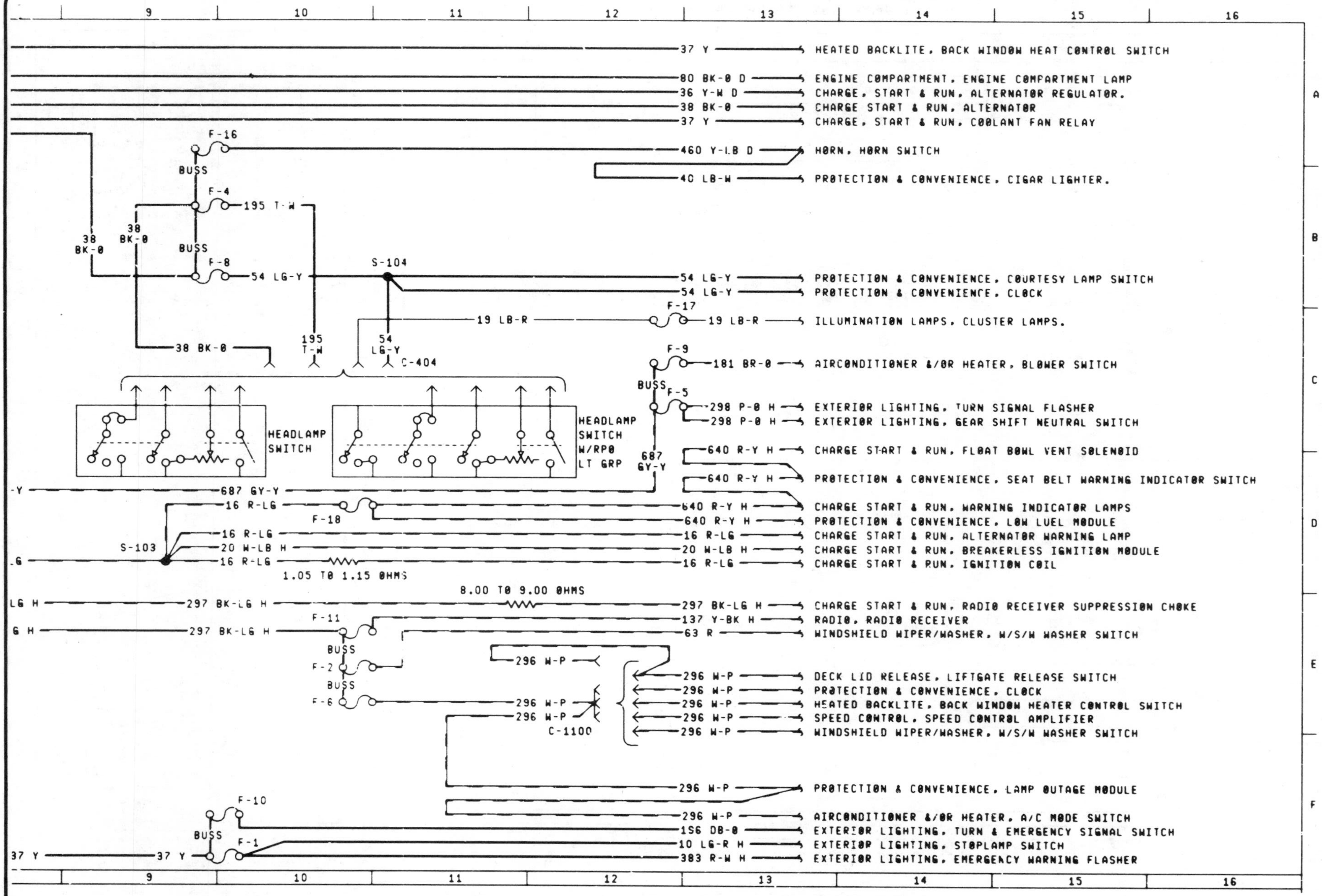

Fig. 10.27 Wiring diagram, power distribution (cont.), 1981 models

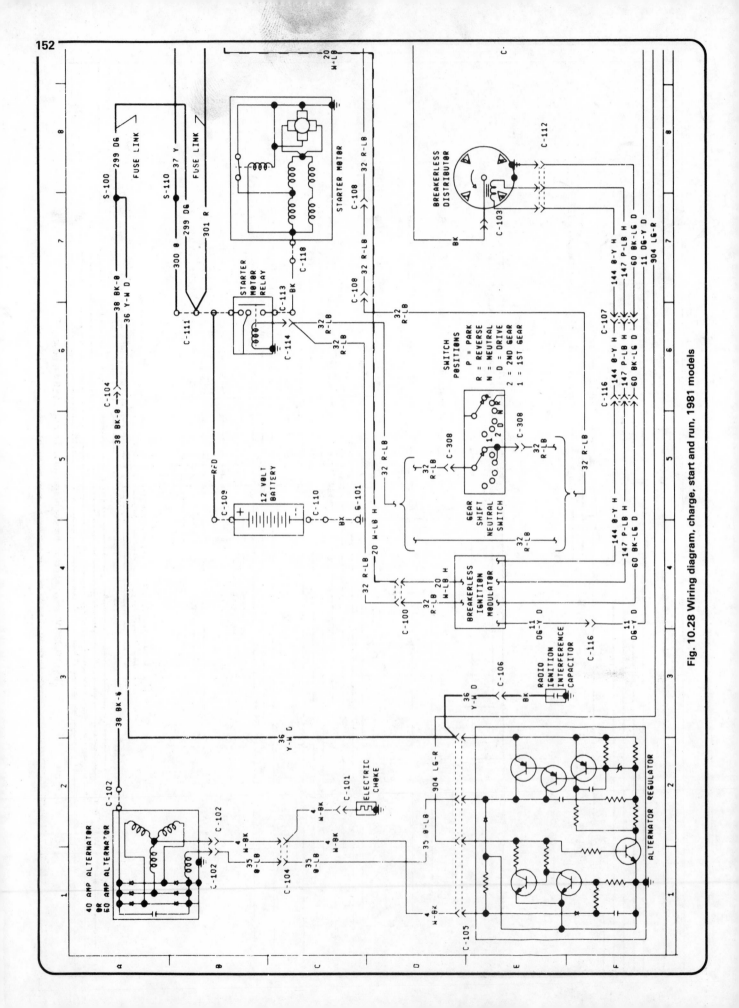

Fig. 10.28 Wiring diagram, charge, start and run, 1981 models

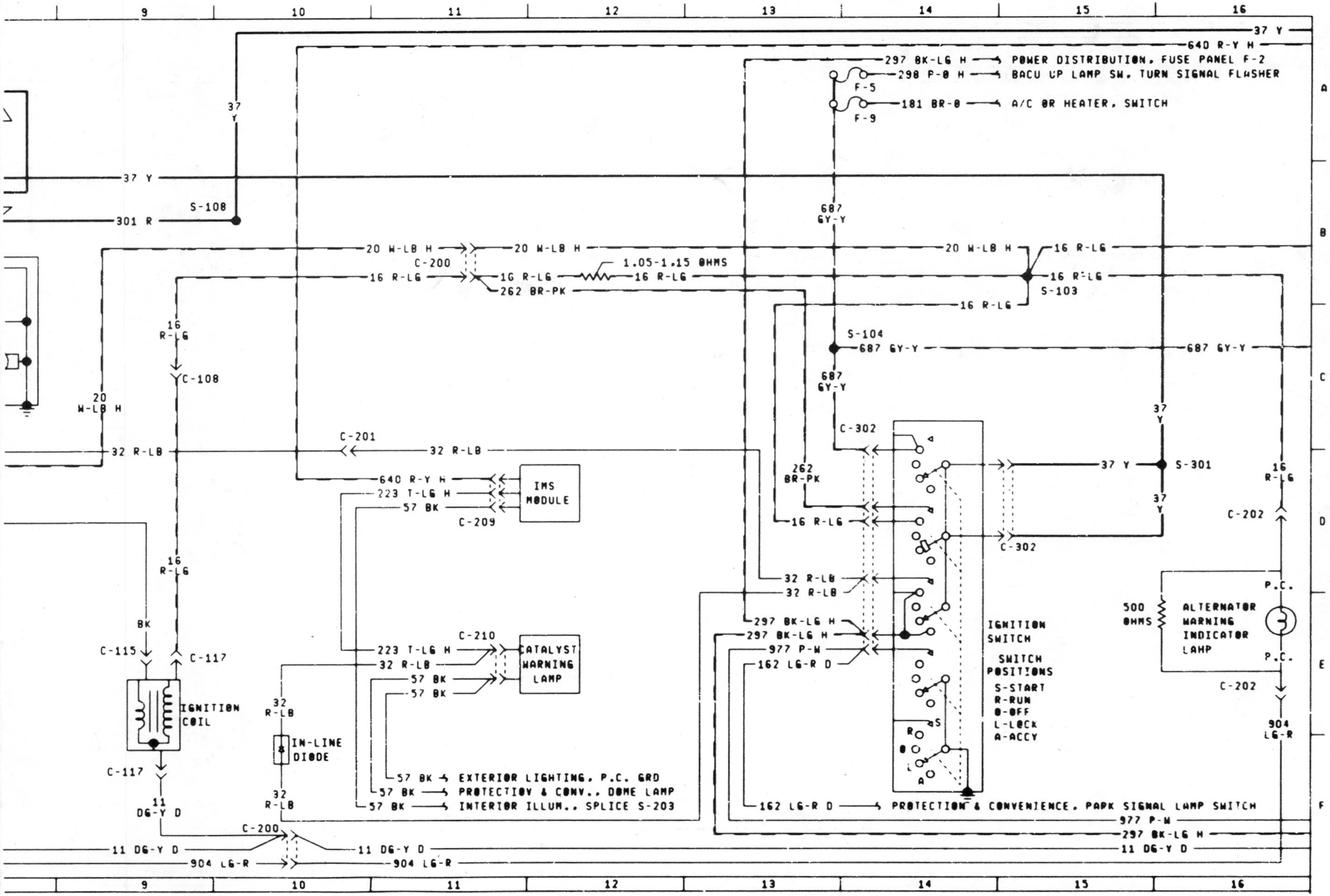

Fig. 10.28 Wiring diagram, charge, start and run (cont.), 1981 models

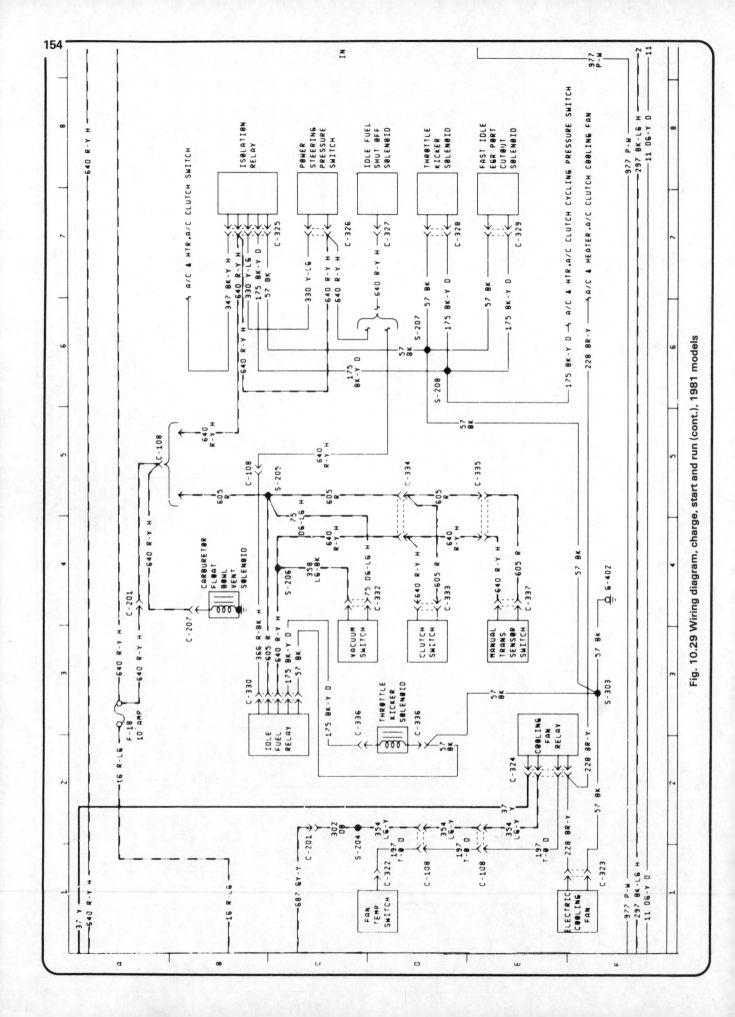

Fig. 10.29 Wiring diagram, charge, start and run (cont.), 1981 models

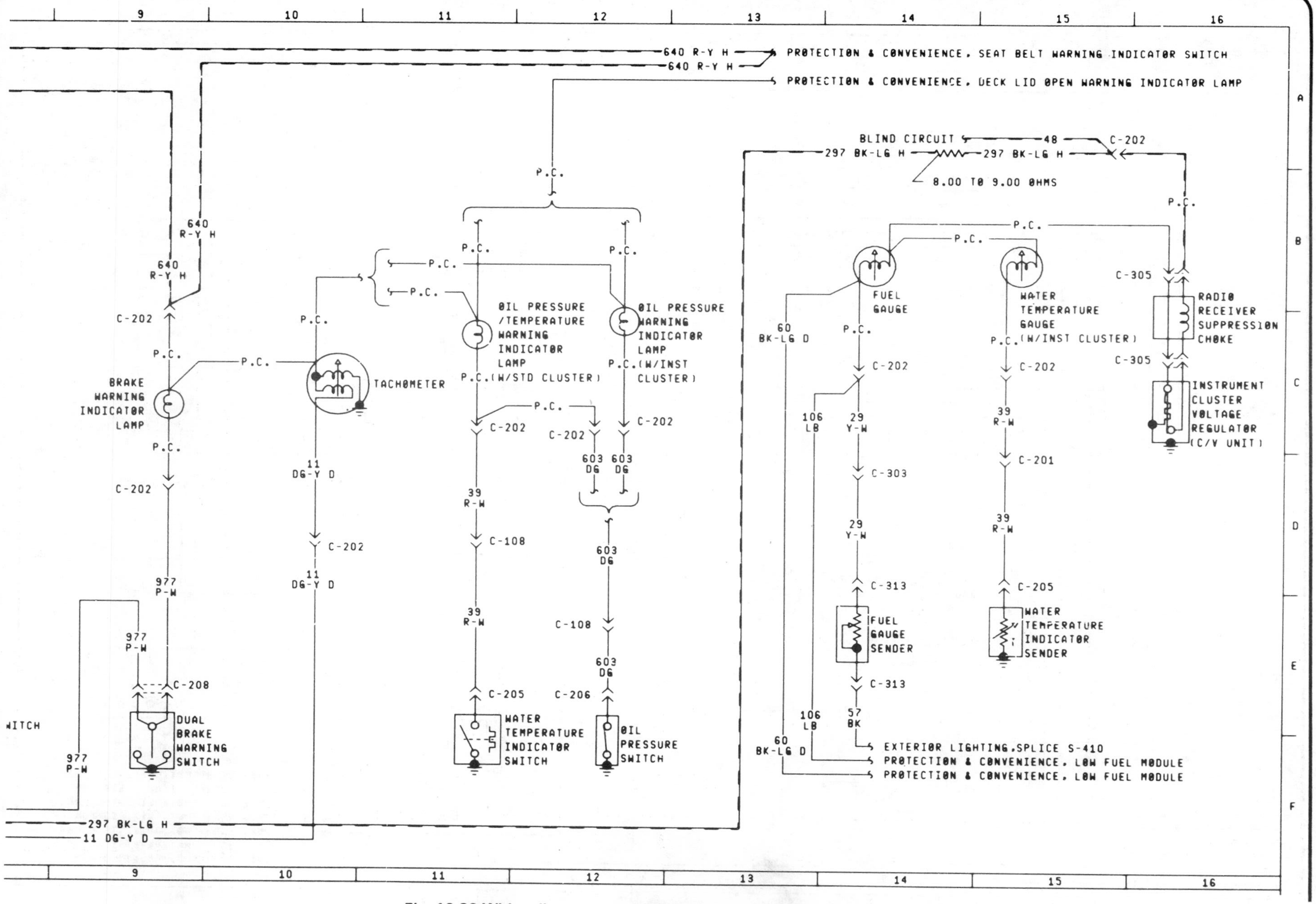

Fig. 10.29 Wiring diagram, charge, start and run (cont.), 1981 models

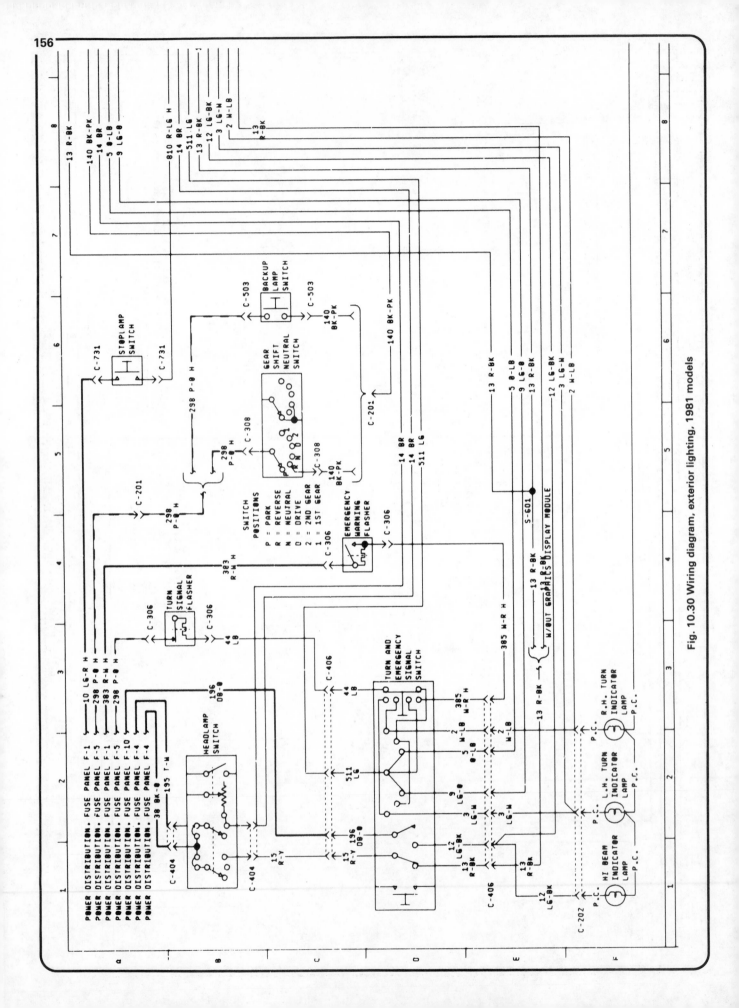

Fig. 10.30 Wiring diagram, exterior lighting, 1981 models

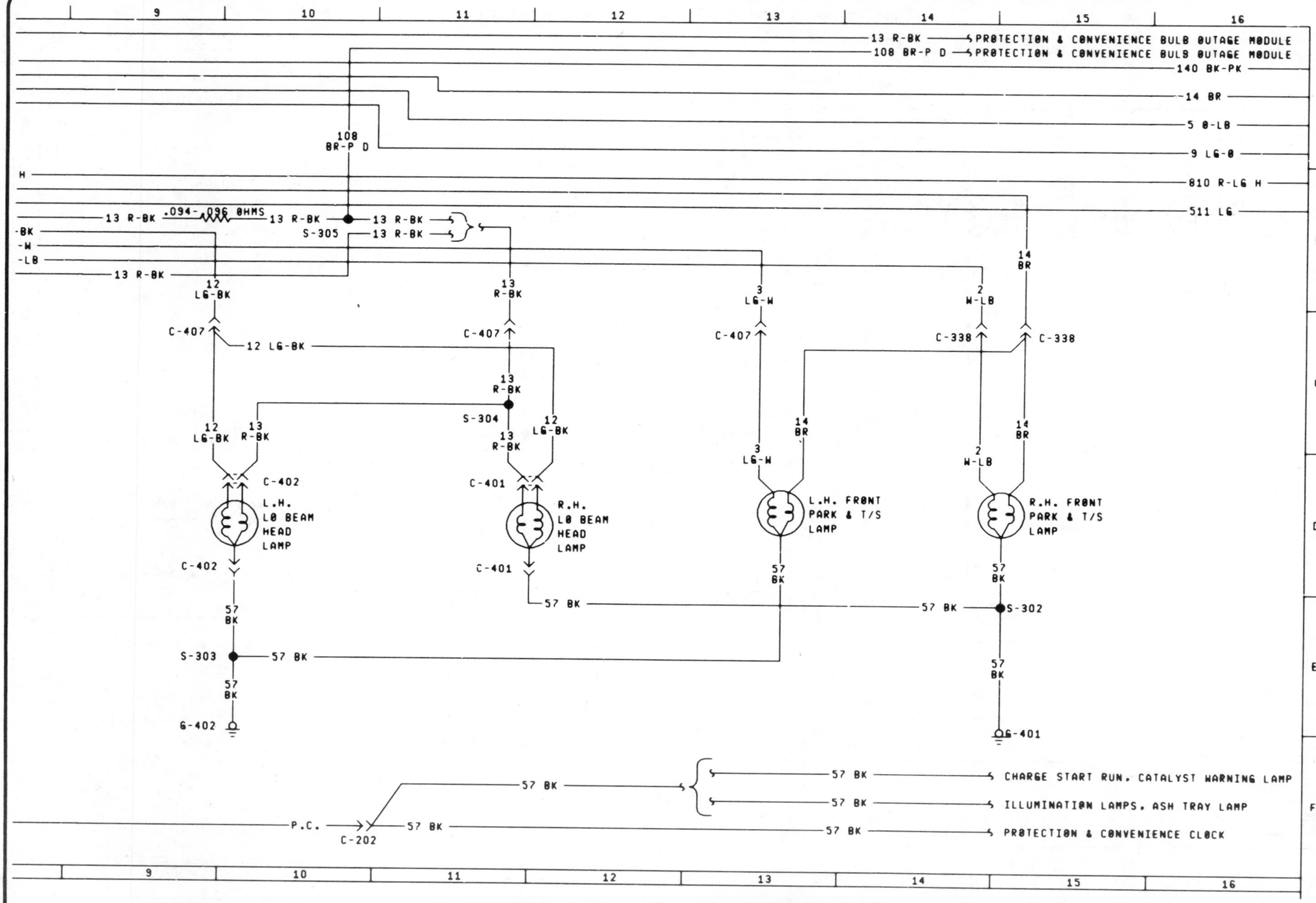

Fig. 10.30 Wiring diagram, exterior lighting (cont.), 1981 models

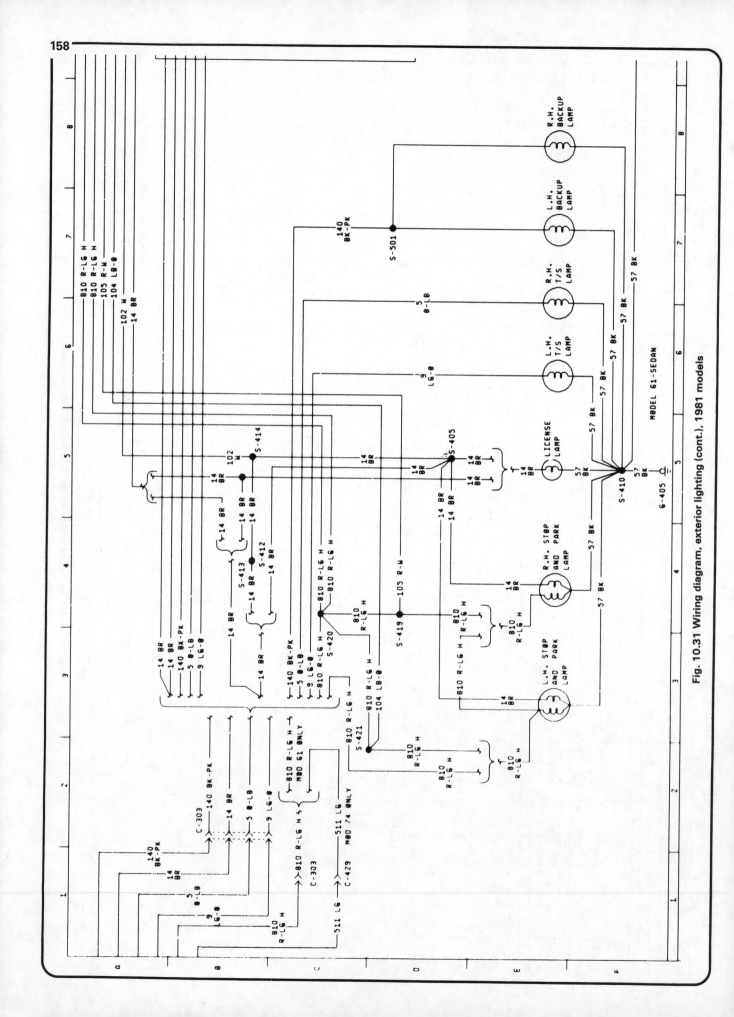

Fig. 10.31 Wiring diagram, exterior lighting (cont.), 1981 models

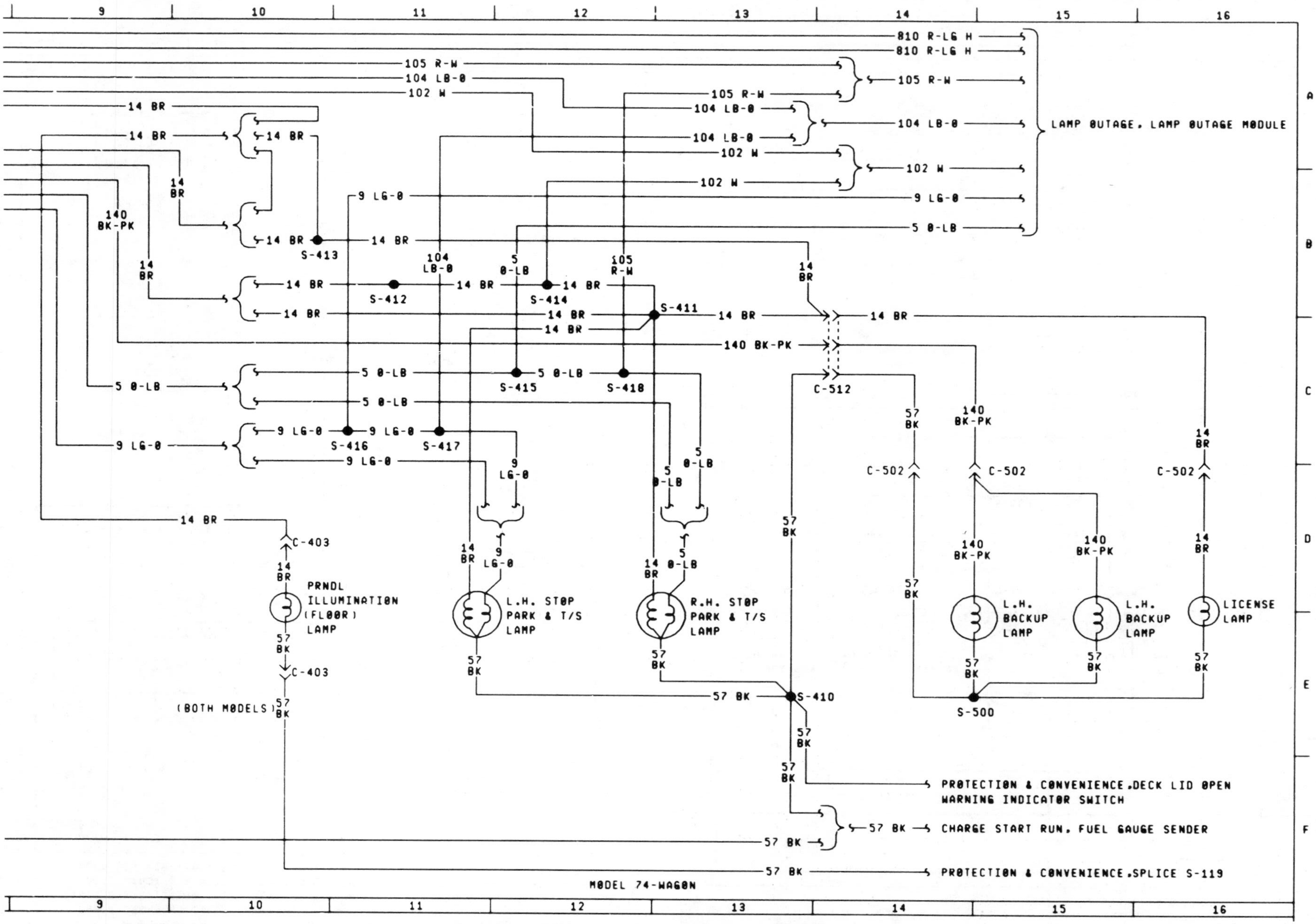

Fig. 10.31 Wiring diagram, exterior lighting (cont.), 1981 models

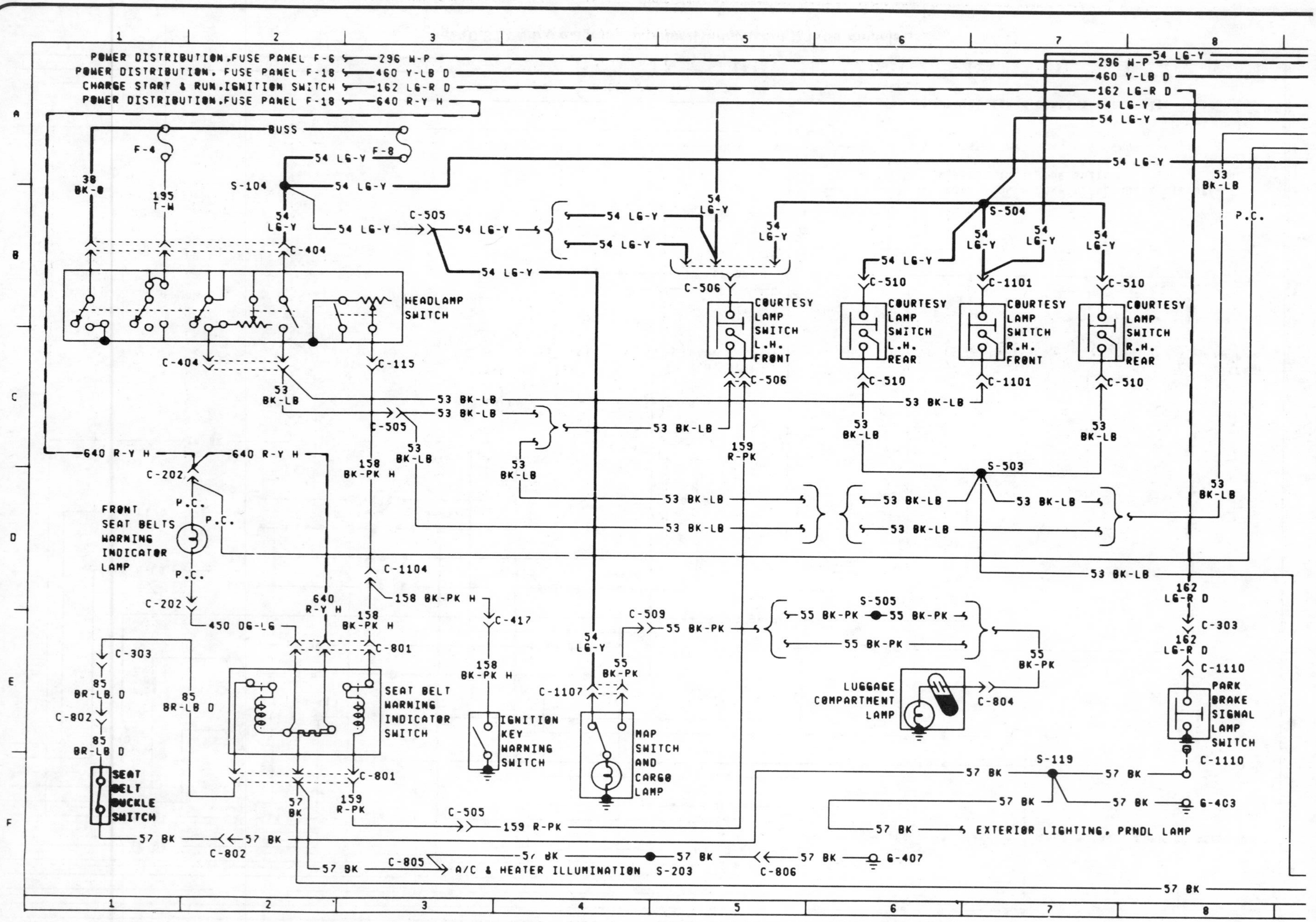

Fig. 10.32 Wiring diagram, protection and convenience, 1981 models

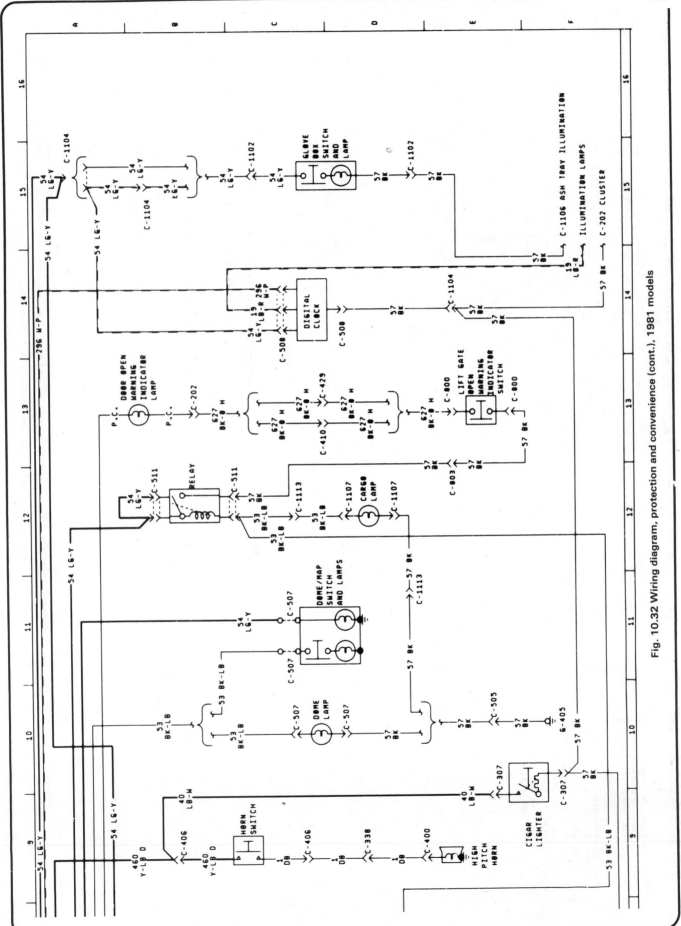

Fig. 10.32 Wiring diagram, protection and convenience (cont.), 1981 models

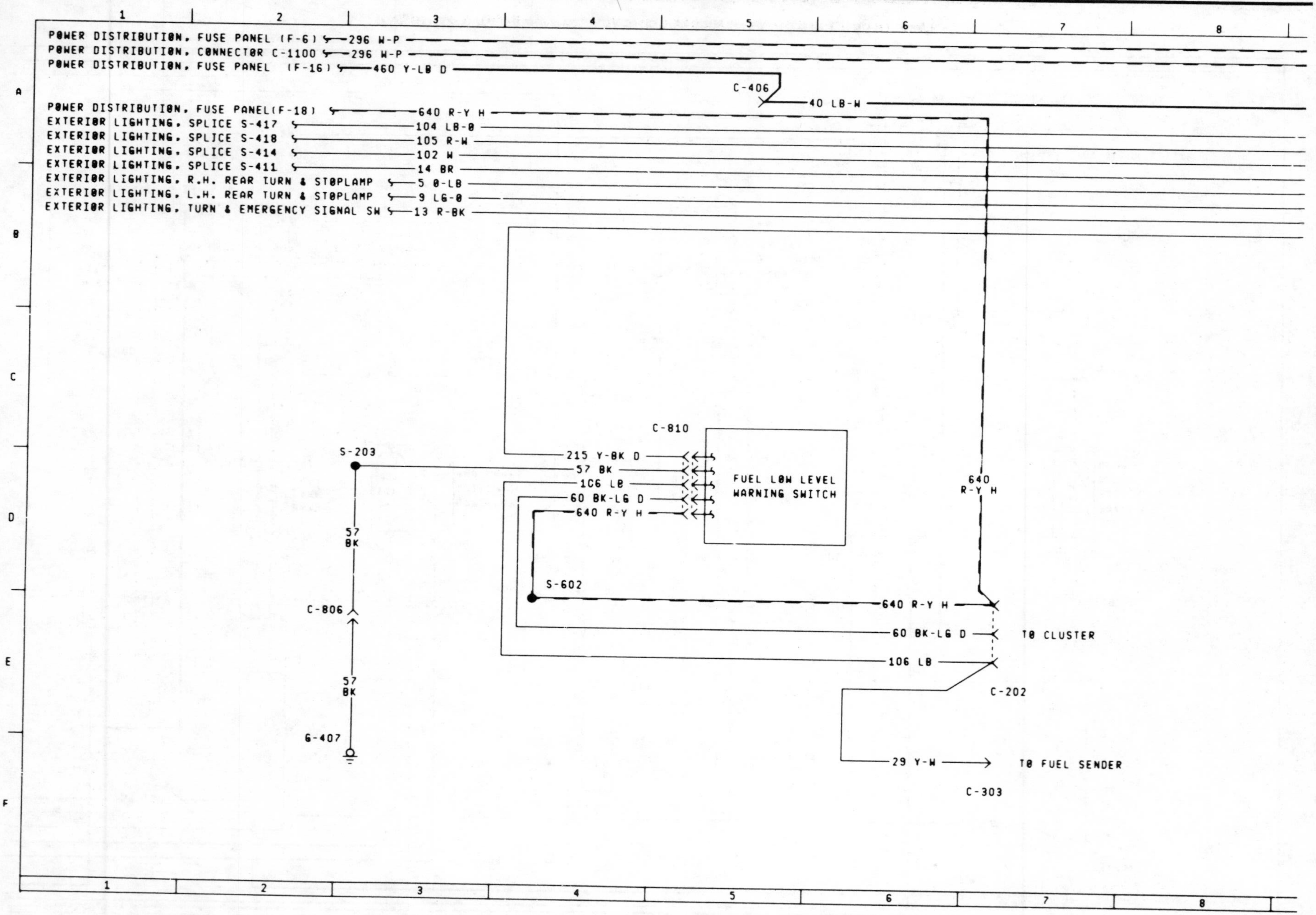

POWER DISTRIBUTION, FUSE PANEL (F-6) ⊱ 296 W-P
POWER DISTRIBUTION, CONNECTOR C-1100 ⊱ 296 W-P
POWER DISTRIBUTION, FUSE PANEL (F-16) ⊱ 460 Y-LB D

POWER DISTRIBUTION, FUSE PANEL(F-18) ⊱ 640 R-Y H
EXTERIOR LIGHTING, SPLICE S-417 ⊱ 104 LB-B
EXTERIOR LIGHTING, SPLICE S-418 ⊱ 105 R-W
EXTERIOR LIGHTING, SPLICE S-414 ⊱ 102 W
EXTERIOR LIGHTING, SPLICE S-411 ⊱ 14 BR
EXTERIOR LIGHTING, R.H. REAR TURN & STOPLAMP ⊱ 5 B-LB
EXTERIOR LIGHTING, L.H. REAR TURN & STOPLAMP ⊱ 9 LG-B
EXTERIOR LIGHTING, TURN & EMERGENCY SIGNAL SW ⊱ 13 R-BK

C-406 ⊱ 40 LB-W

640 R-Y H

TO CLUSTER

C-202

TO FUEL SENDER

29 Y-W ⟶ C-303

FUEL LOW LEVEL
WARNING SWITCH

C-810

215 Y-BK D
57 BK
106 LB
60 BK-LG D
640 R-Y H

640 R-Y H
60 BK-LG D
106 LB

S-602

S-203

57 BK
C-806

57 BK
G-407

Fig. 10.33 Wiring diagram, protection and convenience (cont.), 1981 models

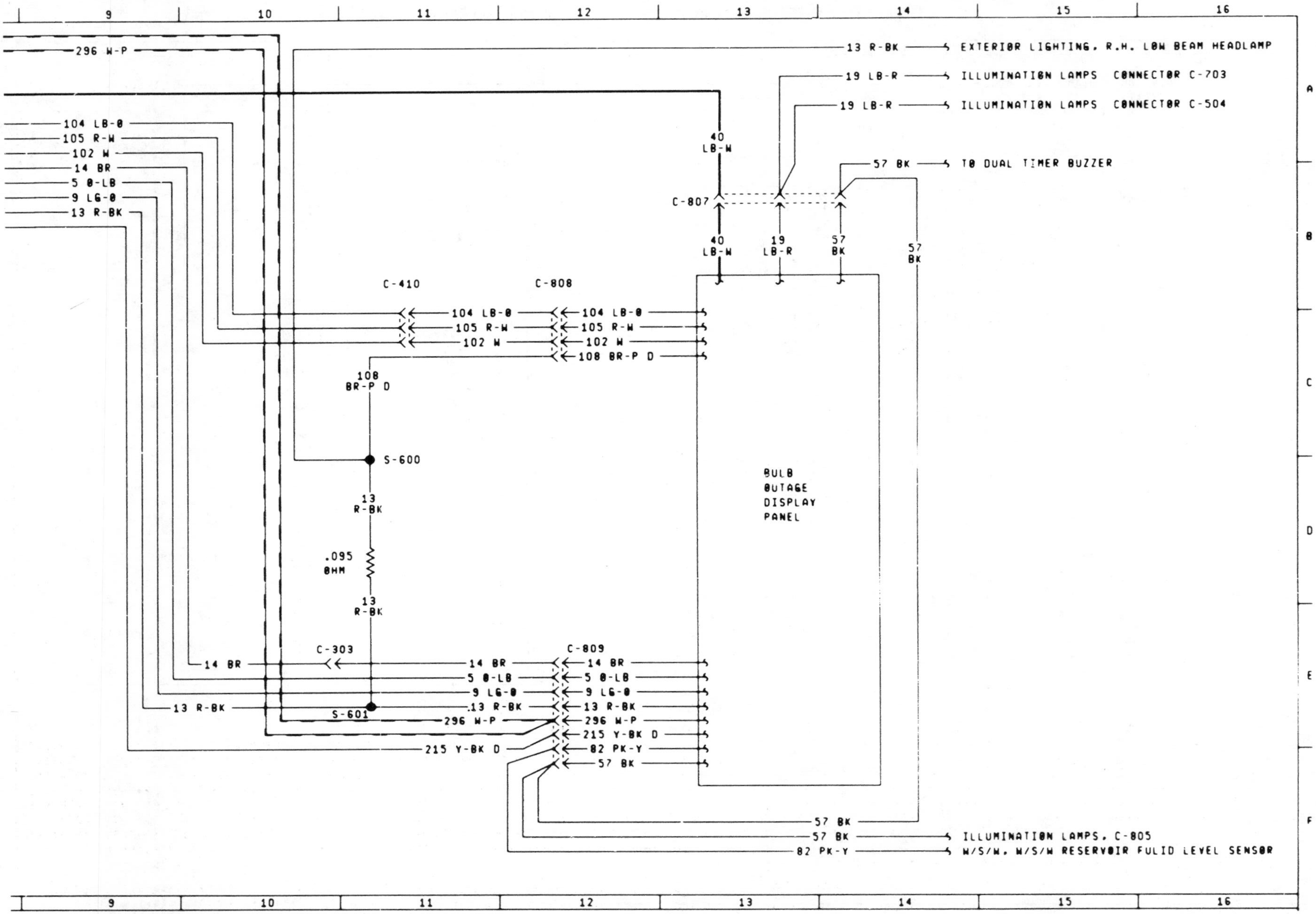

Fig. 10.33 Wiring diagram, protection and convenience (cont.), 1981 models

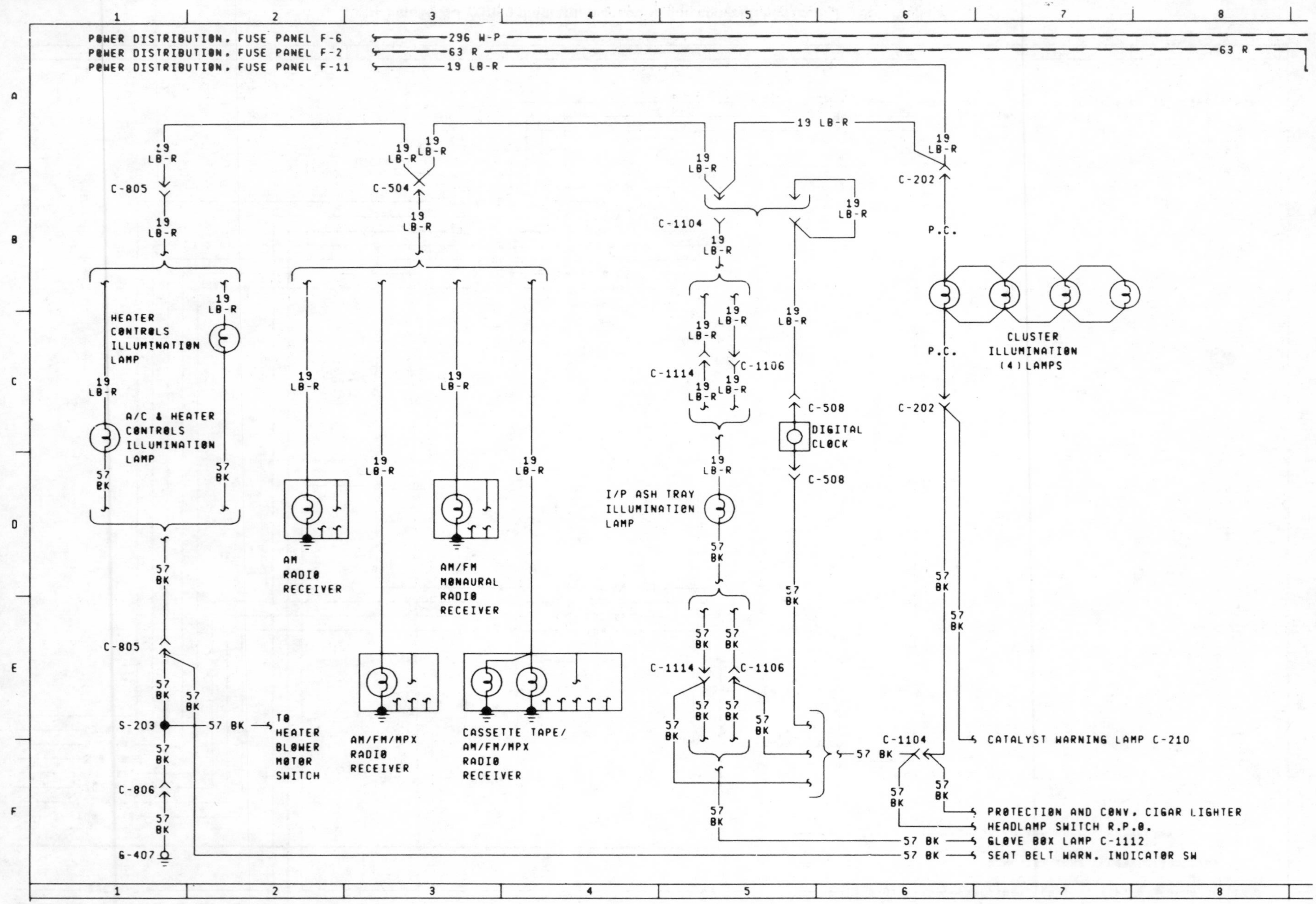

Fig. 10.34 Wiring diagram, illumination lamps, windshield washer/wiper, 1981 models

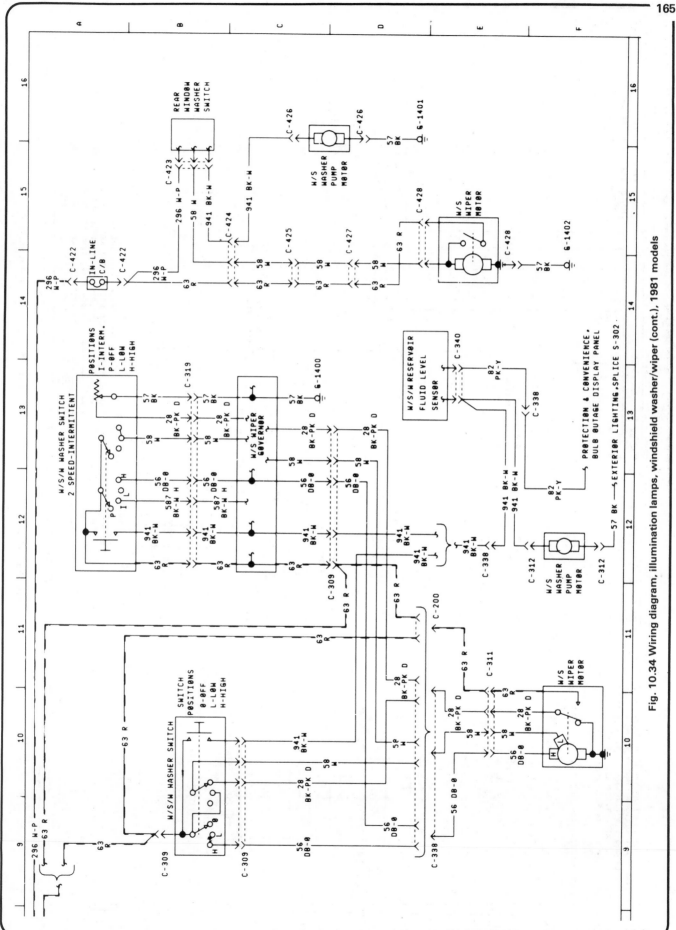

Fig. 10.34 Wiring diagram, illumination lamps, windshield washer/wiper (cont.), 1981 models

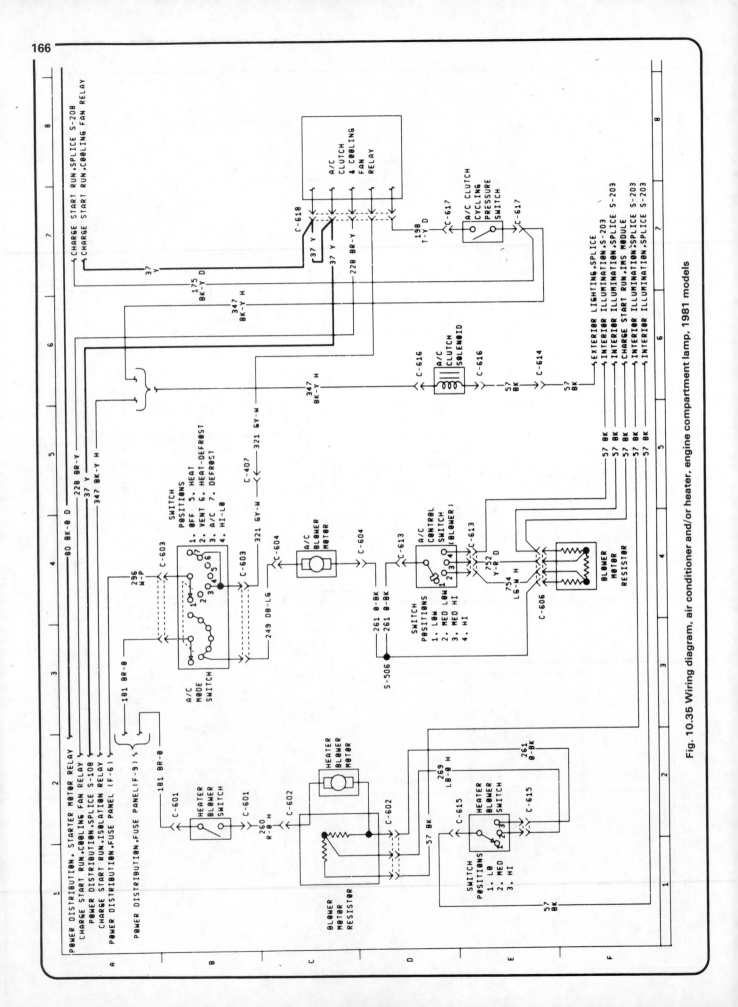

Fig. 10.35 Wiring diagram, air conditioner and/or heater, engine compartment lamp, 1981 models

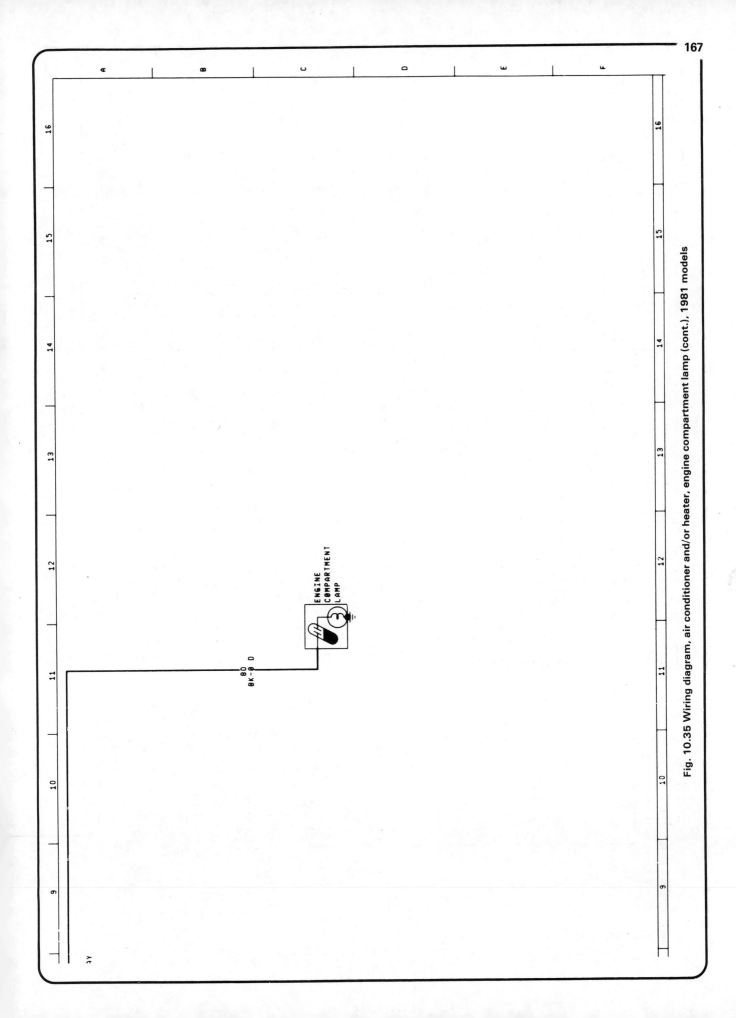

Fig. 10.35 Wiring diagram, air conditioner and/or heater, engine compartment lamp (cont.). 1981 models

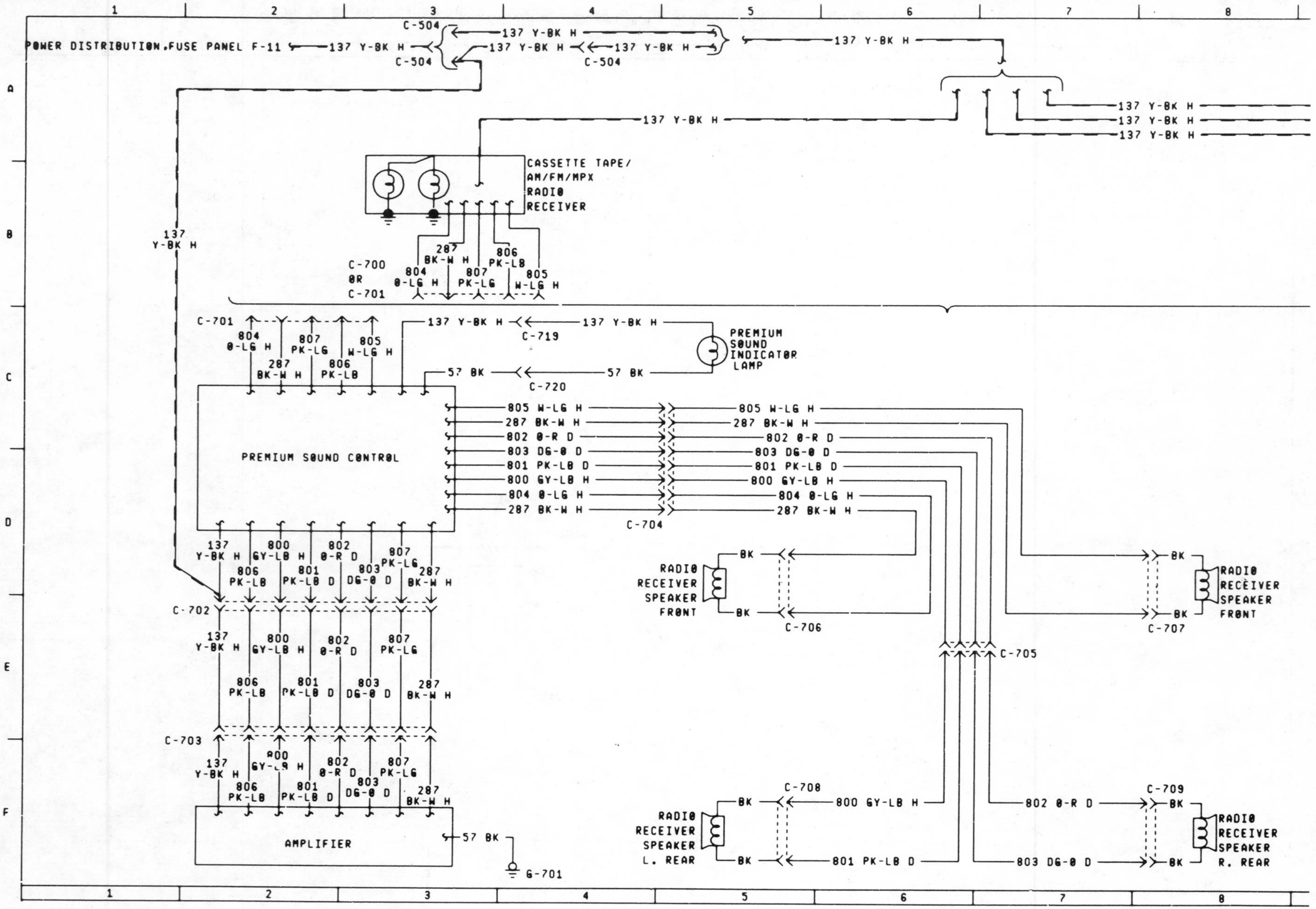

POWER DISTRIBUTION, FUSE PANEL F-11

137 Y-BK H

CASSETTE TAPE/ AM/FM/MPX RADIO RECEIVER

PREMIUM SOUND INDICATOR LAMP

PREMIUM SOUND CONTROL

AMPLIFIER

RADIO RECEIVER SPEAKER FRONT

RADIO RECEIVER SPEAKER R. REAR

RADIO RECEIVER SPEAKER FRONT

RADIO RECEIVER SPEAKER L. REAR

Fig. 10.36 Wiring diagram, radio circuits, 1981 models

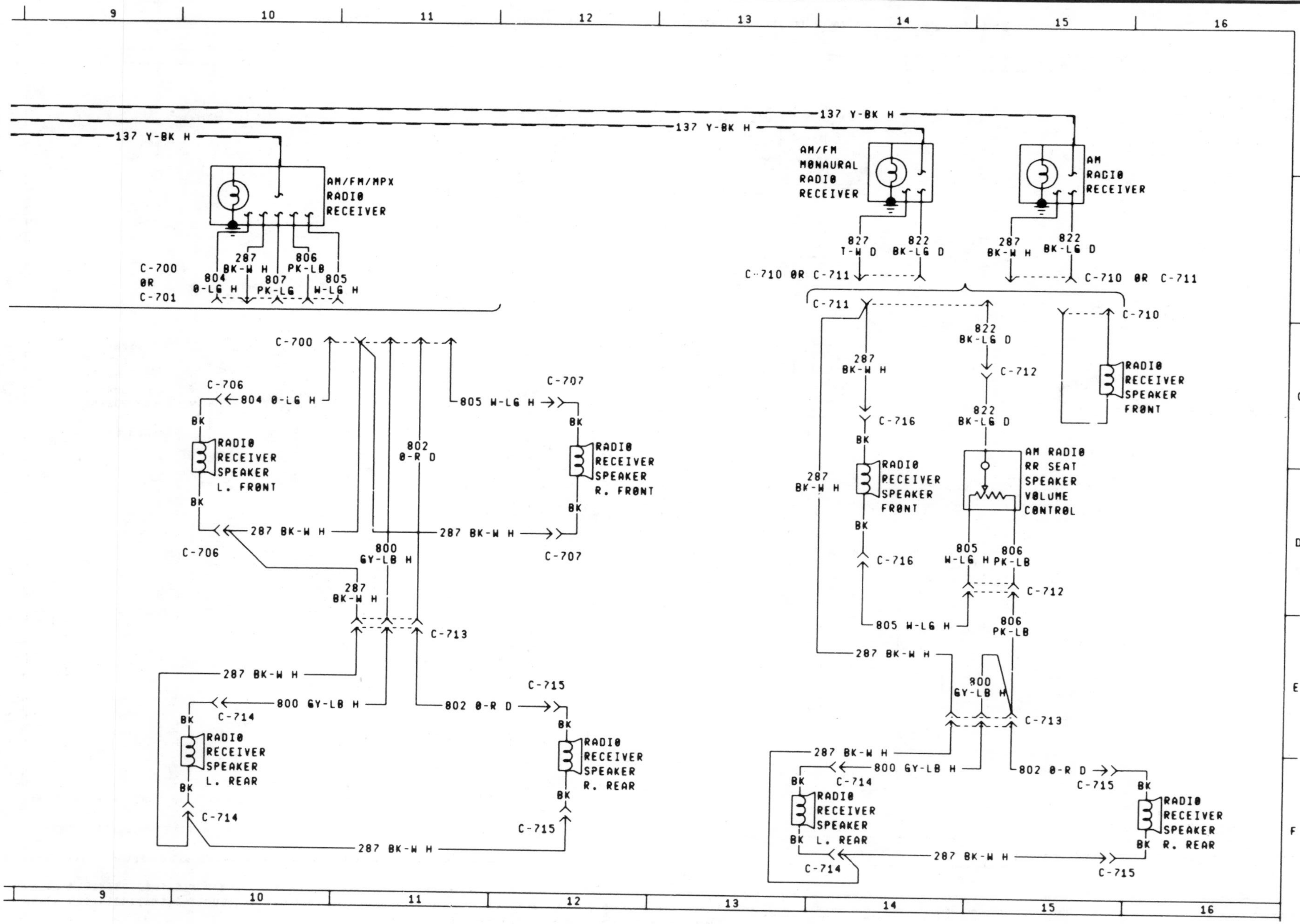

Fig. 10.36 Wiring diagram, radio circuits (cont.), 1981 models

170

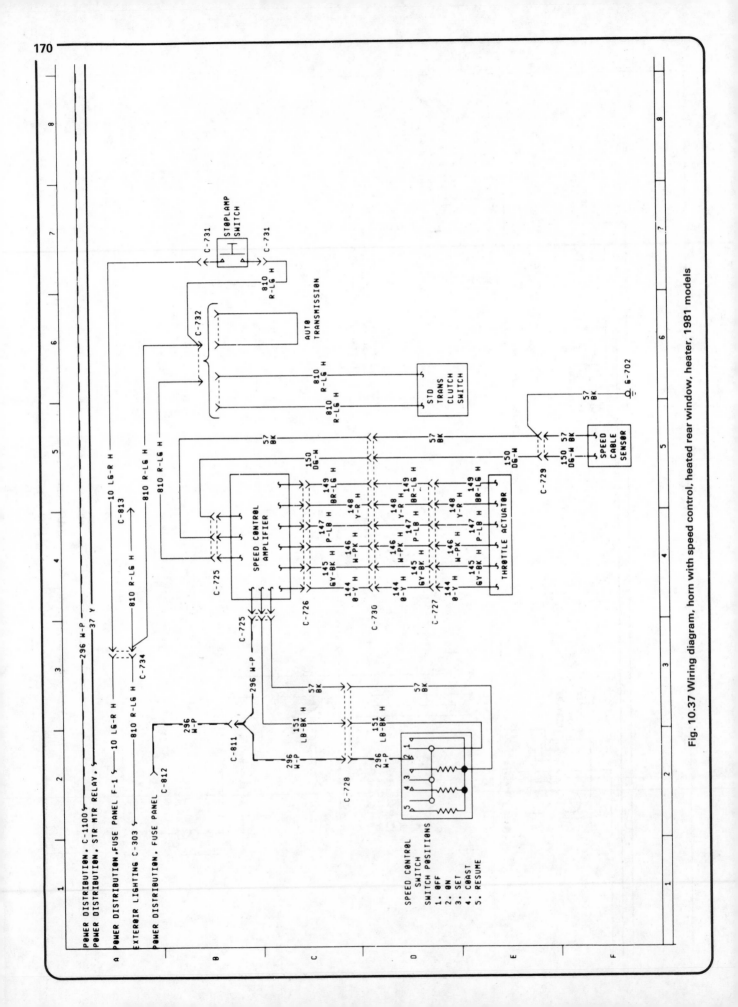

Fig. 10.37 Wiring diagram, horn with speed control, heated rear window, heater, 1981 models

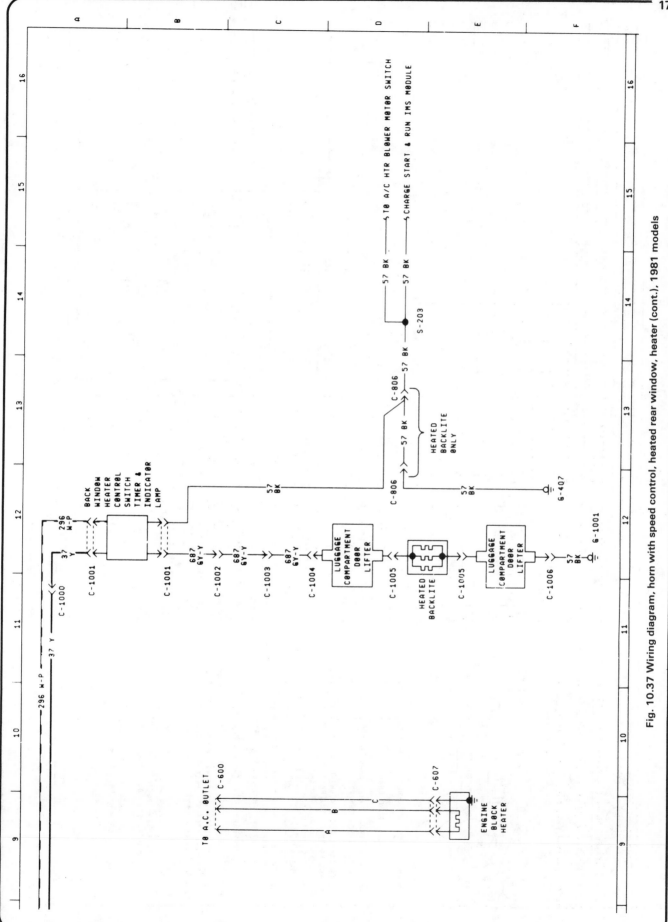

Fig. 10.37 Wiring diagram, horn with speed control, heated rear window, heater (cont.), 1981 models

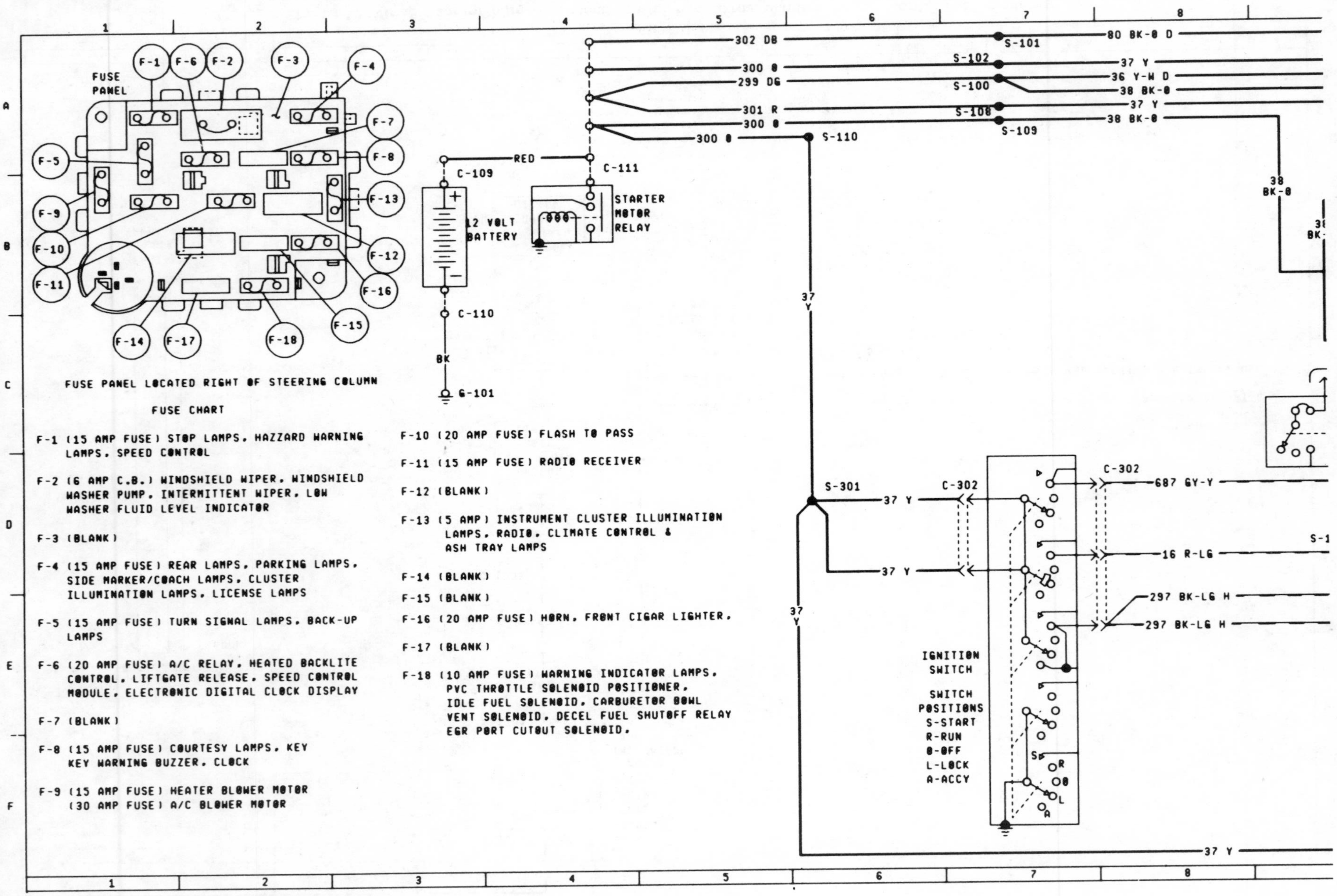

FUSE PANEL LOCATED RIGHT OF STEERING COLUMN

FUSE CHART

F-1 (15 AMP FUSE) STOP LAMPS, HAZZARD WARNING LAMPS, SPEED CONTROL

F-2 (6 AMP C.B.) WINDSHIELD WIPER, WINDSHIELD WASHER PUMP, INTERMITTENT WIPER, LOW WASHER FLUID INDICATOR

F-3 (BLANK)

F-4 (15 AMP FUSE) REAR LAMPS, PARKING LAMPS, SIDE MARKER/COACH LAMPS, CLUSTER ILLUMINATION LAMPS, LICENSE LAMPS

F-5 (15 AMP FUSE) TURN SIGNAL LAMPS, BACK-UP LAMPS

F-6 (20 AMP FUSE) A/C RELAY, HEATED BACKLITE CONTROL, LIFTGATE RELEASE, SPEED CONTROL MODULE, ELECTRONIC DIGITAL CLOCK DISPLAY

F-7 (BLANK)

F-8 (15 AMP FUSE) COURTESY LAMPS, KEY KEY WARNING BUZZER, CLOCK

F-9 (15 AMP FUSE) HEATER BLOWER MOTOR (30 AMP FUSE) A/C BLOWER MOTOR

F-10 (20 AMP FUSE) FLASH TO PASS

F-11 (15 AMP FUSE) RADIO RECEIVER

F-12 (BLANK)

F-13 (5 AMP) INSTRUMENT CLUSTER ILLUMINATION LAMPS, RADIO, CLIMATE CONTROL & ASH TRAY LAMPS

F-14 (BLANK)

F-15 (BLANK)

F-16 (20 AMP FUSE) HORN, FRONT CIGAR LIGHTER.

F-17 (BLANK)

F-18 (10 AMP FUSE) WARNING INDICATOR LAMPS, PVC THROTTLE SOLENOID POSITIONER, IDLE FUEL SOLENOID, CARBURETOR BOWL VENT SOLENOID, DECEL FUEL SHUTOFF RELAY EGR PORT CUTOUT SOLENOID.

FUSE PANEL

STARTER MOTOR RELAY

12 VOLT BATTERY

C-111
C-109
C-110
G-101
RED
BK

IGNITION SWITCH

SWITCH POSITIONS
S-START
R-RUN
0-OFF
L-LOCK
A-ACCY

Fig. 10.38 Wiring diagram, power distribution, 1982 models

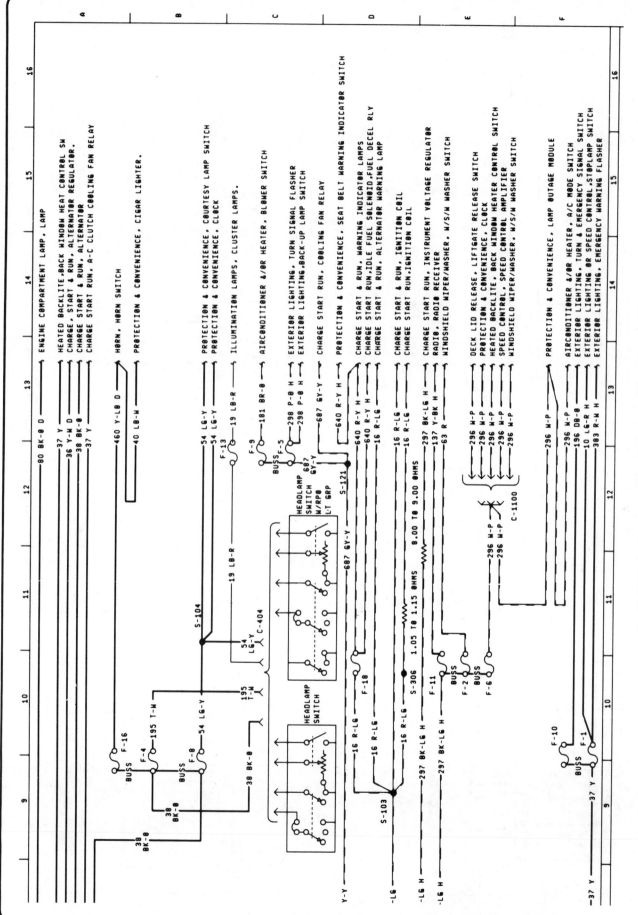

Fig. 10.38 Wiring diagram, power distribution (cont.), 1982 models

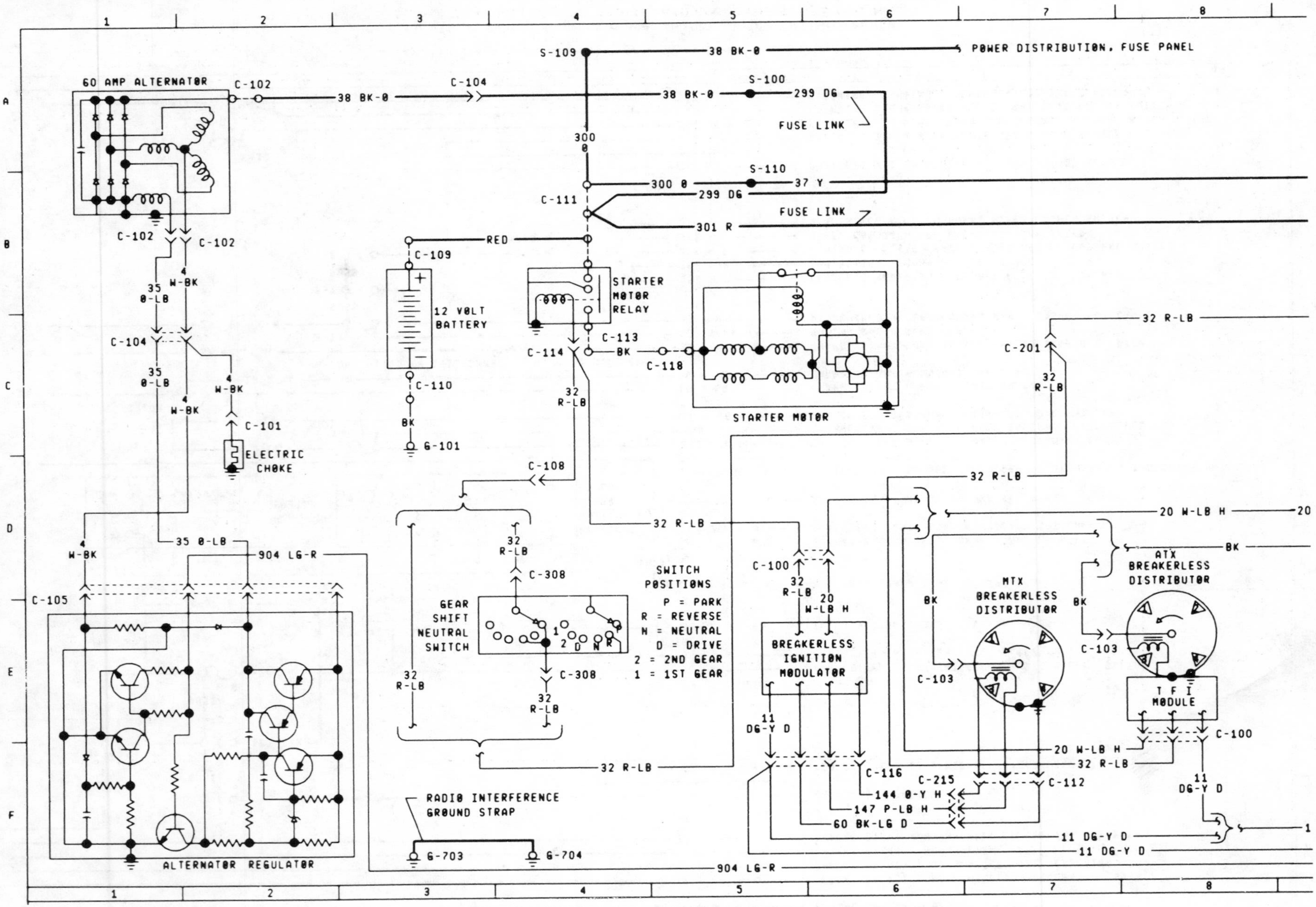

POWER DISTRIBUTION, FUSE PANEL

60 AMP ALTERNATOR

ALTERNATOR REGULATOR

STARTER MOTOR

STARTER MOTOR RELAY

12 VOLT BATTERY

ELECTRIC CHOKE

GEAR SHIFT NEUTRAL SWITCH

RADIO INTERFERENCE GROUND STRAP

ATX BREAKERLESS DISTRIBUTOR

MTX BREAKERLESS DISTRIBUTOR

TFI MODULE

BREAKERLESS IGNITION MODULATOR

SWITCH POSITIONS
P = PARK
R = REVERSE
N = NEUTRAL
D = DRIVE
2 = 2ND GEAR
1 = 1ST GEAR

FUSE LINK

RED

38 BK-0
299 DG
37 Y
300 0 299 DG
301 R
32 R-LB
20 W-LB H
BK
11 DG-Y D
904 LG-R
35 0-LB
W-BK
144 0-Y H
147 P-LB H
60 BK-LG D

S-100 S-109 S-110
C-100 C-101 C-102 C-103 C-104 C-105 C-108 C-109 C-110 C-111 C-112 C-113 C-114 C-116 C-118 C-201 C-215 C-308
G-101 G-203 G-704 G-704

Fig. 10.39 Wiring diagram, charge, start and run, 1982 models

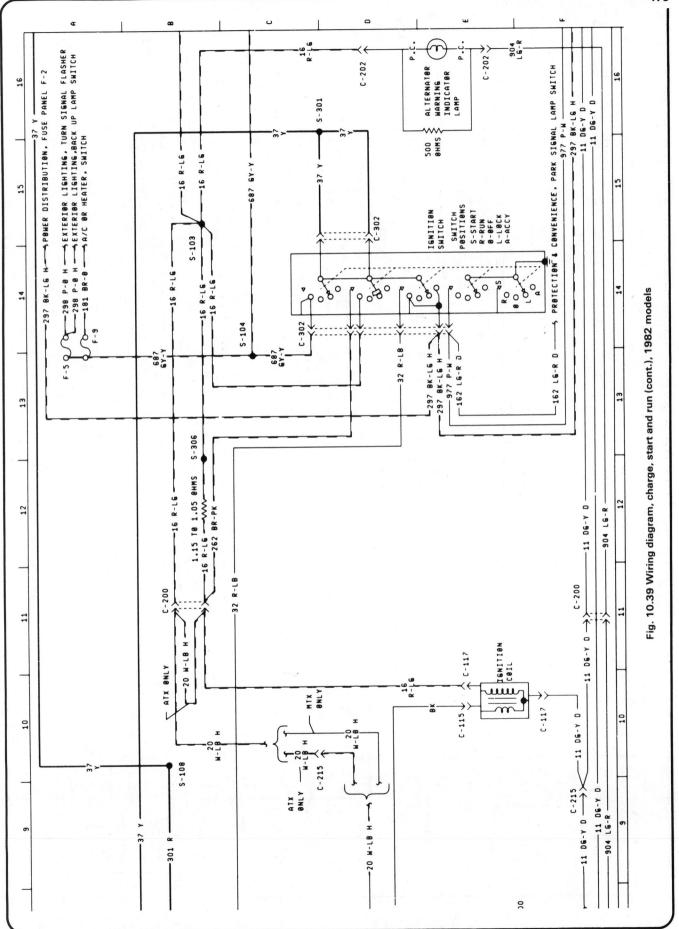

Fig. 10.39 Wiring diagram, charge, start and run (cont.), 1982 models

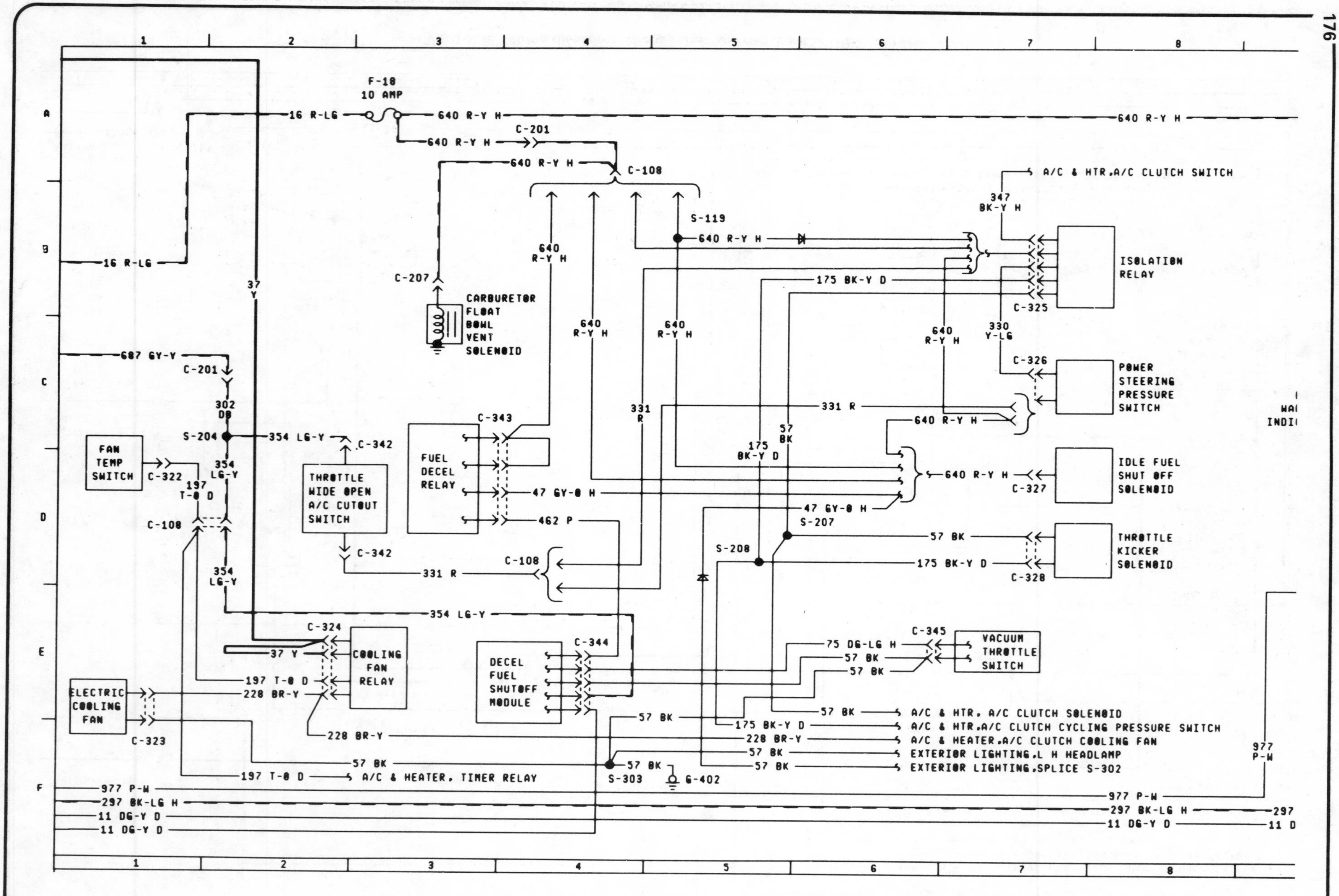

Fig. 10.40 Wiring diagram, charge, start and run (cont.), 1982 models

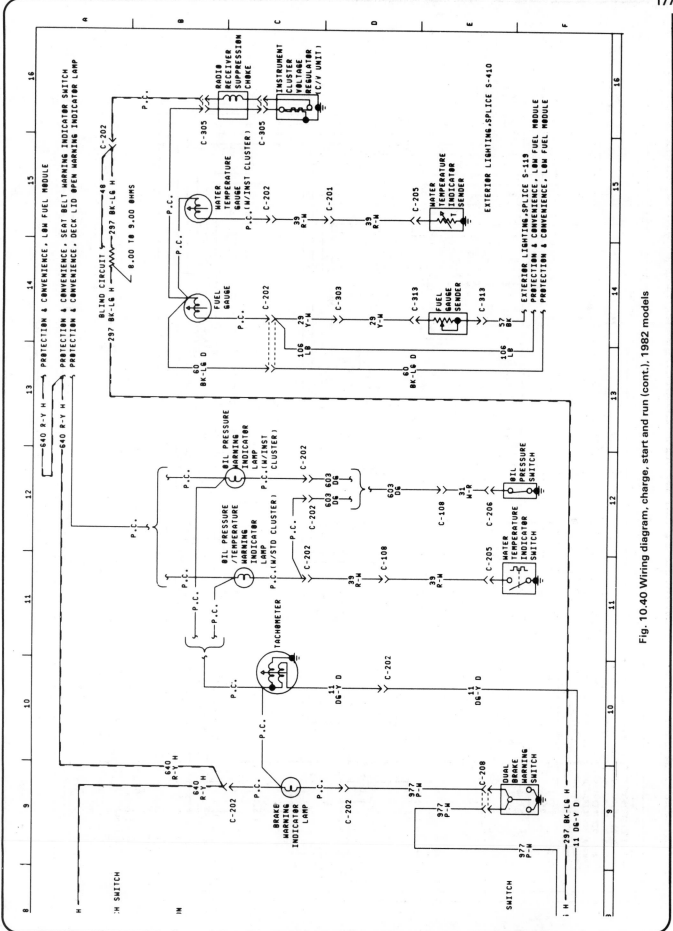

Fig. 10.40 Wiring diagram, charge, start and run (cont.), 1982 models

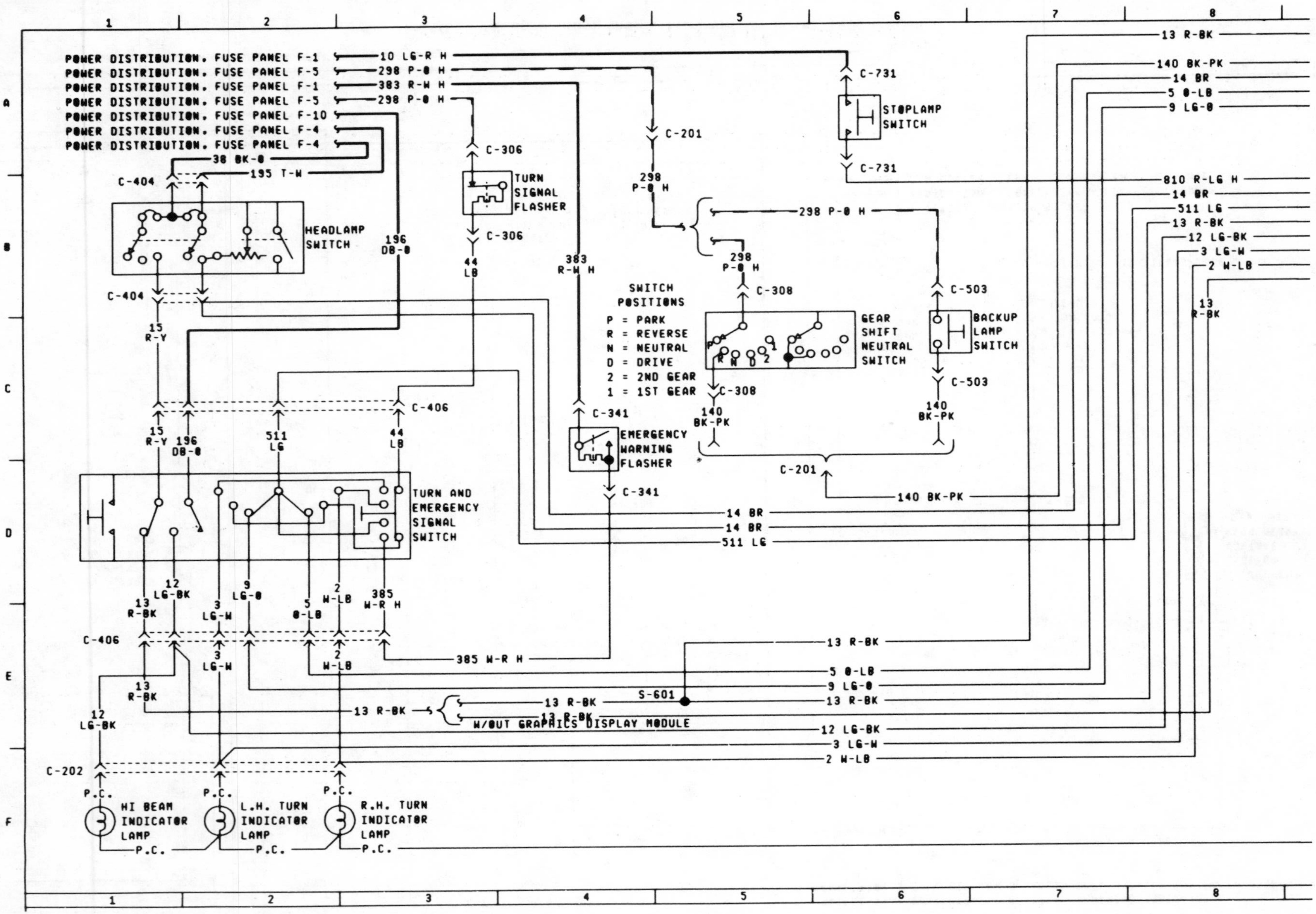

Fig. 10.41 Wiring diagram, exterior lighting, 1982 models

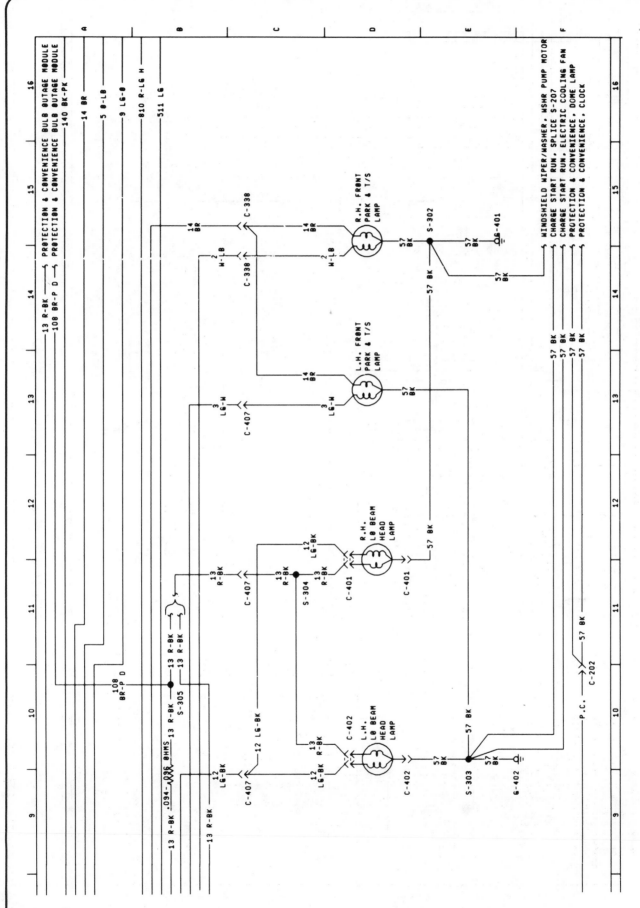

Fig. 10.41 Wiring diagram, exterior lighting (cont.), 1982 models

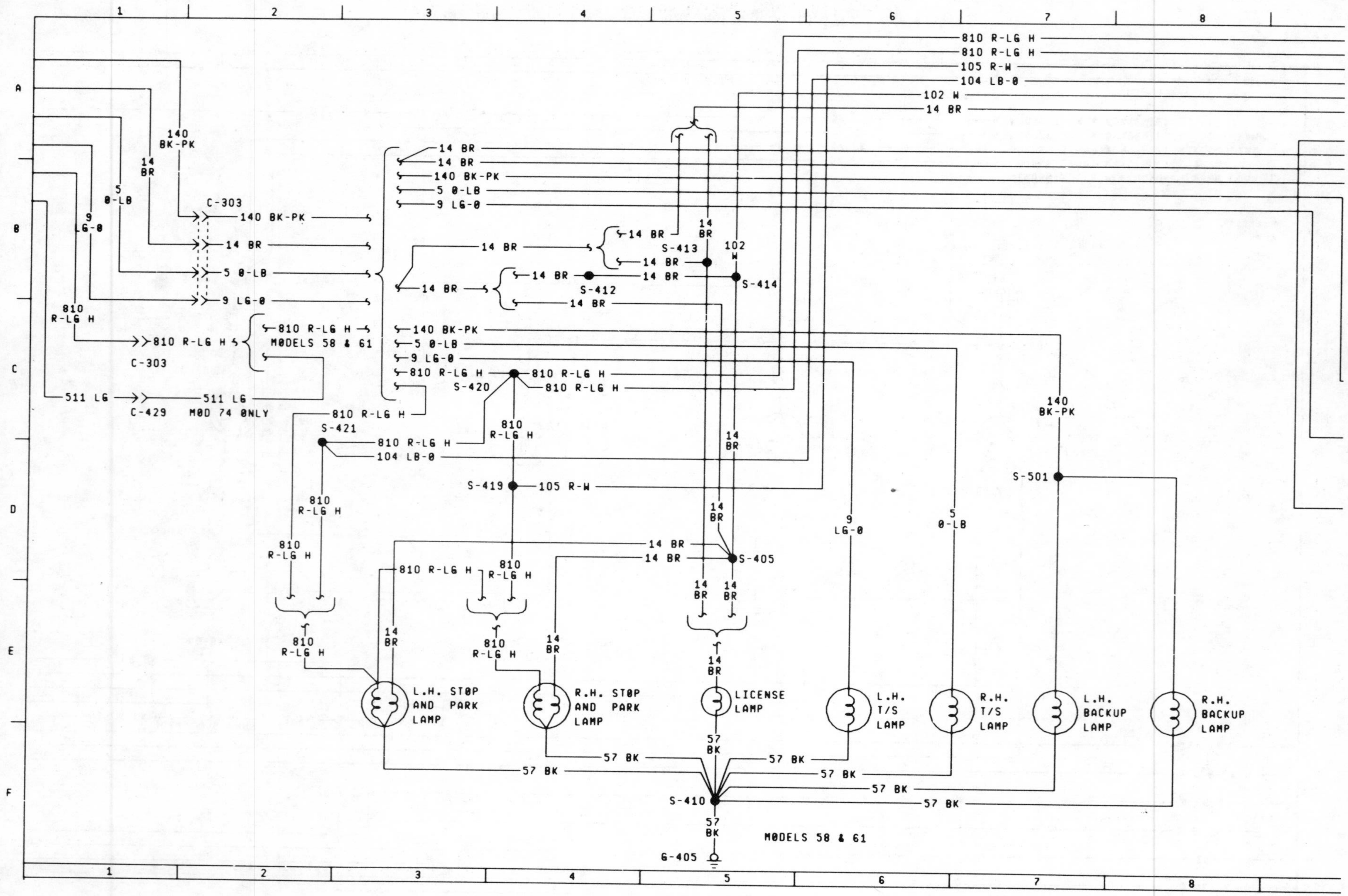

Fig. 10.42 Wiring diagram, exterior lighting (cont.), 1982 models

R.H. BACKUP LAMP

L.H. BACKUP LAMP

R.H. T/S LAMP

L.H. T/S LAMP

LICENSE LAMP

R.H. STOP AND PARK LAMP

L.H. STOP AND PARK LAMP

MODELS 58 & 61

810 R-LG H
810 R-LG H
105 R-W
104 LB-0
102 W
14 BR

140 BK-PK
S-501

0-LB
57 BK
57 BK

LG-0
57 BK
57 BK

102 W
S-414
S-413
S-412
14 BR
14 BR
14 BR

14 BR
14 BR
S-405
14 BR
14 BR
14 BR
57 BK
S-410
57 BK
G-405

810 R-LG H
810 R-LG H
S-420

810 R-LG H
S-419 105 R-W

810 R-LG H
810 R-LG H

14 BR
57 BK

14 BR
14 BR

810 R-LG H

810 R-LG H
810 R-LG H
MODELS 58 & 61

810 R-LG H
810 R-LG H
S-421
104 LB-0

810 R-LG H
810 R-LG H

810 R-LG H

14 BR
14 BR
140 BK-PK
5 0-LB
9 LG-0
14 BR

14 BR
140 BK-PK
5 0-LB
9 LG-0
810 R-LG H

C-303
140 BK-PK
14 BR
5 0-LB
9 LG-0

140 BK-PK
14 BR
5 0-LB
9 LG-0
810 R-LG H

810 R-LG H
MODELS 58 & 61

C-303
511 LG MOD 74 ONLY

511 LG
C-429

14 BR
14 BR

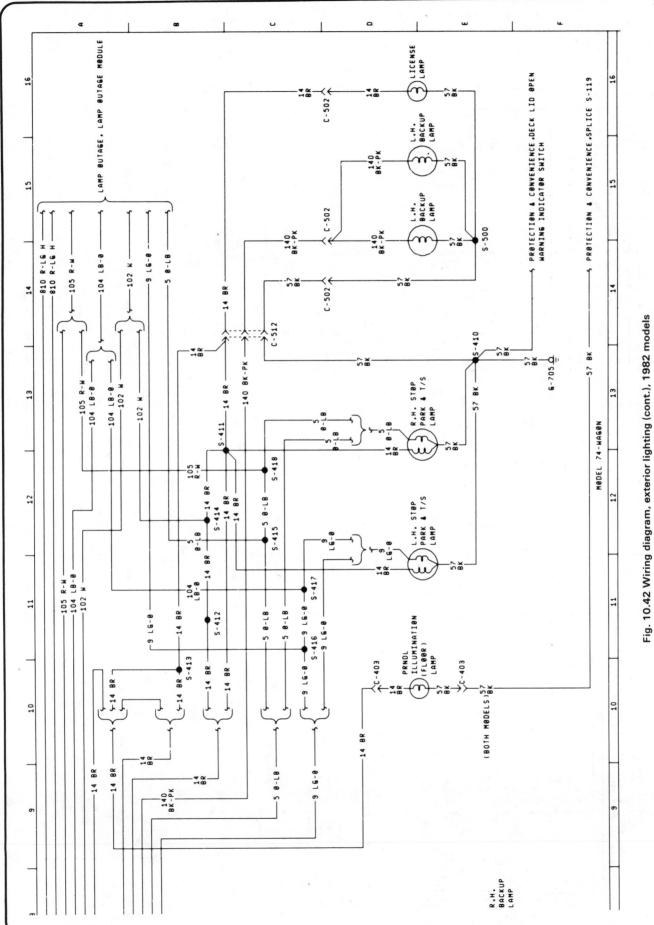

Fig. 10.42 Wiring diagram, exterior lighting (cont.), 1982 models

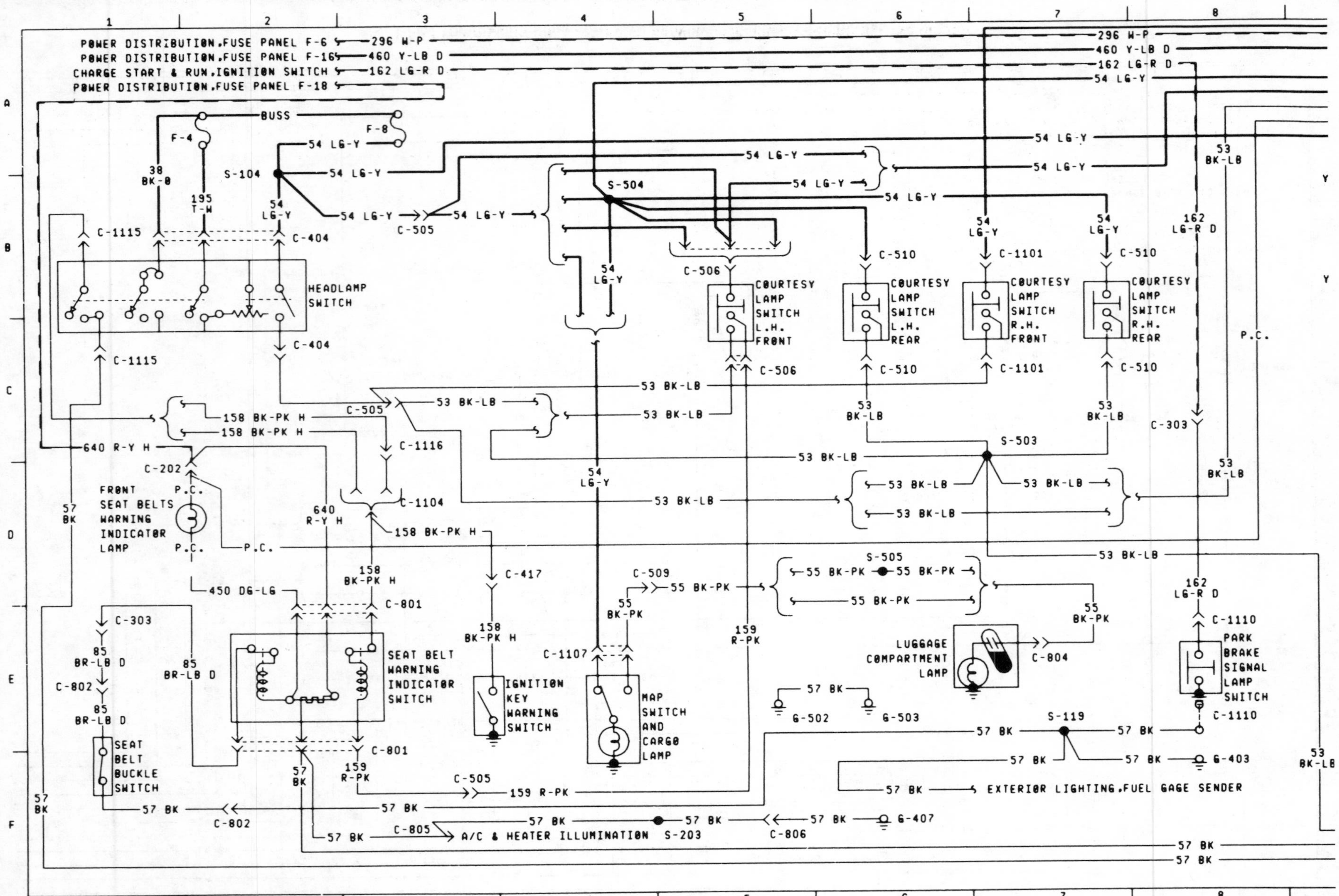

Fig. 10.43 Wiring diagram, protection, convenience and horn, 1982 models

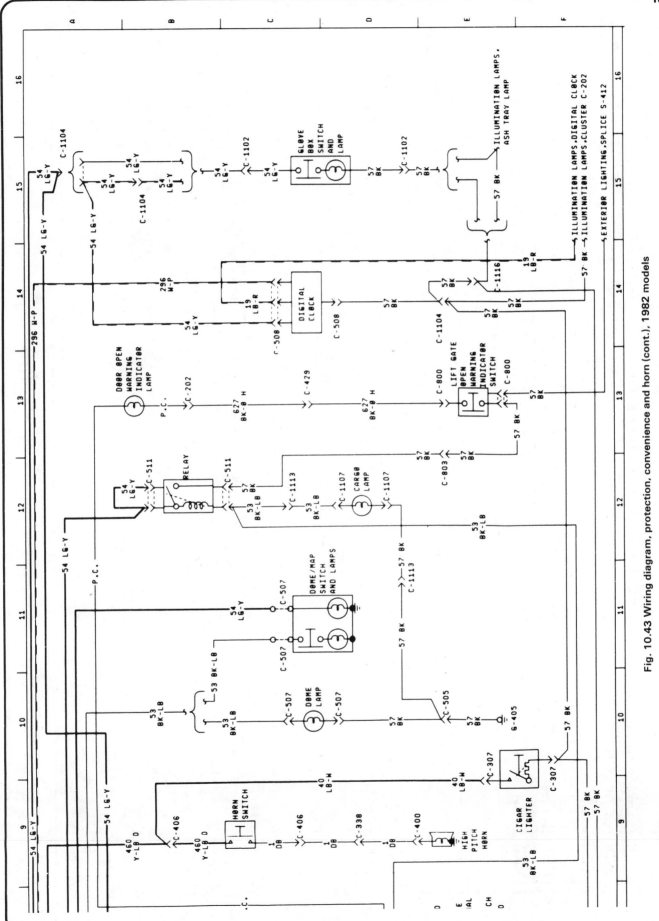

Fig. 10.43 Wiring diagram, protection, convenience and horn (cont.), 1982 models

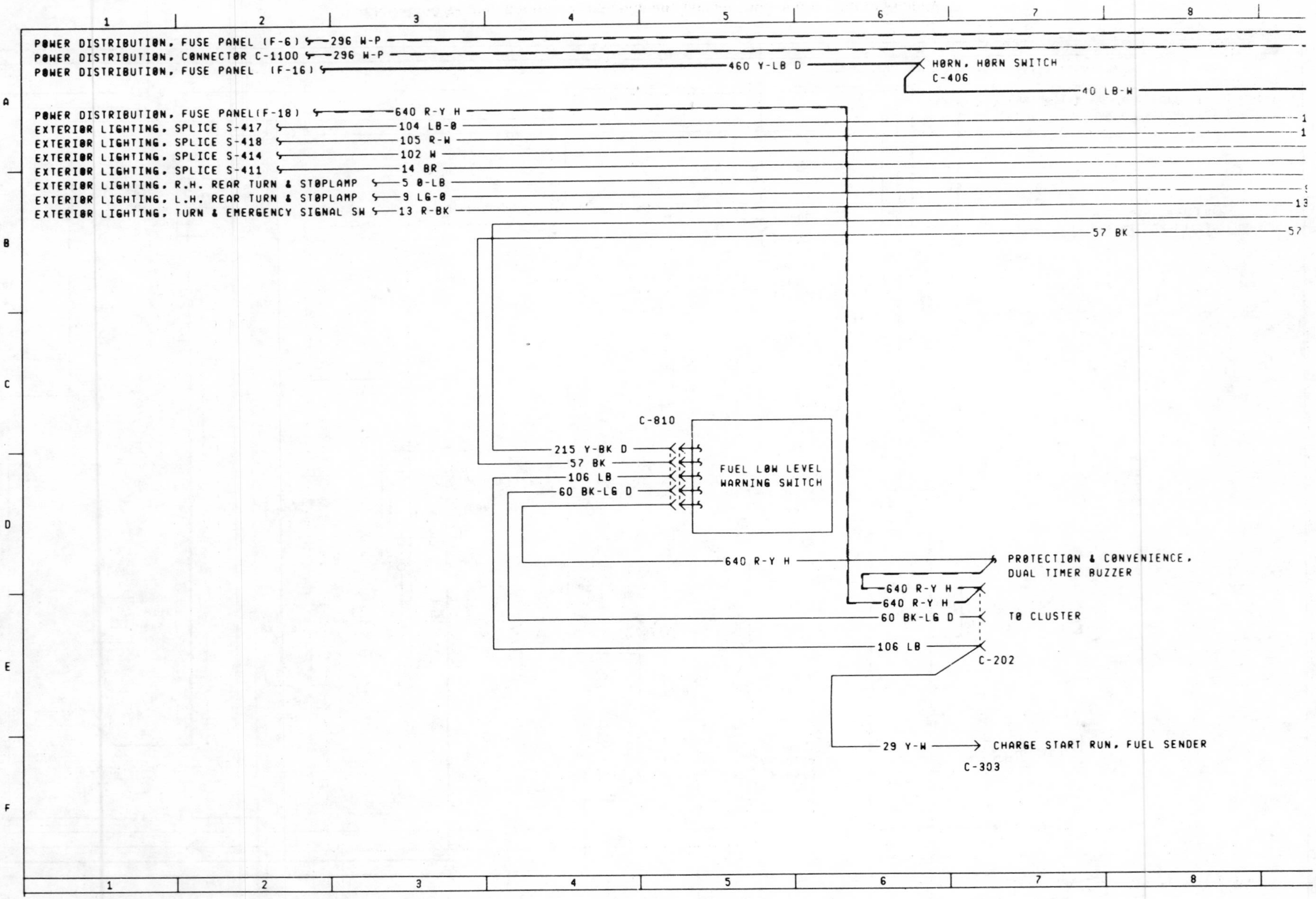

POWER DISTRIBUTION, FUSE PANEL (F-6) ⟩—296 W-P
POWER DISTRIBUTION, CONNECTOR C-1100 ⟩—296 W-P
POWER DISTRIBUTION, FUSE PANEL (F-16)

POWER DISTRIBUTION, FUSE PANEL(F-18) ⟩———640 R-Y H
EXTERIOR LIGHTING, SPLICE S-417 ⟩————104 LB-O
EXTERIOR LIGHTING, SPLICE S-418 ⟩————105 R-W
EXTERIOR LIGHTING, SPLICE S-414 ⟩————102 W
EXTERIOR LIGHTING, SPLICE S-411 ⟩————14 BR
EXTERIOR LIGHTING, R.H. REAR TURN & STOPLAMP ⟩——5 O-LB
EXTERIOR LIGHTING, L.H. REAR TURN & STOPLAMP ⟩——9 LG-O
EXTERIOR LIGHTING, TURN & EMERGENCY SIGNAL SW ⟩——13 R-BK

HORN, HORN SWITCH
C-406

460 Y-LB D

57 BK

FUEL LOW LEVEL
WARNING SWITCH

C-810

215 Y-BK D
57 BK
106 LB
60 BK-LG D

640 R-Y H

PROTECTION & CONVENIENCE,
DUAL TIMER BUZZER

640 R-Y H
640 R-Y H
60 BK-LG D

TO CLUSTER

106 LB

C-202

29 Y-W ——→ CHARGE START RUN, FUEL SENDER

C-303

Fig. 10.44 Wiring diagram, protection and convenience (cont.), 1982 models

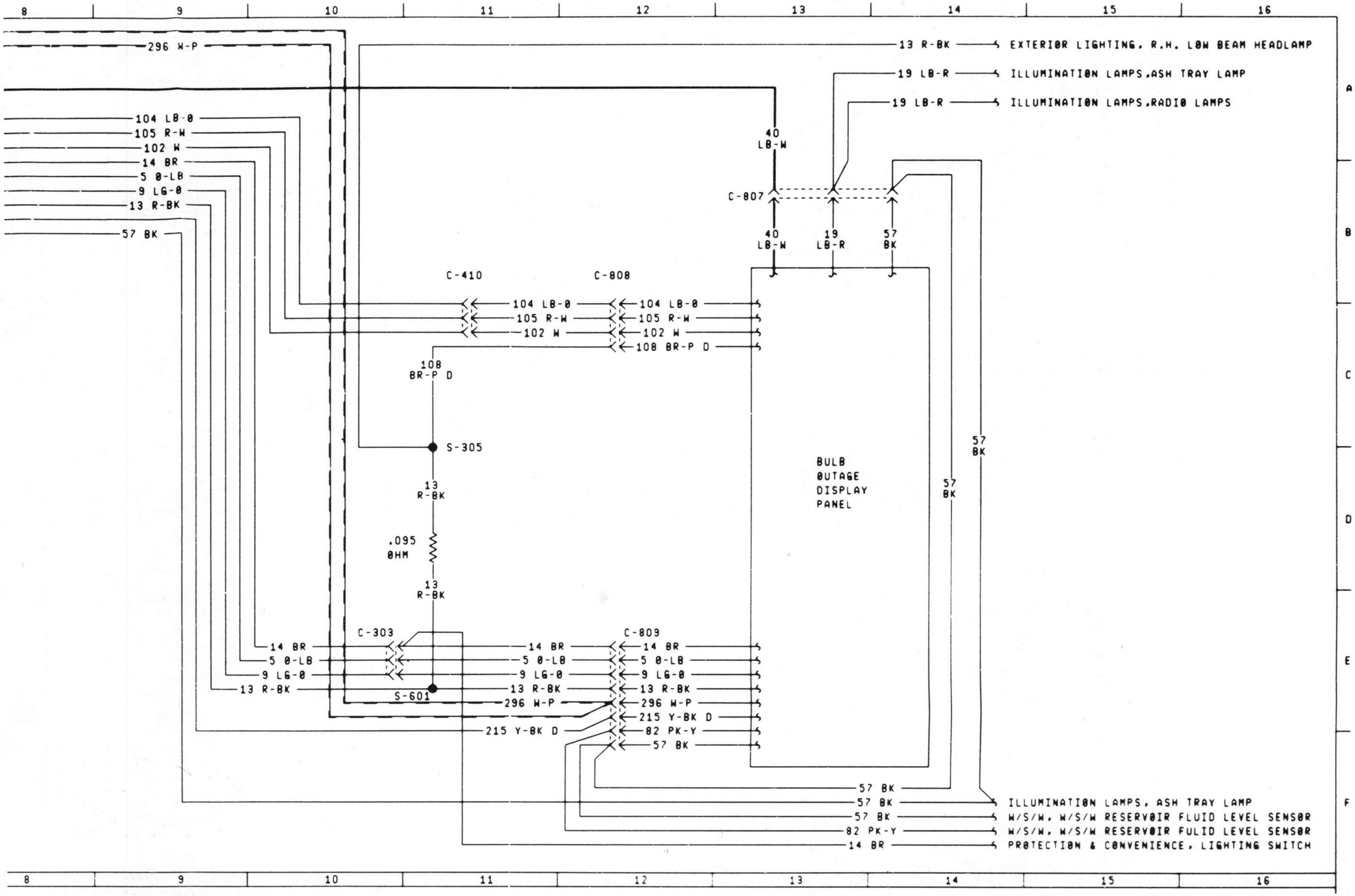

Fig. 10.44 Wiring diagram, protection and convenience (cont.), 1982 models

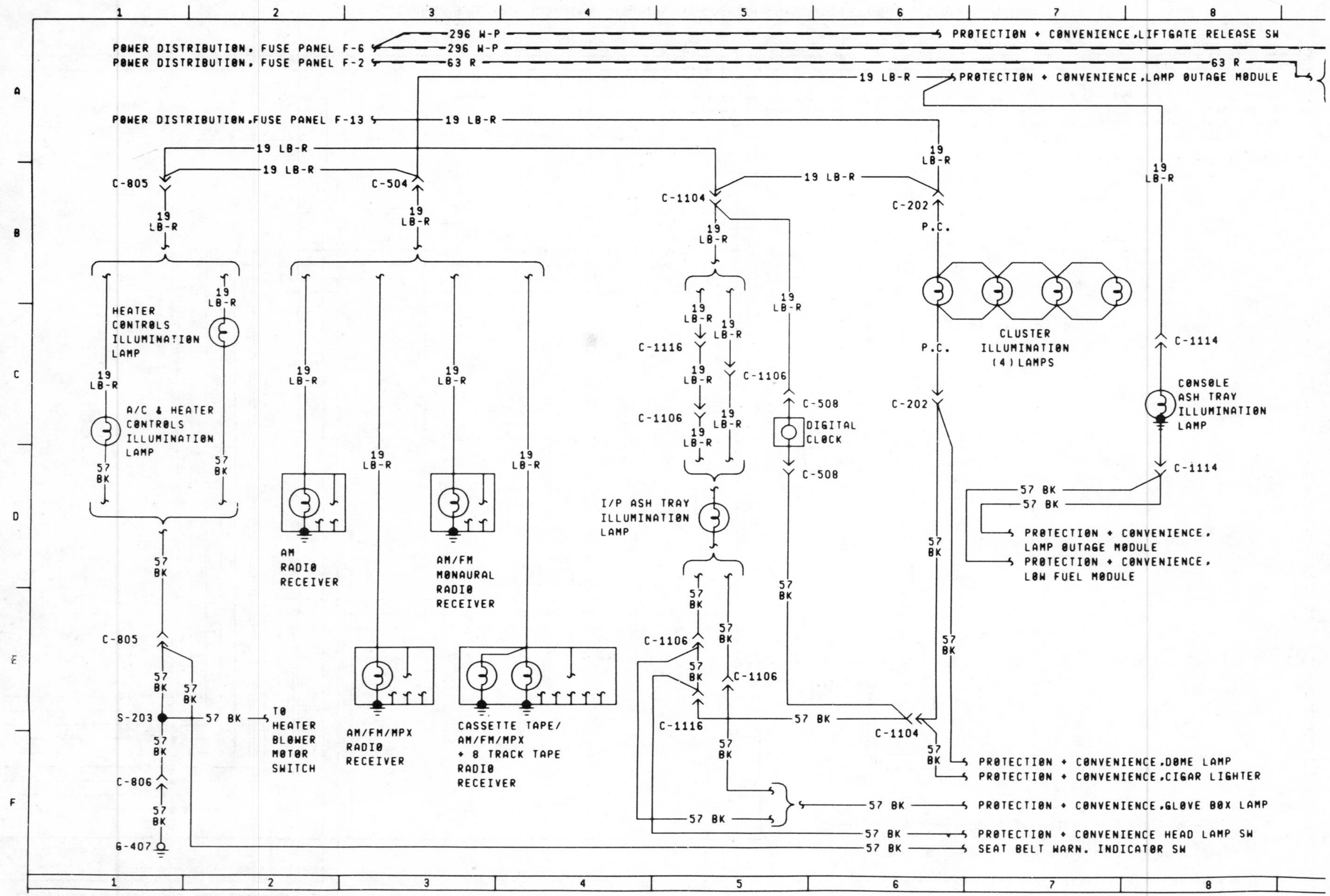

Fig. 10.45 Wiring diagram, illumination lamps, windshield wiper/washer, 1982 models

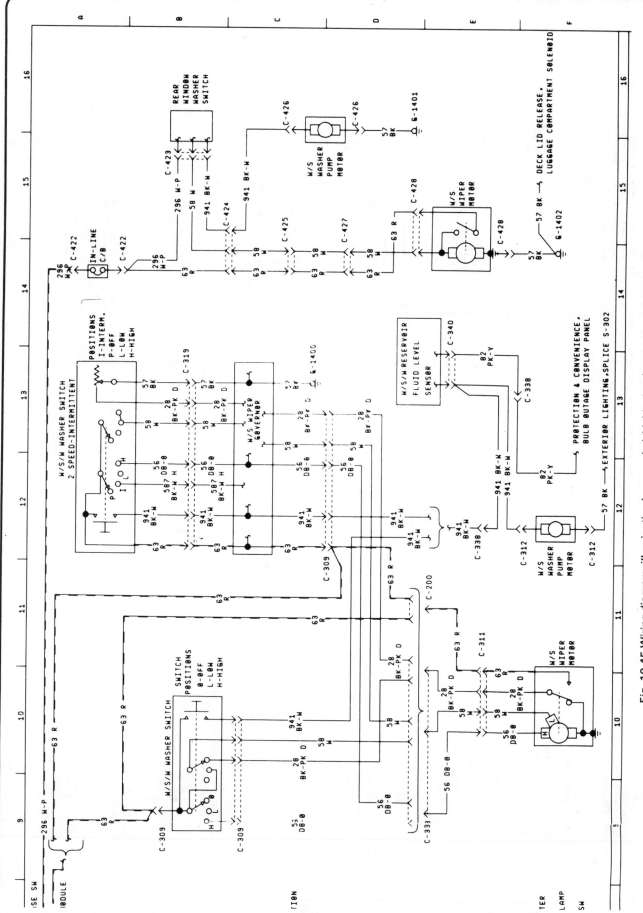

Fig. 10.45 Wiring diagram, illumination lamps, windshield wiper/washer (cont.), 1982 models

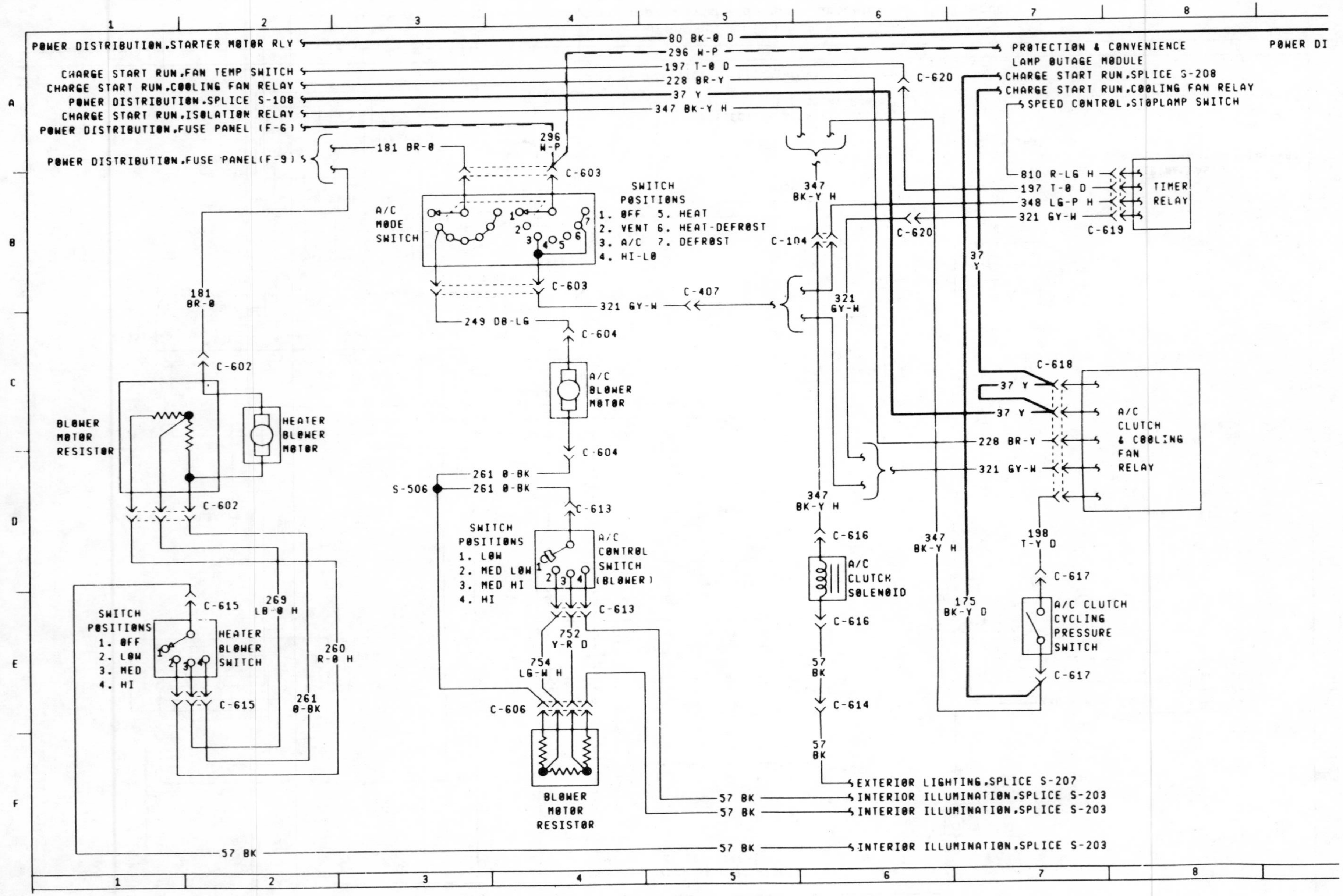

188

Fig. 10.46 Wiring diagram, air conditioner and/or heater, engine compartment lamp, deck lid release, 1982 models

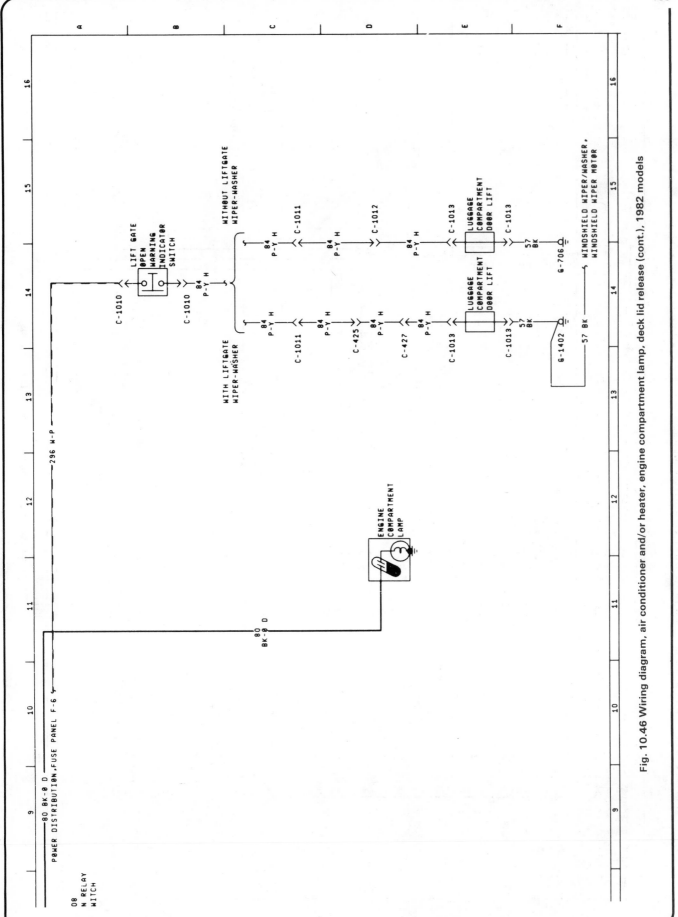

Fig. 10.46 Wiring diagram, air conditioner and/or heater, engine compartment lamp, deck lid release (cont.), 1982 models

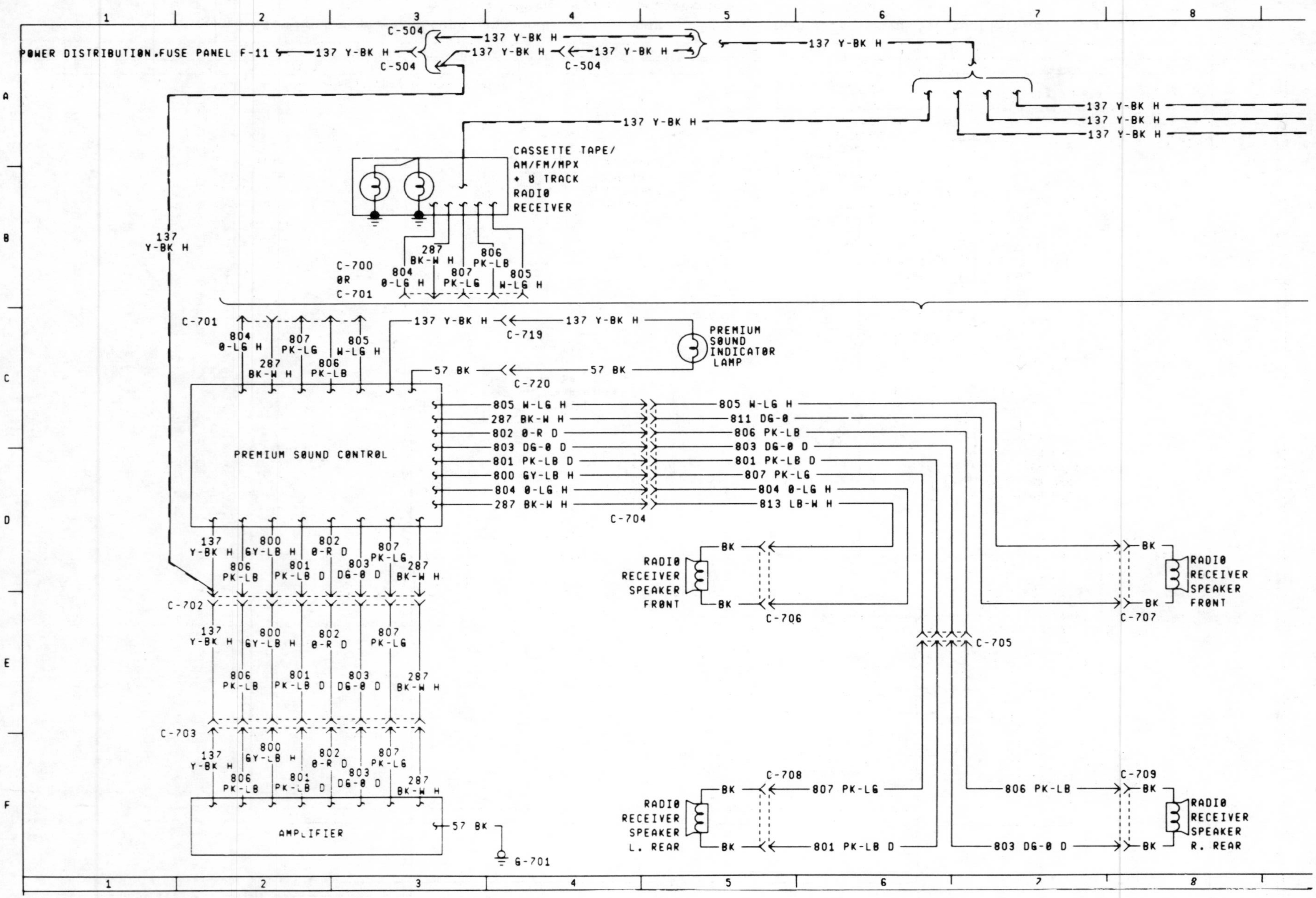

Fig. 10.47 Wiring diagram, radio circuits, 1982 models

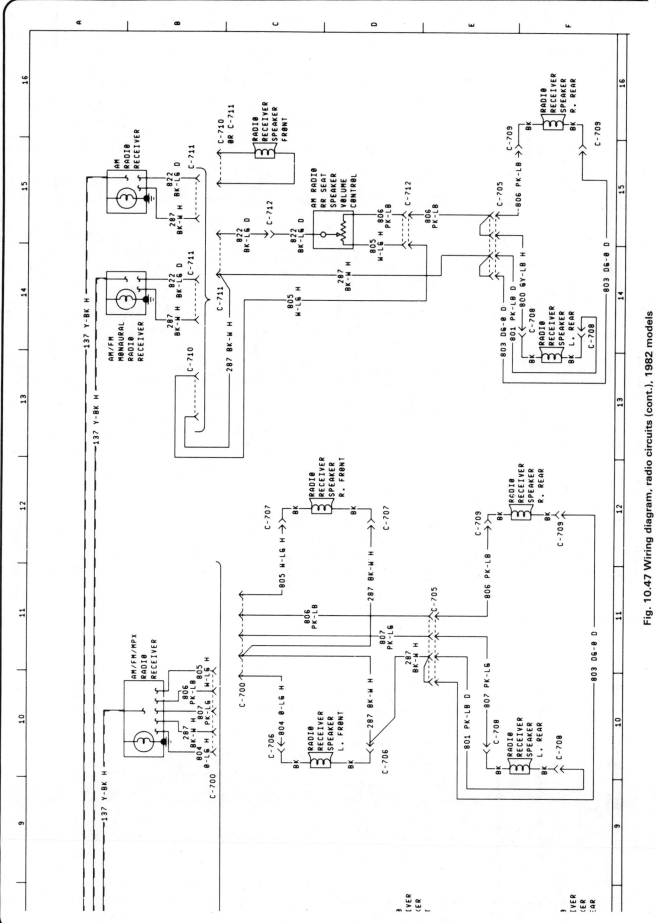

Fig. 10.47 Wiring diagram, radio circuits (cont.), 1982 models

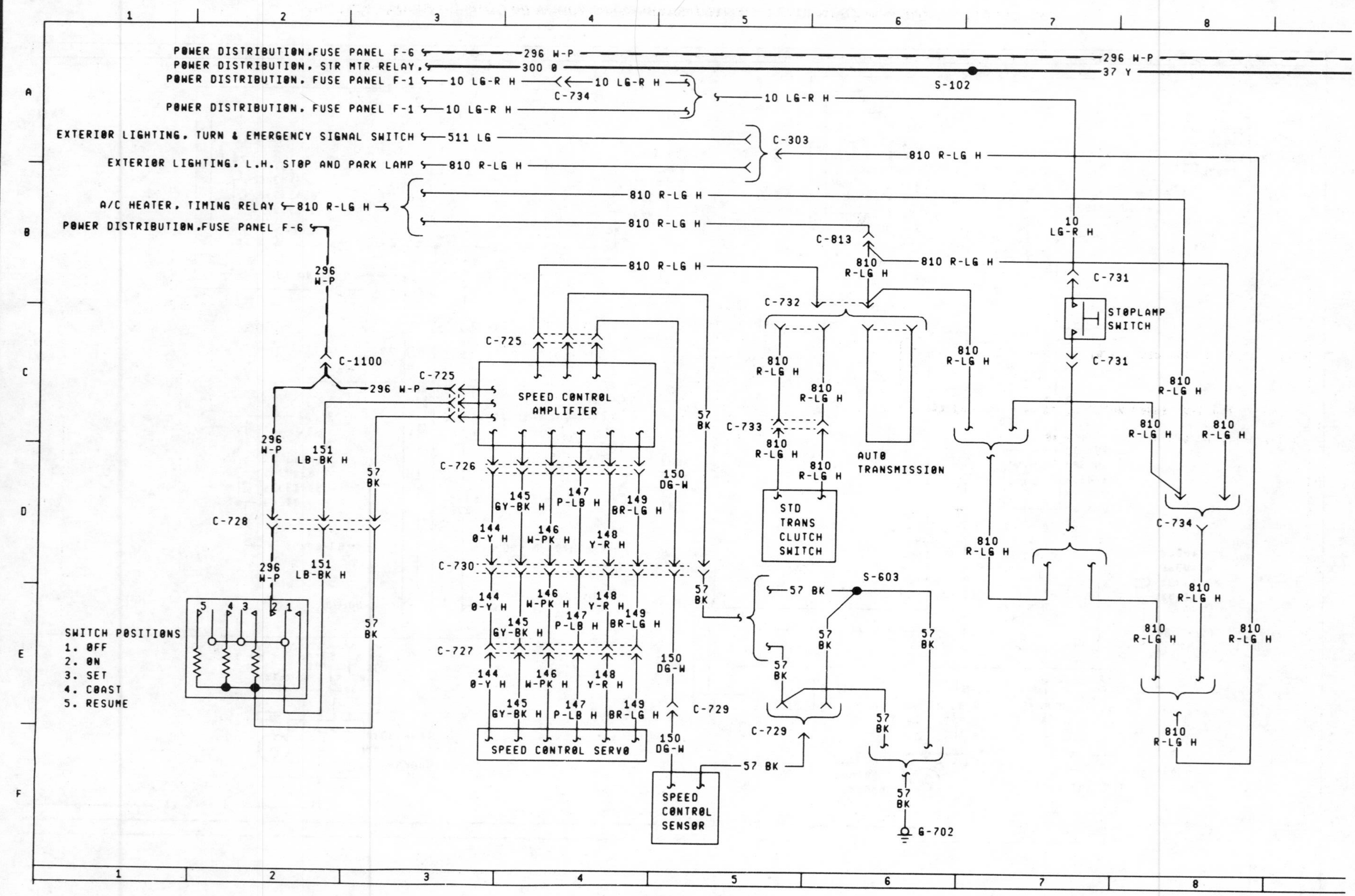

Fig. 10.48 Wiring diagram, horn with speed control, heated rear window, heater, 1982 models

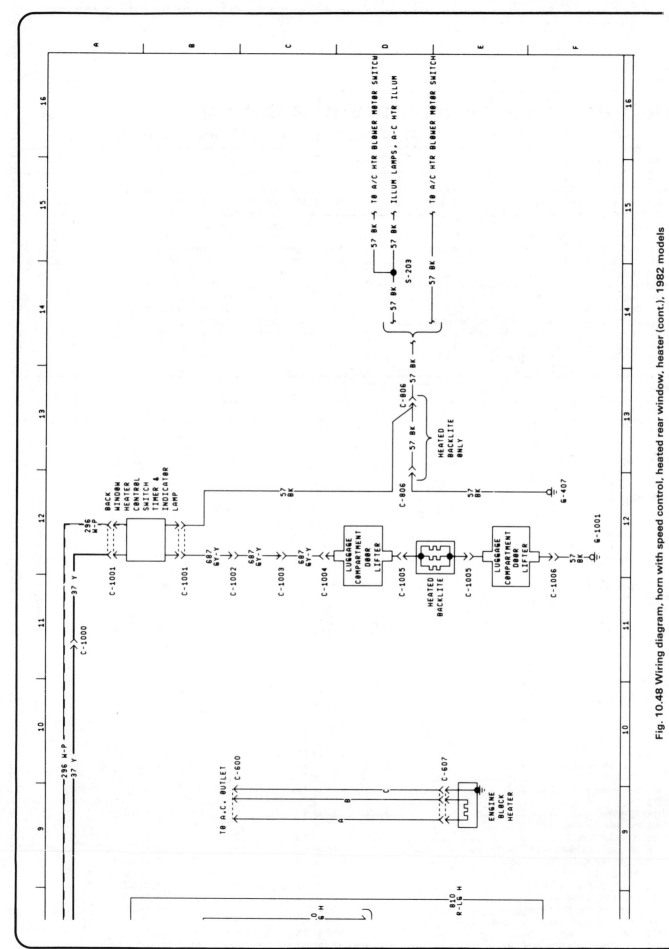

Fig. 10.48 Wiring diagram, horn with speed control, heated rear window, heater (cont.), 1982 models

Chapter 11 Suspension and steering

Refer to Chapter 13 for specifications and information related to 1983 thru 1985 models

Contents

Specifications

Front suspension type .... Independent MacPherson strut with integral shock absorber and strut mounted coil spring

Rear suspension type .... Independent modified MacPherson strut with integral shock absorber and coil spring mounted on the lower arm

Steering gear
Type .... Rack and pinion with optional power assist
Lubricant type .... Fluid grease, Ford specification D8AZ-19578-A or equiv.
Lubricant capacity .... 0.2 pts (3.2 oz)
Power steering fluid type .... Type F
Power steering pump capacity .... 786 milliliters

Torque specifications

	Ft-lb	Nm
Front suspension		
Shock absorber shaft retaining nut	48 to 70	65 to 95
Shock absorber-to-body	23 to 30	31 to 40
Shock absorber-to-knuckle	66 to 81	90 to 110
Control arm-to-body	44 to 55	60 to 75
Control arm-to-knuckle	37 to 44	50 to 60
Stabilizer bar-to-control arm	80 to 115	108 to 156
Stabilizer bar bracket-to-body	50 to 60	69 to 81
Stabilizer bar insulator U-clamp-to-bracket	60 to 70	81 to 95
Tie rod end-to-steering knuckle	23 to 35	31 to 47
Rear suspension		
Shock absorber-to-body	35 to 55	48 to 75
Shock absorber-to-spindle	90 to 100	122 to 135
Control arm-to-body	65 to 75	88 to 102
Control arm-to-spindle	90 to 100	122 to 135
Tie-rod-to-body	90 to 100	122 to 135
Tie-rod-to-spindle	88 to 102	65 to 75
Steering		
Steering wheel nut	30 to 40	41 to 54
Steering column mount nut	17 to 25	23 to 33
Steering column shaft clamp nut	20 to 30	27 to 40
Steering gear mounting bolts	48 to 55	65 to 75
Connecting rod end-to-spindle arm	27 to 32	36 to 43
Connecting rod end-to-inner tie-rod jam nut	42 to 50	57 to 68
Pinion shaft-to-flex coupling	20 to 37	28 to 50
Power steering oil pressure line	10 to 15	13 to 20
Power steering oil return line	10 to15	13 to 20
Power steering pump pivot and mounting bolts	30 to 45	41 to 61
Oil pressure hose-to-pump fitting	10 to 15	13 to 20
Oil return hose-to-pump clamp	1 to 2	2 to 3

1   General information

The front suspension on all models is of the MacPherso strut type which features a shock absorber strut and spring mounted on top of the steering knuckle. The steering knuckle is located by the front stabilizer bar and the lower control arm.

The rear suspension is a modifed MacPherson strut design consisting of a shock absorber strut attached to a spindle mounted to the end of the lower control arm. The spring is mounted between the control arm and the chassis crossmember. The assembly is located by a rubber bushed tie-rod running forward from the spindle to the chassis.

The shock absorber is an integral part of the strut and can be replaced only by disassembling the strut assembly.

Steering is of the rack-and-pinion type with power assist as an option.

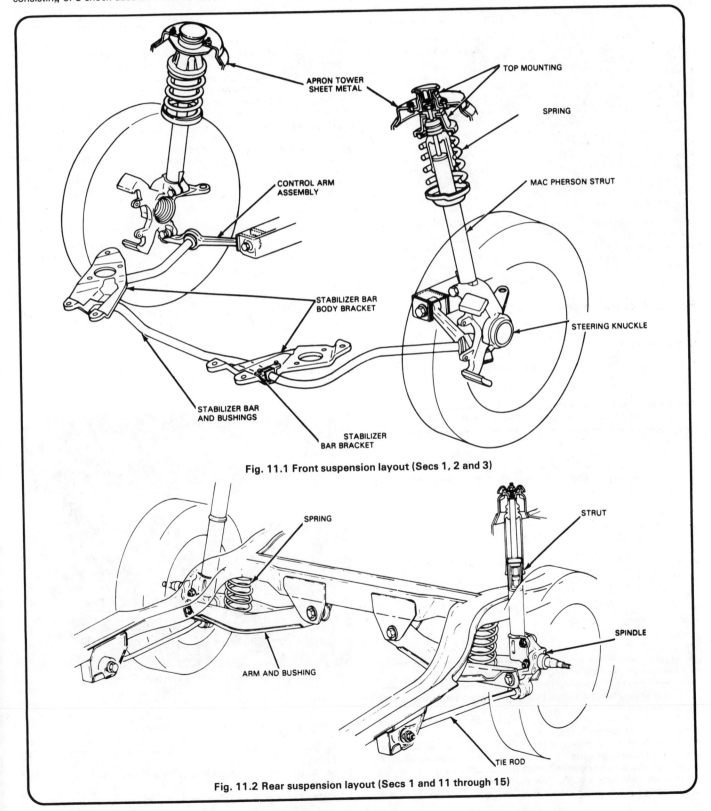

APRON TOWER SHEET METAL

CONTROL ARM ASSEMBLY

STABILIZER BAR BODY BRACKET

STABILIZER BAR AND BUSHINGS

STABILIZER BAR BRACKET

TOP MOUNTING

SPRING

MAC PHERSON STRUT

STEERING KNUCKLE

Fig. 11.1 Front suspension layout (Secs 1, 2 and 3)

SPRING

STRUT

ARM AND BUSHING

SPINDLE

TIE ROD

Fig. 11.2 Rear suspension layout (Secs 1 and 11 through 15)

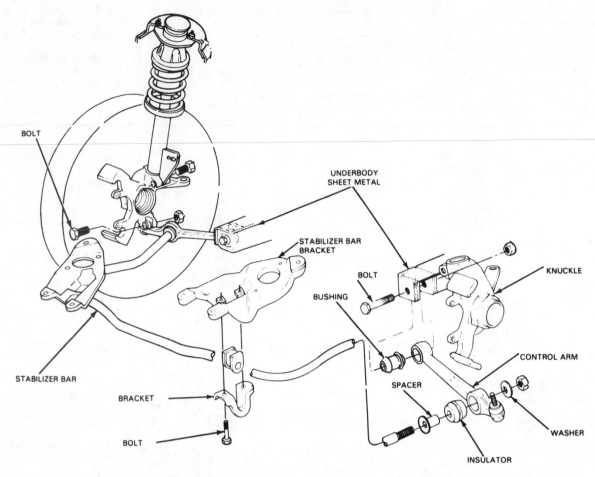

Fig. 11.3 Front suspension components (Secs 1 through 9)

2 Stabilizer bar and insulators – removal and installation

1 Raise the vehicle and support it securely.
2 Remove the nuts from the stabilizer bar ends at the control arms and withdraw the dished washers.
3 Unbolt the stabilizer bar insulator mounting brackets and remove the bar.
4 Cut the worn insulators carefully and remove them from the bar.
5 Prior to installation, lubricate the stabilizer bar and insulators with rubber lubricant.
6 Slide the new insulators onto the stabilizer bar to their approximate installed locations.
7 Install the washer spacers onto the end of the car and place the mounting brackets over the insulators.
8 Position the ends of the bar in the lower control arms and install the insulator brackets, using new bolts.
9 Install new nuts on the ends of the stabilizer bar at the control ends and tighten to specification.
10 Lower the vehicle.

3 Lower control arm – removal and installation

1 Raise the vehicle, support it securely and remove the front wheels.
2 Disconnect the stabilizer bar at the control arm.
3 Remove the pivot bolt and nut at the inner end of the control arm.
4 Remove the pinch bolt on the lower control arm (photo).
5 With the steering column unlocked, use a screwdriver to spread the pinch joint and separate the control arm from the steering knuckle. A suitable drift punch and hammer are useful in removing the steering knuckle, but take care not to strike the knuckle.
6 To install, insert the control arm ballstud into the steering knuckle.

3.4 Loosening the steering knuckle pinch bolt

7 Install a new pinch bolt and nut, tightening to specification.
8 Place the lower control arm on the stabilizer bar and position the arm to the inner mounting. Install a new pivot bolt and nut and tighten to specification.
9 Install the stabilizer bar washer and install a new nut, tightening to specification.
10 Install the wheels and lower the vehicle.

4 Control arm stabilizer bushing – removal and installation

1 Raise the vehicle, support it securely and remove the front wheels.
2 Remove the stabilizer bar-to-control arm nut and washer.

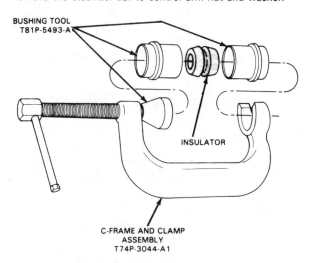

Fig. 11.4 Stabilizer bar bushing tool (Sec 2)

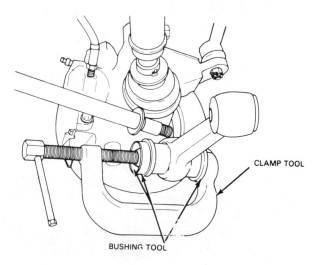

Fig. 11.5 Stabilizer bar bushing removal (Sec 2)

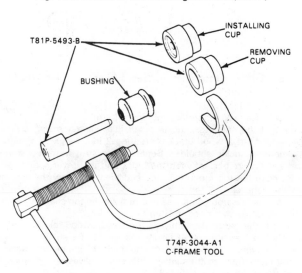

Fig. 11.7 Inner bushing removal and replacement tool (Sec 5)

3 Remove the control arm inner pivot bolt and nut, pull the arm downward and disconnect the arm from the stabilizer bar.
4 Using Ford C-clamp tool T74P-3044-A1 and bushing tool T81P-5493-A or equivalent, press the old bushing out of the control arm (Figs. 11.4 and 11.5).
5 Prior to installation, thoroughly lubricate the new bushing and the lower control arm contact area with vegetable cooking oil. Use only vegetable oil as mineral-, or petroleum-based oils or brake fluid will cause the rubber bushing to deteriorate.
6 Use the Ford tools to push the new bushing into the lower control arm by slowly turning the C-clamp until the bushing pops into place (Fig. 11.6).
7 Install the outer end of the control arm to the stabilizer bar and the inner end to the chassis, using new bolts and nuts.
8 Install the wheels and lower the vehicle.

5 Control arm inner pivot bushing – removal and installation

1 Raise the vehicle, support it securely and remove the front wheels.
2 Disconnect the stabilizer bar at the outer end and remove the inner pivot bolt and nut. Remove the control arm by pulling it downward and away from the stabilizer bar.
3 Carefully cut away the bushing's retaining lip.
4 Use Ford tool T74P-3044-A1 and T81P-5493-B or equivalent to push the old bushing from the control arm (Figs. 11.7 and 11.8).
5 Prior to installation, thoroughly lubricate the new bushing and the control arm with vegetable oil. Use only vegetable oil as any other lubricant will accelerate the deterioration of the rubber bushing.
6 Install the new bushing into the control arm using the Ford tools (Fig. 11.9).

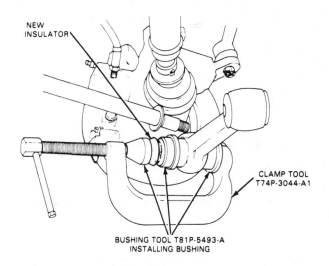

Fig. 11.6 Pressing the new bushing into the control arm with the Ford tool (Sec 4)

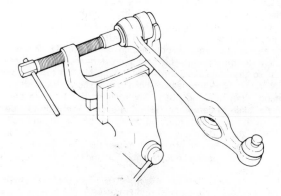

Fig. 11.8 Removing the control arm inner pivot bushing (Sec 5)

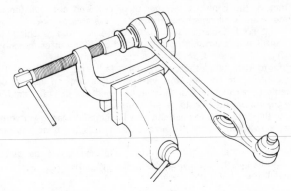

Fig. 11.9 Installing a new lower control arm inner bushing (Sec 5)

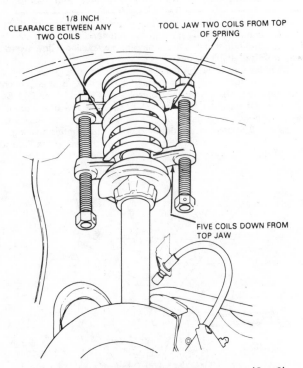

Fig. 11.11 Properly installed spring compressor (Sec 6)

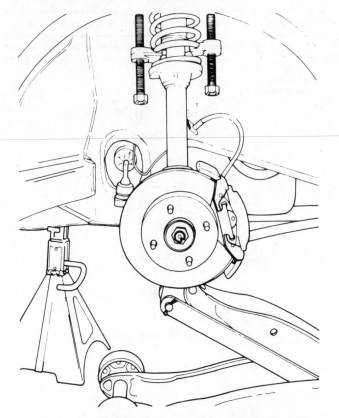

Fig. 11.10 Raising the strut but not the vehicle (Sec 6)

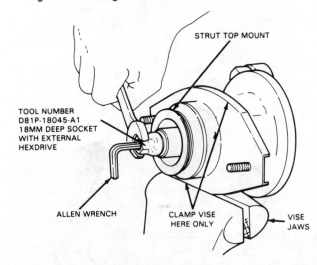

Fig. 11.12 Strut top shaft nut removal or loosening (Sec 6)

7   Install the control arm to the stabilizer bar and chassis, using new bolts.
8   Reinstall the front wheels and lower the vehicle.

6   Spring, strut and upper mount – removal and installation

1   Raise the vehicle, support it securely and remove the front wheels.
2   Disconnect the brake hose flex clips from the strut.
3   Place a jack under the lower control arm and raise the strut until just short of lifting the vehicle (Fig. 11.10).
4   Install a spring compressor tool such as Ford tool T81P-5301-A or equivalent to the spring. The spring must be compressed prior to removal so that excessive force will not be applied to the constant velocity joints. The compressor tool threads should be oiled prior to use, hand wrenches and not power tools should be used and care should be taken to compress the spring evenly from side to side. The top jaw of the compressor should be placed on the second coil from the top with the bottom jaw gripping five coils down from the top jaw. The spring should be compressed until there is $\frac{1}{8}$ in between the coils.
5   Remove the steering knuckle pinch bolt and loosen the top mount-to-apron bolts.
6   Loosen the top shaft nut using an 18 mm deep socket with an external hex drive such as Ford tool D81P-18045-A1. Hold the shaft end with the hex nut and loosen the shaft nut with an 18 mm Allen

wrench (Fig. 11.12).
7   Lower the jack supporting the control arm.
8   Spread the steering knuckle pinch joint slightly, using a screw-driver and insert a wood block measuring 2 in x 4 in x 7$\frac{1}{2}$ in against the steering knuckle shoulder. Separate the strut from the knuckle, using a short pry bar between the block and the lower spring seat.
9   Remove the top mounting nuts and then withdraw the assembly from the vehicle.
10   Place the assembly in a vise and remove the top shaft nut with an Allen wrench as described in Step 6 (Fig. 11.12).
11   When the strut assembly is removed, wood blocks can be fabricated to clamp the strut firmly in a vise. Cut a standard 2 in x 4 in block of wood to a 7$\frac{1}{2}$ in length and drill a 1$\frac{5}{8}$ in hole in the center. Cut the block through the center, into equal halves and chamfer the edges of the drilled areas (Fig. 11.14).
12   Place the assembly in a vise, taking care not to clamp the lower

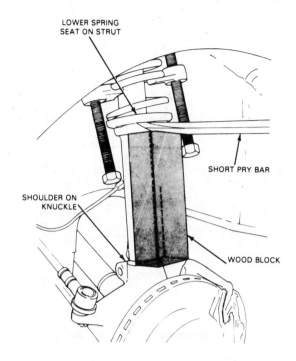

Fig. 11.13 Separating the steering knuckle from the strut seat
(Sec 6)

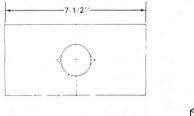

Fig. 11.14 Wood strut clamp block fabrication (Sec 6)

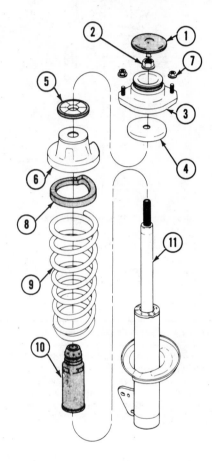

Fig. 11.16 Front strut components (Sec 6)

1 Dust cap
2 Nut and washer
3 Upper mount
4 Thrust plate
5 Bearing and seal
6 Spring seat
7 Nut
8 Spring insulator
9 Spring
10 Front jounce bumper
11 Shock absorber strut

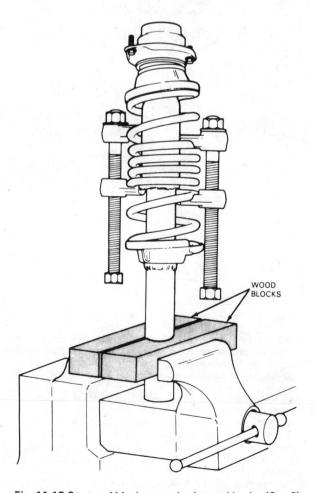

Fig. 11.15 Strut and block properly clamped in vise (Sec 6)

four inches of the strut (Fig. 11.15).

13 Remove any components to be worked on or replaced. If only the strut and top mount are to be worked on, the spring compressor can be left in place.

14 Prior to installation, check that the spring compressor is properly installed 90 degrees from the metal tab on the strut. Also make sure that the upper jaw is two coils and the lower jaw is five coils from the top, the coils are approximately $\frac{1}{8}$ in apart and the lower pigtail is seated in the spring seat (Fig. 11.17).

15 Tighten the upper shaft nut to specification.

16 Install the compressor and strut assembly to the vehicle, positioning the top mounting stud through the apron. Install but do not tighten the nuts.

17 Install the strut to the steering knuckle pinch joint and install a

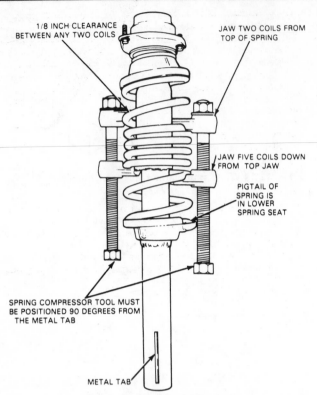

Fig. 11.17 Compressor and strut assembly ready for installation (Sec 6)

new nut and bolt, tightening to specification.
18   Tighten the upper mounting bolts to specification at this time.
19   Remove the spring compressor.
20   Install the brake hose clip onto the strut.
21   Install the front wheels and lower the vehicle.

7 Steering knuckle lower balljoint – checking

1   Raise the front of the vehicle and support it securely.
2   Have an assistant grasp the lower edge of the front wheel and rock it in and out as you observe the lower balljoint for movement.
3   If any movement is visible, the balljoint is worn and the lower control arm must be replaced with a new one (Section 3).

8 Steering knuckle – removal and installation

1   Raise the vehicle, support it securely and remove the front wheels.
2   Remove the tie-rod end strut nut and cotter pin.
3   Disconnect the tie-rod from the steering knuckle, using a suitable tool (photo).
4   Remove the brake caliper (Chapter 9).
5   Remove the hub from the driveshaft (Section 10, Steps 10 and 11).
6   Disconnect the lower control arm at the steering knuckle pinch bolt (Section 3, Step 5).
7   Remove the steering knuckle from the strut assembly (Section 6, Step 5).
8   Place the hub assembly on a workbench and remove the seals and bearings (Section 10).
9   Install the steering knuckle onto the shock absorber strut with a new pinch bolt and nut, tightening to specification.
10   Install the hub onto the driveshaft (Section 10, Steps 28 to 30).
11   Install the lower control arm to the steering knuckle using a new bolt and nut, tightening to specification.
12   Install the brake caliper (Chapter 9).
13   Connect the tie-rod to the steering knuckle, using a new nut, tighten to specification and advance the nut to align the slot if necessary to insert the cotter pin.
14   Install the front wheels and lower the vehicle.

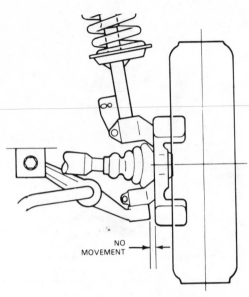

Fig. 11.18 Checking balljoint wear (Sec 7)

8.3 Disconnecting the tie rod

9 Tie-rod end – removal and installation

1   Raise the vehicle, support it securely and remove the front wheel(s).
2   Remove the nut and cotter pin from the tie-rod end ball stud.
3   Disconnect the tie-rod end using a suitable tool to separate the rod end from the steering knuckle.
4   Hold the tie-rod end with a wrench and loosen the jam nut (Fig. 11.19).
5   Mark the depth to which the rod end is threaded into the rod. Use a pair of locking pliers and remove the rod end.
6   Clean and lubricate the tie-rod threads. Thread the new rod end into the rod to the marked position and tighten the jam nut.
7   Install the rod end to the steering knuckle arm using a new nut. Tighten to specification and advance the nut to the next slot if necessary for the installation of the cotter pin.
8   Install the front wheels, lower the vehicle and have the front end alignment checked.

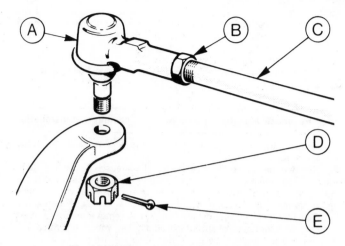

Fig. 11.19 Tie-rod end components (Sec 9)

A Balljoint   D Lock nut
B Jam nut   E Cotter pin
C Tie-rod

10 Front hub bearings – removal and installation

1 Slacken the wheel bolts, raise the front of the vehicle and remove the wheel.

2 Install two of the wheel bolts as a means of anchorage for the disc when the hub nut is unscrewed.

3 Have an assistant apply the brake and then unscrew the staked hub nut and remove it together with the plain washer. This nut is very tight.

4 Remove the temporary wheel bolts.

5 Unbolt the brake caliper and tie it up to the suspension strut to avoid strain on the flexible hose.

6 Withdraw the hub/disc. If it is tight, use a two-legged puller.

7 Extract the split pin and unscrew the castellated nut from the tie-rod end balljoint.

8 Using a suitable balljoint splitter, separate the balljoint from the steering arm.

9 Unscrew and remove the pinch-bolt which holds the lower arm balljoint to the stub axle carrier.

10 Support the driveshaft on a block of wood and remove the bolt which holds the stub axle carrier to the base of the suspension strut.

11 Using a suitable lever, separate the carrier from the strut by prying open the clamp jaws.

12 Support the driveshaft at the outboard CV joint and pull the stub

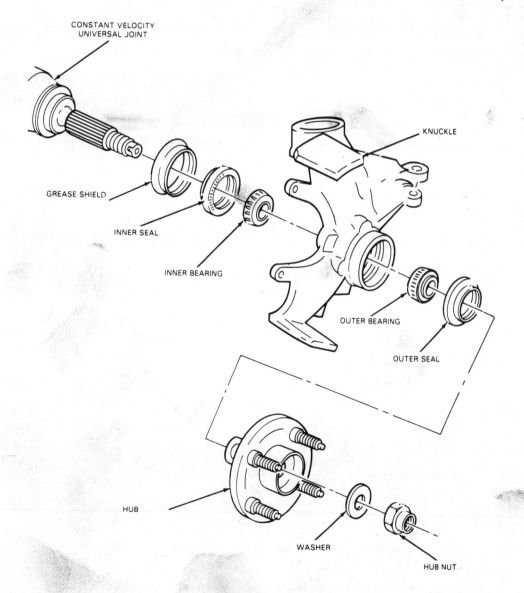

Fig. 11.20 Front hub components (Sec 10)

axle carrier clear of the driveshaft.

13 Remove the stub axle carrier and grip it in a vise fitted with jaw protectors.

14 Using pliers, pull out the dust shield from the groove in the stub axle carrier.

15 Pry out the inner and outer oil seals.

16 Lift out the bearings.

17 With a suitable drift, drive out the bearing cups.

18 Clean away all the old grease from the stub axle carrier.

19 Drive the new bearing cups squarely into their seats using a piece of suitable diameter tubing.

20 Liberally pack grease into the bearings, making sure to work plenty into the spaces between the rollers.

21 Install the bearing to one side of the carrier, then fill the lips of the new oil seal with grease and tap it squarely into position.

22 Fit the bearing and its seal to the opposite side in a similar way.

23 Fit the dust shield by tapping it into position using a block of wood.

24 Smear the driveshaft splines with grease, then install the carrier over the end of the driveshaft.

25 Connect the carrier to the suspension strut and tighten the bolt to the specified torque.

26 Reconnect the suspension lower arm balljoint to the carrier and secure by passing the pinch-bolt through the groove in the balljoint stud.

27 Reconnect the tie-rod to the steering arm, tighten the castellated nut to the specified torque and secure with a new split pin.

28 Install the hub/disc and push it on to the driveshaft as far as it will go using hand pressure.

29 In the absence of the special hub installer tool draw the hub/disc onto the driveshaft by using a two or three-legged puller with legs engaged behind the carrier. On no account try to knock the hub/disc into position using hammer blows or the CV joint will be damaged.

30 Grease the threads at the end of the driveshaft, fit the plain washer and screw on a new nut, finger tight.

31 Install the brake caliper, tightening the mounting bolts to the

specified torque.

32 Screw in two wheel bolts and have an assistant apply the brake.

33 Tighten the hub nut to the specified torque.

34 Stake the nut into the driveshaft groove.

35 Remove the temporary wheel bolts.

36 Fit the wheel and lower the vehicle to the floor. Fully tighten the wheel bolts.

11 Rear shock absorber strut – removal, testing and installation

1 Remove any interior panels necessary to gain access to the top of the shock absorber strut.

2 Remove the cap and loosen the top shock absorber nut by holding the strut rod with a 6 mm Allen wrench and turning the shock absorber with a 43 mm socket ot wrench. If the shock absorber is to be used again, do not grip the shaft with pliers as this will cause damage.

3 Raise the vehicle, support it securely and remove the rear wheels. Support the lower control arm of the side being worked on with a jack.

4 Release the brake hose from the shock absorber.

5 Loosen but do not remove the shock absorber-to-spindle attaching bolts.

6 Remove the shock absorber top mounting nut, washer and insulator.

7 Remove the bottom mounting bolts and withdraw the shock absorber assembly from the vehicle.

8 Inspect the shock absorber for signs of fluid leakage. A thin film of fluid is permissible but the strut should be replaced with a new one if the leakage is excessive. Place the shock absorber in a vise and compress and extend it fully several times. If there is lag or skip in the action or a clicking noise, replace with a new unit.

9 Prior to installation, turn the shock absorber upside down and extend and compress it fully several times to expel any trapped air.

10 Extend the shock absorber to its full length and install the lower washer and insulator, using rubber lubricant for ease of installation into the shock tower.

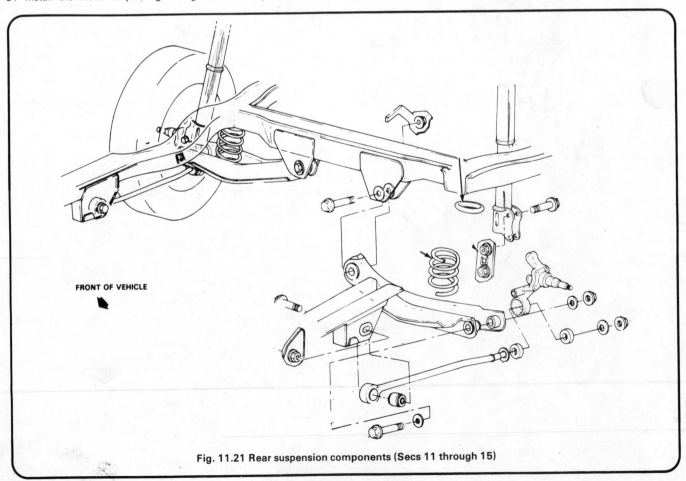

FRONT OF VEHICLE

Fig. 11.21 Rear suspension components (Secs 11 through 15)

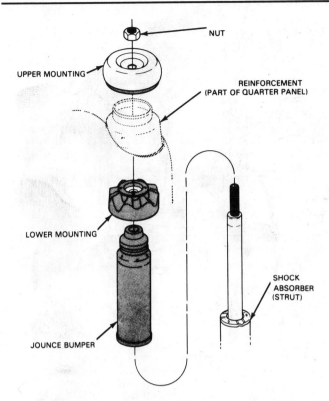

Fig. 11.22 Rear shock absorber top mount components (Sec 11)

11 Place the upper end of the shock absorber into the shock tower and slowly push it upward to align the mounting holes.
12 Install but do not tighten the mounting bolts, with the bolt heads facing towards the rear of the vehicle.
13 Install the upper insulator, washer and nut assembly onto the upper shock absorber shaft.
14 Tighten the nut to specification, using the Allen wrench to hold the strut shaft while turning the socket or wrench.
15 Tighten the lower mounting bolts to specification at this time.
16 Install the brake hose to the shock absorber.
17 Install the rear wheels, remove the jack from the suspension arm and lower the vehicle.
18 Replace any access panels.

12 Lower control arm and spring – removal and installation

1 Raise the vehicle, support it securely and remove the rear wheels.
2 With the rear suspension fully extended, support the control arm with a jack.
3 Remove the nuts attaching the control arm to the spindle and the chassis, leaving the bolts in place. It will not be necessary to remove the control arm-to-body nut and bolt if only the spring is to be removed. The manufacturer recommends that new nuts and bolts be installed any time they are loosened or removed.
4 Remove the arm-to-spindle bolt and slowly lower the control arm with the jack until the spring and insulator can be removed.
5 Remove the inner end bolt and lift the control arm from the vehicle.
6 Install the inner end of the arm to the body using a new nut and bolt. Do not tighten at this time.
7 Install the insulator to the top of the spring, making sure to properly index the spring end. The standard and TRX-type suspensions vary somewhat in detail (Figs. 11.24 and 11.25).
8 Install the spring in the lower control arm spring pocket with the spring pigtail properly indexed and with the insulator in place (Fig. 11.26).
9 Raise the control arm with the jack until the arm and spindle bolt holes are aligned.
10 With the bolt head to the rear of the vehicle, install a new bolt and nut. Do not tighten at this time.

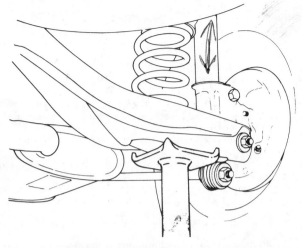

Fig. 11.23 Supporting the rear control arm (Sec 12)

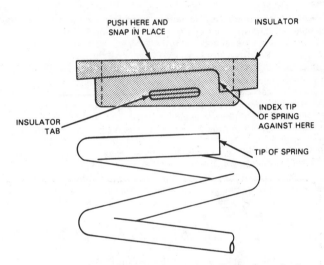

Fig. 11.24 Spring upper insulator installation (standard suspension) (Sec 12)

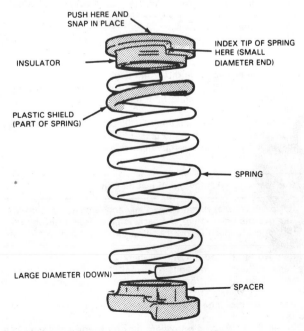

Fig. 11.25 TRX-type rear spring insulator installation (Sec 12)

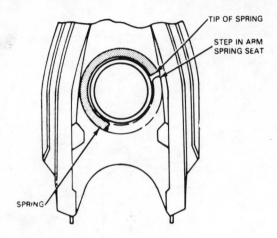

Fig. 11.26 Proper indexing of the spring to the lower suspension arm (Sec 12)

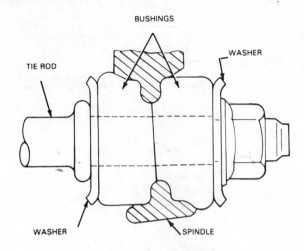

Fig. 11.27 Rear suspension tie-rod end installation (Sec 13)

11 Raise the control arm to normal operating level and tighten the spindle bolt and the control arm inner bolt to specification.
12 Install the wheels and lower the vehicle.

---

13 Rear suspension tie-rod – removal and installation

1 Raise the vehicle, support it securely and remove the rear wheels.
2 Remove the tie-rod-to-spindle nut, washers and insulators.
3 Mark the tie-rod front bracket bolt location for ease of installation and remove the bolt.
4 Lift the tie-rod away from the vehicle. It may be necessary to pry apart the front bracket sheet metal when removing.
5 Install the washer with the larger internal diameter on the tie-rod. With the new bushings installed in the spindle, insert the tie-rod. Install the washer with the smaller internal diameter and a new nut, tightening to specification.
6 Raise the control arm with a jack to operating height, align the scribe mark on the bolt and front body bracket and tighten to specification.
7 Install the wheels and lower the vehicle.

---

14 Rear suspension tie-rod bushings – removal and installation

1 Remove the tie-rod (Section 13).
2 The old bushing can be removed using a vise or large C-clamp and suitable sized socket or Ford tools T74P-3044-A1 and T81P-5896-A to press the bushing from the rod. Whichever tools are used, always work from the beveled side of the rod (Fig. 11.28).
3 The new bushing is pressed into place in the same manner as during removal, again working from the beveled side of the rod (Fig. 11.29).
4 The tie-rod bushings in the spindle can be pried out using a screwdriver and new ones hand-pressed into place.
5 Install the tie-rod as described in Section 13.

---

15 Rear spindle – removal and installation

1 Raise the vehicle, support it securely and remove the rear wheels.
2 Remove the brake drum and backing plate assembly (Chapter 9).
3 Use a jack under the lower control arm to raise it to the normal operating level.
4 Remove the tie-rod nut and washer.
5 Remove the nuts and bolts retaining the strut to the spindle.
6 Unbolt the spindle from the lower control arm and remove the spindle.
7 Install the bushings to the spindle, position the spindle over the end of the tie-rod.
8 Install the new spindle-to-shock strut nuts and bolts (bolt heads facing toward the rear) and tighten to specification.

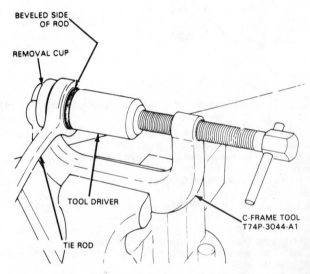

Fig. 11.28 Removing the tie-rod bushing using the Ford tool (Sec 14)

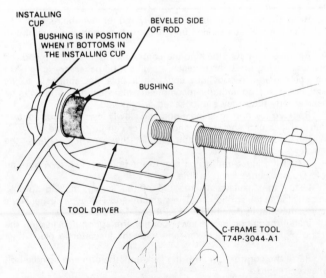

Fig. 11.29 Installing the tie-rod bushing with the Ford tool (Sec 11.14)

9   Install a new washer and nut on the tie-rod, tightening to specification.
10 Install the brake and backing plate assembly (Chapter 9).
11 Adjust the rear wheel bearings (Section 17).
12 Install the rear whels and lower the vehicle.

16   Rear wheel bearing – removal, inspection and installation

1   Raise the rear of the vehicle, support it securely and remove the rear wheels.
2   Remove the grease cap, cotter pin, nut retainer and adjusting nut and remove the hub, taking care not to drop the outer bearing.
3   Pry out the inner grease seal with a screwdriver (Fig. 11.31).
4   Wipe the spindle and hub bearing surfaces clean of grease and brake dust. Wash the bearings and grease cups in a suitable solvent, drying thoroughly. Inspect the bearings and cups for wear, scratches, pits and excessive looseness, replacing any worn parts.
5   If the bearing cups are to be removed, they can be driven out of the hub with a suitable punch after supporting the hub on a block of wood.
6   To install the bearing cups, support the hub on the block of wood, position the cup in the hub recess and use a suitable-size socket and hammer to gently tap into place.
7   Lubricate the wheel bearings thoroughly, working the specified grease into the rollers and cages. Lightly grease the cup surfaces.
8   Install the inner bearing into the hub, lightly grease the lips of the new seal and tap it into position.
9   Lightly grease the spindle and install the hub.
10 Install the outer bearing, flat washer and spindle nut.
11 Adjust the bearings as described in Section 17.
12 Lower the vehicle.

17   Rear wheel bearings – adjustment

1   If the wheel is loose on the spindle when it is grasped at the edge and rocked back and forth or does not rotate freely, the bearing should be adjusted.
2   Raise the vehicle, support it securely and remove the hub cap or nut caps and grease cup.
3   Clean off excess grease and remove the cotter pin and nut retainer.
4   While rotating the wheel, tighten the adjusting nut to the specification in the accompanying figure (Step 1 in Fig. 11.32).
5   Back the adjusting nut ½ turn (Step 2 in the Figure).
6   Tighten the nut to the specification in Step 3 in the Figure.
7   Install the nut retainer over the adjusting nut with the slots aligned with the cotter pin hole and install the pin (Step 4).
8   Reinstall any removed components and lower the vehicle.

18   Rear wheel toe (dog tracking) – checking

1   Improper rear wheel toe (dog tracking) is a condition where the rear wheels are out of alignment with the front wheels.
2   The easiest way to check this is to drive the vehicle straight across a puddle of water onto a dry area of pavement. The dog tracking will be evident as the rear tire tracks are overlapping the front ones (Fig. 11.33).
3   If the overlap exceeds 1½ in, the rear toe on the vehicle will have to be adjusted. This procedure should be left to your dealer or a properly-equipped alignment shop.

19   Steering – general information

Steering is of the rack-and-pinion type with the steering column incorporating a double universal joint shaft and a collapsible section.

The pinion gear engages the rack and rotating the steering shaft causes lateral movement of the rack which is transmitted through the steering rods to the steering knuckle arms.

The power steering is of the integral type which is operated by hydraulic pressure provided by a belt-driven pump.

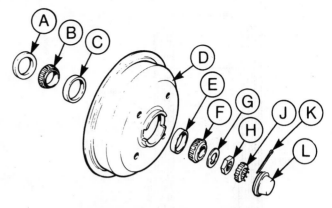

Fig. 11.30 Rear hub components (Sec 16)

A Inner grease seal	G Washer
B Bearing	H Nut
C Bearing cup	J Nut retainer
D Drum/hub	K Cotter pin
E Bearing cup	L Cap
F Bearing	

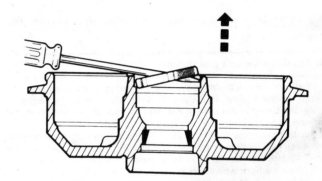

Fig. 11.31 Prying the inner grease seal out of the hub (Sec 16)

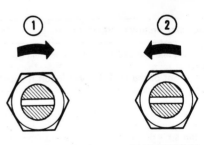

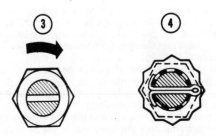

WITH WHEEL ROTATING, TORQUE ADJUSTING NUT, TO 23-34 N·m (17-25 LB-FT)

BACK ADJUSTING NUT OFF 1/2 TURN

TIGHTEN ADJUSTING NUT TO 1.1-1.7 N·m (10-15 LB-IN)

INSTALL THE RETAINER AND A NEW COTTER PIN

Fig. 11.32 Rear wheel bearing adjustment (Sec 17)

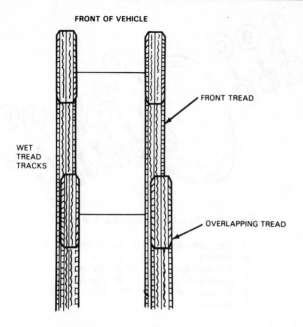

FRONT OF VEHICLE

FRONT TREAD

WET
TREAD
TRACKS

OVERLAPPING TREAD

Fig. 11.33 Checking for incorrect rear toe (dog tracking) (Sec 18)

20 Maintenance and precautions

1   Regularly check the condition of the steering gear bellows and the tie-rod balljoint dust excluders. If split, they must be replaced immediately and in the case of the steering gear, the lubricant cleared out and fresh injected (see Section 21).
2   With an assistant turning the steering wheel from side-to-side, check for lost motion at the tie-rod end balljoints. If evident, replace the balljoints (see Section 22) as no repair or lubrication is possible.
3   When the front wheels are raised, avoid turning the steering wheel rapidly from lock-to-lock. This could cause hydraulic pressure build-up, with consequent damage to the bellows.

21 Steering gear bellows – replacement

1   At the first indication of a split or grease leakage from the bellows, replace them.
2   Raise the front of the vehicle and support it securely.
3   Turn the wheels slowly to full lock to give access to the tie-rod balljoint.
4   Release the tie-rod end lock nut, but only unscrew it one quarter of a turn.
5   Extract the split pin and remove the nut from the balljoint taper pin.
6   Using a suitable balljoint extractor, separate the balljoint taper pin from the eye of the steering arm.
7   Unscrew the balljoint from the end of the tie-rod.
8   Release the clips from both ends of the damaged bellows and slide them from the rack and the tie-rod.
9   Turn the steering wheel gently to expel as much lubricant as possible from the rack housing. It is recommended that the bellows on the opposite side are released by detaching their inboard clip, turning the bellows back and clearing the lubricant as it is also ejected at this end of the rack housing.
10 Smear the narrow neck of the new bellows with specified grease and slide them over the tie-rod into position on the rack housing.
11 If new bellows are being fitted to the pinion end of the rack, leave both ends of the bellows unclamped at this stage.
12 If the bellows are being fitted to the rack support bush end of the rack housing, clamp only the inner end of the bellows and leave the outer end unfastened.
13 Screw on the tie-rod end until the lock nut requires only $\frac{1}{4}$ turn to lock it.
14 Connect the tie-rod end balljoint to the steering arm, tighten the

nut to the specified torque and insert a new split pin.
15 Add 95 cc (0.17 pint) of the specified lubricant to the pinion end of the rack housing. Move the steering slowly from lock-to-lock to assist the entry of the lubricant into the steering gear.
16 When all the lubricant is injected, install the bellows clamps. Where the original bellows clamping was by means of soft wire, this should be discarded and screw-type clips used instead.
17 Lower the vehicle to the floor.
18 If the position of the tie-rod lock nut was not altered from its original setting, the front wheel alignment (toe) will not have altered, but it is recommended that the alignment is checked at the earliest opportunity as described in Section 24.

22 Tie-rod end balljoint – replacement

1   If as the result of inspection the tie-rod end balljoints are found to be worn, remove them as described in the preceding Section.
2   When the balljoints nuts are unscrewed, it is sometimes found that the balljoint taper pin turns in the eye of the steering arm to prevent the nut from unscrewing. Should this happen, apply pressure to the top of the balljoint using a length of wood as a lever to seat the taper pin while the nut is unscrewed. When this condition is met with, a balljoint extractor is unlikely to be required to free the taper pin from the steering arm.
3   With the tie-rod end removed, wire brush the threads of the tie-rod and apply grease to them.
4 Screw on the new tie-rod end to take up a position similar to the original. Due to manufacturing differences, the fitting of a new component will almost certainly mean that the front wheel alignment will require some adjustment. Check this as described in Section 24.
5   Connect the balljoint to the steering arm as described in Section 21.

23 Steering gear – removal and installation

1   Set the front wheels in the straight-ahead position and disconnect the battery negative cable.
2   Raise the front of the vehicle and support it on safety stands.
3   Working under the hood remove the pinch-bolt from the coupling at the base of the steering column shaft.
4   Extract the split pins from the tie-rod balljoint taper pin nuts, unscrew the nuts and remove them. On power steering equipped models, connect the hydraulic lines and drain them into a suitable container.
5   Separate the balljoints from the steering arms using a suitable tool.
6   Flatten the lock tabs on the steering gear securing bolts and unscrew and remove the bolts. Withdraw the steering gear downwards to separate the coupling from the steering shaft and then take it out from under the front fender.
7   Installation is a reversal of removal. If a new rack-and-pinion assembly is being installed, the tie-rod ends will have to be removed from the original unit and screwed onto the new tie-rods to approximately the same setting. If a note was not made of the position of the original tie-rod ends on their rods, inspection of the threads will probably indicate their original location. In any event it is important that the new tie-rod ends are screwed on an equal amount at this stage.
8   Make sure that the steering gear is centered. Do this by turning the pinion shaft to full lock in one direction and then count the number of turns required to rotate it to the opposite lock. Now turn the splined pinion shaft through half the number of turns just counted.
9   Check that the wheels and the steering wheel are in the straight-ahead attitude, install the steering gear and connect the shaft coupling without inserting the pinch-bolt.
10 Bolt up the gear housing and lock the bolts with their lock plate tabs.
11 Reconnect the tie-rod ends to the steering arms. Use new split pins.
12 Tighten the coupling pinch-bolt to the specified torque. Lower the vehicle to the floor and reconnect the battery negative cable.
13 If the tie-rod ends were disturbed or if a new assembly was installed, check and adjust the front wheel alignment as described in Section 24.

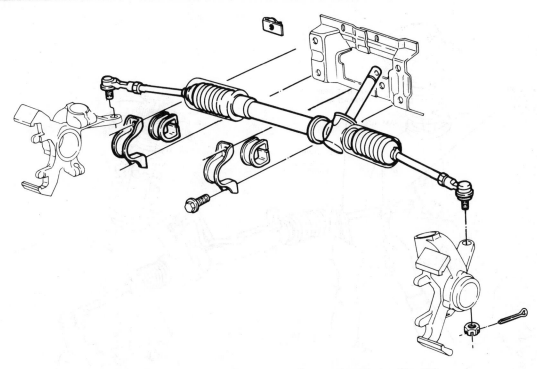

Fig. 11.34 Typical rack and pinion steering gear installation (Sec 23)

24 Steering angles and wheel alignment

1 When reading this Section, reference should also be made to the appropriate Figures.

2 Accurate front wheel alignment is essential to good steering and for even tire wear. Before considering the steering angles, check that the tires are correctly inflated, that the wheels are not buckled, the hub bearings are not worn or incorrectly adjusted and that the steering linkage is in good order.

3 Wheel alignment consists of four factors,:

Camber is the angle at which the wheels are set from the vertical when viewed from the front or rear of the vehicle. Positive camber is the angle (in degrees) that the wheels are tilted outwards at the top, from the vertical.

Caster is the angle between the steering axis and a vertical line when viewed from each side of the vehicle. Positive caster is indicated when the steering axis is inclined towards the rear of the vehicle at its upper end.

Steering axis inclination is the angle when viewed from the front or rear of the vehicle, between the vertical and an imaginary line drawn between the upper and lower suspension swivel balljoints or upper and lower strut mountings.

Toe is the amount by which the distance between the front inside edges of the roadwheel runs differs from that between the rear inside edges. If the distance at the front is less than that at the rear, the wheels are said to toe-in. If the distance at the front inside edges is greater than that at the rear, the wheels toe-out.

4 Due to the need for precision gauges to measure the small angles of the steering and suspension settings, it is preferable to leave this work to your dealer. Camber and caster angles are set in production and are not adjustable. If these angles are ever checked and found to be outside specification then either the suspension components are damaged or distorted, or wear has occurred in the bushes at the attachment points.

5 If you wish to check front wheel alignment yourself, first make sure that the lengths of both tie-rods are equal when the steering is in the straight-ahead position. This can be measured reasonably accurately by counting the number of exposed threads on the tie-rod adjacent to the balljoint assembly.

6 Adjust if necessary by releasing the lock nut from the balljoint assembly and the clamp at the small end of the bellows.

7 Obtain a tracking gauge. These are available in various forms from accessory stores, or one can be fabricated from a length of steel tubing, suitably cranked to clear the oil pan and bellhousing, and having a setscrew and lock nut at one end.

8 With the gauge, measure the distance between the two inner rims of the front wheels (at hub height) at the rear of the wheel. Push the vehicle forward to rotate the wheel through 180° (half a turn) and measure the distance between the wheel inner rims, again at hub height, at the front of the wheel. This last measurement should differ from the first one by the specified toe-in/toe-out (see Specifications).

9 Where the toe setting is found to be incorrect, release the tie-rod balljoint lock nuts and turn the tie-rods by an equal amount. Only turn them through a quarter turn at a time before re-checking the alignment. Do not grip the threaded part of the tie-rod during adjustment and make sure that the bellows outboard clip is released otherwise the bellows will twist as the tie-rod is rotated. When each tie-rod is viewed from the rack housing, turning the rods clockwise will increase the toe-out. Always turn the tie-rods in the same direction when viewed from the center of the vehicle, otherwise they will become unequal in length. This would cause the steering wheel spoke alignment to alter and also cause problems on turning with tire scrubbing.

10 On completion of adjustment, tighten the tie-rod end lock nuts without altering the setting of the tie-rods. Hold the balljoint assembly at the mid-point of its arc of travel (flats are provided on it for a wrench) while the lock nuts are tightened (Fig. 11.35).

11 Finally, tighten the bellows clamps.

12 Rear wheel alignment is set in production and adjustable only with the proper equipment, and when dismantling the tie bar, it is essential that all washers are reinstalled in their original positions as they control the wheel setting for the life of the vehicle.

25 Power steering pump – removal and installation

1 Disconnect the battery negative cable.

2 Remove the air cleaner, Thermactor air pump and belt and the power steering pump reservoir filler extension. Plug the dipstick opening to prevent the entrance of dirt or foreign matter.

3 From underneath the vehicle, loosen an adjusting bolt and remove the pump-to-mounting bracket bolts. Disconnect the pump return hose.

4 In the engine compartment, loosen an adjusting bolt and a pivot bolt and remove the drivebelt.

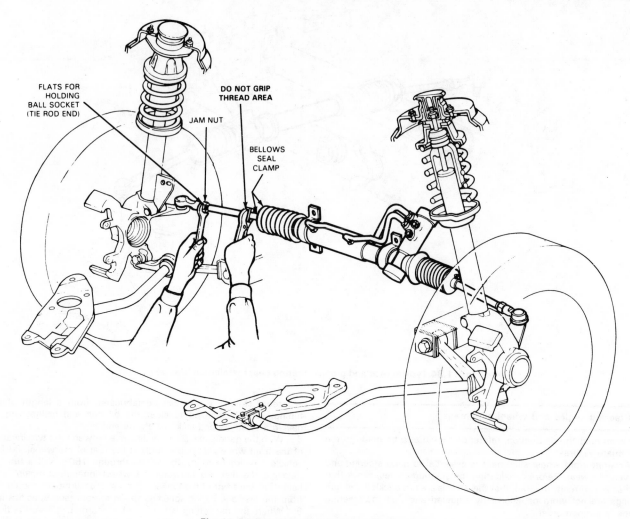

Fig. 11.35 Adjusting steering tie-rods (Sec 24)

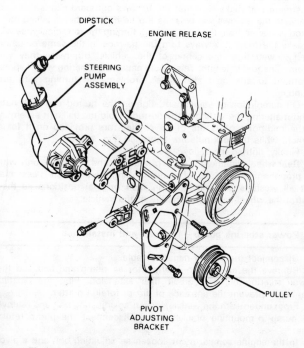

Fig. 11.36 Power steering pump installation (Sec 25)

5   Remove the two pump-to-bracket bolts and pass the pump through the bracket to remove it. Remove the pressure hose from the pump.
6   To install it, place the pump in position in the adjusting bracket, install the mounting bolts and tighten to specification.
7   From underneath the vehicle, connect the pressure hose.
8   Install the drivebelt and adjust the tension (Chapter 3).
9   Install the return line to the pump.
10 Install the reservoir fill extension, Thermactor pump and air cleaner.
11 Fill the pump reservoir to the proper level with the specified lubricant.

26 Power steering – bleeding

1   The power steering system will only need bleeding in the event of air being introduced into the system, ie, where pipes have been disconnected or where leakage has occurred. To bleed the system proceed as described in the following paragraphs.
2   Open the hood and check the fluid level in the fluid reservoir. Top up if necessary using the specified type of fluid.
3   If fluid is added, allow two minutes then run the engine at approximately 1500 rpm. Slowly turn the steering wheel from lock-to-lock, while checking and topping-up fluid level until the level remains steady, and no more bubbles appear in the reservoir. Do not hold the steering wheel in the far right or left positions.
4   Clean and replace the reservoir cap, and close the hood.

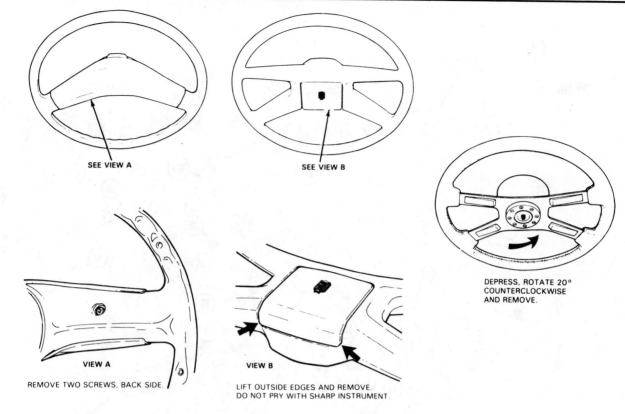

Fig. 11.37 Removal of the two types of steering wheel hub cover (Sec 27)

27 Steering wheel – removal and installation

Refer to Figure 11.39 for component numbering
1   Disconnect the battery negative cable.
2   Remove the steering wheel hub cover (Fig. 11.37).
3   Remove the steering wheel nut (43).
4   Remove the steering wheel with a suitable wheel puller. Do not use a knock-off type puller or strike the steering column shaft.
5   On speed control-equipped models, remove the control from the steering wheel spokes.
6   To install, place the steering wheel on the shaft, making sure that the front wheels are in the straight ahead position.
7   Install the steering wheel nut and tighten to specification.
8   Install the steering wheel hub cover.
9   Connect the battery negative cable.

28 Steering column – removal and installation

Refer to Figure 11.39 for component numbering
1   Disconnect the battery negative cable.
2   Remove the cover from the lower portion of the steering column to gain access to the instrument panel reinforcement section.
3   Remove the two instrument panel reinforcement section retaining screws.
4   Remove the screw retaining the lower steering column shroud (32).
5   Loosen but do not remove the two nuts (49) and bolts (41) which retain the upper shroud (33).
6   Disconnect all steering column electrical connectors which would interfere with removal.
7   Loosen the clamps (28) retaining the shaft to the column and remove the bolt (46) and nut (47).
8   Remove the two nuts (49) and bolts (41) which retain the steering column (29) to the bracket (40) and lower the steering column to the vehicle floor.
9   In the area of the clamp (28), pry open the steering column on each side of the bolt groove. Open sufficiently to carefully disengage the shafts.

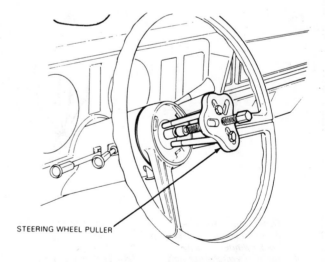

STEERING WHEEL PULLER

Fig. 11.38 Steering wheel removal (Sec 27)

10 Inspect the steering column bracket clips (2) for damage, replace them if they are bent or distorted.
11 When installing, measure the distance which the steering shaft (21) extends past the outer tube assembly (1). This measurement must be between 1.44 and 1.63 in (36.6 to 41.5 mm) (Fig. 11.40).
12 Insert the lower shaft (21) into the intermediate shaft (38P or 38M) and install the clamp bolt and nut (46 and 47) finger tight.
13 Position the steering column under the instrument panel and install the two nuts (49) on the bracket assembly (40). Check to make sure that the clips are present on the outer bracket. Install the two bolts (41) through the outer tube upper bracket and the clip into the bracket nuts.
14 Reconnect all electrical connectors to the steering column.
15 Install the upper shroud (32) and tighten the steering column mounting nut (49) and bolts (41).

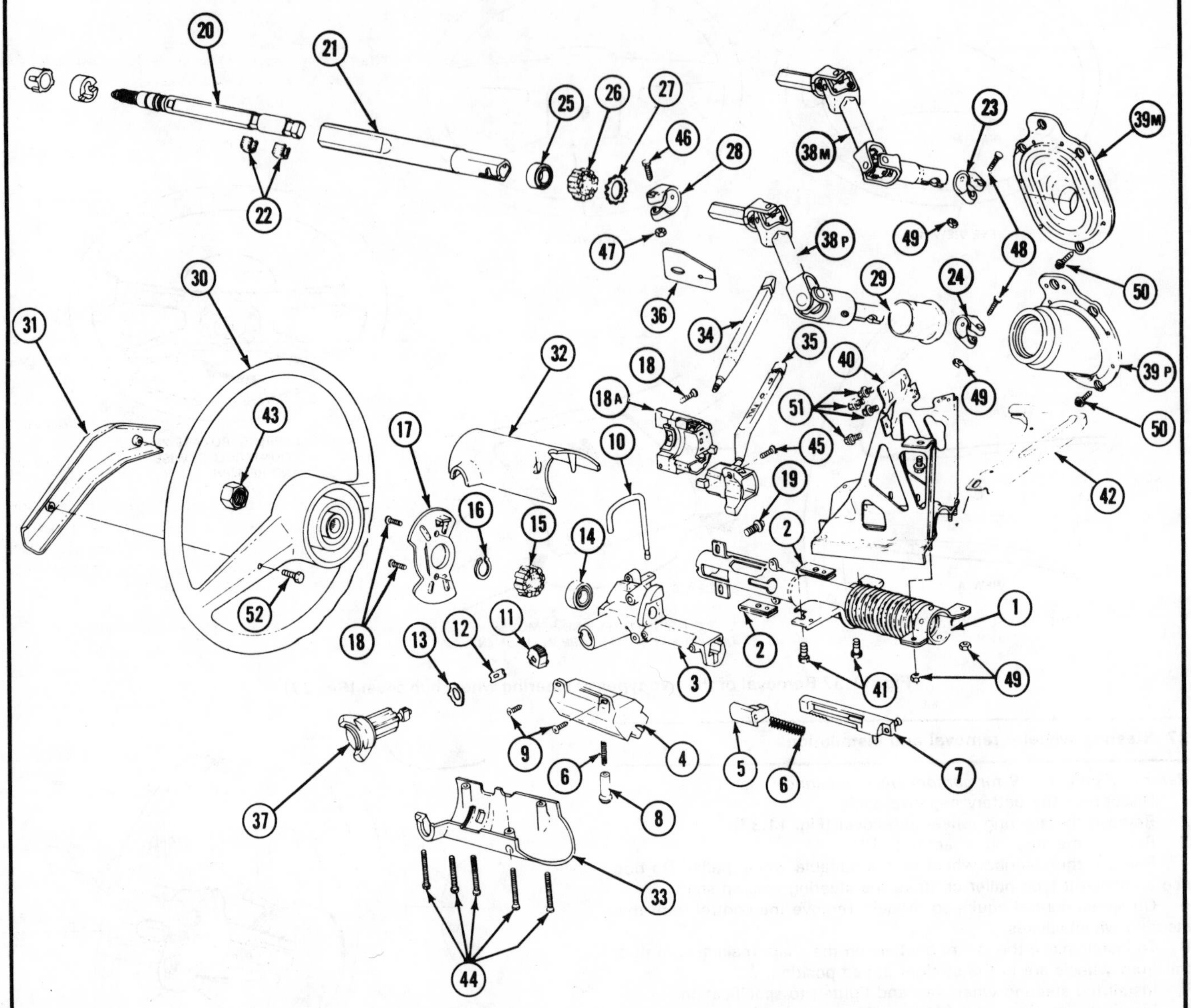

Fig. 11.39 Steering column components (Secs 27 and 28)

1	Outer tube assembly
2	Steering column bracket clip
3	Lock cylinder housing
4	Ignition switch assembly
5	Steering column lock pawl
6	Steering column lock spring
7	Actuator assembly
8	Column lock actuator knob
9	Break-off head bolt
10	Lock actuator lever
11	Column lock gear
12	Lock housing bearing
13	Lock gear retainer
14	Upper steering column bearing assembly
15	Upper bearing sleeve
16	Upper bearing retainer
17	Upper bearing retainer plate
18	Screw
18A	Switch assembly
19	Hex head bolt
20	Upper steering shaft
21	Lower steering shaft
22	Steering shaft insulator
23	Manual steering clamp
24	Power steering clamp
25	Lower steering shaft bearing assembly
26	Lower steering column bearing sleeve
27	Retainer ring
28	Lower steering column clamp
29	Seal
30	Steering wheel assembly
31	Steering wheel cover assembly
32	Upper shroud
33	Lower shroud
34	Turn signal handle and shank assembly
35	Washer/wiper switch
36	Turn signal and washer/wiper switch
37	Lock cylinder
38M	Manual steering lower shaft assembly
38P	Power steering lower shaft assembly
39M	Manual steering boot and seal assembly
39P	Power steering boot and seal assembly
40	Steering column support bracket assembly
41	Hex head bolt
42	Lateral brace
43	Steering wheel nut
44	Pan head screw
45	Screw
46	Bolt
47	Nut
48	Bolt
49	Nut
50	Screw
51	Bolt
52	Screw

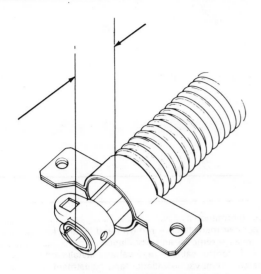

Fig. 11.40 Measurement of the distance the steering shaft extends past the outer tube (Sec 28)

16 With the engine running on power steering models, rotate the steering column one turn to the left and then one to the right to line up the intermediate shaft into the column shaft. Tighten to specification.
17 Install the lower trim shroud (33) with the five screws (44) and the instrument panel reinforcement section (two screws).
18 Install the column cover onto the instrument panel.
19 Reconnect the battery negative cable.
20 Check the steering column for proper operation.

29 Wheels and tires

1 Check the tire pressures weekly (when they are cold).
2 Frequently inspect the tire walls and treads for damage and pick out any large stones which have become trapped in the tread pattern.
3 If the wheels and tires have been balanced on the car then they should not be moved to a different axle position. If they have been balanced off the car then, in the interests of extending tread life, they can be moved between the front and rear on the same side of the car and the spare incorporated in the rotational pattern.
4 Never mix tires of different construction or very dissimiliar tread patterns.
5 Always keep the wheels tightened to the specified torque and if the bolt holes become elongated or flattened, replace the wheel.
6 Occasionally, clean the inner faces of the wheels and if there is any sign of rust or corrosion, paint them with metal preservative paint.
Note: *Corrosion of aluminum alloy wheels may be evidence of a more serious problem which could lead to wheel failure. If corrosion is evident, consult your local authorized dealer for advice.*
7 Before removing a wheel which has been balanced on the car, always mark one wheel stud and bolt hole so that the wheel may be refitted in the same relative position to maintain the balance.

Chapter 12 Bodywork

Contents

Specifications

Torque specifications

	Ft-lb	Nm
Bumper-to-isolator bolts	26 to 40	35 to 55
Bumper extension screw	1.5 to 2	2 to 3
Door latch-to-door	3 to 6	4 to 8
Door hinge bolt	14 to 21	18 to 29
Door vent window-to-intrusion bar	5 to 8	7 to 11
Hood-to-hinge bolt	7 to 11	9 to 14
Hood latch	7 to 11	9 to 14
Liftgate-to-hinge bolts	5 to 8	7 to 11
Liftgate-to-body screws	12 to 20	17 to 27
Steering column attaching bolts	15 to 25	23 to 33
Window glass to regulator nuts	3 to 5	4 to 7

1 General information

Models are available in 2-door, 4-door and station wagon body styles.

The body is of unitized construction and certain components which are particularly vulnerable to accident can be unbolted and replaced with new units. Among these are the front fenders, grille, inner fender skirts, bumpers and radiator support panel.

2 Body exterior – maintenance

1 The condition of your vehicle's bodywork is of considerable importance as it is on this that the resale value will mainly depend. It is much more difficult to repair neglected bodywork than to replace mechanical assemblies. The hidden portions of the body, such as the wheel arches, fender skirts, the underframe and the engine compartment, are equally important, although obviously not requiring such frequent attention as the immediately visible paint.
2 Once a year or every 12 000 miles it is a sound idea to visit your local dealer and have the underside of the body steam cleaned. All traces of dirt and oil will have to be removed and the underside can then be inspected carefully for rust, damaged hydraulic pipes, frayed electrical wiring and similar trouble areas. The front suspension should be greased on completion of this job.
3 At the same time, clean the engine and the engine compartment either using a steam cleaner or a water-soluble cleaner.
4 The fender wells should be given particular attention as undercoating can easily come away here and stones and dirt thrown up from the wheels can soon cause the paint to chip and flake, and allow rust to set in. If rust is found, clean down to the bare metal and apply an anti-rust paint.
5 The bodywork should be washed once a week or when dirty. Thoroughly wet the vehicle to soften the dirt and then wash down with a soft sponge and plenty of clean water. If the surplus dirt is not washed off very gently, in time it will wear the paint down.
6 Spots of tar thrown up from the road surfaces are best removed with a cloth soaked in a cleaner made especially for this purpose.
7 Once every six months, or more frequently depending on the weather conditions, give the bodywork and chrome trim a thoroughly good wax polish. If a chrome cleaner is used to remove rust on any of the vehicle's plated parts, remember that the cleaner can also remove part of the chrome, so use it sparingly.

3 Upholstery and carpets – maintenance

1   Remove the carpets or mats and thoroughly vacuum clean the interior of the vehicle every three months or more frequently if necessary.
2   Beat out the carpets and vacuum clean them if they are very dirty. If the upholstery is soiled apply an upholstery cleaner with a damp sponge and wipe off with a clean dry cloth.
3   Consult your local dealer or auto parts store for cleaners made especially for newer automotive upholstery fabric. Always test the cleaner in an inconspicuous place.

4 Body repair – minor damage

See color photo sequence on pages 214 and 215.

Repair of minor scratches

If the scratch is very superficial, and does not penetrate to the metal of the body, repair is very simple. Lightly rub the area of the scratch with a fine rubbing compound to remove loose paint from the scratch and to clear the surrounding paint of wax buildup. Rinse the area with clean water.

Apply touch-up paint to the scratch using a small brush. Continue to apply thin layers of paint until the surface of the paint in the scratch is level with the surrounding paint. Allow the new paint at least two weeks to harden, then blend it into the surrounding paint by rubbing with a very fine rubbing compound. Finally, apply a coat of wax to the scratch area.

Where the scratch has penetrated the paint and exposed the metal of the body, causing the metal to rust, a different repair technique is required. Remove any loose rust from the bottom of the scratch with a pocket knife, then apply rust inhibiting paint to prevent the formation of rust in the future. Using a rubber or nylon applicator, coat the scratched area with glaze type filler. If required, this filler can be mixed with thinner to provide a very thin paste which is ideal for filling narrow scratches. Before the glaze filler in the scratch hardens, wrap a piece of smooth cotton cloth around the top of a finger. Dip the cloth in thinner and then quickly wipe it along the surface of the scratch. This will ensure that the surface of the filler is slightly hollowed. The scratch can now be painted over as described earlier in this Section.

Repair of dents

When deep denting of the vehicle's bodywork has taken place, the first task is to pull the dent out until the affected area nearly attains its original shape. There is little point in trying to restore the original shape completely as the metal in the damaged area will have stretched on impact and cannot be reshaped fully to its original contours. It is better to bring the level of the dent up to a point which is about $\frac{1}{8}$ in below the level of the surrounding metal. In cases where the dent is very shallow, it is not worth trying to pull it out at all.

If the underside of the dent is accessible, it can be hammered out gently from behind using a mallet with a wooden or plastic head. Whilst doing this, hold a suitable block of wood firmly against the metal to absorb the hammer blows and thus prevent a large area of the metal from being stretched out.

If the dent is in a section of the body which has double layers, or some other factor making it inaccessible from behind, a different technique is in order. Drill several small holes through the metal inside the damaged area, particularly in the deeper sections. Screw long self-tapping screws into the holes just enough for them to get a good grip in the metal. Now the dent can be pulled out by pulling on the protruding head of the screws with a pair of locking pliers.

The next stage of the repair is the removal of paint from the damaged area and from an inch or so of the surrounding 'sound' metal. This is accomplished most easily by using a wire brush or sanding disk in a drill motor, although it can be done just as effectively by hand with sandpaper. To complete the preparation for filling, score the surface of the bare metal with a screwdriver or the tang of a file (or drill small holes in the affected area). This will provide a really good 'key' for the filler material. To complete the repair, see the Section on filling and painting.

Repair of rust holes or gashes

Remove all paint from the affected area and from an inch or so of the surrounding 'sound' metal using a sanding disk or wire brush mounted in a drill motor. If these are not available a few sheets of sandpaper will do the job just as effectively. With the paint removed you will be able to determine the severity of the corrosion and therefore decide whether to replace the whole panel if possible, or to repair the affected area. New body panels are not as expensive as most people think and it is often quicker to install a new panel than to attempt to repair large areas of rust.

Remove all trim pieces from the affected area (except those which will act as a guide to the original shape of the damaged body ie. headlamp shells etc). Then, using metal snips or a hacksaw blade, remove all loose metal and any other metal that is badly affected by rust. Hammer the edges of the hole inwards to create a slight depression for the filler material.

Wire brush the affected area to remove the powdery rust from the surface of the metal. If the back of the rusted area is accessible, treat it with rust-inhibiting paint.

Before filling can be done it will be necessary to block the hole in some way. This can be accomplished with sheet metal riveted or screwed into place, or by stuffing the hole with wire mesh.

Once the hole is blocked off the affected area can be filled and painted (see the following section on filling and painting).

Filling and painting

Many types of body fillers are available, but generally speaking, body repair kits which contain filler paste and a tube of resin hardener are best for this type of repair work. A wide, flexible plastic or nylon applicator will be necessary for imparting a smooth and contoured finish to the surface of the filler material.

Mix up a small amount of filler on a clean piece of wood or cardboard (use the hardener sparingly). Follow the maker's instructions on the package, otherwise the filler will set incorrectly.

Using the applicator, apply the filler paste to the prepared area. Draw the applicator across the surface of the filler to achieve the desired contour and to level the filler surface. As soon as a contour that approximates the correct one is achieved, stop working the paste. If you continue, the paste will begin to stick to the applicator. Continue to add thin layers of filler paste at 20-minute intervals until the level of the filler is just proud of the surrounding metal.

Once the filler has hardened, excess can be removed using a body file. From then on, progressively finer grades of sandpaper should be used, starting with a 180-grit paper and finishing with 600-grit wet-or-dry paper. Always wrap the sandpaper around a flat rubber or wooden block, otherwise the surface of the filler will not be completely flat. During the sanding of the filler surface the wet-or-dry paper should be periodically rinsed in water. This will ensure that a very smooth finish is produced in the final stage.

At this point, the repair area should be surrounded by a ring of bare metal, which in turn should be encircled by the finely feathered edge of the good paint. Rinse the repair area with clean water until all of the dust produced by the sand operation has gone.

Spray the entire area with a light coat of primer. This will reveal any imperfections in the surface of the filler. Repair these imperfections with fresh filler paste or glaze filler and once more smooth the surface with sandpaper. Repeat this spray-and-repair procedure until you are satisfied that the surface of the filler and the feathered edge of the paintwork are perfect. Rinse the area with clean water and allow to dry fully.

The repair area is now ready for painting. Paint spraying must be carried out in warm, dry, windless and dustfree atmosphere. These conditions can be created if you have access to a large indoor working area, but if you are forced to work in the open, you will have to pick your day very carefully. If you are working indoors, dousing the floor in the work area with water will help to settle the dust which would otherwise be in the air. If the repair area is confined to one body panel, mask off the surrounding panels. This will help to minimise the effects of a slight mis-match in paint color. Trim pieces such as chrome strips, door handles, etc., will also need to be masked off or removed. Use masking tape and several thicknesses of newspaper for the masking operations.

Before spraying, shake the paint can thoroughly, then spray a test area until the technique is mastered. Cover the repair area with a thick coat of primer. The thickness should be built up using several thin layers of primer rather than one thick one. Using 600-grit wet-or-dry

This photo sequence illustrates the repair of a dent and damaged paintwork. The procedure for the repair of a hole is similar. Refer to the text for more complete instructions

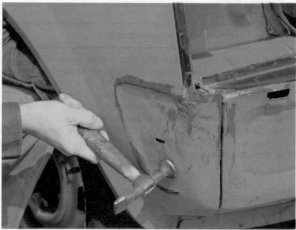

After removing any adjacent body trim, hammer the dent out. The damaged area should then be made slightly concave

Use coarse sandpaper or a sanding disc on a drill motor to remove all paint from the damaged area. Feather the sanded area into the edges of the surrounding paint, using progressively finer grades of sandpaper

The damaged area should be treated with rust remover prior to application of the body filler. In the case of a rust hole, all rusted sheet metal should be cut away

Carefully follow manufacturer's instructions when mixing the body filler so as to have the longest possible working time during application. Rust holes should be covered with fiberglass screen held in place with dabs of body filler prior to repair

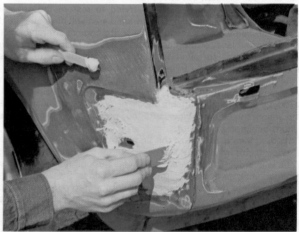

Apply the filler with a flexible applicator in thin layers at 20 minute intervals. Use an applicator such as a wood spatula for confined areas. The filler should protrude slightly above the surrounding area

Shape the filler with a surform-type plane. Then, use water and progressively finer grades of sandpaper and a sanding block to wet-sand the area until it is smooth. Feather the edges of the repair area into the surrounding paint.

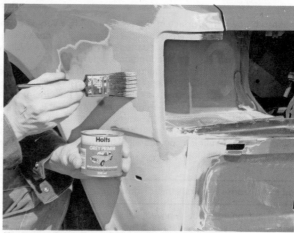

Use spray or brush applied primer to cover the entire repair area so that slight imperfections in the surface will be filled in. Prime at least one inch into the area surrounding the repair. Be careful of over-spray when using spray-type primer

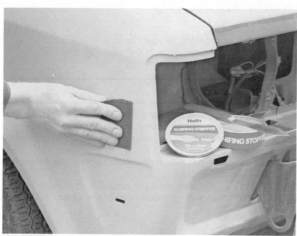

Wet-sand the primer with fine (approximately 400 grade) sandpaper until the area is smooth to the touch and blended into the surrounding paint. Use filler paste on minor imperfections

After the filler paste has dried, use rubbing compound to ensure that the surface of the primer is smooth. Prior to painting, the surface should be wiped down with a tack rag or lint-free cloth soaked in lacquer thinner

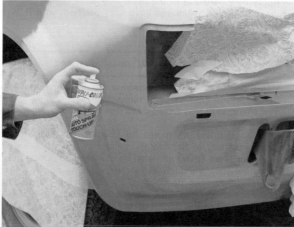

Choose a dry, warm, breeze-free area in which to paint and make sure that adjacent areas are protected from over-spray. Shake the spray paint can thoroughly and apply the top coat to the repair area, building it up by applying several coats, working from the center

After allowing at least two weeks for the paint to harden, use fine rubbing compound to blend the area into the original paint. Wax can now be applied

sandpaper, rub down the surface of the primer until it is very smooth. While doing this, the work area should be thoroughly rinsed with water, and the wet-or-dry sandpaper periodically rinsed as well. Allow the primer to dry before spraying additional coats.

Spray on the top coat, again building up the thickness by using several thin layers of paint. Begin spraying in the center of the repair area and then, using a circular motion, work out until the whole repair area and about two inches of the surrounding original paint is covered. Remove all masking material 10 to 15 minutes after spraying on the final coat of paint. Allow the new paint at least two weeks to harden, then using a very fine rubbing compound, blend the edges of the paint into the existing paint. Finally, apply a coat of wax.

5 Body and frame repairs – major damage

1   Major damage must be repaired by an auto body/frame repair shop with the necessary welding and hydraulic straightening equipment.
2   If the damage has been serious, it is vital that the frame be checked for correct alignment, as the handling of the vehicle will be affected. Other problems, such as excessive tire wear and wear in the transmission and steering may also occur.

6 Vinyl trim maintenance

Vinyl body trim should not be cleaned with detergents, caustic soaps or petroleum based cleaners. Plain soap and water or a mild vinyl cleaner is best for stains. Test a small area for color fastness. Bubbles under the vinyl can be corrected by piercing with a pin and then working the air out.

7 Maintenance – hinges and locks

Every 3000 miles (5000 km) or 3 months the door, hood and trunk hinges and locks shuld be lubricated with a few drops of oil. The door striker plates should also be given a thin smear of grease to reduce wear and ensure free movement.

8 Door – removal and installation

1   Use a pencil or scribe to mark the hinge location for ease of reinstallation.
2   With an assistant supporting the weight of the door, remove the upper and lower hinge retaining bolts. Lift the door away and stand it on an old blanket.
3   Installation is a reversal of removal, using the marks scribed around the hinges in step 1 as a guide. If it is necessary to realign the door, refer to Section 11.

9 Door hinges – removal and installation

1   Support the door and scribe or mark the hinge location on the door and body.
2   Remove the cowl side trim panel to give access to the hinge-to-body attaching bolts. On some models it will also be necessary to remove air conditioning ducts, body shake braces or glove box (photo).
3   Remove the hinge bolts and hinges (Fig. 12.1).
4   Remove the door support and adjust as necessary (Section 11).
5   Replace any components which were removed to gain access.

10 Door hinge check – removal and installation

1   If the door hinge check, located on the lower hinge, is broken it can be replaced without removing the hinge or door.
2   Remove the bolt whch retains the hinge to the body.
3   Insert a suitable length chisel which a $\frac{3}{4}$ inch blade between the hinge on the body and the back of the hinge check. Use a hammer to remove the rivet which retains the hinge check.
4   Place a new hinge check in position in the door hinge and install

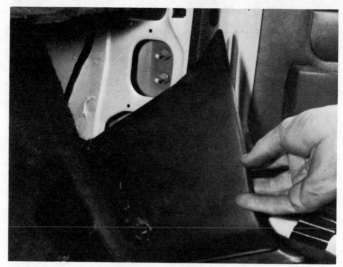

9.2 The front door hinge bolts are accessible after removing the cowl side trim

the hinge bolt, tightening to specification.
5   Lubricate the assembly with the specified lubricant.

11 Door – alignment

1   The door hinge bolt holes are elongated or enlarged so that hinge and door alignment can be accomplished.
2   Loosen the hinge bolts just enough so that the door can be moved with a padded pry bar.
3   After the door has been adjusted, tighten the hinge bolts and check the door fit.
4   Repeat this operation until the proper fit is obtained.
5   After the alignment is made, check the striker plate for proper closing.

12 Door weatherstripping – removal and installation

1   Remove the old weatherstripping by pulling it away from the door to break it loose from the adhesive.
2   Clean the old adhesive off the door.
3   Apply new adhesive to the door.
4   Press the new weatherstriping into position until it is secure, referring to the accompanying figure.

13 Door latch striker – removal, installation and adjustment

1   Use a pair of vise grips to unscrew the door latch striker stud.
2   Installation is the reverse of removal.
3   The striker stud may be adjusted vertically and laterally as well as fore-and-aft.
4   The latch striker must not be used to compensate for door misalignment (refer to Section 1).
5   The door latch striker can also be shimmed to obtain the correct clearance between the latch and striker.
6   The clearance can be checked by cleaning the latch jams and striker area and applying a thin layer of dark grease to the striker.
7   Close and open the door, noting the pattern of the grease.
8   Move the striker assembly laterally to provide a flush fit at the door and pillar or quarter panel.
9   Tighten the striker stud after adjustment.

14 Door trim panel – removal and installation

1   Remove the door handle and cup.
2   Remove the window crank.

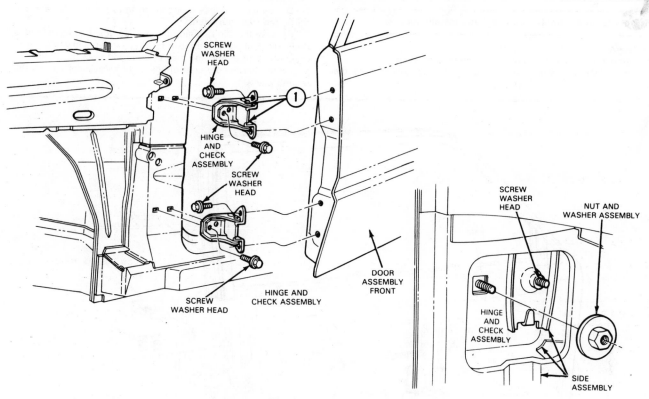

Fig. 12.1 Door hinge layout (Secs 8 through 11)

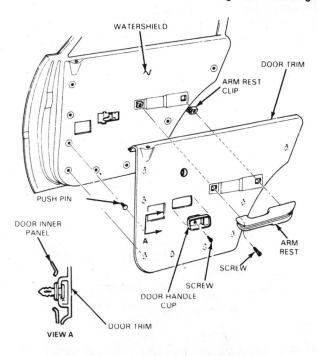

Fig. 12.2 Door trim panel installation (Sec 14)

14.4 Be careful not to damage the plastic retaining pins when removing the trim. Release the pins with a screwdriver, do not pry them out by pulling the trim panel

14.5 Do not damage the watershield adhesive surface during removal

3   Remove the armrest.
4   Use a screwdriver to pry the panel away from the door and remove the panel (photo).
5   Carefully peel the watershield away from the door inner panel (photo).
6   To install, position the watershield against the inner panel so that the adhesive on the back aligns with the adhesive on the door and press into place.
7   The rest of installation is the reverse of removal.

15 Door latch assembly – removal and installation

Front door

1   Remove the door trim panel and watershield (Section 14).
2   Disconnect the remote control assembly clip and remove the assembly.

3   Disconnect the lock cylinder rod from the cylinder and the push rod button from the latch.
4   Remove the clip retaining the outside door handle rod to the latch assembly, remove the three attaching screws and remove the latch assembly, control link and lock cylinder rod from the door.
5   Attach the remote control link and lock cylinder rods to the latch assembly levers.

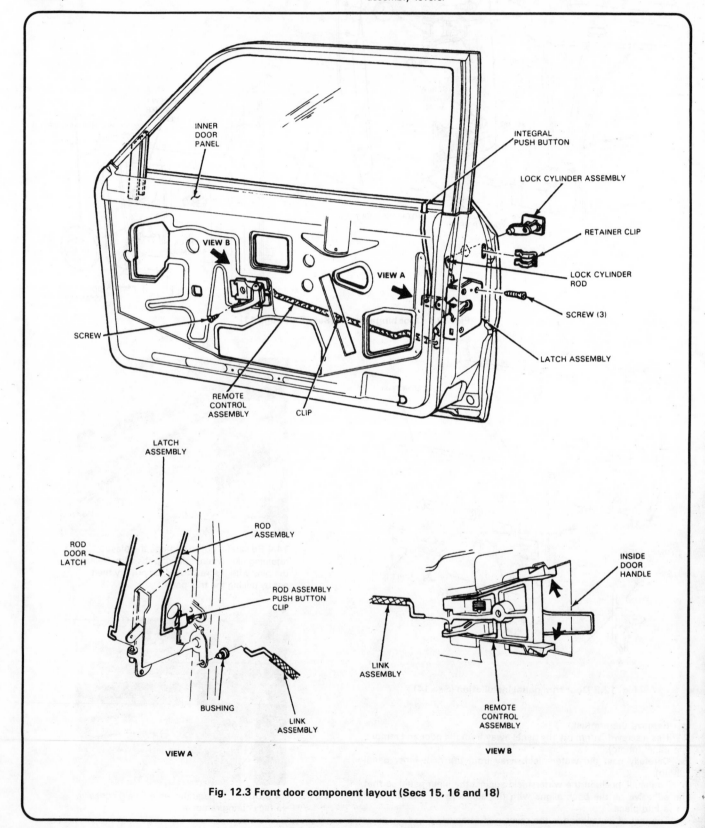

Fig. 12.3 Front door component layout (Secs 15, 16 and 18)

6   Position the latch to the door, install the attaching screws and then attach the push button, lock cylinder and remote control links.
7   Install the door trim and watershield.

Rear door
8   Remove the door trim and watershield (Section 14).
9   Disconnect the remote control assembly.

10 Remove the nut retaining the bellcrank to the door panel and remove the bellcrank from the door.
11 Disconnect the door latch bracket assembly from the latch.
12 Prior to installation, connect the remote control and bellcrank links to the latch assembly.
13 Install the latch and link assembly to the door and install the screws.

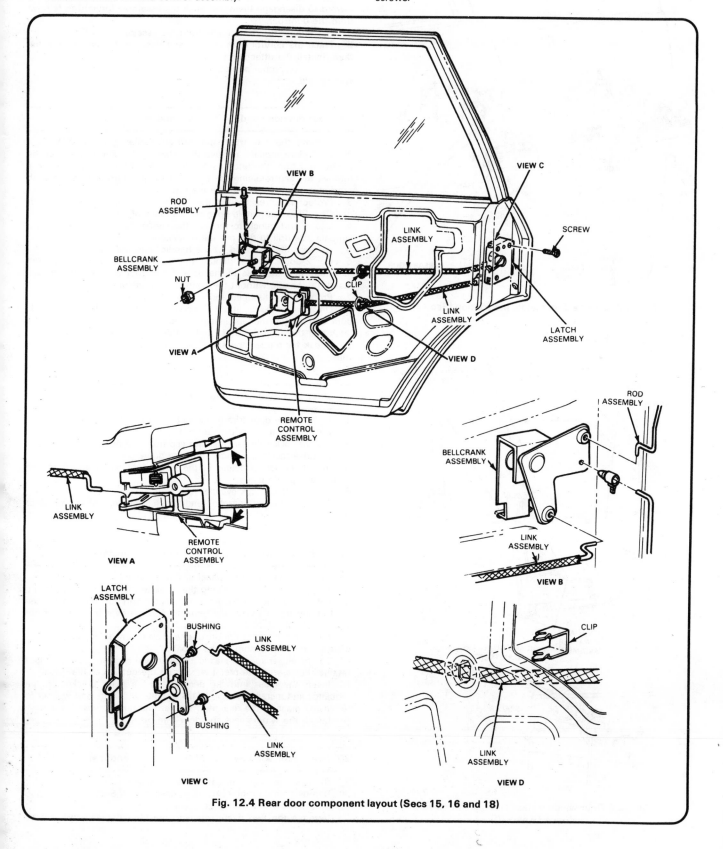

Fig. 12.4 Rear door component layout (Secs 15, 16 and 18)

14 Connect the bellcrank links and pushbutton rod to the bellcrank.
15 Install the bellcrank to the door inner panel and tighten the nut until it is snug.
16 Check the door and latch for proper operation and install the trim and watershield.

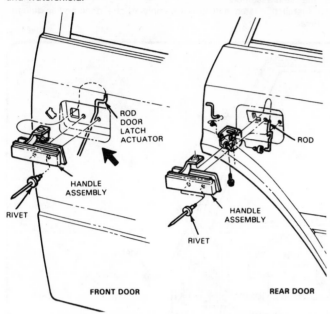

Fig. 12.5 Outside door handle installation (Sec 17)

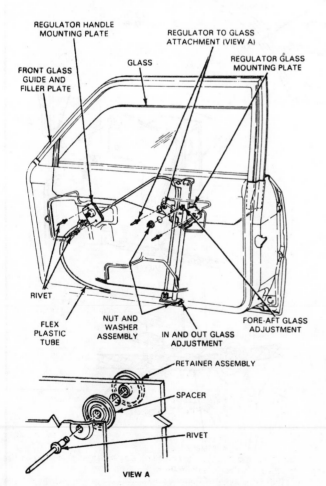

Fig. 12.6 Door window glass and regulator layout (Secs 19 and 20)

16 Door latch remote control – removal and installation

1   Remove the door trim and watershield.
2   To remove the remote control link retaining clip, squeeze it and then disengage it from the hole in the inner door panel.
3   Remove the remote control attaching screw, squeeze the tabs inward to disengage them and push the assembly forward to remove from the door panel.
4   Disconnect the remote link from the assembly.
5   Place the control onto the rod and position the assembly in the door. Install the attaching screw.
6   Check for proper operation and reinstall the door trim panel and watershield.

17 Door outside handle – removal and installation

1   Remove the door trim panel and watershield (Section 14).
2   On 2-door models, remove the retaining clip and disconnect the control rod from the latch assembly. On 4-door and wagon models, remove the clip retaining the outside handle control rod to the latch bracket assembly and remove the rod.
3   Protect the area around the handle from damage with tape or padding. Prop the handle open with a piece of wood.
4   Use a drift punch to remove the center pin of the rivets and a suitable size drill to drill out the remainder.
5   Remove the prop and lift the handle from the door.
6   On 2-door models, install the door handle and control rod assembly into the hole in the door. On 4-door and wagon models, install the handle without the control rod attached.
7   Prop the handle open and attach it by installing the two rivets.
8   On 2-door models, attach the control rod to the latch lever. On 4-door and wagon models, install the control rod into the hole in the latch and then clip the other end to the latch bracket assembly.
9   Check for proper operation and install the watershield and door trim.

18 Door lock cylinder – removal and installation

1   Remove the door trim panel and watershield.
2   Disconnect the lock cylinder rod.
3   Pry the lock cylinder retaining clip from the door.
4   Remove the lock cylinder from the door.
5   Install the lock cylinder in the outer door panel and push the retaining clip into place.
6   Reconnect the lock cylinder rod.
7   Check for proper operation and reinstall the watershield and door trim panel.

19 Front door window glass – removal and installation

1   Remove the door trim panel and watershield.
2   Remove the rivets retaining the glass to the regulator by placing a suitable block behind the glass and using a drift punch to remove the rivet center pin. Remove the remainder of the rivet by drilling it out with a suitable sized drill bit.
3   Remove the glass from the door and clean any drilling or remnants of rivet from the bottom of the door.
4   To install, snap the plastic retainer and spacer into the glass retainer holes with the metal washer on the outside of the glass.
5   Insert the glass into the door, place the glass bracket on the regulator and install two 1 in X 1/4 in bolts with nuts and washer to retain the glass to the regulator. Tighten the nuts to specification.
6   Install the watershield and door trim panel.

20 Front door window regulator – removal and installation

1   Remove the door trim panel and watershield.
2   Remove the door glass rivets as described in Section 19, Step 2. Prop the glass in the full up position.
3   Remove the two rivets retaining the regulator assembly to the

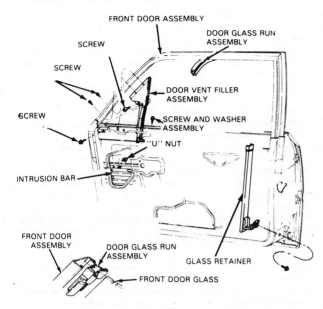

Fig. 12.7 Front door window vent installation (Sec 19)

inner door panel.

4 Remove the two nuts attaching the regulator and remove it through the door access hole.

5 To install, position the assembly in the door and install the nuts and washers loosely.

6 Install two $\frac{1}{2}$ in X 1 in bolts with nuts and washers to secure the regulator assembly mounting plate to the door.

7 Route the drain tube to the bottom of the door.

8 Install the door glass to the regulator as described in Section 19, Step 5.

9 Move the glass to the full up position and tighten the nuts and washers installed in Step 5 of this Section.

10 Check for proper operation and reinstall the watershield and door trim panel.

21 Rear door window glass – removal and installation

1 Remove the door trim panel and watershield.

2 Remove the glass bracket retaining rivets as described in Section 19, Step 2 and lower the glass to the bottom of the door.

3 Remove the glass guide run from the front of the division bar and the top of the door frame.

4 Remove the division bar retaining screws, tilt the bar forward and remove it, the quarter glass and weather stripping.

5 Lift the window glass up and remove it from the door.

6 Install the plastic retainer and spacers to the window glass and insert the window into the door.

7 Install the quarter window glass and weather stripping into the rear of the door, using soapy water to ease installation. Seat the weather stripping firmly into the door frame.

8 Install the division bar, firmly seating the weather stripping. Install and tighten the top retaining screw, but installing the lower screw loosely.

9 Install the glass guide into the door frame and division bar.

10 Raise the window glass and install two 1 in X $\frac{1}{2}$ in bolts with nuts and washers to fasten the glass to the regulator mounting bracket.

11 Check for proper operation and install the watershield and door trim panel.

22 Rear door window regulator – removal and installation

1 Remove the door trim and watershield.

2 Remove the two rivets attaching the glass to the regulator as described in Section 19, step 2.

3 Remove the rivets retaining the regulator clutch plate assembly to the door inner panel.

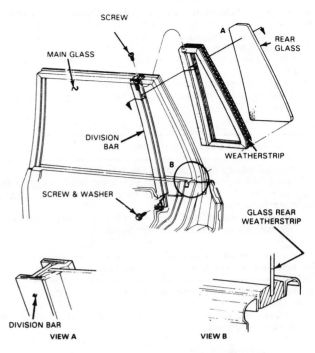

Fig. 12.8 Rear door glass installation (Sec 21)

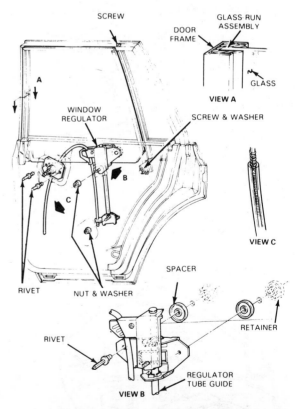

Fig. 12.9 Rear door window regulator installation (Secs 21 and 22)

4 Remove the nuts attaching the regulator tube guide to the door panel.

5 Disconnect the door latch remote rods at the latch and remove the regulator through the access hole in the door panel.

6 Install the regulator through the access hole and loosely install the nuts and washers.

7 Install the regulator mounting plate to the door inner panel, using

two 1 in X ½ in bolts with nuts and washers to replace the drilled out rivets.
8   Install the door glass to the regulator, replacing the rivets with 1 X ½ in bolts with nuts and washers.
9   With the glass in the full up position, tighten the nuts installed in Step 6.
10   Connect the remote rods to the door latch.
11   Check for proper operation and install the watershield and door trim panel.

23   Door window glass – adjustment

1   Remove the door trim panel and watershield.
2   Loosen the nut and washer assemblies and move the glass fore and aft or in and out in the guide runs in the door until smooth operation is reached.
3   Tighten the nuts to specification and check for proper operation.
4   Reinstall the watershield and trim panel.

24   Rear quarter window – removal and installation

1   Remove the screws retaining the glass hinge and disconnect the cable retainer.
2   Remove the glass from the vehicle, noting the number and location of the spacers.

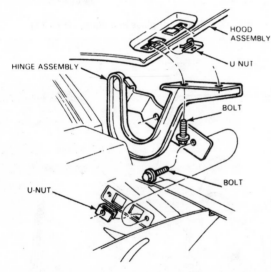

Fig. 12.10 Hood hinge components (Secs 26 and 27)

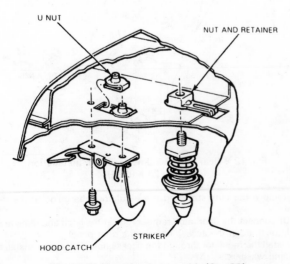

Fig. 12.11 Hood latch assembly (Sec 28)

3   Remove the plastic hinge cover by prying it loose with a screwdriver.
4   Remove the pop rivet which retains the hinge to the glass and the screw and washer attaching it to the pillar. Remove the hinge.
5   Install the hinge assembly and install the glass, taking care that the spacers go in their original holes.
6   Install the screws and reconnect the cable retainer.

25   Windshield, stationary quarter window and rear glass – removal and installation

The windshield, stationary quarter window and rear glass on all models are sealed in place with a special butyl compound. Removal of the existing sealant requires the use of an electric knife specially made for the operation and glass replacement is a complex operation.
In view of this, it is not recommended that stationary glass removal be attempted by the home mechanic. If replacement is necessary due to breakage or leakage, the work should be referred to your dealer or a qualified glass or body shop.

26   Hood – removal and installation

1   Open the hood and support it in the open position.
2   Protect the fenders and cowl with suitable covering to prevent damage to the paint.
3   Scribe around the hinges for ease of reinstallation.
4   Have an assistant support the weight of the hood and remove the hinge-to-hood bolts.
5   Lift the hood over the front of the car.
6   Installation is a reversal of removal, taking care to align the hinges with the previously scribed marks.

27   Hood hinges – removal and installation

1   Open the hood and support it in the open position.
2   Remove the hood as described in Section 26.
3   Scribe around the hinge housing with a pencil for ease of installation.
4   Remove bolts and washers securing the hinge to the body and remove the hinge.
5   Installation is the reverse of removal.

28   Hood latch – removal, installation and adjustment

1   Open the hood and support it in the open position.
2   Remove the hood latch cable retainer plate and disengage the cable from the hood latch assembly.
3   Remove the latch attaching screws and remove the latch.
4   Installation is the reverse of removal. Do not fully tighten the latch screws until adjustment is made.
5   The hood latch can be adjusted from side-to-side to align it with the hood latch hook. It can also be adjusted up and down to obtain a flush fit between the hood and fenders.
6   Move the hood latch from side-to-side until it is properly aligned with the opening in the hood inner panel.
7   Loosen the hood bumper lock nuts and lower the bumpers.
8   Move the latch up and down until the proper fit is obtained when the hood is pulled up. Tighten the hood latch screws.
9   Raise the hood bumpers to eliminate any hood looseness and then tighten the bumper lock nuts.

29   Hood latch control cable – removal and installation

1   Prop the hood securely in the open position.
2   Remove the hood latch cable retainer screws, plate and cable clip.
3   Disengage the cable and ferrule from the latch assembly.
4   Remove the cable retaining clips.
5   From inside the vehicle, remove the bracket and screws and carefully pull the cable assembly through the retaining wall.
6   To install, insert the cable assembly through the retaining wall and seat the grommet securely.

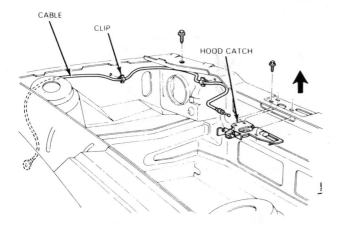

Fig. 12.12 Hood latch control cable layout (Sec 29)

7   Install the cable mounting bracket and screws.
8   Route the cable and install the retaining clips, referring to the accompanying figure.
9   Install the cable clip and hood latch retaining plate.
10 Prior to closing the hood, check the cable release for proper operation.

30 Hood support rod – removal and installation

1   Open the hood and support it in the open position with a long piece of wood.
2   Remove the support rod from its stowed position.
3   Remove the bolt which attached the support rod mounting bracket to the left side of the radiator support.
4   Remove the rod and bracket.
5   Installation is the reverse of removal.

31 Tailgate – removal and installation

1   Open the tailgate fully and disconnect the leads from the heated rear window and the wiper (where fitted).
2   From the top edge of the tailgate aperture, remove the weatherstrip and then peel back the headlining.
3   With an assistant supporting the tailgate, unbolt and remove the struts. The strut balljoint is released by prying out the small plastic peg.
4   Unscrew the hinge screws, remove them with the washers and lift the tailgate from the vehicle.
5   The tailgate lock and (if fitted) the wiper motor are accessible for removal once the trim panel has been released from its securing clips, which should be turned through 90° to release them.
6   The tailgate lock cylinder is retained by a spring clip. The two tailgate stops are secured with pop rivets which will have to be drilled out if the stops must be removed.
7   Installation is a reversal of removal, but do not fully tighten the hinge screws until the tailgate has been adjusted to give an equal gap all round.

32 Glove compartment latch – removal and installation

1   Open the glove compartment and pry the lock retainer out with a small screwdriver.
2   Withdraw the latch from the glove compartment door.
3   Insert the latch assembly and install the lock retainer.
4   Check for proper operation.

33 Instrument panel – removal and installation

1   Disconnect the battery negative cable.
2   Remove the steering column opening cover, the reinforcement retaining screws and disconnect the speed control wires (if equipped).
3   Remove the steering column retaining screws, lower the steering column, remove the column shrouds and disconnect the wiring connectors.

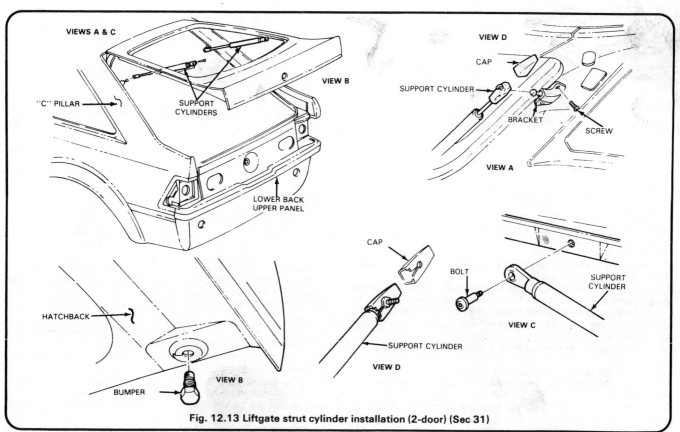

Fig. 12.13 Liftgate strut cylinder installation (2-door) (Sec 31)

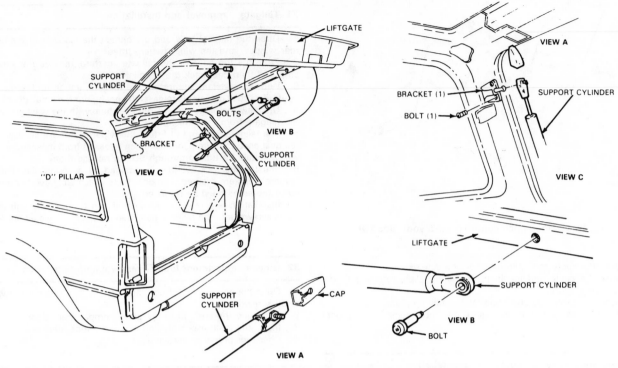

Fig. 12.14 Wagon liftgate strut cylinder installation (Sec 31)

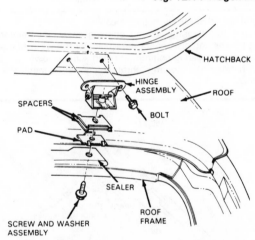

Fig. 12.15 Liftgate hinge installation (Sec 31)

4   Remove the cluster opening finish panel retaining screws, rock the upper edge of the panel toward the rear and remove it.
5   Disconnect the speedometer cable by reaching under the dash and pressing on the flat surface of the connector.
6   Remove the cluster retaining screws, disconnect the wiring and remove the cluster.
7   Remove the glove compartment hinge screws, depress the sides of the compartment bin and remove.
8   Disconnect all vacuum, electrical and other connections which would interfere with the removal of the instrument panel.
9   Remove the instrument panel-to-support bracket screw, the two lower instrument panel-to-cowl screws and the instrument panel brace retaining screw.
10   Remove the center radio speaker grille and snap the grille out to remove it.
11   Remove the left and right speaker grilles.
12   Remove the instrument panel retaining screws and remove the instrument panel.
13   If a new instrument panel is to be installed, transfer all components from the old unit.
14   Installation is the reverse of removal.

34   Ignition switch – removal and installation

1   Disconnect the battery negative cable.
2   Remove the steering column shroud, unbolt the steering column and lower it.
3   Remove the shrouds from the steering column and disconnect the ignition connector.
4   On 1982 models, move the ignition key lock cylinder to the On position.
5   Use a $\frac{1}{8}$ in drill to drill out the break-off head bolts retaining the switch.
6   Remove the bolts, using an easy-out type tool or equivalent.
7   Remove the ignition switch from the actuator pin.
8   On 1981 models, adjust the switch to the Lock position by inserting a $\frac{1}{16}$ in drill bit or equivalent tool through the switch housing and into the carrier. This will prevent the carrier from moving in relation to the switch housing. A new switch will have a pin already installed. On 1982 models, the actuator pin and ignition switch should be set in the On position. Rotating the key lock cylinder 90 degrees from the Lock position will locate it in approximately the On position.
9   Place the ignition switch in position and install it onto the actuator pin.
10   Install break-off head bolts finger tight.
11   On 1982 models, tighten the bolts until the heads break off. On 1981 models, slide the switch up the steering column until all of the screw slot travel is used up, hole it in this position and tighten the bolts until the heads break off.
12   On 1981 models, remove the adjustment pin.
13   Connect the electrical connector and install the column shrouds.
14   Reinstall the steering column and tighten the nuts to specification.
15   Connect the battery negative cable.
16   Check the switch for proper operation.

35   Console – removal and installation

Console

1   Move the parking brake lever forward sufficiently so that a finger can be inserted into the lever slot finish panel. Pull the rear of the panel upward, pull the parking brake fully upward and remove the finish panel.
2   Remove the four screws retaining the console base and the two

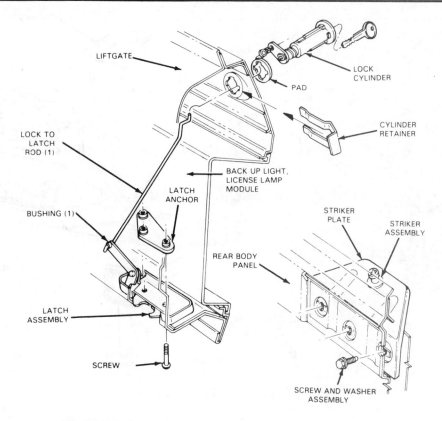

LIFTGATE

LOCK CYLINDER

PAD

CYLINDER RETAINER

LOCK TO LATCH ROD (1)

BACK UP LIGHT, LICENSE LAMP MODULE

LATCH ANCHOR

BUSHING (1)

STRIKER PLATE

STRIKER ASSEMBLY

REAR BODY PANEL

LATCH ASSEMBLY

SCREW

SCREW AND WASHER ASSEMBLY

Fig. 12.16 4-door and wagon rear liftgate latch assembly (Sec 31)

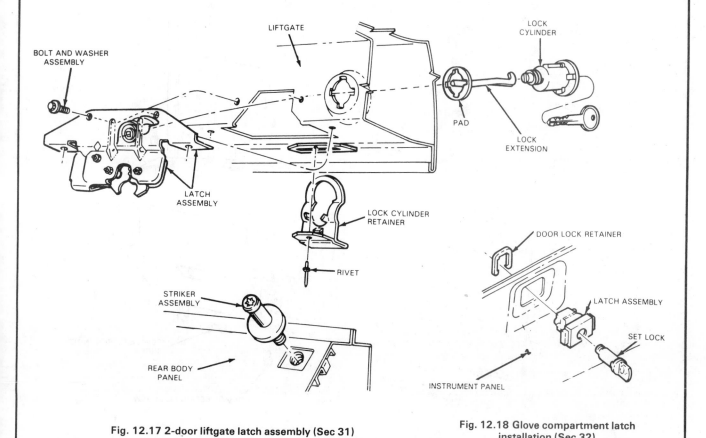

LIFTGATE

LOCK CYLINDER

BOLT AND WASHER ASSEMBLY

PAD

LOCK EXTENSION

LATCH ASSEMBLY

LOCK CYLINDER RETAINER

RIVET

DOOR LOCK RETAINER

LATCH ASSEMBLY

STRIKER ASSEMBLY

SET LOCK

REAR BODY PANEL

INSTRUMENT PANEL

Fig. 12.17 2-door liftgate latch assembly (Sec 31)

Fig. 12.18 Glove compartment latch installation (Sec 32)

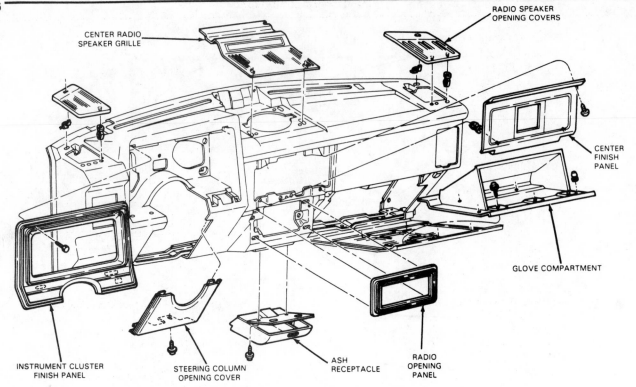

CENTER RADIO
SPEAKER GRILLE

RADIO SPEAKER
OPENING COVERS

CENTER
FINISH
PANEL

GLOVE COMPARTMENT

INSTRUMENT CLUSTER
FINISH PANEL

STEERING COLUMN
OPENING COVER

ASH
RECEPTACLE

RADIO
OPENING
PANEL

Fig. 12.19 Instrument panel layout (Sec 33)

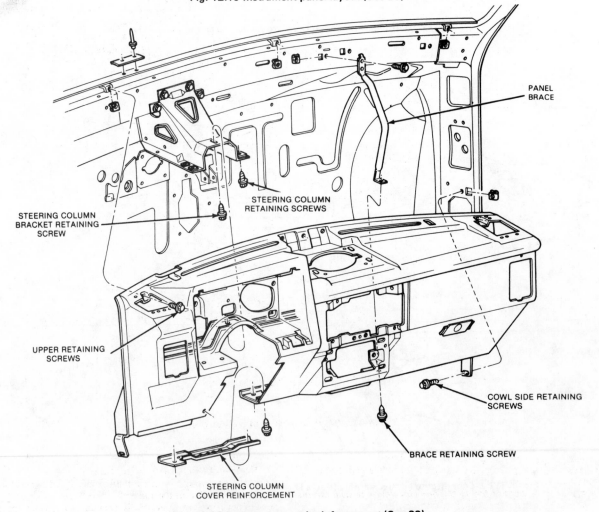

PANEL
BRACE

STEERING COLUMN
BRACKET RETAINING
SCREW

STEERING COLUMN
RETAINING SCREWS

UPPER RETAINING
SCREWS

COWL SIDE RETAINING
SCREWS

BRACE RETAINING SCREW

STEERING COLUMN
COVER REINFORCEMENT

Fig. 12.20 Instrument panel reinforcement (Sec 33)

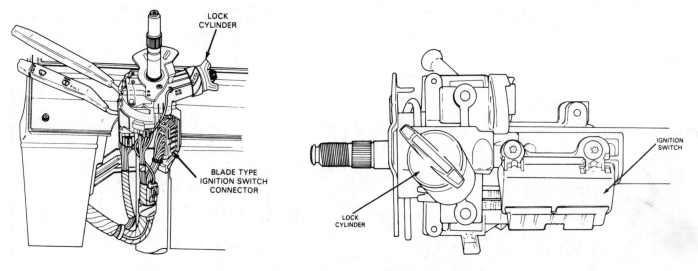

Fig. 12.21 Ignition switch and lock cylinder (Sec 34)

Fig. 12.22 Ignition switch installation (Sec 34)

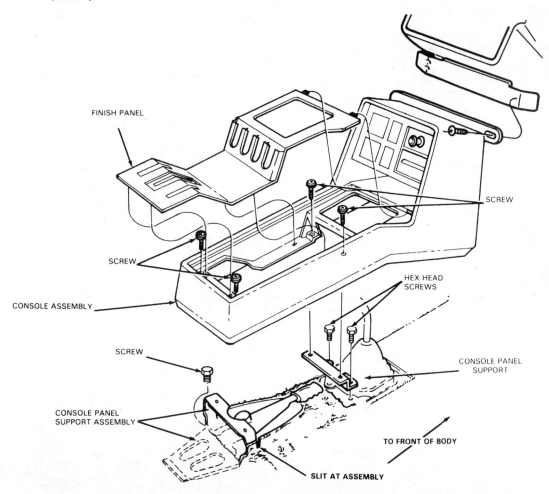

Fig. 12.23 Console installation (Sec 35)

screws holding the console to the instrument panel.
3   Release the parking brake and move the transaxle shift lever into Low (automatic) or Fourth (manual).
4   Pull the console upward and to the rear sufficiently to gain access to the wiring connectors and disconnect them.
5   Remove the console.
6   Installation is the reverse of removal.

Consolette

7   Remove the drill screw in the tray.
8   Use a screwdriver or putty knife to pry the consolette top up from the bottom section at the rear.
9   Remove the remaining three screws and remove the consolette bottom.
10 Installation is a reversal of removal.

36 Radiator grille – removal and installation

1   Remove the attaching screws and withdraw the grille assembly from the vehicle.

2   To install, position the grille on the locating tabs extending from the headlamp doors and loosely install the five retaining screws. Adjust the grille so that there is an even gap between the grille sides and the headlamp doors and tighten the retaining screws.

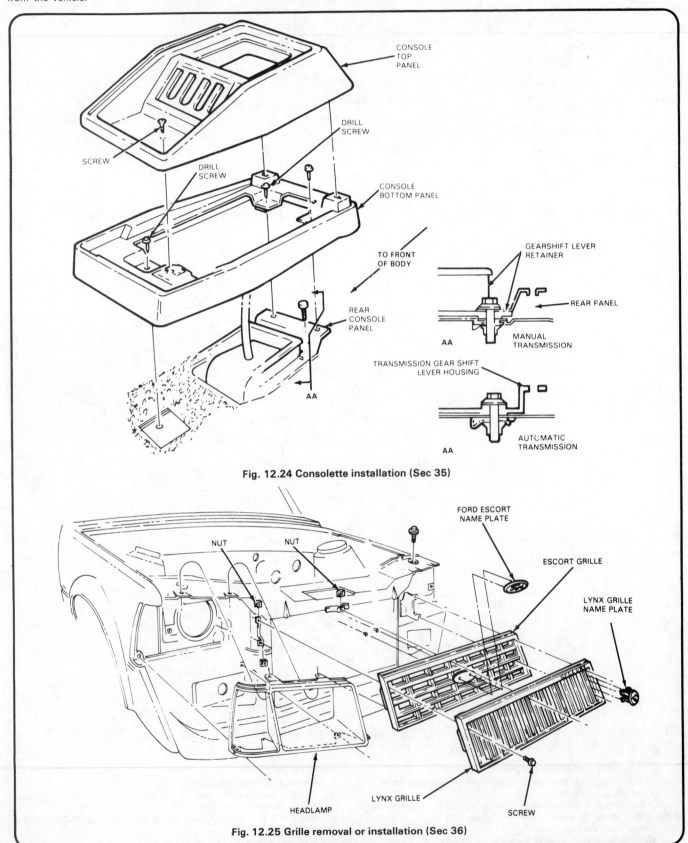

Fig. 12.24 Consolette installation (Sec 35)

Fig. 12.25 Grille removal or installation (Sec 36)

37 Front and rear bumpers – removal and installation

1   Scribe around the bumper isolator attaching bolts for ease of reinstallation. Remove the bolts and with the help of an assistant remove the bumper, making sure to note the number and order of removal of the spacers.

2   If the bumper is to be replaced, transfer the bumper guards, pads, extensions and other components to the new bumper.

3   To install, with an assistant holding the bumper in place on the isolator brackets, install the bolts and tighten to specification.

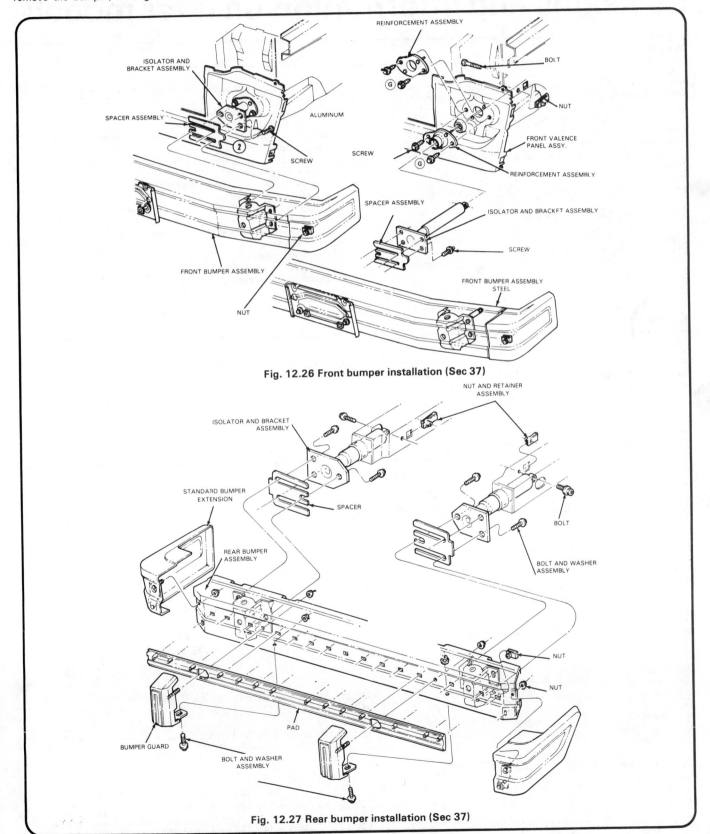

Fig. 12.26 Front bumper installation (Sec 37)

Fig. 12.27 Rear bumper installation (Sec 37)

Chapter 13 Supplement:
Revisions and information on later models

Contents

1 Introduction

This supplement contains specifications and service procedure changes that apply to all Ford Escort/Mercury Lynx models produced between 1983 and 1985. Also included is information related to previous models that was not available at the time of original publication of this manual.

Where no differences (or very minor differences) exist between 1981/82 models and 1983 through 1985 models, no information is given. In those instances, the original material included in Chapters 1 through 12 pertaining to 1981/82 models should be used.

2 Specifications

Note: *The specifications listed here include only the items which differ from those listed in Chapters 1 through 12. For information not specifically listed here refer to the appropriate Chapter.*

General dimensions and capacities (1983 thru 1985)
Cooling system capacity
1.6L, 1.6L H.O . . . . 7.3 qts.
1.6L EFI, 1.6L turbo . . . . 7.8 qts.

Manual transaxle capacity
5-speed . . . . 6.1 pts.

Engine
Valve stem-to-guide clearance
Exhaust . . . . 0.0018 to 0.0037 in (0.046 to 0.095 mm)

Valve springs
Compression pressure @ specified length
    loaded . . . . 200 lbs. @ 1.09 in (892.7 Nm @ 27.71 mm)
    unloaded . . . . 95 lbs. @ 1.461 in (422 Nm @ 37.1 mm)
Free length . . . . 1.86 in. (47.2 mm)
Assembled height . . . . 1.48 to 1.44 in (37.5 to 36.9 mm)
Service limit . . . . 5% pressure loss @ specified height

Camshaft bore inside diameter (1985 only)
No. 1 . . . . 1.7636 to 1.7646 in (44.796 to 44.821 mm)
No. 2 . . . . 1.7735 to 1.7745 in (45.046 to 45.071 mm)
No. 3 . . . . 1.7833 to 1.7843 in (45.298 to 45.321 mm)
No. 4 . . . . 1.7931 to 1.7941 in (45.546 to 45.571 mm)
No. 5 . . . . 1.8030 to 1.8040 in (45.796 to 45.821 mm)

Camshaft bore inside diameter (1985 only) — oversize (not applicable to HO, EFI and Turbo)
No. 1 . . . . 1.7796 to 1.7786 in (45.201 to 45.176 mm)
No. 2 . . . . 1.7894 to 1.7884 in (45.451 to 45.426 mm)
No. 3 . . . . 1.7993 to 1.7983 in (45.701 to 45.676 mm)
No. 4 . . . . 1.8091 to 1.8081 in (45.951 to 45.926 mm)
No. 5 . . . . 1.8189 to 1.8179 in (46.201 to 46.176 mm)

Camshaft (base engine)
Lobe lift
  Intake . . . . 0.229 in. (5.805 mm)
  Exhaust . . . . 0.229 in. (5.805 mm)
  Allowable lobe loss . . . . 0.005 in. (0.127 mm)
Theoretical maximum valve lift
  Intake and exhaust . . . . 0.377 in. (9.58 mm)

Camshaft (HO and EFI)
Lobe lift
  Intake . . . . 0.240 in. (6.094 mm)
  Exhaust . . . . 0.240 in. (6.094 mm)
  Allowable lobe loss . . . . 0.005 in. (0.127 mm)
Theoretical maximum valve lift
  Intake and exhaust . . . . 0.436 in. (10.06 mm)
End play . . . . 0.006 to 0.0018 in (0.152 to 0.046 mm)
  Service limit . . . . 0.0078 in. (0.20 mm)
Journal-to-bearing clearance . . . . 0.0008 to 0.0028 in (0.0205 to 0.0705 mm)
Journal diameter — oversize (not applicable to HO)
No. 1 . . . . 1.7773 to 1.7763 in (45.1425 to 45.1175 mm)
No. 2 . . . . 1.7871 to 1.7861 in (45.3925 to 45.3675 mm)
No. 3 . . . . 1.7969 to 1.7960 in (45.6425 to 45.6175 mm)
No. 4 . . . . 1.8068 to 1.8058 in (45.8925 to 45.8675 mm)
No. 5 . . . . 1.8166 to 1.8156 in (46.1425 to 46.1175 mm)
Runout limit . . . . 0.005 in. (0.127 mm) (runout of center bearing relative to #1 and #5)

Connecting rod bearings
Clearance to crankshaft
  Desired . . . . 0.008 to 0.0015 in (0.020 to 0.028 mm)
  Allowable . . . . 0.008 to 0.0026 in (0.020 to 0.066 mm)
Bearing wall thickness (std) . . . . 0.0581 to 0.0585 in (1.477 to 1.487 mm)

Connecting rod
Out-of-round limit, piston pin bore . . . . 0.0003 in. (0.008 mm)
Taper limit, piston pin bore . . . . 0.00015 in per inch (0.0038 mm per 25.4 mm)
Alignment (bore-to-bore max. diff.)
  Twist . . . . 0.002 in. (0.05 mm)
  Bend . . . . 0.0015 in. (0.038 mm)

Piston
Diameter
  Coded red . . . . 3.1463 to 3.157 in (79.915 to 79.900 mm)
  Coded blue . . . . 3.1474 to 3.1468 in (79.945 to 79.930 mm)
  .004 inch (0.1 mm) oversize . . . . 3.1502 to 3.1496 in (80.015 to 80.000 mm)
Piston-to-bore clearance . . . . 0.0018 to 0.0026 in (0.045 to 0.065 mm)
Pin bore diameter . . . . 0.8123 to 0.8128 in (20.632 to 20.644 mm)
Pin-to-piston clearance . . . . 0.0003 to 0.0005 in (0.007 to 0.013 mm)
Piston rings
  Ring width
    Compression (top) . . . . 0.0626 to 0.0621 in
  Side clearance
    1st ring . . . . 0.002 to 0.0032 in (0.05 to 0.82 mm)
    2nd ring . . . . 0.0016 to 0.0032 in (0.04 to 0.80 mm)

Lubrication system
Oil pump
  Relief valve spring tension, 1984 . . . . 8.0 to 8.8 lbs @ 1.1 in (39.1 to 35.6 Nm @ 25.8 mm)
  Relief valve spring tension, 1985 . . . . 5.3 to 4.7 lbs @ 1.65 in (23.6 to 20.9 Nm @ 42.5 mm)
  Relief valve to bore clearance . . . . 0.0007 to 0.0031 in (0.02 to 0.08 mm)
  Outer gear to housing clearance . . . . 0.003 to 0.0065 in (0.0074 to 0.161 mm)
  Inner and outer gear to cover clearance (end play)
    1983 . . . . 0.000 to 0.003 in (0.000 to 0.077 mm)
    1984 . . . . 0.000 to 0.0035 in (0.000 to 0.089 mm)
    1985 . . . . 0.0005 to 0.0035 in (0.013 to 0.0089 mm)
  Inner to outer gear tip clearance
    1984 and 1985 only . . . . 0.002 to 0.007 in (0.05 to 0.18 mm)

Torque specifications

	Ft-lb	Nm
Distributor clamp to block	6 to 8	8 to 11
Flywheel to crankshaft	54 to 63	73 to 87
Intake manifold stud to head	1.5 to 7.4	2 to 10
Exhaust manifold to head	1.5 to 7.4	2 to 10
Oil pump cover	6 to 9	8 to 12
Oil pump main discharge plug	21 to 23	28 to 32
Oil pump relief valve plug	12 to 15	16 to 20
Spark plug	8 to 15	10 to 20

Cooling system

Torque specifications

	Ft-lb	Nm
Water pump attaching bolts	30 to 40	40 to 55
Water outlet connection bolts	6 to 8	8 to 11
Water pump inlet tube to water pump	5 to 7	6 to 9
Water pump inlet tube to block	30 to 40	40 to 55
Clamps	1.5 to 2.5	1.8 to 2.8
Pipe plug (water outlet)	5 to 8	7 to 11

Fuel and exhaust systems

Torque specifications

	Ft-lb	Nm
Lower intake manifold to head	12 to 15	16 to 20
EGR tube	6 to 8.5	8 to 11.5
Air supply tube clamps	17 to 26*	2 to 3
Upper to lower intake manifold	15 to 22	20 to 30
Throttle body to intake manifold	12 to 15	16 to 20
Air bypass valve to throttle body	71 to 97*	8 to 11
Throttle sensor to throttle body	14 to 16*	1.2 to 1.8
Fuel pressure relief valve	48 to 84*	6 to 10
Fuel pressure relief valve cap	4 to 6*	0.5 to 0.7
Fuel manifold to charging assembly	15 to 22	20 to 30
Fuel pressure regulator to injector manifold	2.7 to 4.0	3 to 4.5
Fuel return line fitting	15 to 18	20 to 25
Vane air meter mounting screws	6 to 9	8 to 12
Air cleaner to air vane meter	6 to 9	8 to 12

* In-lbs

Manual transaxle

Transaxle type	5-speed, synchromesh on all forward gears
Oil capacity	6.2 US pts
Oil type	Type 'F' automatic transmission fluid

Torque specifications

	Ft-lb	Nm
Transaxle to engine bolts	98 to 115	139 to 156
Air management valve bracket bolt to transaxle	28 to 31	38 to 42
Switch actuator bracket bolt	7 to 10	9 to 14
Control arm to steering knuckle	37 to 44	50 to 60
Rear mounting bolts	35 to 50	47 to 68
Transaxle mounting stud	38 to 41	52 to 56
Front mounting bracket bolts	25 to 35	34 to 47
Stiffener brace bolts	28 to 38	38 to 51
Starter stud bolts	30 to 40	41 to 54
Roll restrictor bolts	25 to 30	34 to 40
Shift stabilizer bar to transaxle case	23 to 35	31 to 47
Speedometer	2.5 to 3.5	3.4 to 4.5

Automatic transaxle

Oil capacity	8.3 US qts.
Oil type	Dexron II or equivalent

Braking system

Caliper cylinder bore diameter	2.362 in. (60 mm)

---

3   Tune-up and maintenance

1   No extra service has been added to late model base engines, but on turbocharged engines it is recommended that the oil and oil filter be changed every 5,000 miles or 12 months, whichever comes first. In the interest of turbo longevity we recommend that the oil and oil filter be changed every 3,000 miles.

2   On turbocharged engines it is recommended that the spark plugs be changed every 15,000 miles and the crankcase oil separator filter replaced every 30,000 miles.

Engine idle speed adjustment (EFI engines only)

Note: *Engine idle speed is computer controlled on EFI engines. This procedure is for checking the engine base idle with the computer disconnected. If the engine is not within specifications after performing this procedure the vehicle should be taken to a qualified service technician.*

3   With the transmission in Park or Neutral, bring the engine to normal operating temperature and then turn it off.

4   Disconnect and plug both vacuum connections at the EGR solenoid.

5   Disconnect the idle speed controller (ISC) power lead.

6   The electric cooling fan must be running during this procedure. To accomplish this:

233

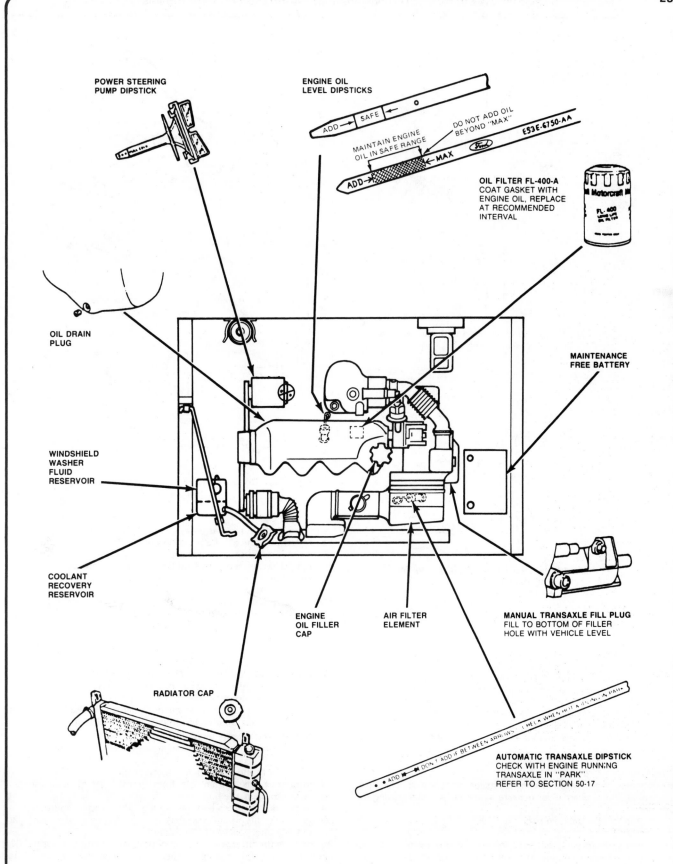

Fig. 13.1   Engine service points (EFI and turbo)(Sec 3)

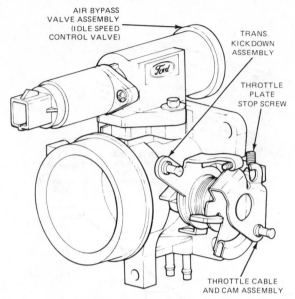

Fig. 13.2   Base idle speed is adjusted with the throttle plate stop screw (Sec 3)

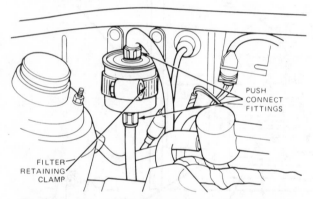

Fig. 13.4   Note the direction of the 'flow' arrow before removing the filter (Sec 3)

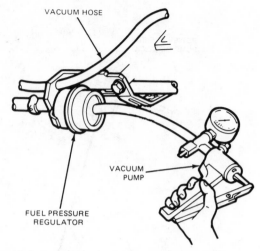

Fig. 13.3   A vacuum pump is used to relieve fuel system pressure (Sec 3)

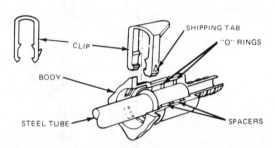

Fig. 13.5   Do not reuse the hairpin clip on 3/8 and 5/16-in. fittings (Sec 3)

a) Disconnect the power lead at the fan motor.
b) Connect a jumper wire between the fan motor and the positive (+) battery terminal.

7   Run the engine at 2000 RPM for one minute.

8   With the parking brake set and the transmission in Neutral (manual transmission) or Drive (automatic transmission) check/adjust the engine RPM within 120 seconds. Adjustment is by turning the throttle plate screw clockwise to raise RPM or counterclockwise to lower RPM. **Note:** *If engine RPM is not adjusted within 120 seconds, shut the engine off and repeat Steps 7 and 8.*

9   Turn the engine off and reconnect the vacuum and electrical connections.

Fuel system pressure relief

10   A pressure relief valve has been installed in the fuel supply line in the engine compartment. Fuel pressure is relieved by first removing the gas cap.

11   Disconnect the vacuum hose from the fuel pressure regulator on the fuel rail.

12   With a vacuum pump apply 25 in. HG to the regulator. The fuel pressure will be released into the gas tank through the return line.

Fuel filter replacement (EFI engine)

Warning: *Fuel supply lines on EFI models remain pressurized for long periods of time after the engine has been shut off. This pressure must be relieved any time the fuel system is being serviced.*

13   The fuel filter on fuel injected models is located on the dash panel

extension in the right rear corner of the engine compartment.

14   With the engine off and the fuel system depressurized, remove the two push-connect fittings at the ends of the fuel filter (see Steps 21 through 32 for push-connect fitting removal procedure).

15   Note the direction of the 'flow' arrow on the side of the filter for future reference.

16   Loosen the filter retainer clamp enough to remove the filter.

17   Install a new filter with the 'flow' arrow in the same direction as the old filter. Tighten the retaining clamp.

18   Reinstall the fuel lines.

19   Start the engine and check the system for leaks.

Push-connect fittings — removal and installation

20   Two types of push-connect fittings are used on fuel injected models. The 3/8 and 5/16-inch diameter hoses use a 'hairpin' clip in the fitting. The 1/4-inch diameter hose uses a 'duck bill' clip in the fitting. Each type of fitting uses a different removal and installation procedure.

3/8 and 5/16-in. fittings (hairpin clip)

21   Clean the fitting of any grease or dirt before proceding with this procedure.

22   Twist the fitting to break loose the seal.

23   To remove the 'hairpin' clip from the fitting first bend the tab downward to clear the body.

24   Using your hand, spread the clip legs 1/8-in. apart and push the clip up into the fitting. Remove the clip by pulling up on the triangular tab and working it clear of the fitting.

25   Remove the fitting by pulling the fitting off the tube. After the fitting is separated from the tube inspect it for any damage or loose parts that may have come out.

26   Do not use the old clip for reinstallation. Any time the fitting is separated a new clip must be used. Insert a new clip into the fitting with the triangular tab pointing away from the fitting opening.

27   With the tube end clean and free of any obstructions, insert the fitting onto the tube end. A 'click' will be heard when the fitting is ful-

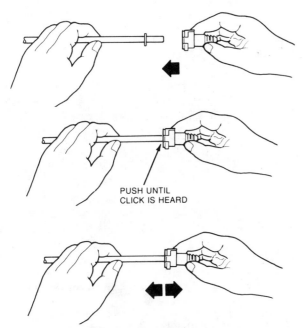

Fig. 13.6   After engaging the fitting on the tube a pull will confirm that it is locked in place (Sec 3)

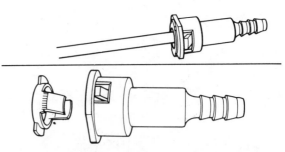

Fig. 13.7   A pair of needle nose pliers can be used to disconnect the fitting (Sec 3)

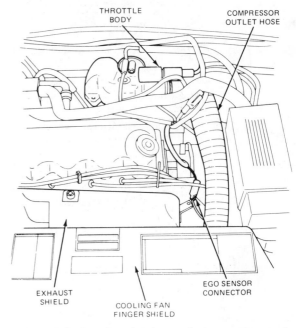

Fig. 13.8   Location of various turbocarger components (Sec 4)

ly engaged with the tube. Pull on the fitting to check that it is fully engaged.

1/4-in. fittings (duck bill clip)
28   Removal requires a pair of needle nose pliers (jaw width of 0.2 in. or less). Align the jaws with the opening in the side of the case and compress the part of the retaining clip that engages the fitting case.
29   With the retaining clip disengaged, pull the fitting off the tube.
30   The retaining clip will remain with the tube. Disengage it from the tube and remove it. Inspect the fitting for any damage or loose parts.
Note: *It is recommended that the old retaining clip not be reused.*
31   For reinstallation insert one of the edges of the clip at the window opening of the fitting. Push on the other side until the clip snaps into place.
32   After checking to see that the tube end is clean, reinstall the fitting onto the tube until a 'click' is heard. Pull on the fitting to check on full engagement.

Ignition timing Non-EFI engine
33   Place the transmission in Park or Neutral, with the air conditioning in the Off position.
34   Remove and plug the vacuum hoses at the distributor vacuum advance canister.
35   Connect an inductive timing light and a hand-held tachometer according to the manufacturer's instructions.
36   If the vehicle is equipped with a barometric pressure sensor, disconnect it from the ignition module and place a jumper between the pins on the ignition module connector (yellow and black wires).
37   Start the engine and let it reach operating temperature.
38   With the engine at timing RPM check and adjust the ignition timing to specification (refer to the emissions decal located under the hood).
39   Unplug and reconnect the vacuum hoses.
40   Remove the jumper wire from the ignition module connector and reattach it to the module.

EFI and turbocharged engines
41   Place the transmission in Park or Neutral, with the air conditioning in the Off position.
42   Connect an inductive timing light and a hand-held tachometer according to the manufacturer's instructions.
43   Disconnect the single white connector (black on some models) wire near the distributor.
44   Start the engine and let it reach operating temperature.
45   With the engine at timing RPM check and adjust the ignition tim-

ing to specification (refer to the emissions decal located under the hood).
46   Unplug and reconnect the vacuum hoses.
47   Reconnect the single wire connector.

---

4   Engine

Cylinder head (turbocharged engines) — removal and installation
1   The procedures in Chapter 2 (Sec 7) should be followed with the addition of the following steps:
2   Disconnect the upper radiator hose at the cylinder head.
3   Disconnect the cooling fan switch lead and any EFI related wires that may interfere with removal. **Note:** *When disconnecting EFI wires each should be marked to aid in reinstallation.*
4   Remove the air intake hose at the throttle body.
5   Remove the PCV oil separator system.
6   Disconnect the EGO sensor and the EGR valve vacuum hose.
7   Remove the turbocharger air inlet hose.
8   Disconnect and remove the oil supply tube at the turbocharger coolant outlet and the engine block.
9   Disconnect the exhaust pipe from the turbocharger, then disconnect the oil return line at the turbocharger.
10   Remove the head with the turbocharger attached. **Note:** *Before installing the cylinder head on a turbocharged engine the piston 'squish'*

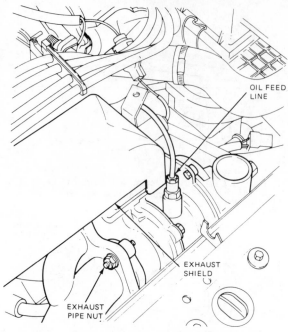

Fig. 13.9   Turbocharger oil feed line (Sec 4)

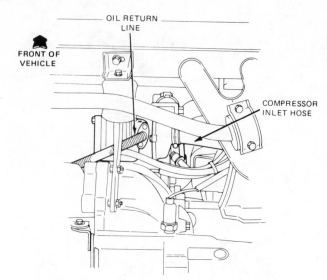

Fig. 13.10   Turbocharger oil return line (Sec 4)

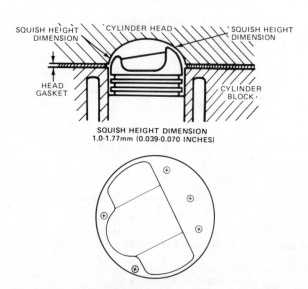

Fig. 13.11   Lead solder positioning for checking 'squish' height (Sec 4)

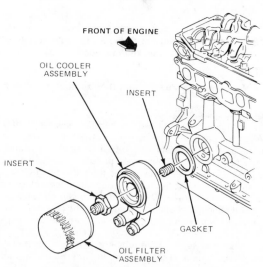

Fig. 13.12   Oil cooler installation (Sec 4)

the tightening sequence).

16 Rotate the crankshaft to move the piston through its TDC position.

17 Remove the cylinder head and measure the thickness of the solder to determine the 'squish' height. It should be between 0.039 and 0.070 in. If it is not double-check to make sure that any new parts installed which might affect 'squish' height, such as the head gasket or pistons, are the parts specified for this engine. If you have the correct parts and the 'squish' height is still not within specifications consult your Ford dealer.

Oil pan (turbocharged engine) — removal and installation

18 The procedure in Chapter 2 should be followed with the addition of the following steps:

19 Remove the knee-braces at the transaxle.

20 Remove the EGR tube at the exhaust inlet pipe and disconnect the exhaust pipe between the turbocharger and the converter.

21 Installation is the reverse of the removal procedure.

Engine (turbocharged) — removal and installation

22 The procedure in Chapter 2 should be used with the addition of the following steps:

23 While the vehicle is still on the ground remove the radiator cooling fan guard and radiator.

24 After the vehicle is in the air remove the oil cooler (see Steps 27 through 32).

height must be checked (see Steps 12 to 17).

11 Installation is the reverse of the removal procedure. **Note:** *The head gasket on a turbocharged engine is different than on a nonturbocharged engine. Be sure the correct gasket is installed!*

Piston 'squish' height — checking

Note: *Any replacement of parts (crankshaft, pistons and connecting rods) or modifications to the head affecting the 'squish' height are not permitted. If no parts other than a head gasket are replaced, the piston 'squish' height should be within specifications. If parts other than the head gasket are replaced the 'squish' height should be checked.*

12 Clean both gasket surfaces (cylinder head and engine block) of all old gasket material.

13 Place a small amount of soft lead solder on the piston in the areas shown in the accompanying illustration.

14 Rotate the crankshaft to lower the piston and install the head gasket and the cylinder head. **Note:** *A compressed (used) gasket is preferred.*

15 Install the head bolts and tighten them to 30 to 44 ft-lb (40 to 60 Nm) in the proper tightening sequence (see Chapter 2 Fig. 2.7 for

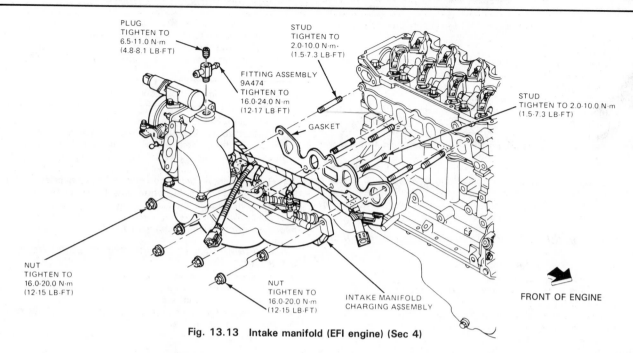

Fig. 13.13   Intake manifold (EFI engine) (Sec 4)

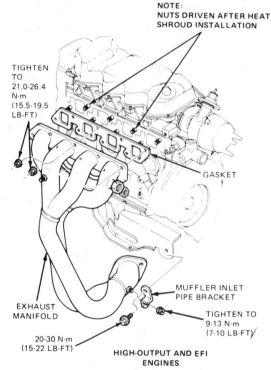

Fig. 13.14   Exhaust manifold (HO and EFI engines) (Sec 4)

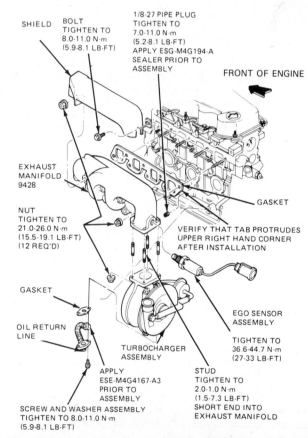

Fig. 13.15   Exhaust manifold (turbocharged engine) (Sec 4)

25 After disconnecting the exhaust pipe from the turbocharger remove the exhaust pipe support bracket.

26 Installation is the reverse of the removal procedure.

Oil cooler — removal and installation

27 Disconnect the negative battery cable.

28 Drain the engine oil and remove the oil filter.

29 Drain the engine coolant.

30 Disconnect the two coolant hoses at the oil cooler.

31 Remove the oil filter adapter from the cooler and remove the oil cooler.

32 Installation is the reverse of removal. Use a new oil cooler gasket and refill the cooling system with the proper mixture of water and coolant (see Chapter 3).

Intake manifold (turbocharged and EFI engines) — removal and installation

33 Disconnect the negative battery cable.

34 Remove the air intake from the throttle body.

35 Disconnect and label the vacuum hoses connected to the intake manifold.
36 Remove the EGR tube.
37 Disconnect the electrical connector at the air by-pass valve and the engine wiring harness at the shock absorber tower.
38 Raise the vehicle and support it securely on jackstands.
39 Remove the bottom three manifold nuts.
40 From the top of the engine remove the fuel lines (inlet and return) at the manifold.
41 Disconnect the throttle cable from the throttle body.
42 Remove the PCV valve and hose from the intake manifold and rocker arm cover.
43 Remove the three remaining nuts from the intake manifold and carefully remove the intake manifold. **Note:** *To avoid damage to the machined surface do not lay the intake manifold on its gasket surface.*
44 Installation is the reverse of removal. Use a new gasket and torque all manifold bolts to the proper specification.

Exhaust manifold (turbocharged engine) — removal and installation

45 Disconnect the negative battery cable.
46 Remove the radiator fan shield.
47 Disconnect the turbocharger outlet hose at the turbocharger and rotate it up out of the way.
48 Remove the alternator and bracket (see Chapter 5 Sec 6).
49 Disconnect the electrical connector at the EGO sensor.
50 Disconnect the oil supply line at the turbocharger.
51 Remove the oil return line by unbolting it at the engine block and turbocharger.
52 Disconnect the exhaust pipe from the turbocharger.
53 Remove the bolt connecting the heat shield to the water outlet.
54 Remove the eight exhaust manifold nuts and slide the manifold assembly back to remove the heat shield.
55 Remove the turbocharger and manifold as an assembly.
56 Installation is the reverse of the removal procedure with the following additions:
57 Use a new gasket. **Note:** *The exhaust gasket has a top and bot-*
tom. Make sure it is installed correctly.
58 If a new exhaust manifold is being installed be sure to install the EGO sensor from the old manifold.
59 Use a new gasket at the oil return line to avoid leaks.

5   Cooling, heating and air conditoning

1   The major change in the cooling system is for the turbocharged engine. Due to engine compartment space limitations and heat generated by the turbocharger it was necessary to mount twin fans in front of the radiator and condenser. The fans operate in the same manner as the conventional cooling system except the controller module contains an overload protection circuit. If the fan is jammed, such as by snow or road debris, the controller will open the fan circuit, preventing costly damage to the electrical system. **Caution:** *When working near the cooling fans the ignition must be in the Off position and the negative battery cable disconnected.*

Cooling fan motor (turbocharged engine) — removal and installation

2   Disconnect the negative battery cable.
3   Remove the radiator fan shield and disconnect the electrical connector from the fan motor.
4   Remove the two bolts from the fan motor bracket and remove the fan assembly from the vehicle.
5   To separate the fan motors from the brackets remove the four retaining nuts.
6   Installation is the reverse of the removal procedure with the addition of the following:
7   After installing the four retaining nuts on the fan motors torque them to 44 to 66 in-lb.
8   After installing the fan motor bracket assembly in the vehicle torque the retaining bolts to 35 to 45 in-lb.
9   Thread the fan motor wire loom through the radiator support. Reconnect the wire connector to the vehicle harness, making sure the two lock fingers on the connector snap firmly into place.

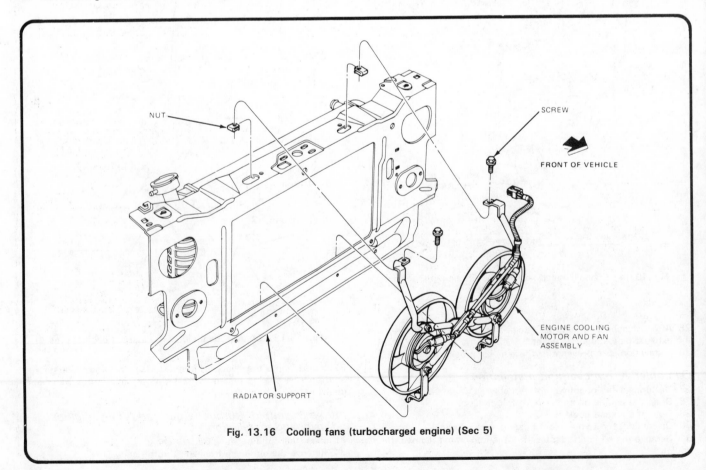

Fig. 13.16   Cooling fans (turbocharged engine) (Sec 5)

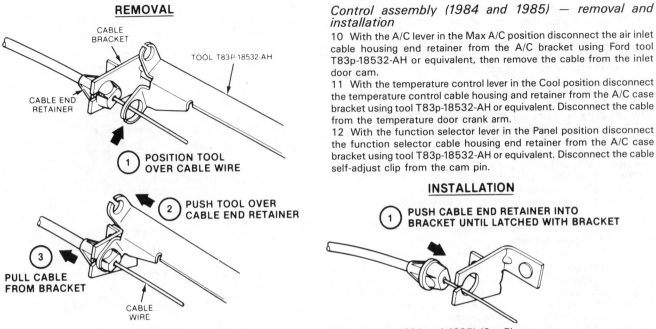

REMOVAL

① POSITION TOOL OVER CABLE WIRE

② PUSH TOOL OVER CABLE END RETAINER

③ PULL CABLE FROM BRACKET

Control assembly (1984 and 1985) — removal and installation

10 With the A/C lever in the Max A/C position disconnect the air inlet cable housing end retainer from the A/C bracket using Ford tool T83p-18532-AH or equivalent, then remove the cable from the inlet door cam.

11 With the temperature control lever in the Cool position disconnect the temperature control cable housing and retainer from the A/C case bracket using tool T83p-18532-AH or equivalent. Disconnect the cable from the temperature door crank arm.

12 With the function selector lever in the Panel position disconnect the function selector cable housing end retainer from the A/C case bracket using tool T83p-18532-AH or equivalent. Disconnect the cable self-adjust clip from the cam pin.

INSTALLATION

① PUSH CABLE END RETAINER INTO BRACKET UNTIL LATCHED WITH BRACKET

Fig. 13.17 Control cable end removal and installation (1984 and 1985) (Sec 5)

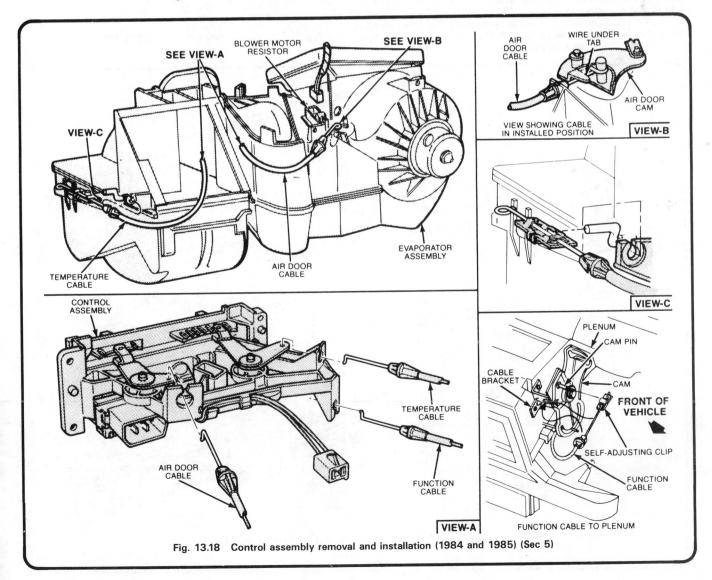

Fig. 13.18 Control assembly removal and installation (1984 and 1985) (Sec 5)

13 Remove the instrument panel finish center.
14 Remove the control assembly by removing the four attaching screws.
15 With the control levers in the Cool, Panel and Recirc positions, disconnect the three cables.
16 Disconnect the electrical connectors and remove the control assembly.
17 Installation is the reverse of the removal procedure.

Heater core — removal and installation

18 Drain the coolant from the radiator.
19 Disconnect the two heater core hoses.
20 From underneath the glove box remove the floor duct (two screws), the instrument panel screw and the evaporator assembly.
21 Remove the heater core cover (two screws).
22 Remove the heater core.
23 Installation is the reverse of the removal procedure.

6 Fuel and exhaust systems

1   The 1984 and 1985 Escort/Lynx is equipped with an Electronic Fuel Injection (EFI) system in place of the conventional carburetor. Electronic fuel injection provides optimum mixture ratios at all stages of combustion, and this, together with the immediate response characteristics of fuel injection, permits the engine to run on the weakest possible fuel/air mixture, vastly reducing exhaust emissions. The EFI system is interrelated with and works in conjunction with the emission control and exhaust systems.
2   The EFI system consists of four sub-systems: the fuel flow system, the air flow system, the electrical sensors and the electronic control unit. The various components that make up the entire EFI system are

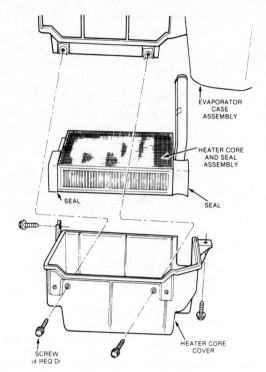

Fig. 13.19   Heater core assembly (1984 and 1985) (Sec 5)

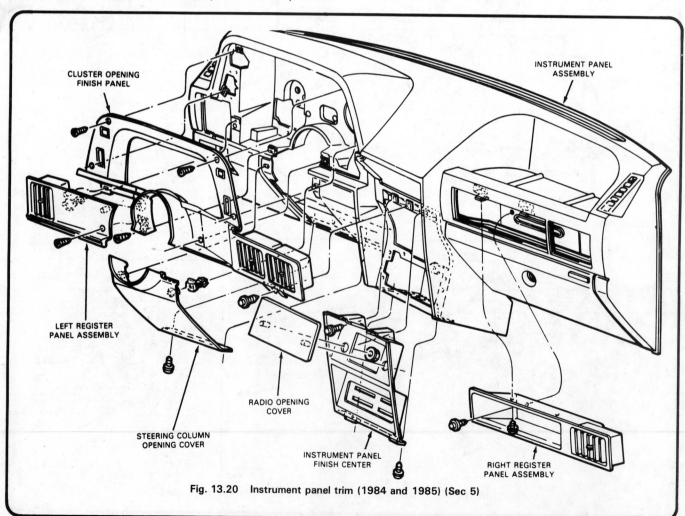

Fig. 13.20   Instrument panel trim (1984 and 1985) (Sec 5)

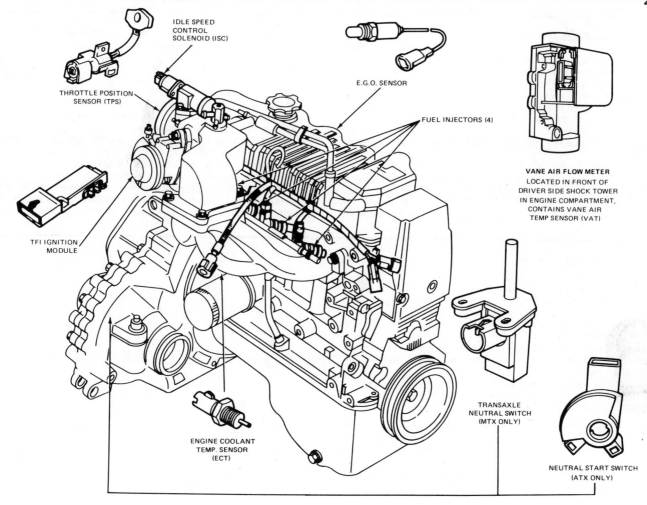

IDLE SPEED
CONTROL
SOLENOID (ISC)

THROTTLE POSITION
SENSOR (TPS)

E.G.O. SENSOR

FUEL INJECTORS (4)

TFI IGNITION
MODULE

VANE AIR FLOW METER
LOCATED IN FRONT OF
DRIVER SIDE SHOCK TOWER
IN ENGINE COMPARTMENT,
CONTAINS VANE AIR
TEMP SENSOR (VAT)

ENGINE COOLANT
TEMP. SENSOR
(ECT)

TRANSAXLE
NEUTRAL SWITCH
(MTX ONLY)

NEUTRAL START SWITCH
(ATX ONLY)

Fig. 13.21   EFI component location (Sec 6)

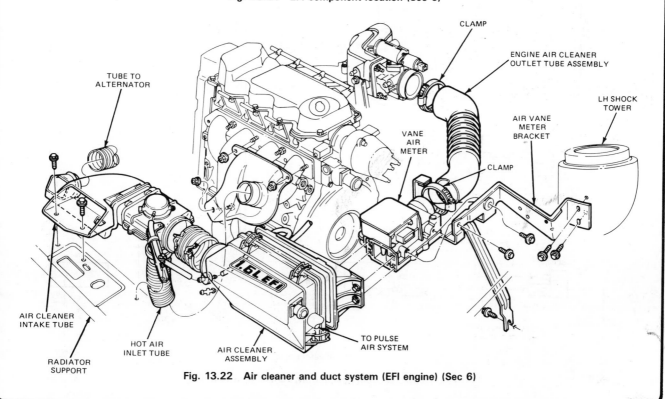

CLAMP

ENGINE AIR CLEANER
OUTLET TUBE ASSEMBLY

TUBE TO
ALTERNATOR

LH SHOCK
TOWER

VANE
AIR
METER

AIR VANE
METER
BRACKET

CLAMP

AIR CLEANER
INTAKE TUBE

RADIATOR
SUPPORT

HOT AIR
INLET TUBE

AIR CLEANER
ASSEMBLY

TO PULSE
AIR SYSTEM

1.6L EFI

Fig. 13.22   Air cleaner and duct system (EFI engine) (Sec 6)

detailed later in this Section.

3   Fuel from the tank is delivered under pressure from the electric fuel pump through a fuel filter and a pressure regulator. It is then injected into the intake manifold. The pressure regulator is designed to maintain a constant pressure difference between the fuel line pressure and the intake manifold vacuum. Where manifold conditions are such that the fuel pressure could be beyond that specified, the pressure regulator returns surplus fuel to the tank.

4   An injection of fuel occurs once every rotation of the crankshaft. Because the injection signal comes from the control unit, all four injectors operate simultaneously and independent of the engine stroke. Each injection supplies half the amount of fuel required by the cylinder, and the length of the injection period is determined by information fed to the control unit by the various sensors included in the system.

5   Elements affecting the injection duration include: engine rpm, quantity and temperature of the intake air, throttle valve opening,

temperature of the engine coolant, position of the ignition switch, intake manifold vacuum pressure and amount of oxygen in the exhaust gases.

6   Because the EFI system operates at high fuel pressure a slight leak can affect the system's efficiency and present a serious fire risk. Also, since the intake air flow is critical to the operation of the system, even a slight air leak will cause wrong air/fuel mixtures.

Note: *Certain precautions should be observed when working on the EFI system because of its critical and sensitive components.*

Do not disconnect either battery cable while the engine is running.

Prior to any operation in which a fuel line will be disconnected the high pressure in the system must first be eliminated. This procedure is described in Section 3.

Disconnect the negative battery cable to eliminate the possibility of sparks occuring while fuel is present. Prior to removing an EFI component be sure the ignition switch is Off and the negative battery cable

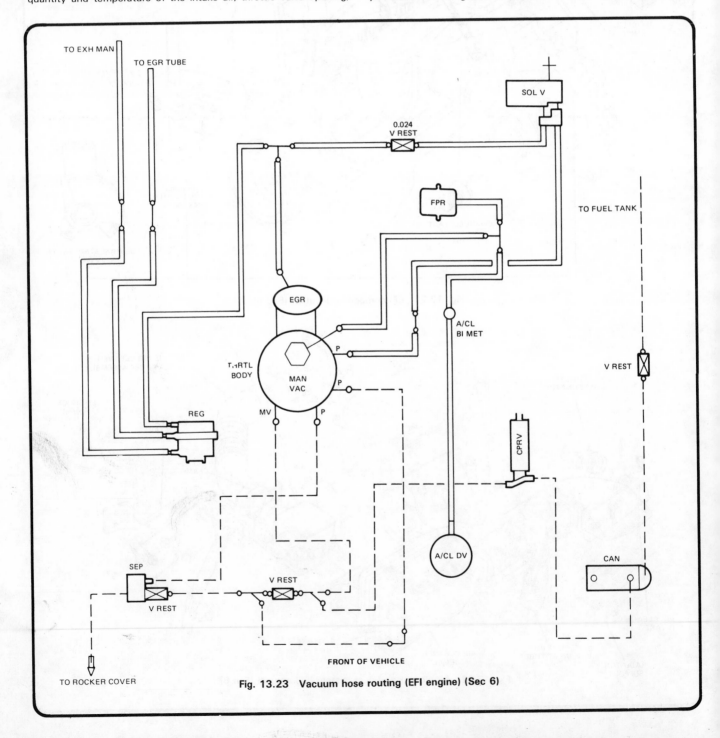

Fig. 13.23 Vacuum hose routing (EFI engine) (Sec 6)

is disconnected.

The EFI wiring harness should be kept at least four (4) inches (10 mm) away from adjacent harnesses. This includes a CB antenna feeder cable as well. This is to prevent electrical pulses in other systems from interferring with the EFI operation. Be sure all EFI wiring connections are tight, clean and secure as a poor connection can cause extremely high voltage surges in the ignition coil, which could drain the IC circuit.

7   While a basic check of the EFI system is included in this Chapter, the complexity of the system prevents most problems from being accurately diagnosed by the home mechanic. If a problem develops in the system, but cannot be pinpointed by the checks listed here, take the vehicle to a Ford/Mercury dealer to locate the fault.

EFI components — general description

Control unit

8   The essential role of this unit is to generate a pulse to the injectors. Upon receiving an electrical signal from each sensor the control unit generates a pulse whose duration (injector open time period) is controlled to provide the exact amount of fuel, according to engine characteristics at that particular time.

Air vane meter

9   The air vane meter measures the volume and temperature of the intake air and sends the signal to the control unit. This is achieved by a potentiometer which is linked to the air intake flap shaft. The more air that enters the flow meter, the further the flap valve rotates, which in turn rotates the potentiometer wiper through a variable resistance coil. This increasing or decreasing resistance (dependent upon the flap angle) sends the signal to the control unit. In order to dampen any excessive movement of the flap, due to vacuum depressions in the intake manifold, a helical spring and compensating plate in a damper chamber are provided. Also built into the airflow meter is an air temperature sensor, which sends a signal to the control unit. This signal will define the duration of the injection time. Air that flows into the meter is first passed through the air cleaner assembly.

Throttle body assembly

10   The throttle body controls air flow into the engine in response to the accelerator pedal. Mounted to the throttle body are various other sensors, including the throttle position sensor and idle air bypass valve.

Air bypass valve

11   The air bypass valve controls the engine idle by regulating the amount of air that passes around the throttle plate. Besides controlling normal idle it also controls cold start fast idle and over-temperature idle boost.

Injectors

12   An injector is mounted on each branch portion of the intake manifold. Each injector is actuated by a small solenoid valve built into the injector body. Actuating the solenoid valve pulls the needle valve

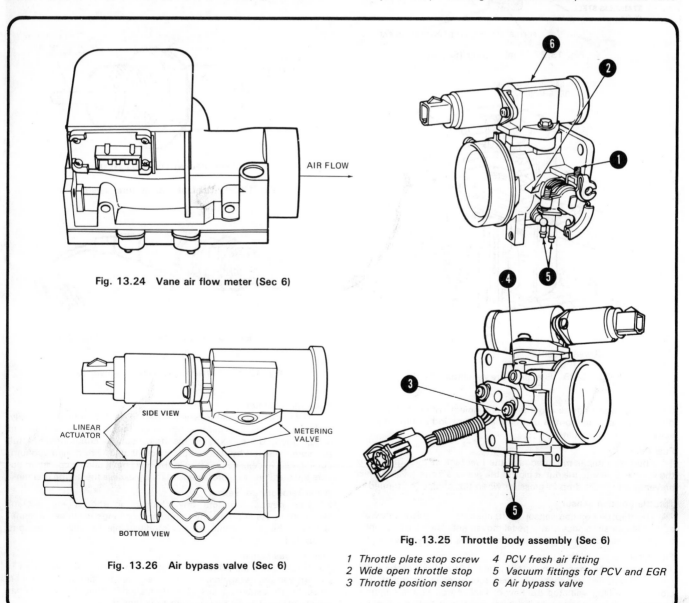

Fig. 13.24   Vane air flow meter (Sec 6)

AIR FLOW

SIDE VIEW

LINEAR ACTUATOR

METERING VALVE

BOTTOM VIEW

Fig. 13.26   Air bypass valve (Sec 6)

Fig. 13.25   Throttle body assembly (Sec 6)

1 Throttle plate stop screw   4 PCV fresh air fitting
2 Wide open throttle stop   5 Vacuum fittings for PCV and EGR
3 Throttle position sensor   6 Air bypass valve

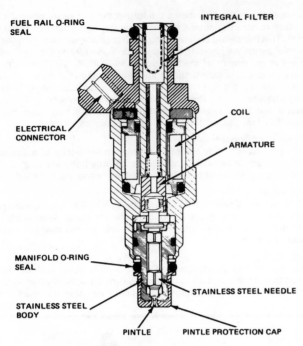

Fig. 13.27   Fuel injector (Sec 6)

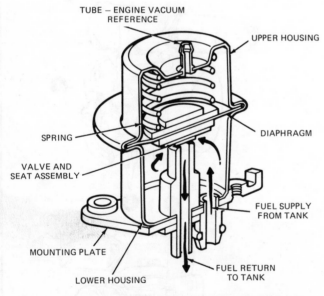

Fig. 13.29   Fuel pressure regulator (Sec 6)

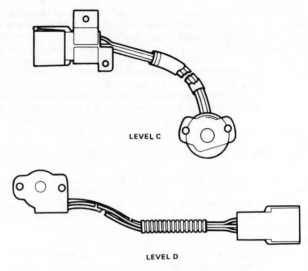

Fig. 13.28   Throttle position sensor (Sec 6)

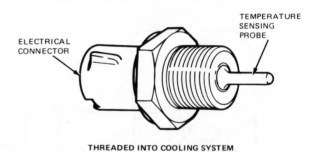

Fig. 13.30   Coolant temperature sensor (Sec 6)

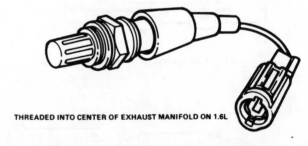

Fig. 13.31   Exhaust gas oxygen sensor (Sec 6)

into the open position to allow the fuel to inject. The duration of the pulse sent from the control unit defines the period of time that the solenoid valve is actuated.

Fuel Pump

13 The fuel pump is mounted near the fuel tank at the right rear of the vehicle. Built into the outlet pipe of the pump is a check valve which prevents an abrupt drop in pressure when the engine is stopped.

Throttle position sensor

14 The throttle position sensor is attached to the throttle body and acts in response to accelerator pedal movement. The sensor supplies a signal to the control unit proportional to the throttle plate angle.

Fuel filter

15 The fuel filter, which is mounted in the right-hand side of the engine compartment, ensures that only clean fuel reaches the injectors. A clogged fuel filter will stop the flow of fuel and cause the engine to operate in a sluggish manner, hesitate, and eventually stop running.

Pressure regulator

16 The pressure regulator, which is part of the fuel supply assembly, maintains a constant fuel pressure at all stages of acceleration and deceleration. Under extreme manifold vacuum conditions the full pressure delivered by the fuel pump, combined with a high vacuum, could cause excessive pressure in the fuel line. If such a condition occurs the pressure regulator opens to return excess fuel to the fuel tank.

Water temperature sensor

17 This device monitors any changes in the engine coolant temperature. As soon as any temperature change is sensed a signal is sent to the control unit, where a modified injector pulse duration is computed.

Exhaust gas sensor

18 The exhaust gas sensor, which works in conjunction with the EFI system and the catalytic converter, measures the amount of oxygen present in the exhaust gases. This information is fed to the control unit, which adjusts the air/fuel mixture to compensate.

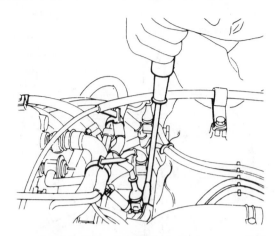

Fig. 13.32   A screwdriver can be used as a stethoscope to check injector operation (Sec 6)

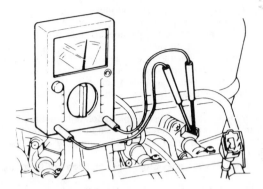

Fig. 13.33   Use an ohmmeter to check injector continuity (Sec 6)

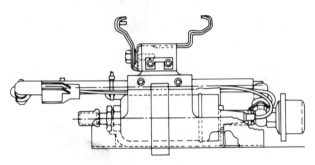

Fig. 13.34   Electric fuel pump mounting (EFI engine) (Sec 6)

EFI components — testing

Note: *Most problems in the EFI system are caused by dirty connectors or improperly connected wires. Therefore, a check should be made of all connectors to make sure they are all tight and clean. Prior to disconnecting any wiring, turn the ignition switch to the Off position.*

EFI basic system check

19 If the EFI system is suspected, a simple test can be performed to check if all the injectors are functional.

20 To trace a single faulty injector with the engine running use a screwdriver as a stethoscope. Position the blade of the screwdriver on the injector and hold the handle against your ear. You should hear a click every time the injector operates. Compare the noise of the suspect injector with the other three injectors. If the volume of the click is noticeably less than at the other injectors, that particular injector could be faulty and should be checked by a trained professional.

21 If the engine will not run, the injectors can still be checked individually as described above. With the assistance of a second person operating the ignition switch to crank the engine, use the screwdriver method described in Step 20 to determine if the problem is in the EFI system.

22 Once you have isolated a possibly faulty injector the fault can be verified by carrying out a continuity check. To do this, first disconnect the battery ground cable.

23 Disconnect the electrical connector from the suspect injector.

24 With the probes of an ohmmeter connected to the terminals on the injector, ensure that continuity exists (Fig. 13.33). If there is no continuity, the solenoid coil windings could be open-circuited (broken) or the terminal leads supplying the coil with current may be broken inside the injector. In such cases the only remedy is to replace the faulty injector.

Electric fuel pump (EFI and turbocharged engines)

Diagnosis

25 Almost any electric fuel pump malfunction that can occur will result in a loss or reduction of fuel flow and/or pressure. Loss of pressure and/or

flow will be detected by a reduction in engine performance. This diagnosis procedure will concentrate on determining if the electric fuel pump is operating properly.

26 Check the fuel tank for adequate fuel supply.

27 Check for fuel leakage at all fittings and lines.

28 Check for electrical continuity to the fuel pump by disconnecting the electrical connector at the fuel pump inlet.

29 Connect a voltmeter to the body wiring harness connector.

30 Turn the key to On while watching the voltmeter.

31 The voltage should rise to battery voltage, then return to zero after approximately one second.

32 If the voltage is not as specified check the inertia switch and electrical system.

33 Connect a continuity tester (ohmmeter) to the pump wiring harness connector. If there is no continuity, check continuity directly at the pump terminals.

34 If there is no continuity at the pump terminals, replace the pump. If continuity is present here but not in Step 33, service or replace the wiring harness.

35 To check electric fuel pump operation, disconnect the return line at the fuel rail, being careful to avoid fuel spillage.

36 Connect a hose from the fuel rail fitting to a calibrated container of at least one quart.

37 Connect a pressure gauge (T80L-9974-A or equivalent) to the fuel diagnostic valve on the fuel rail.

38 Disconnect the electrical connector to the electric fuel pump just forward of the pump outlet if not already disconnected from Step 28.

39 Connect an auxillary wiring harness to the electical connector to the fuel pump.

40 Energize the fuel pump for 10 seconds by connecting the auxiliary wiring harness to a fully charged 12-volt battery; observe pressure while energized. If there is no pressure check the polarity of the wiring harness. Also check the terminal connectors at the fuel pump.

41 Allow fuel to drain from the hose into the container and observe the volume.

42 The fuel pump is operating properly if:
   a) The fuel pressure reaches 35-45 psi.
   b) Fuel flow is a minimum of 7.5 oz. in 10 seconds.
   c) Fuel pressure remains at a minimum of 30 psi after de-energization.

43 When all three conditions are met, the fuel pump is operating normally.

44 If pressure condition is met but flow is not, check for a blocked filter or fuel supply lines. After correcting any blockages recheck using the above procedure. If flow conditions are still not met replace the fuel pump.

45 If both pressure and flow conditions are met but pressure will not maintain after de-energization, check for a leaking regulator or injectors. If both check OK then replace the fuel pump.

46 If no flow or pressure is seen the fuel system should be checked as in Step 44. If no trouble is found replace the fuel pump and the sock filter in the fuel tank.

Removal and installation

Refer to Fig. 13.34

47 Depressurize fuel system (refer to Section 3).

48 Disconnect the negative battery cable.

49 Raise vehicle and support it on jackstands.

50 Loosen the mounting until the pump assembly can be removed from the bracket, then remove the parking brake cable clip on the pump.

51 Disconnect the electrical connector from the body harness. Remove the inlet and outlet lines from the fuel pump. **Note:** *During fuel pump removal the fuel tank should be empty or the fuel line held above the level of fuel to prevent a siphoning action.*

52 Installation is basically the reverse of removal with the following additions:

53 After installing the pump mounting bolt tighten it to 20 to 30 in-lb.

54 With a fuel pressure gauge installed on the fuel rail turn the ignition On and Off at 2 second intervals to bring the fuel pressure up to 35 psi.

55 Start vehicle and check for proper operation of the pump and for leaks.

56 Recheck the system for leaks after the pressure gauge has been removed.

Turbocharger

General description

57 The turbocharger which is mounted on the 1.6 liter engine increases the horsepower output by approximately 35% with a 25% increase in torque. This is not a constant increase, as the turbocharger assembly works on a 'demand' basis only. This means that additionally compressed gases are not fed into the engine except under load conditions (acceleration and climbing). The rest of the time the engine is 'normally aspirated' and operates on normal amounts of fuel.

58 The turbocharger unit consists of two turbine wheels mounted on a common shaft. Each wheel is enclosed by a shroud which directs air flow. One shroud connects to the exhaust manifold. This is the turbine unit. The other shroud is linked to the carburetor and the intake manifold and is known as the compressor. In practice, these units operate as follows:

59 Compression in the cylinder of the engine is not just a mechanical action. When the fuel/air mixture is burned it gains heat (superheats)

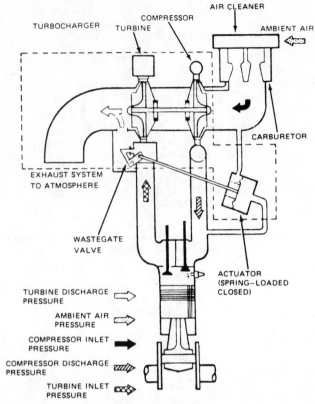

Fig. 13.35 Turbocharged engine air flow diagram (Sec 6)

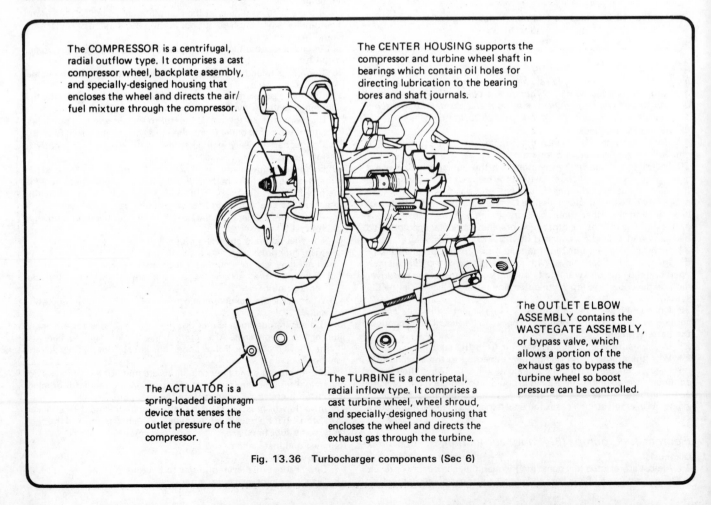

Fig. 13.36 Turbocharger components (Sec 6)

and therefore pressure. When this pressurized gas is routed through a small exhaust port and along a narrow exhaust pipe it gains velocity. Directing this stream of gases into the turbine unit provides power to the turbine. The turbine housing is 'snail-shaped', keeping the gases tightly compressed as they enter the housing and allowing them to expand and cool as they leave. The change in heat and velocity provides power to the turbine wheel.

60 On the opposite end of the shaft the compressor wheel is driven by the turbine. As the carburetor sits on top of the compressor, the air/fuel mixture is drawn out of the carburetor and compressed. The compressor housing is also 'snail-shaped', but in the opposite direction from that of the turbine housing. The air/fuel charge is drawn through a large orifice and gradually compressed, until a charge of compressed gases exits the compressor. This charge carries a much greater amount of fuel and air and packs it into the same space (the cylinder) as a normally-aspired engine. With a greater initial charge each cylinder produces more power.

61 As the superheated gases escape through the exhaust ports, the process is begun again. Turbine speeds can reach 120,000 rpm during normal opertion of the engine. Since the speed of the engine also determines the speed of the turbine and the size of the charge, certain safety measures are provided to prevent damage to the engine and turbocharger.

62 A wastegate is installed to control turbine speed and pressure build-up. The wastegate is operated by an actuator, which is a canister containing a spring-loaded diaphragm. As the pressure in the compressor housing changes, the actuator diphragm moves, opening and closing the wastegate by means of an actuating lever.

63 The opening of the wastegate allows exhaust gases to bypass the turbine, slowing turbine and compressor wheel speeds. This prevents two conditions which would occur without the wastegate. On acceleration, exhaust gases are driving the turbine at a speed higher than the compressed air/fuel is being demanded. The packing of pressurized gases slows the compressor blades so that if acceleration occurred at that moment, there would be a 'throttle lag' while the turbocharger worked back up to operating speed. On acceleration, the closing of the wastegate directs all exhaust gases into the turbine housing, preventing lag and helping maintain turbine speed.

Cautions

64 The turbocharger is driven by superheated exhaust gases and routinely operates at extremely high temperatures. The turbocharger castings retain heat for a very long time and must not be touched for a period of at least three hours after the car engine was last run. Even at this time it is advisable to wear heavy gloves to prevent burns.

65 High rotation speed in the turbocharger unit means that bearing life is dependent upon a constant flow of engine oil. Careful attention should be paid to the condition of the oil lines and the tightness of their fittings. Never overtighten the hollow bolts, as this will deform the unions and cause leakage.

66 Because the turbocharger is dependent upon clean oil, drain the engine oil and change the oil filter any time the turbocharger is removed. Interruption or contamination of the oil supply to the bearings in the center housing, which support the rotating assembly, can result in major turbocharger damage. If a bearing fails in the turbocharger or the engine, flush all engine and turbocharger oil passageways completely before reassembling. When the engine of a turbocharged car is torn down for rebuilding perform all the standard passageway routines, as you would for a normally aspirated engine, then flush all oilways once again with fresh oil. When flushing is completed drain the engine oil and fill once again with fresh oil and install a new oil filter. After changing oil and the oil filter on a turbocharged engine, or when performing any service operation, start the engine and let idle for 30-60 seconds before driving.

67 A turbocharger is a turbine, and, like any turbine, its greatest enemy is dirt and foreign objects. A stray nut, metal chip or rock passing through a turbine rotating at 120,000 rpm can cause major damage. The best defense against foreign object damage is to work on your engine and turbocharger unit only after the engine has been cleaned. Cover all inlets and pipes. Account for each and every nut, screw and washer before starting the engine after assembly is complete. When removing the turbocharger assembly take special care not to bend, nick or in any way damage the turbine or compressor wheel blades. Any damage to the turbine or compressor wheels may result in rotating assembly imbalance and failure of the bearings and oil seals. Finally, never rush your engine work. Work only as fast as 100% accuracy permits.

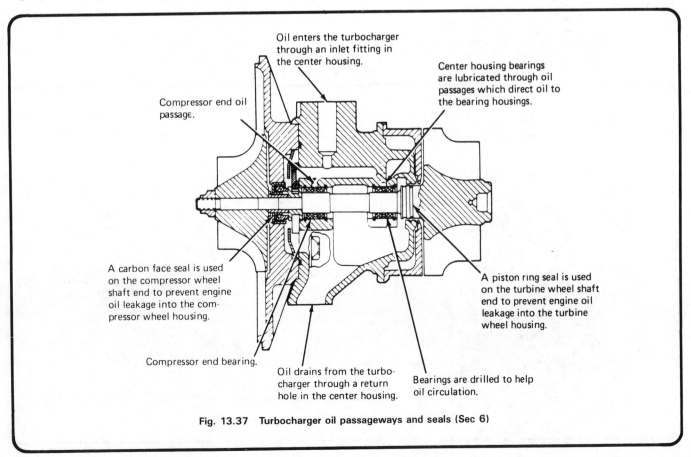

Fig. 13.37 Turbocharger oil passageways and seals (Sec 6)

68 Turbocharged engines are very simple to understand and most work is a straightforward operation. Observe the cautions above and you will add significantly to the operating life of your engine.
69 The turbocharger is not repairable and serviced by replacement only.

Bearing clearance check

70 Push the turbocharger shaft assembly as far in one direction as possible. Spin the shaft by hand.
71 Next push the shaft in the opposite direction as far as possible and spin the shaft again.
72 If either the turbine blade or the compressor blade contacts any portion of the housing, the bearings are no good.
73 The tubine should spin freely with no unusal noise or rough feeling in the bearing.
74 Inspect the inlet and outlet passages for signs of oil. If any oil is present the seals are failing.
75 If any of these tests come up negative the entire turbocharger must be replaced as an asembly.

Wastegate — testing

76 To correctly preform this test compressed air at 10 to 11 psi and an air nozzle will be needed.
77 Disconnect the wastegate actuator hose.
78 Apply between 10 and 11 psi air pressure to the actuating diaphragm while watching the actuating rod. There should be noticable movement. **Note:** *To avoid serious damage do not apply any more than the recommended air pressure to the wastegate diaphragm.*
79 If the wastegate fails this test the turbocharger will have to be replaced as an assembly.

Turbocharger — Removal and installation
Refer to Fig. 13.8 through 13.15 and Fig. 13.40
80 Disconnect the battery ground cable.
81 Remove the radiator fan guard at the radiator support.
82 With the compressor hose loose at the throttle housing, remove the hose from the turbocharger compressor outlet and rotate the hose up and out of the way.
83 Remove the compressor inlet hose.
84 Remove the alternator and bracket (Chapter 5).
85 Disconnect the electrical connector at the EGO sensor.
86 Raise the vehicle and support it securely on jackstands.
87 Disconnect the oil return line from the bottom of the turbocharger.
88 Disconnect the exhaust pipe from the turbocharger.
89 Remove the bolt attaching the exhaust shield to the water outlet connector.
90 Disconnect the oil feed line at the top of the turbocharger.

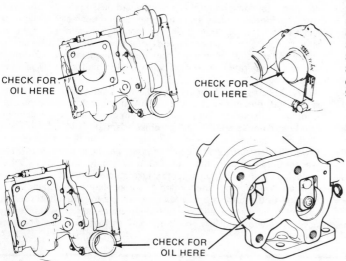

CHECK FOR OIL HERE

CHECK FOR OIL HERE

CHECK FOR OIL HERE

Fig. 13.38 Any indication of oil at these points indicates failing oil seals (Sec 6)

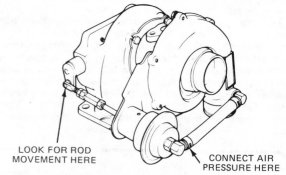

LOOK FOR ROD MOVEMENT HERE

CONNECT AIR PRESSURE HERE

Fig. 13.39 Use caution when testing the wastegate not to use excessive air pressure (Sec 6)

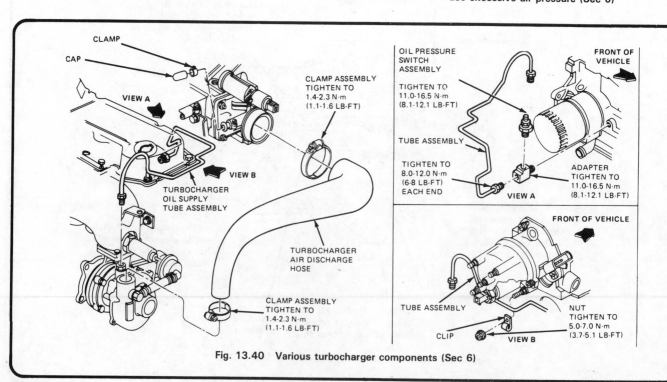

CLAMP

CAP

VIEW A

CLAMP ASSEMBLY TIGHTEN TO 1.4-2.3 N·m (1.1-1.6 LB·FT)

VIEW B

TURBOCHARGER OIL SUPPLY TUBE ASSEMBLY

TURBOCHARGER AIR DISCHARGE HOSE

CLAMP ASSEMBLY TIGHTEN TO 1.4-2.3 N·m (1.1-1.6 LB·FT)

OIL PRESSURE SWITCH ASSEMBLY

TIGHTEN TO 11.0-16.5 N·m (8.1-12.1 LB·FT)

TUBE ASSEMBLY

TIGHTEN TO 8.0-12.0 N·m (6-8 LB·FT) EACH END

FRONT OF VEHICLE

ADAPTER TIGHTEN TO 11.0-16.5 N·m (8.1-12.1 LB·FT)

VIEW A

FRONT OF VEHICLE

TUBE ASSEMBLY

CLIP

VIEW B

NUT TIGHTEN TO 5.0-7.0 N·m (3.7-5.1 LB·FT)

Fig. 13.40 Various turbocharger components (Sec 6)

91 Remove the exhaust manifold to cylinder head nuts. Slide the exhaust manifold and turbocharger away from the cylinder head enough to remove the exhaust shield.
92 The turbocharger and exhaust manifold are removed as an assembly.
93 To disconnect the turbocharger from the exhaust manifold remove the four retaining nuts.
94 Installation is the reverse of the removal procedure. Use new gaskets and tighten all the bolts to specification.

7 Engine electrical

General information

1 Due to the use of fuel injection, the distributor has become an integral part of the computer system which runs the engine. This means more precise ignition timing and a distributor with fewer moving parts. The basic construction of the distributor has remained the same, with the exception of the advance diaphram being replaced by a stationary octane rod (Fig. 13.41). The procedure in Chapter 5 (Sec 19) should be used for disassembly, inspection and reassembly along with the illustration.

Alternator and starter, exploded view

2 The exploded views provided in this Chapter apply to all year models and should be used along with the procedures in Chapter 5.

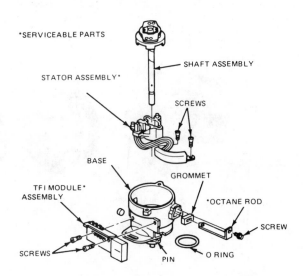

Fig. 13.41 Distributor — exploded view (EFI engine) (Sec 7)

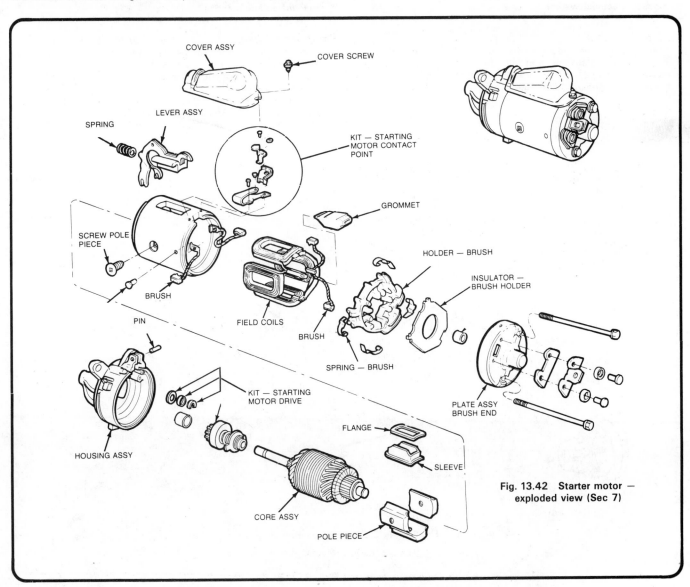

Fig. 13.42 Starter motor — exploded view (Sec 7)

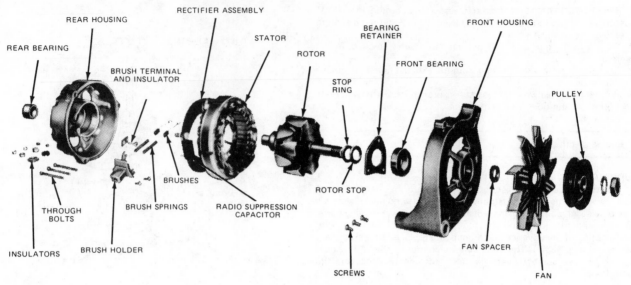

Fig. 13.43 Alternator — exploded view (Sec 7)

8 Chassis electrical system

Wiring diagrams

1   Note that the updated wiring diagrams for the later model years have been included at the end of this Chapter. Due to space limitations we are not able to provide every diagram for all years. However, a representative sampling is included.

9 Suspension and steering

Front wheel bearings — removal and installation

1   The two tapered roller bearings used on previous models have been replaced by one sealed bearing pressed into the steering knuckle. Service is limited to replacement, which requires an arbor press and is best left to a machine shop.
2   The procedure for steering knuckle removal in Chapter 11 should be used to remove the knuckle/hub assembly. The assembly should then be taken to a qualified machine shop for bearing replacement.

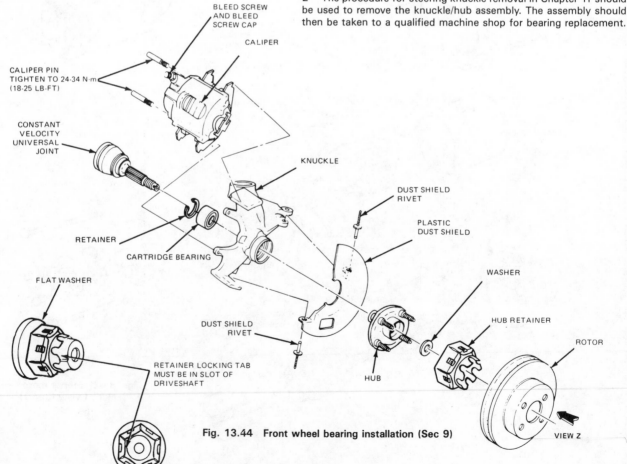

Fig. 13.44 Front wheel bearing installation (Sec 9)

LEGEND
WIRE IDENTIFICATION

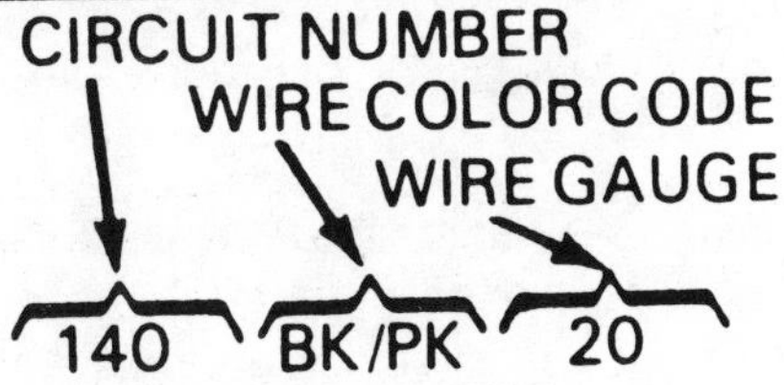

CIRCUIT NUMBER
WIRE COLOR CODE
WIRE GAUGE

140   BK/PK   20

WIRING COLOR CODE
(PRIMARY COLORS)

BLACK	BK
BROWN	BR
TAN	T
RED	R
PINK	PK
ORANGE	O
YELLOW	Y
DARK GREEN	DG
LIGHT GREEN	LG
DARK BLUE	DB
LIGHT BLUE	LB
PURPLE	P
GRAY	GY
WHITE	W
HASH	(H)
DOT	(D)

The presence of a tracer on the wire is indicated by a secondary color followed by an "H" for Hash or a "D" for Dot. A stripe is understood if no letter follows.

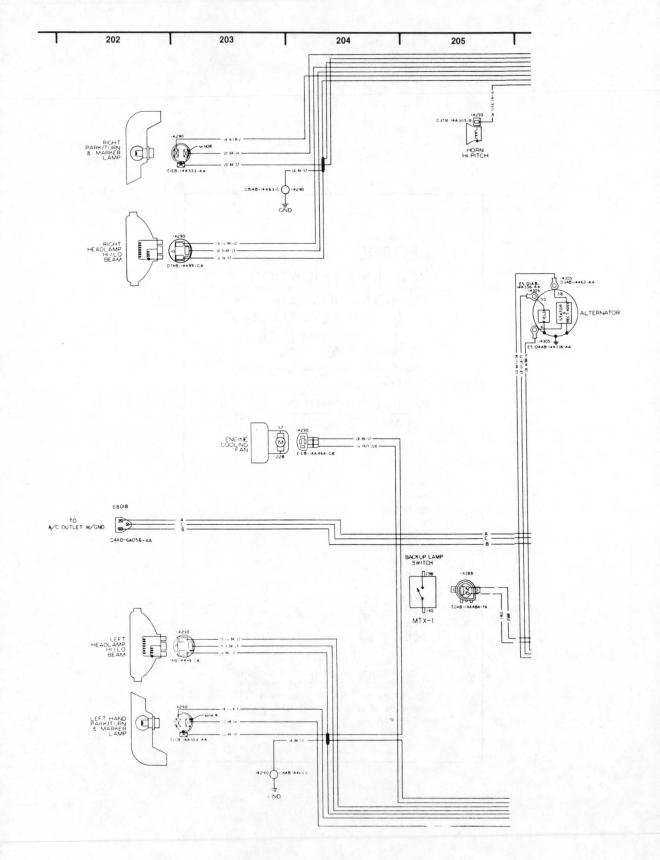

Wiring diagram — Front end — typical

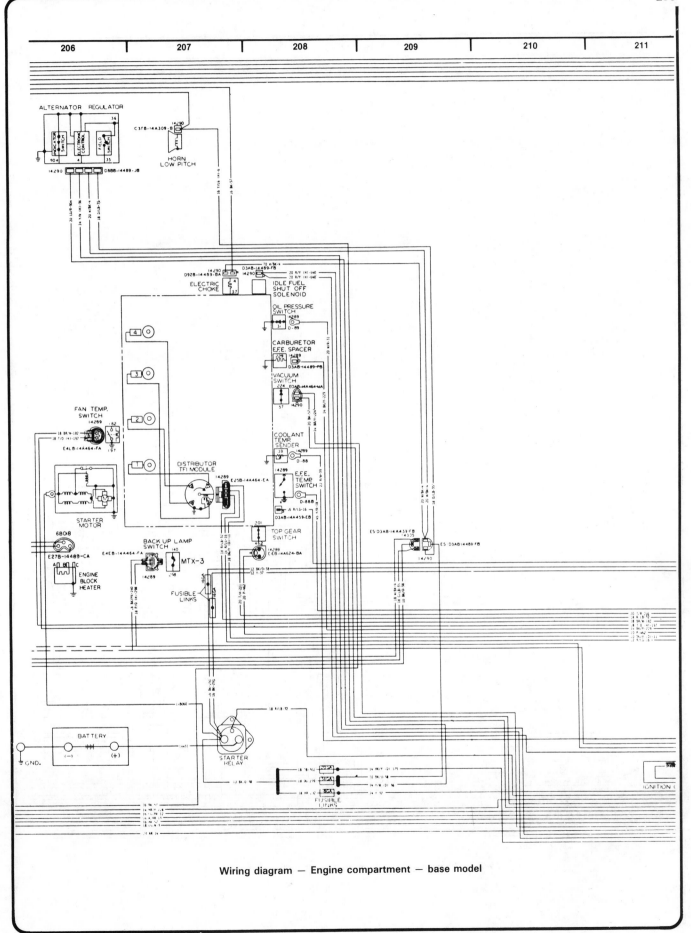

Wiring diagram — Engine compartment — base model

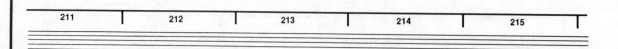

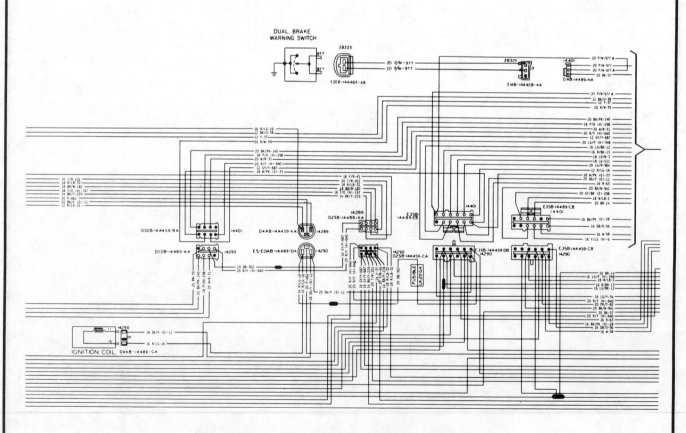

Wiring diagram — Engine compartment (cont.) — base model

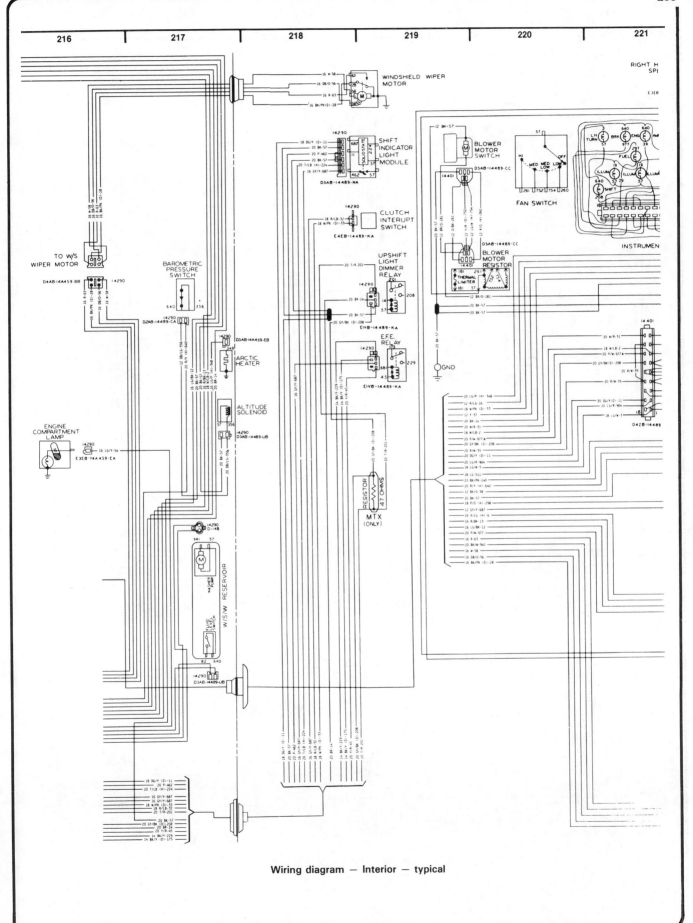

Wiring diagram – Interior – typical

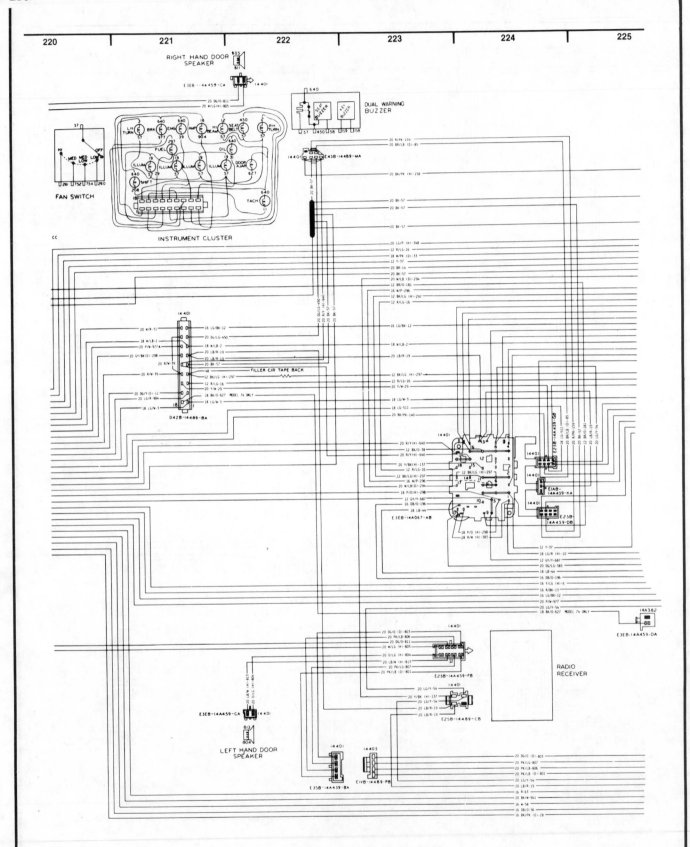

Wiring diagram — Interior (cont.) — typical

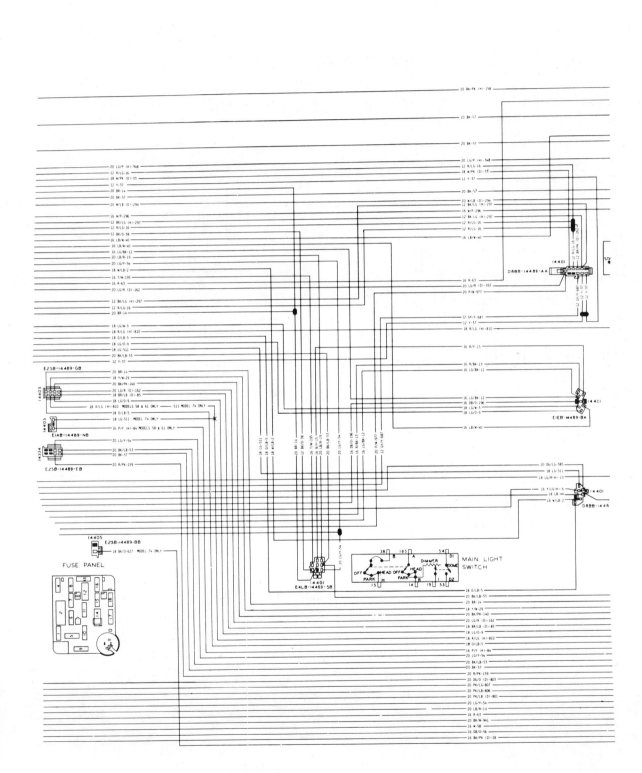

Wiring diagram — Interior (cont.) — typical

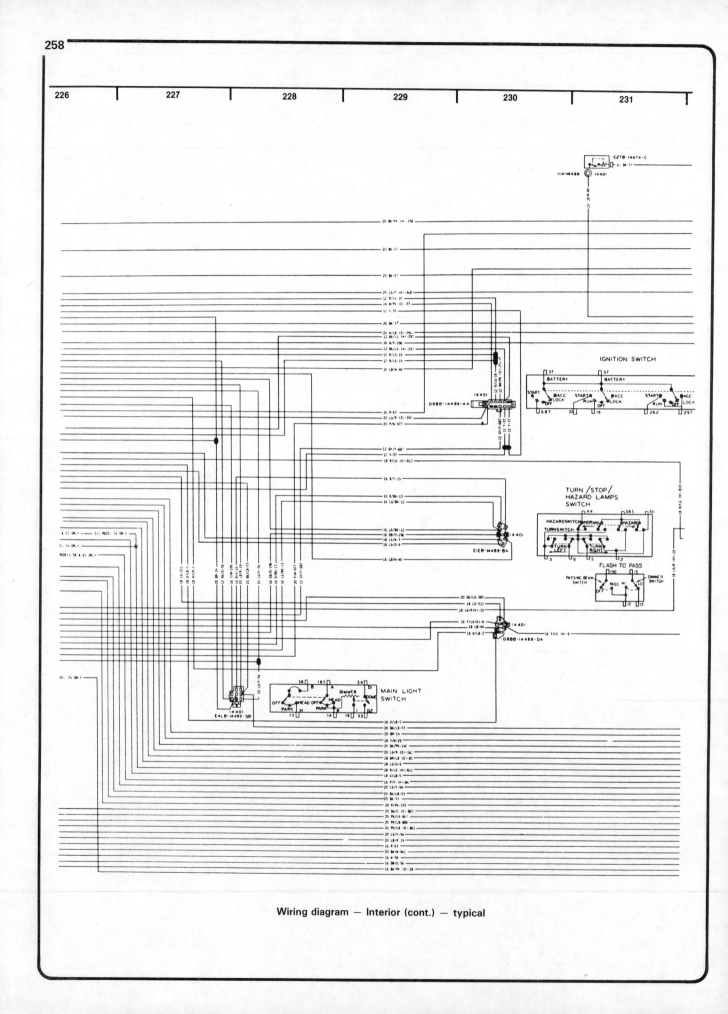

Wiring diagram — Interior (cont.) — typical

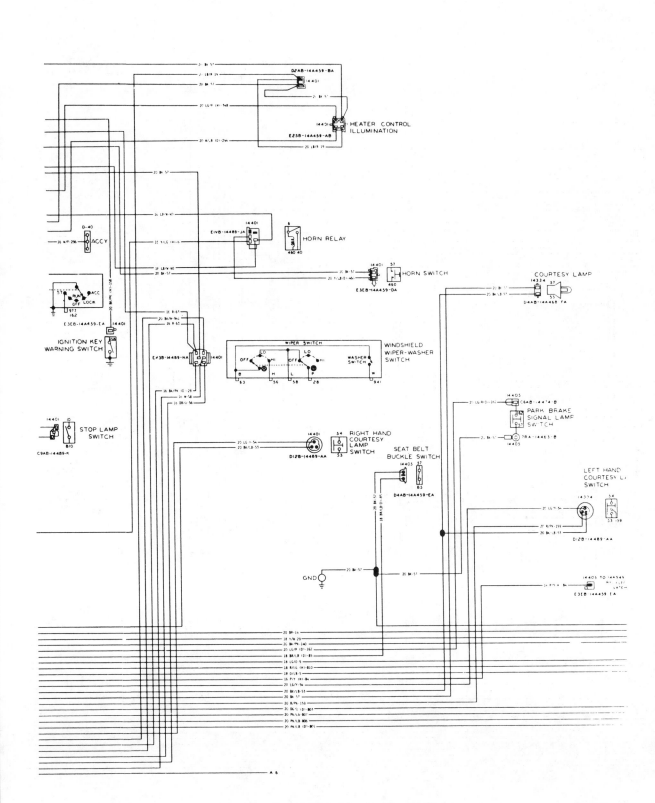

Wiring diagram — Interior (cont.) — typical

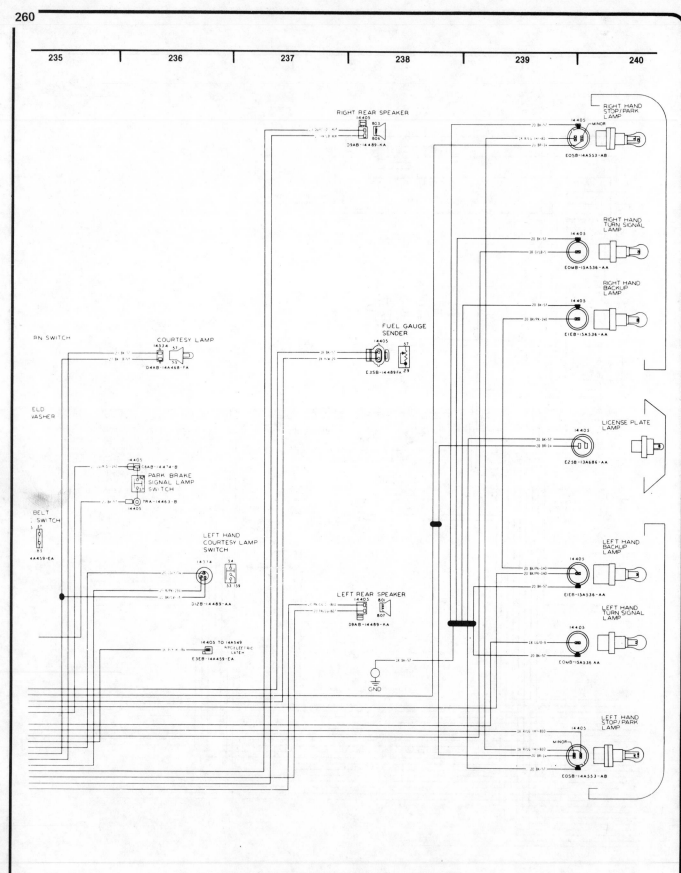

Wiring diagram — Rear compartment — base model

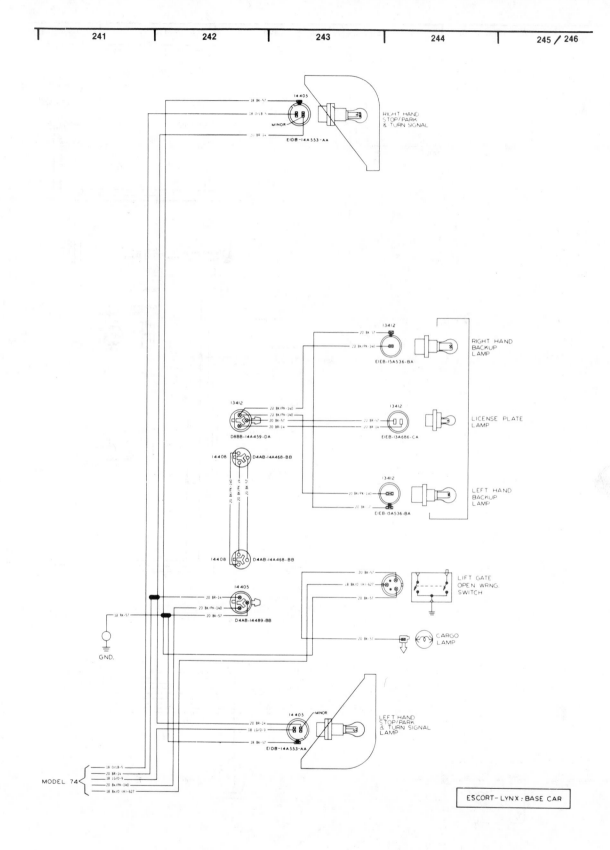

Wiring diagram — Rear compartment — hatchback

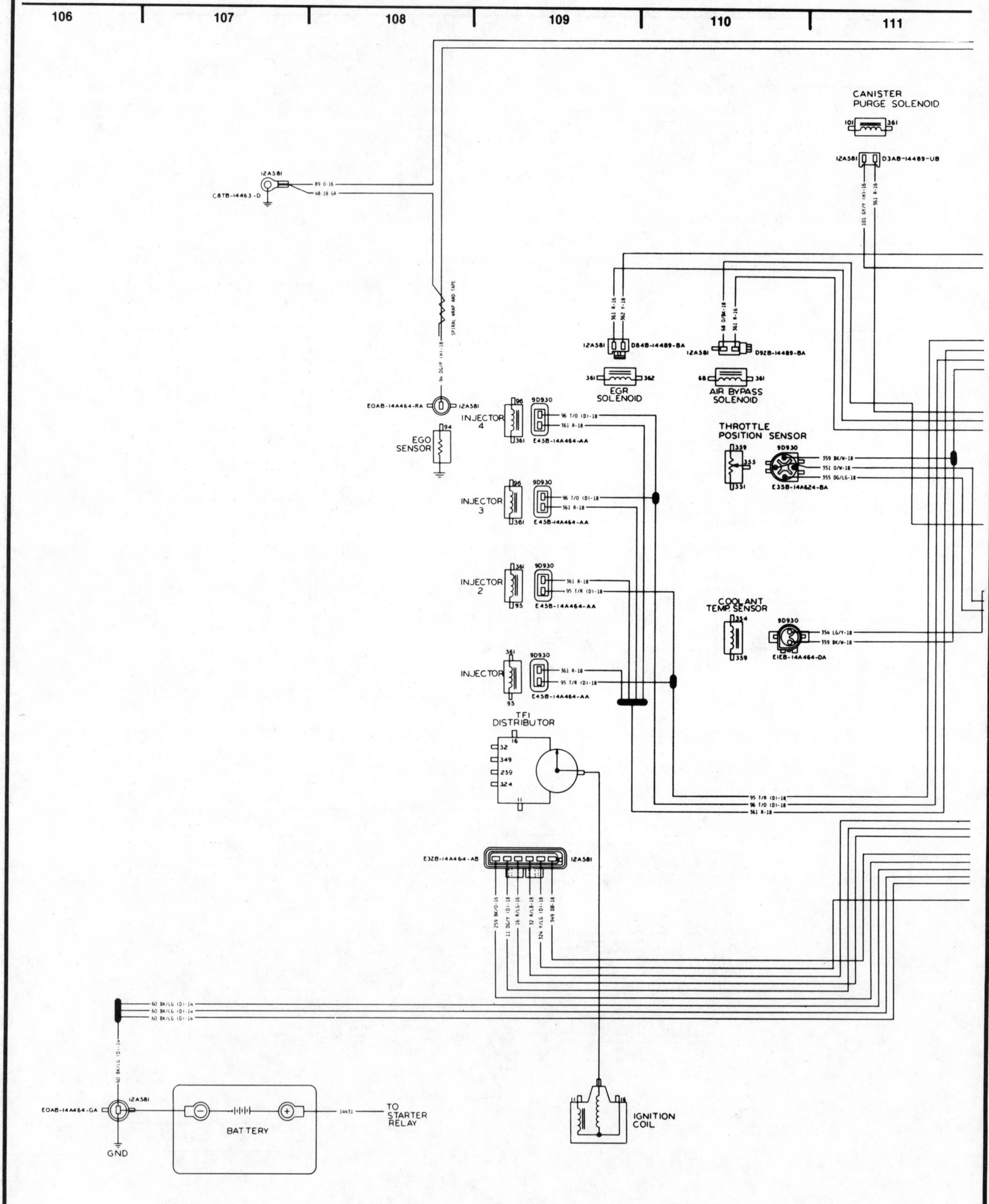

106	107	108	109	110	111

CANISTER
PURGE SOLENOID

12A58I   D3AB-14489-UB

C8TB-14463-D
89 0-16
48-18 GA

12A58I
361 R-16   362 Y-18
D84B-14489-BA

58 0/PK-18
361 R-16
D92B-14489-BA

EGR
SOLENOID

AIR BYPASS
SOLENOID

EOAB-14A464-RA   12A58I

EGO
SENSOR

INJECTOR 4
9D930
96 T/O (D)-18
361 R-18
E45B-14A464-AA

THROTTLE
POSITION SENSOR
9D930
359 BK/W-18
351 O/W-18
355 DG/LG-18
E35B-14A624-BA

INJECTOR 3
9D930
96 T/O (D)-18
361 R-18
E45B-14A464-AA

INJECTOR 2
9D930
361 R-18 (D)
95 T/R (D)-18
E45B-14A464-AA

COOLANT
TEMP SENSOR
9D930
354 LG/Y-18
359 BK/W-18
E1EB-14A464-DA

INJECTOR 1
9D930
361 R-18 (D)
95 T/R (D)-18
E45B-14A464-AA

TFI
DISTRIBUTOR
16
32
349
259
324
11

95 T/R (D)-18
96 T/O (D)-18
361 R-18

E3ZB-14A464-AB   12A58I

TO
STARTER
RELAY

EOAB-14A464-GA   12A58I

BATTERY

GND

IGNITION
COIL

Wiring diagram — EFI engine — EFI model

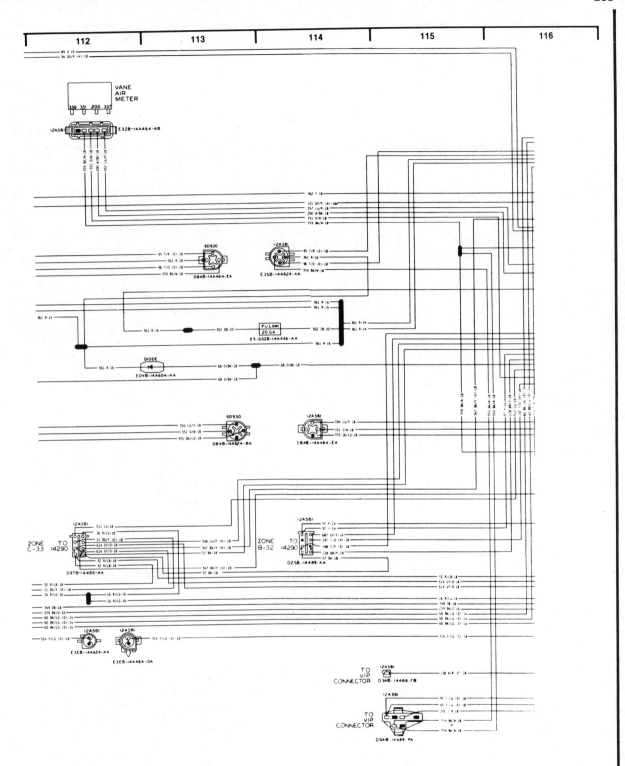

Wiring diagram — EFI engine (cont.) — EFI model

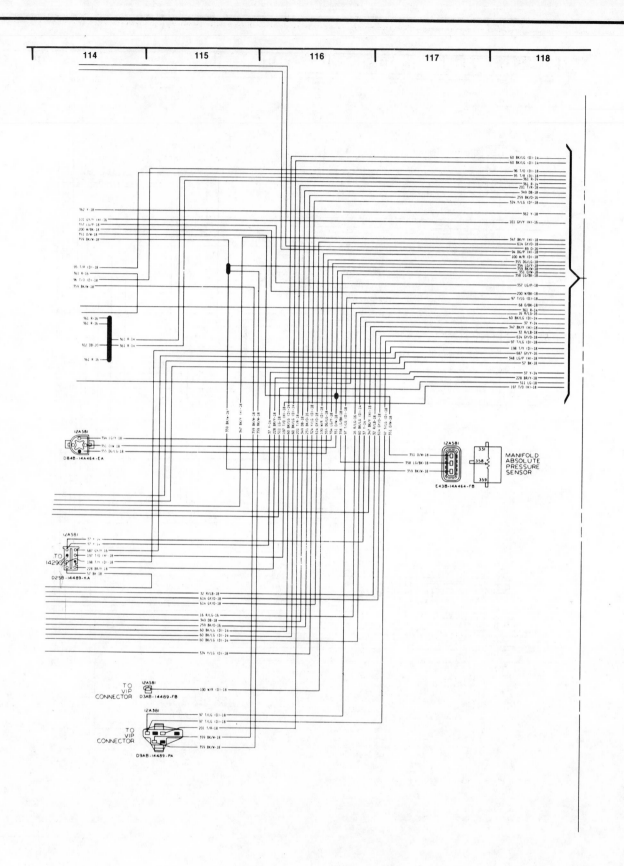

Wiring diagram — EFI engine (cont.) — EFI model

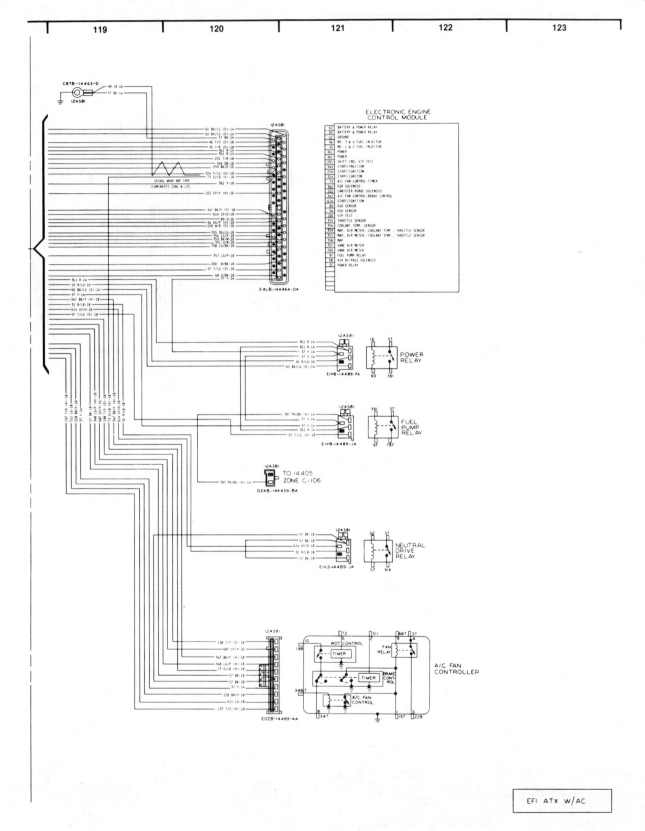

Wiring diagram — EFI engine (cont.) — EFI model

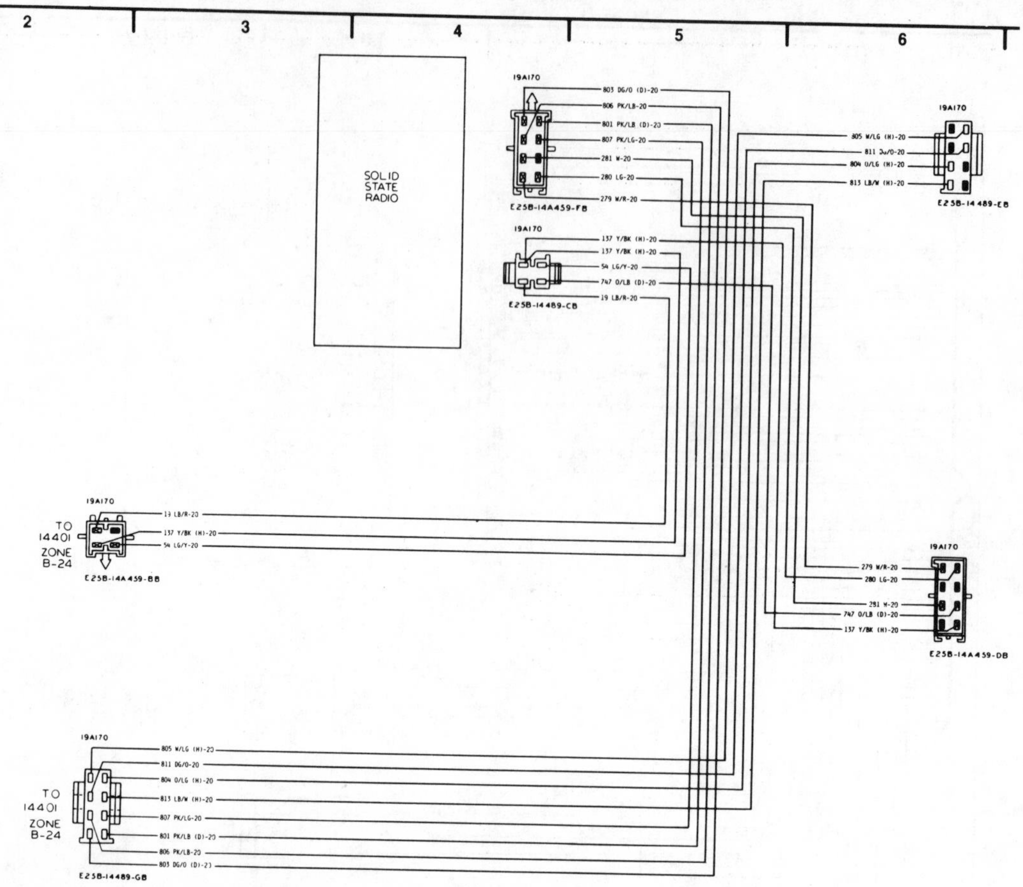

1	2	3	4	5	6

SOLID
STATE
RADIO

19A170
E25B-14A459-FB

803 DG/O (D1-20)
806 PK/LB (D1-20)
801 PK/LG (D1-23)
807 PK/LG-20
281 W-20
280 LG-20
279 W/R-20

19A170
E25B-14489-EB

805 W/LG (HI-20)
811 DW/O-20
804 O/LG (HI-20)
813 LB/W (HI-20)

19A170
E25B-14489-CB

137 Y/BK (HI-20)
137 Y/BK (HI-20)
54 LG/Y-20
747 O/LB (D1-20)
19 LB/R-20

TO
14401
ZONE
B-24

19A170
E25B-14A459-BB

19 LB/R-20
137 Y/BK (HI-20)
54 LG/Y-20

19A170
E25B-14A459-DB

279 W/R-20
280 LG-20
281 W-20
747 O/LB (D1-20)
137 Y/BK (HI-20)

TO
14401
ZONE
B-24

19A170
E25B-14489-GB

805 W/LG (HI-20)
811 DG/O-20
804 O/LG (HI-20)
813 LB/W (HI-20)
807 PK/LG-20
801 PK/LB (D1-23)
806 PK/LB-20
803 DG/O (D1-2)

Wiring diagram — Sound system — typical

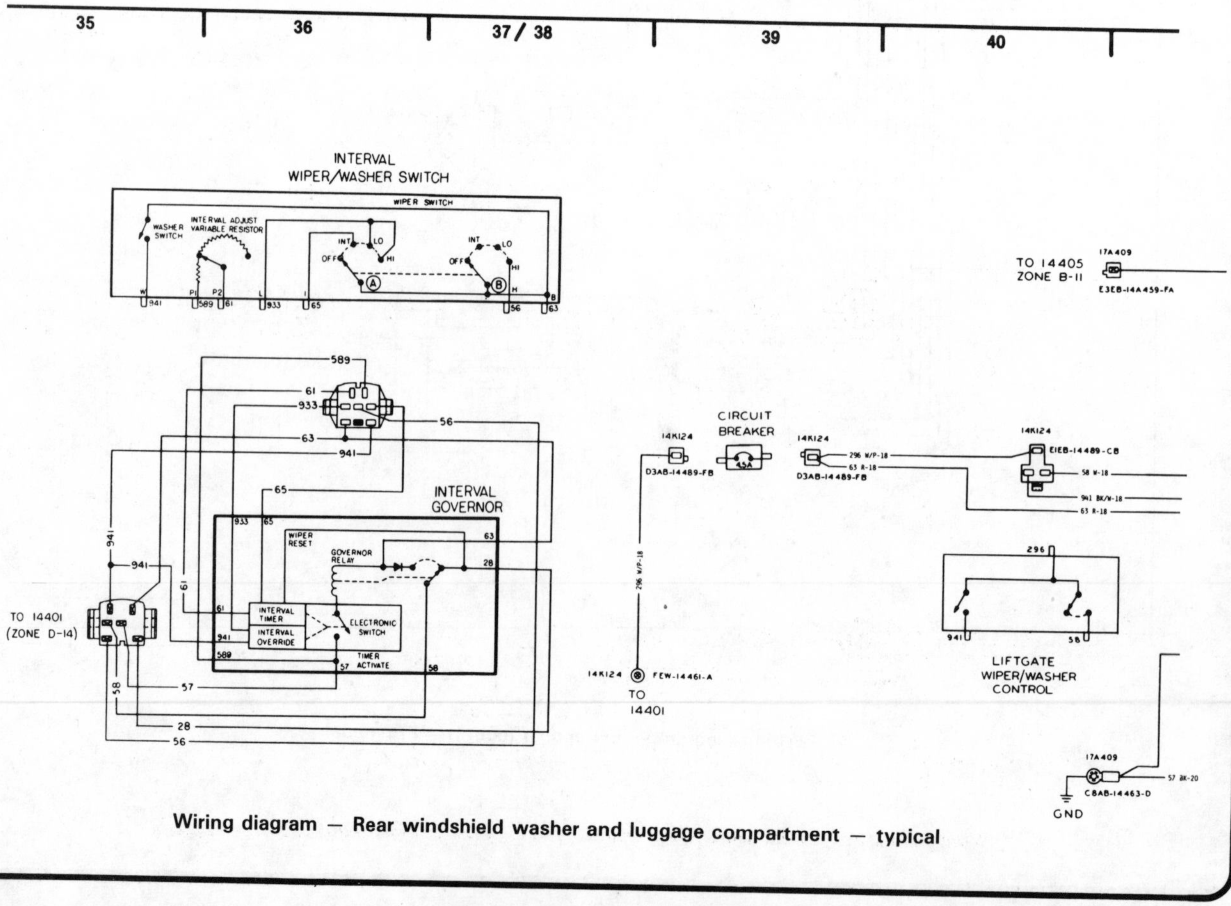

35	36	37 / 38	39	40

INTERVAL
WIPER/WASHER SWITCH

WIPER SWITCH

WASHER
SWITCH

INTERVAL ADJUST
VARIABLE RESISTOR

INT   LO   INT   LO
OFF   HI   OFF   HI
        A   B

W   P1   P2   589 61   L   933   L 65   56   63

TO 14405
ZONE B-11

17A409
E3EB-14A459-FA

589
61
933
56
63
941
65

INTERVAL
GOVERNOR

INTERVAL
GOVERNOR

WIPER
RESET

GOVERNOR
RELAY

63
28

INTERVAL
TIMER

INTERVAL
OVERRIDE

ELECTRONIC
SWITCH

TIMER
ACTIVATE

941
589
57   58

TO 14401
(ZONE D-14)

941
61

58
57
28
56

CIRCUIT
BREAKER

14K124
D3AB-14489-FB

14K124
D3AB-14489-FB

45A

296 W/P-18
63 R-18

14K124
E1EB-14489-CB

58 W-18
941 BK/W-18
63 R-18

296 W/P-18

14K124   FEW-14461-A
TO
14401

296
941   58

LIFTGATE
WIPER/WASHER
CONTROL

17A409
C8AB-14463-D

57 BK-20

GND

Wiring diagram — Rear windshield washer and luggage compartment — typical

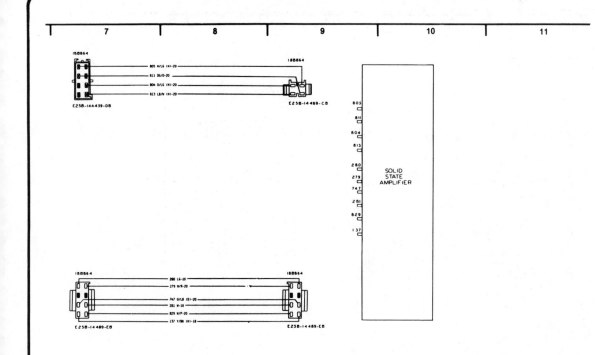

Wiring diagram — Sound system (cont.) — typical

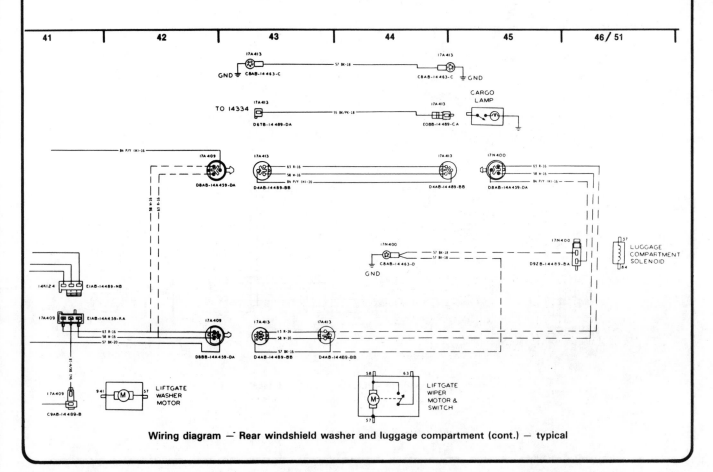

Wiring diagram — Rear windshield washer and luggage compartment (cont.) — typical

52   53   54   55

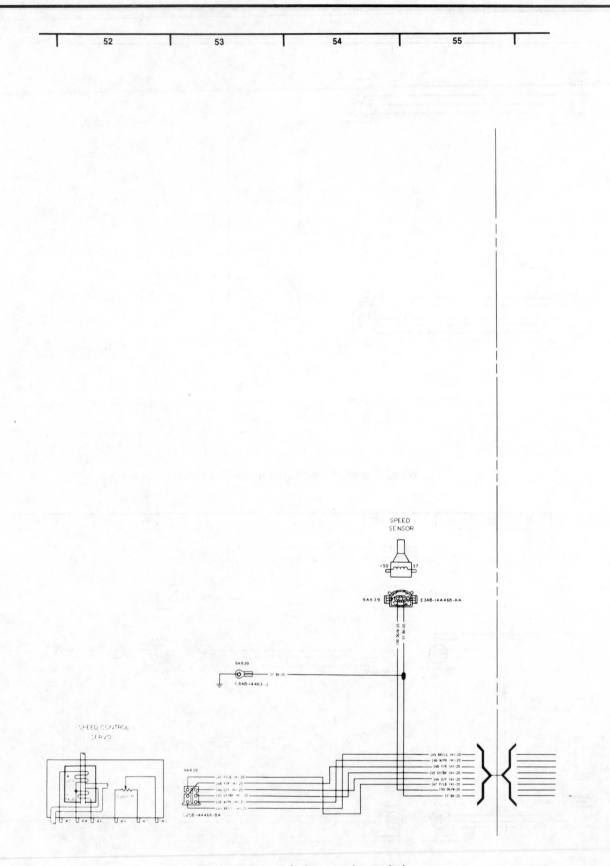

SPEED
SENSOR

SPEED CONTROL
SERVO

Wiring diagram — Cruise control — typical

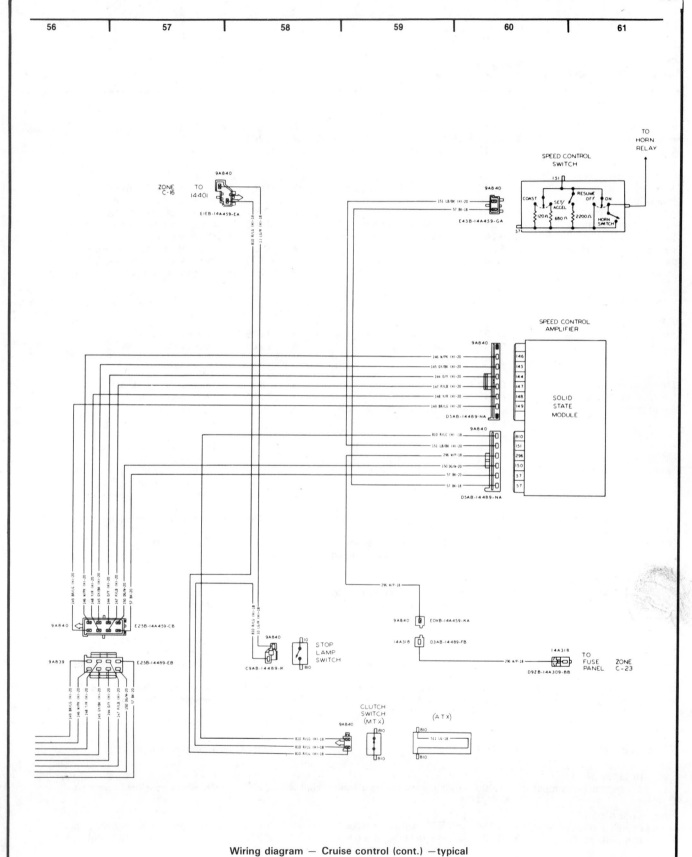

Wiring diagram — Cruise control (cont.) —typical

Conversion factors

Length (distance)

Inches (in)	X	25.4	= Millimetres (mm)	X 0.0394	= Inches (in)
Feet (ft)	X	0.305	= Metres (m)	X 3.281	= Feet (ft)
Miles	X	1.609	= Kilometres (km)	X 0.621	= Miles

Volume (capacity)

Cubic inches (cu in; in^3)	X	16.387	= Cubic centimetres (cc; cm^3)	X 0.061	= Cubic inches (cu in; in^3)
Imperial pints (Imp pt)	X	0.568	= Litres (l)	X 1.76	= Imperial pints (Imp pt)
Imperial quarts (Imp qt)	X	1.137	= Litres (l)	X 0.88	= Imperial quarts (Imp qt)
Imperial quarts (Imp qt)	X	1.201	= US quarts (US qt)	X 0.833	= Imperial quarts (Imp qt)
US quarts (US qt)	X	0.946	= Litres (l)	X 1.057	= US quarts (US qt)
Imperial gallons (Imp gal)	X	4.546	= Litres (l)	X 0.22	= Imperial gallons (Imp gal)
Imperial gallons (Imp gal)	X	1.201	= US gallons (US gal)	X 0.833	= Imperial gallons (Imp gal)
US gallons (US gal)	X	3.785	= Litres (l)	X 0.264	= US gallons (US gal)

Mass (weight)

Ounces (oz)	X	28.35	= Grams (g)	X 0.035	= Ounces (oz)
Pounds (lb)	X	0.454	= Kilograms (kg)	X 2.205	= Pounds (lb)

Force

Ounces-force (ozf; oz)	X	0.278	= Newtons (N)	X 3.6	= Ounces-force (ozf; oz)
Pounds-force (lbf; lb)	X	4.448	= Newtons (N)	X 0.225	= Pounds-force (lbf; lb)
Newtons (N)	X	0.1	= Kilograms-force (kgf; kg)	X 9.81	= Newtons (N)

Pressure

Pounds-force per square inch (psi; lbf/in^2; lb/in^2)	X	0.070	= Kilograms-force per square centimetre (kgf/cm^2; kg/cm^2)	X 14.223	= Pounds-force per square inch (psi; lbf/in^2; lb/in^2)
Pounds-force per square inch (psi; lbf/in^2; lb/in^2)	X	0.068	= Atmospheres (atm)	X 14.696	= Pounds-force per square inch (psi; lbf/in^2; lb/in^2)
Pounds-force per square inch (psi; lbf/in^2; lb/in^2)	X	0.069	= Bars	X 14.5	= Pounds-force per square inch (psi; lbf/in^2; lb/in^2)
Pounds-force per square inch (psi; lbf/in^2; lb/in^2)	X	6.895	= Kilopascals (kPa)	X 0.145	= Pounds-force per square inch (psi; lbf/in^2; lb/in^2)
Kilopascals (kPa)	X	0.01	= Kilograms-force per square centimetre (kgf/cm^2; kg/cm^2)	X 98.1	= Kilopascals (kPa)

Torque (moment of force)

Pounds-force inches (lbf in; lb in)	X	1.152	= Kilograms-force centimetre (kgf cm; kg cm)	X 0.868	= Pounds-force inches (lbf in; lb in)
Pounds-force inches (lbf in; lb in)	X	0.113	= Newton metres (Nm)	X 8.85	= Pounds-force inches (lbf in; lb in)
Pounds-force inches (lbf in; lb in)	X	0.083	= Pounds-force feet (lbf ft; lb ft)	X 12	= Pounds-force inches (lbf in; lb in)
Pounds-force feet (lbf ft; lb ft)	X	0.138	= Kilograms-force metres (kgf m; kg m)	X 7.233	= Pounds-force feet (lbf ft; lb ft)
Pounds-force feet (lbf ft; lb ft)	X	1.356	= Newton metres (Nm)	X 0.738	= Pounds-force feet (lbf ft; lb ft)
Newton metres (Nm)	X	0.102	= Kilograms-force metres (kgf m; kg m)	X 9.804	= Newton metres (Nm)

Power

Horsepower (hp)	X	745.7	= Watts (W)	X 0.0013	= Horsepower (hp)

Velocity (speed)

Miles per hour (miles/hr; mph)	X	1.609	= Kilometres per hour (km/hr; kph)	X 0.621	= Miles per hour (miles/hr; mph)

Fuel consumption*

Miles per gallon, Imperial (mpg)	X	0.354	= Kilometres per litre (km/l)	X 2.825	= Miles per gallon, Imperial (mpg)
Miles per gallon, US (mpg)	X	0.425	= Kilometres per litre (km/l)	X 2.352	= Miles per gallon, US (mpg)

Temperature

Degrees Fahrenheit = (°C x 1.8) + 32

Degrees Celsius (Degrees Centigrade; °C) = (°F - 32) x 0.56

*It is common practice to convert from miles per gallon (mpg) to litres/100 kilometres (l/100km),
where mpg (Imperial) x l/100 km = 282 and mpg (US) x l/100 km = 235

Index